CARLYLE AND GERMAN THOUGHT:
1819-1834

BY

CHARLES FREDERICK HARROLD

ARCHON BOOKS

HAMDEN   LONDON

1963

TO ELIZABETH

PREFACE

It is with the consciousness of having attempted a hazardous task that I present in this study a survey and an interpretation of Thomas Carlyle's early relations with German literature and philosophy, and their contribution to the formation of his ultimate point of view.[1] Certainly the pitfalls for unwary conjecture are sufficiently numerous, in a subject so broad, so vaguely defined, and so complex, to impel me to urge the modesty of my claims. My purpose has been threefold: (1) to assemble the conclusions of all the numerous valuable monographs and studies of isolated aspects of the problem; (2) to supply, wherever possible, original information on hitherto neglected or debatable points; and (3) to fuse the various elements of the problem by an interpretation which should do justice to the whole. I have thus hoped to present the first comprehensive study of a subject which has hitherto been accorded a fragmentary and often merely conjectural treatment. How far I have succeeded will be judged differently by different critics of Carlyle, for the problem of Carlyle and German thought is peculiarly open to individual interpretation. Complete certainty on a number of important points is so difficult that perhaps no treatment of the subject as a whole can pretend to finality.

As will be noted later, Carlyle's method with his sources was ambiguous and negligent. In addition to this initial handicap to the inquirer, Carlyle's vast reading gives rise to occasional parallels between his ideas and those of other

[1] The present study first suggested itself during my consideration of Carlyle's conception of history, briefly and incompletely indicated in my doctoral dissertation at Yale University in 1925, on the subject of *Carlyle's General Method in The French Revolution*. (Cf. *Publications of the Modern Language Association*, XLIII (1928), pp. 1150-69; and the *Journal of English and Germanic Philology*, XXVII (1928), pp. 51-66.)

writers which may, for instance, suggest to three different readers no less than as many degrees of influence. Again, we may differ on the precise meaning of certain of his expressions, especially as they relate to a known or possible German source. Thus readers may disagree with me in respect to Carlyle's treatment of Goethe's doctrines of *Entsagen* and the "Worship of Sorrow," or the extent to which the words of Coleridge or Jacobi affected Carlyle's phrasing in a given passage. It may be objected that I have understated the influence of Jean Paul, especially in view of the well-known similarities of their styles, their personalities, and their points of view. Likewise it may appear that I have inadequately presented the sources of Carlyle's interesting remarks on Phantasy. It must be remembered, however, that Carlyle's roving eclecticism, his temperamental indifference to the precise origin and extent of many influences which really touched him, his tendency to say different things at different times, and his casual vagueness on theoretical subjects, all make it impossible for Carlyleans to arrive at any close unanimity on a number of points with which I have dealt. One cannot, for instance, prove with certainty an influence from Jean Paul upon Carlyle's *ideas* equal to that in respect to his aesthetic practice. I have tried to consider all possible approaches to each problem as it has arisen, and I trust that I have made it possible for the reader to form conclusions of his own by turning to liberal extracts from the sources as given in the Notes. I hope, above all, that I have kept it sufficiently clear, throughout the discussion, that when Carlyle began the study of German writers, he already had a fundamental point of view, which he wished *confirmed*, and that he was "influenced" less by actual ideas than by the spirit of German thinkers as they clothed old concepts in new forms. Beneath the variations on the surface of his thinking, even throughout the years of his skepticism and despair, there persisted in him the essential spirit of Calvinism: the belief—at least the will to believe—in the infinite and transcendent sovereignty of God, to know and obey whom is man's supreme end; in the need of personal individual salvation, through action rather than through passive states of soul; in the strenuous morality of "knowing and doing the will of God;" in the constant immanence of God in common things, revealing both love and law. As a "Calvinist without the theology," Carlyle sought, in German thought and elsewhere, an acceptable intellectual restatement of these beliefs. He found, for example, in the doctrine of revelation (*Offenbarung*), common in German metaphysics and literature, a new approach to a reality "whose body Nature is, and God the soul."

The aims and limits of the present study have not included three subordinate elements of the general subject: Carlyle's part in the introduction of German ideas and literature into England; his numerous German allusions, together with his frequent Teutonisms; and his rôle as a critic of German literature. These subjects have already been adequately dealt with, notably by Carré, Kraeger, and Roe, respectively. The dates which limit our inquiry (1819-1834) do not carry us into the field of Carlyle's social theories. There is, furthermore, in this respect, no direct influence from the German comparable to that of Goethe upon Carlyle's ethical theory or that of Fichte upon his early conceptions of the divine. By the time Carlyle had begun the writing of *Past and Present* (toward the end of 1842), his interest in things German had been declining for some ten years. In the turmoil of the "hungry 'forties," whatever influence from German ideas he may have applied in his thinking about social evils appeared in a relatively general and intangible form. And if later, in his occasional tendency toward collectivist doctrines and ideals, he reminds some of us of Fichte in *Der geschlossene Handelsstaat* (1800) or the *Staatslehre*

(1820), the evidence of any direct influence cannot be brought to book.

I have given detailed discussion to Carlyle's interpretation of Kant's distinction between the Reason and the Understanding, and the relativity of space and time, not because they occupy a major place in his final teachings—which, of course, they do not—but because they have been the occasion of a great deal of difference of opinion. The same reason has led me to devote considerable space to his treatment of Fichte's theory of the Divine Idea and of Goethe's ideas in *Wilhelm Meisters Wanderjahre,* especially in the chapters depicting the "Pedagogical Province."

It has seemed worth while to employ several of Fichte's popular works, besides *Ueber das Wesen des Gelehrten* (1806), to which he acknowledges an indebtedness, as well as a greater amount of Schelling's *Methode des akademischen Studiums* (1802) than he probably read, in order to provide an adequate ideological background for several of Carlyle's conceptions. Certain striking parallels of thought would point to his familiarity with Fichte's *Bestimmung des Menschen* (1800), *Die Anweisung zum seligen Leben* (1801), and *Die Grundzüge des gegenwärtigen Zeitalters* (1806). They bear investigation also because they have been granted considerable weight as sources by several of Carlyle's critics.

I need hardly say that I owe a great debt to a number of excellent studies by my predecessors dealing with individual elements of my problem. My task would have been immensely more difficult had it not been for the work of Carré and Cazamian, of Kraeger, Hensel, Fehr, and Baumgarten, of Knut Hagberg and René Wellek, of Margaret Storrs and Werner Leopold.

For material aid in traversing a domain which proved at times, as Carlyle might have said, "wide-weltering," I wish to express my gratitude to the officials of the National Library of Scotland, and of the libraries of Yale University, the University of Michigan, the University of Berlin, and the British Museum.

To Professor Karl Young of Yale University I owe my introduction to the fascination of following the origins and ramifications of Carlyle's ideas. To him I am grateful also for unfailing encouragement and constructive criticism during the preparation of this work.

Professor Werner Leopold of Northwestern University has not only critically examined the work in manuscript but has also contributed an Appendix on "Carlyle's Handbooks on the History of German Literature." Professor Margaret Storrs of Smith College has also given me the benefit of a critical reading of the manuscript and of her special knowledge of the philosophies of Kant and Fichte, particularly as they affected Carlyle.

For stimulating personal advice, during a sabbatical year in Europe, I owe no small debt to Mr. James A. S. Barrett of Peebles, Scotland; to Dr. Gerhart von Schulze-Gaevernitz, Professor of Economics in the University of Freiburg; to Professor Louis Cazamian of the Sorbonne; to Professor Heinrich Kraeger of the Technische Hochschule, Berlin; to Dr. René Wellek of the Czech University at Prague; to Mrs. Henrietta Strong, the present curator of the Carlyle House in Chelsea, for permission to examine Carlyle's library there; and to Carlyle's nephew, the late Alexander Carlyle.

CHARLES FREDERICK HARROLD.

LONDON,
May 31, 1932.

TABLE OF CONTENTS

CARLYLE AND GERMAN THOUGHT

CHAPTER I

INTRODUCTION

1. CARLYLE AND GERMAN IDEAS

To any one acquainted with Thomas Carlyle in the years between 1819 and 1827, there must have been something incongruous in the efforts of the irascible young Calvinist to seek in Kant, Goethe, and the German Romanticists the delivering power of a new evangel. What had Goethe—that serene "soul of light and adamant"[1]—for this harassed and gloomy Puritan? Few observers would have predicted that he would find in Wilhelm Meister's search for a well-rounded self-culture a ray of hope for the crumbling certitudes of Calvinism, and a gospel of action capable of galvanizing the energies of nineteenth-century England. Certainly there was apparently little in common between Carlyle's earliest interests and the aesthetic inquiries of Schiller, the reverberations of the Critical Philosophy, the fantastic world of Jean Paul, or the mystical queries of Novalis. But in 1819 Carlyle was entering upon a stage in his development in which German doctrines were to give new form to his convictions, and later to enable him to convey to his contemporaries a renewed sense of those intuitions which underlay his native faith. Through the study of German, which he undertook early in that year, he set out upon a moral and intellectual journey which ended only after some fourteen years of wayfaring among German ideas. By 1833, when the publication of the essay on *Diderot* definitely indicated his growing interest in the French Revolution, he had assimilated all the German teachings which were relevant to his needs; and had effected an adjustment between the essentials of a religious creed and the form and spirit of a foreign philosophy, which is one of the curious achievements in the history of ideas. By the autumn of 1834, the struggling, self-torturing young man of 1819 had fashioned for himself a fairly consistent philosophy of life; so that while *Sartor Resartus* was stating that philosophy in the pages of *Fraser's Magazine*, the author was "burning his ships" and settling in Chelsea, to apply to the moral and social problems of the day the doctrines which he had formulated under the influence of German literature and thought. Our present concern is the study of those formative years, and of the early elements involved in Carlyle's transformation from an obscure Calvinist made ill and bitter with skepticism into the powerful and quickening prophet of Victorian England.

That such a study is not without value, in the greater study of the ideas underlying Victorian literature, may become clear from several considerations. Before new and vitalizing forces may be released into literature and thought, it is necessary for the old to be shown as inadequate. There must be effective criticism of the moribund and obstructive point of view, and a striking and authentic opening up of new sources of inspiration. The man who undertakes this formidable task must levy either upon the past or upon those of his contemporaries, near or remote, who are opposing the inertia of the age. It was Carlyle's purpose, in so far as he dealt with ideas, to reveal the inadequacy of the reigning British empiricism, and its menace to whatever was creative and dynamic in literature, society, and ethics. He sought to redress the intellectual and moral balance which had been disturbed by eighteenth century skepticism, mechanism, associationism. He was not content to ridicule the frenzy of "psycho-physics" which led Emerson to rank Spurzheim's *Cranilogy* with the work of Lavoisier; or to attack the hollow dogmatism of Allison's essay on *Taste*;

or to reveal, as a base calumny on human nature, Bentham's reduction of all morality to a calculus of motives and sanctions. To advance beyond mere opposition, and to present in a new and illuminating form the essence of what he thought was at once the wisdom of the ages and the answer to his opponents, Carlyle needed new terms and fresh concepts. Until he had penetrated into the heart of German literature, he had little more than an anguished intuition of the fallacies of the prevailing British philosophy. His conviction needed the guidance of an intellectual illumination; his malady—a weakened faith in himself—needed the curative influence of a great personality. In turning to German writers, he found not so much a source as an inspiration. But they enabled him to reassert a point of view which was everywhere speedily losing ground. How he utilized their ideas, and applied their terminology to the task which he undertook, forms a problem of considerable significance in the greater movement of which it was a part.

It is important to remember, however, that in considering Carlyle in relation to German thought, any study of him as a philosopher would have a negative result and very little value. It is more profitable to regard him as a man of letters indebted in a peculiar degree to those metaphysical inquiries which he constantly thought of as symptomatic of disease in a man or an age. It is still more profitable to regard him according to his own theory of the "priest of literature." As such, while his proper vocation is a literary one, his interest is in character, ethics, action, and history, and his work frequently takes the form of popular philosophic exhortation. Yet Carlyle never regarded himself as in any sense a philosopher: his chief Master, Goethe, "never thought about thinking."[2] It is this deeply characteristic aversion in him to any systematic thought which makes the comparison between his teachings and their German background extremely hazardous. It has been aptly said that "he had an irresistible impulse, especially when talking theology, to play with metaphysical language," and that "he was somewhat like a layman who ventures on the terminology of lawyers and finds that he has implied far more than was in his mind."[3]   As a man of letters for whom the realm of philosophy was a remote and attractive province, yet enchanting only from a distance, Carlyle handled metaphysical ideas with the negligence of the gifted amateur.   While he frequently seized the heart of an abstract principle, he seldom acknowledged an indebtedness, and when he did so, it was often to the wrong source.   He gave to certain doctrines the wrong names; altered old concepts without changing his terminology; and employed expressions so ambiguous as to be applicable to various technically incompatible theories. Nor are his purposes always any clearer than his language, except that even at the cost of consistency he seeks a homogeneity in various unmaterialistic philosophies in order to reassure himself about the reality of spirit.   Thus the study of Carlyle as a thinker, and the examination of the sources of his ideas, present a number of peculiar difficulties.

If the German background of his teachings cannot always be inferred from his language, the source of many of his ideas must be found elsewhere.   Carlyle's critics have too often forgotten that almost any specific idea in his works might well have come to him through the processes of his own thought, or through his reading in works other than German.   What Professor Lehman has happily called "a float of solution" undoubtedly characterises the fund of thought which Carlyle acquired through his vast reading, and which at times crystallized into ideas deceptively similar to those of philosophers from whom he probably made no conscious borrowing.   Perhaps more than any other cause, the neglect of this simple observation has led many of Carlyle's critics, especially in Germany, to over-estimate his debt to German writers.[4]   Goethe's influence has been exaggerated by those interested in Carlyle's moral doctrines; the influence of German Idealism has been over-stressed by those attracted to the philosophical passages in *Sartor*. Too few have remembered the fundamental and persistent puritanism in all of his works, from the *Life of Schiller* (1823-1824) to *The Portraits of John Knox* (1875). The simplest criterion in the judgment of sources is the reflection that a similarity in ideas does not necessarily imply a borrowing. It has been easy from the very first, when his early critics accused him of "mysticism," unjustifiably to read into Carlyle's work a great deal more of foreign thought than he ever appropriated. A study of the German background of his point of view, therefore, should perhaps become increasingly a study of affinities. In the present work, only obvious borrowings will be treated as such. A number of secondary elements in Carlyle's doctrines will be seen as indirectly appropriated and then more or less transformed. Still other elements will be considered as strikingly parallel to certain German doctrines, but as of very doubtful German origin. We shall find Carlyle appropriating, rejecting, transforming. He invaded authors like a monarch, and exercised a royal privilege in ordering his newly acquired possessions according to the requirements of his own domain.

2. GENERAL NATURE OF THE GERMAN INFLUENCE

In spite of Carlyle's absorbing interest in German literature rather than in German philosophy, his chief debt was to German thought, either expressed in formal treatises like those of Kant and Fichte, or imaginatively stated in the poetry of Schiller and Goethe, or condensed in memorable phrasing in the *Fragmente* of Novalis or in the didactic passages of *Wilhelm Meister*. It is true that he owed a debt to Goethe and Richter for the aesthetic elements in *Sartor*. The character of Teufelsdröckh and much of the frame-work of his story take us back to Jean Paul; while the unfinished novel, *Wotton Reinfred*, and parts of *Sartor Resartus*, are patterned directly after *Wilhelm Meister*,[5] and represent the character and quality of Carlyle's purely literary dependence upon German literature. But it is also true that, although his first fondness for Schiller and Goethe was largely aesthetic, he was soon pained by their "*palabra* about the nature of the fine arts,"[6] and that he concentrated with moral eagerness upon the ethical content rather than upon the form of their imaginative productions. What finally quickened him into moral health, and enabled him to attain his individual point of view, was what he found in their ethical, religious, and philosophical theories. His hunger was not for dissertations on "Grace and Dignity" or on the "Naïve and Sentimental." He soon rejected Goethe's theory that perfection proceeds from culture rather than from morality, and became alarmed at the doctrine that salvation lies through poetry, art, the theater, rather than through fidelity to the old moral code.[7] It has become a commonplace among Carlyle's critics to cite his alteration of Goethe's phrase in the *Generalbeichte* from "im Ganzen, Guten, Schönen" to "the Whole, the Good, the *True*," as representative of his readiness to find a moral emphasis in unlikely places.[8] There is no evidence that he ever went to the Germans for any artistic purposes. That his description of Richter's style happens also to describe his own does not necessarily imply that he chose Richter as a model; his acknowledgment of the influence of his father's speech, and the echoes in his own works of the styles of Sterne, Swift, and Rabelais, make his formal debt to German literature of secondary significance. It was German thought, the German point of view, and the German spirit which struck him as a revelation. Not that technically philosophical ideas superseded all others in their impress upon him. Ideas in any form, if they expressed his inarticulate convictions, appealed to him independently of their source or their context. We find, for example, that the sentence to which he accorded the central position in his teachings—"Doubt of any sort cannot be removed except by Action"—occurs in one of the most unlikely passages in *Wilhelm Meister*.[9] In Richter's *Des Feldpredigers Schmelzle Reise nach Flätz*, he prizes not the characters of the narrative but certain of the irrelevant but provocative footnotes. In both authors, it is not the artist but the moralist, the *penseur*, who ultimately wins Carlyle. But metaphysical ideas, if they are to appeal to him at all, must come in imaginative dress, for if Carlyle is too much of a moralist to enjoy Goethe the novelist, he is too much of an artist to comprehend Kant the epistemologist. On the whole, the German influence—if indeed it may be so called—was essentially philosophic: it furnished the necessary theoretical basis for the demands of his moral conscience, and permitted him an eclectic study of a number of doctrines by which he could vindicate for himself the spirit and essential truth of the creed of Ecclefechan.

In this effort at adjusting new terms and concepts to old religious convictions, Carlyle's moral and religious needs, as well as his independent, eclectical temperament, played an important part. By nature and circumstance he was predisposed to the new German point of view from the outset. Like Friedrich Schlegel he naturally scoffed at the Enlightenment, and scorned Voltaire, its "withered pontif." Impatient of laborious research without a creative or shaping imagination, he found his own impatience expressed in the theories of Schiller, Fichte, and Novalis. His distrust of speculative reason he found succinctly stated for him in Goethe, and elaborately justified—so he thought—in Kant's *Kritik der reinen Vernunft*. He sought the stimulating power of a great personality, and found it presented in Goethe himself, and its cultivation set forth in admirable detail in *Wilhelm Meister*. He had fought with the demons of skepticism and suicidal despair; and Schiller's triumph and Goethe's progress from *Werther* to the serenity of the *Wanderjahre* and the second part of *Faust* showed him that his problems had been other men's problems and had been solved. What he missed in current English and French thought—the dynamical

element—he found in Fichte, and especially in Novalis.[10]
From his earliest years he had developed a passion for history, which could not be satisfied by Hume, Gibbon, and Robertson, but which found an illuminating response in the theories of Fichte, Schelling, Schiller, Novalis, and the Schlegels. His admiration of great men, and his desire to account for them more adequately than in the light of Gibbon's cynicism or Hume's mechanical psychology, found a great measure of satisfaction in Fichte's doctrine of the "Scholar" and in the Romantic notion of the man of genius. In spite of his native Puritanism, therefore, Carlyle had a number of interests and purposes in common with German writers.

No doubt it was the combination in him of a need to rehabilitate his childhood faith, and of impulses toward new modes of thought and belief, which explains his peculiar method of studying his newly found authors. It is almost as if he read them with a constant mental reservation, never giving himself completely to them, nor seeking to appreciate even for a brief period, their whole *Weltanschauung* with all its implications. It is fairly certain that he was fond of aphoristic passages. They permitted him to pause, and to proceed with his own elaboration, to ignore or to reject without loss of meaning. That this was a kind of reading in which he frequently indulged is suggested by the fact that most of the passages to which he clung, and which he quoted in his works and correspondence to the end of his life, are to be found in such aphoristic sources as Novalis's *Fragmente*, Goethe's *West-Oestlicher Divan, Maximen und Reflexionen, Faust,* and *Wilhelm Meister* (into which Goethe poured numbers of his isolated reflections), in Schlegel's *Ideen,* in Richter's *Wahrheit aus Jean Pauls Leben* and *Des Feldpredigers Schmelzle Reise nach Flätz.* In those works not of an aphoristic nature, Carlyle's mind seems to have acted like a magnet: the sentence or phrase which expressed the essence of his notion appears in his works shorn of all context. We have noted that this was true of his favorite sentence in Goethe. It was true also of his method with Fichte: he seized, for example, upon the concept of the "Divine Idea at the Bottom of Appearance," but ignored the relation between the finite and the infinite Egos. In Novalis, where ideas are presented in a series of "fragments," he admires the idea that religion is the essence of society, but is silent on Novalis's audacious query about the close relation between religion, lust, and cruelty.[11] And if he is silent on the contexts from which he drew the passages he needed, he is also noncommittal on the total significance of the author. In spite of his extended discussions of Richter, Novalis, and Goethe, he never made a complete evaluation of them. As a moralist seeking to preach a regenerating doctrine to a materialistic and hedonistic age, he popularized the ethical ideas of Goethe, the religious implications in Kant, Fichte and Novalis, and, out of all the world of Jean Paul, the moral inspiration.

The proportionate degrees in which these writers were significant for him have been subject to much difference of opinion. To throw any light on this question, it is necessary at once to consider the extent of Carlyle's knowledge of German works and the relative importance of their authors in the construction of his point of view. It is undoubtedly true, as Kraeger says, that a great many of the books which Carlyle mentions he knew only by name.[12] Even after the translation of *Meister* (1824), he knew few German authors; when, in the following year, he undertook the translation of the stories published as *German Romance*, he sought the aid of Henry Crabb Robinson.[13] His knowledge of the German nation as a whole was never very rich; he was nearly sixty years old when he first visited Germany, in 1852. In his early passion for German literature, he followed public opinion in regard to Schiller, and later—in 1828—attributed to Goethe an influence greater than it really was.[14] In fact, Carlyle's knowledge of the Germans and their literature is a curious paradox of wide and detailed learning, and sudden and complete gaps. It is certain that his knowledge of Goethe and his works was extraordinarily full; but, in spite of his authoritative manner in discussing Kant, he knew almost nothing of the true meaning of Kant's doctrines. The number of times in which he mentions a writer is no indication of his acquaintance with the author's works. Although Schelling's name appears several times in his correspondence, his knowledge of Schelling was confined, as we shall see, to a collection of the philosopher's popular lectures, the *Methode des akademischen Studiums*.

Though doubt may be felt in regard to most of Carlyle's "German masters," we may be sure that the great and lasting influence was Goethe. Carlyle was of course most familiar with *Wilhelm Meisters Lehrjahre*, and with the *Wanderjahre* in the edition of 1821 rather than in the later and more extended form. Of secondary importance was the *Dichtung und Wahrheit*, the *Maximen und Reflexionen*, the *West-Oestlicher Divan*, and a number of the *Gedichte*, notably the *Proömion*, the *Symbolum*, and such epigrammatic verses as those in *Gott, Gemüt und Welt* and in the *Zahme Xenien*. The greater part of *Faust* seems to have offered him comparatively little. Though it was this drama that first attracted him to Goethe, he had read it but once by 1828 and was repelled by the ending until Goethe sent him the *Helena*.[15] Apparently but two passages remained memorable to him: Faust's curse, and the Song of the Earth Spirit, with its image of the world as the Garment of God. As his fondness for *Meister* increased, he came more and more to regard *Faust*, curiously enough, as "intrinsically a small poem."[16] Later, though his interest in German literature had diminished with the death of Goethe, he studied *Faust Part II* and placed it above *Part I*; as late as 1872 he read it with renewed pleasure.[17] Carlyle had no need, however, to wait for the appearance of *Faust II*; his evangel had taken form, much earlier, on the reading of *Meister*. The great influence which came to Carlyle through all these works was primarily psychological. That is why Goethe remained for him the chief influence to the end of his life. "My greatly most delightful reading," said Carlyle, "is where some Goethe musically teaches me." What Goethe fundamentally taught him was faith in himself. Thereafter, Carlyle admired increasingly Goethe's union of the singer and the sage, his combination of the real and the ideal in *Werther, Meister*, and *Dichtung und Wahrheit*, his treatment of the actual as the raw materials of the ideal, his conception of renunciation as the preliminary act in true living, his reverence for sorrow, his pantheism—so far as it was present in his teachings—his wise silence on the unseen.[18] Goethe's serenity, breadth, and tolerance, achieved after heroic struggle, gave significance to Carlyle's own problems. Long after the novelty had worn off the doctrines of Kant, Fichte, Schelling, and Novalis, and Carlyle had ceased to ponder the speculative enigmas of the philosophers, Goethe remained the permanent and vitalizing power in his thinking. It may be said, indeed, that all the other German writers had relevance for Carlyle only as they elaborated or confirmed the principles he had derived from Goethe. It is difficult to imagine how he would have interpreted Fichte's doctrine of the hero, Novalis's doctrine of *Selbsttödtung*, or Schelling's doctrine of organism, had he not found in Goethe himself an example of a hero, in *Entsagen* an ideal comparable to "self-annihilation," and in Goethe's general philosophy an expression of the organic character of Nature.

After Goethe the primary influences were Kant, Fichte, and Novalis. How many of Kant's works were known to Carlyle has frequently been disputed. It is certain that he never read the whole of the *Kritik der reinen Vernunft*.[19] In spite of Fehr's assertion that Carlyle studied Kant very thoroughly,[20] the interpretation of Kant's doctrines in *The State of German Literature* and in *Novalis* indicates that his knowledge of the Critical Philosophy must have been largely secondary, probably through the writings of Novalis and the Schlegels.[21] The passages on Kant in the *Life of Schiller* have been perhaps too harshly characterised by Hagberg as "grotesquely unapposite reflections."[22] It is possible that they owe something to Schiller's essays, though Carlyle certainly found little there on the specific doctrines in which he was interested.[23] We shall note later how his transformation of Kant's term *Reason* shows that he probably did not know the *Kritik der praktischen Vernunft* or the *Grundlegung zur Metaphysik der Sitten.* It will become clear also that much in Carlyle's peculiar notions of Kant's doctrines is owing to his early study of Dugald Stewart's *Preliminary Dissertation on the Progress of Metaphysical, Ethical and Political Philosophy.* On the whole, Kant's importance for Carlyle lay in the degree to which the new doctrines of Space, Time, Reason, and Understanding might give conceptual form to Goethe's notion of the world as the vesture of spirit, and of reality as knowable only through a faculty superior to narrow speculative reason. Independent of these doctrines was Kant's conception of the transcendental nature of duty, which of course commended itself to the student of Goethe's doctrine of *Entsagen.*

Of all the German influences upon Carlyle, Kant has been the most exaggerated. There is no evidence, however, that Carlyle ever understood—or sought to understand—Kant's investigation into the limits of knowledge, or truly sensed the significance of the attempt. His enthusiasm for the philosopher was conditioned wholly by his own interpretation. We have noted that his authoritative manner of discussing Kant cannot bear close scrutiny. Behind it lies confusion, preconception, inadequate comprehension. This is true, for example, of his remarks on Kant in a letter to Espinasse in 1841:

> "I may say further that after all the Fichteisms, Schellingisms, Hegelisms, I still understand *Kant* to be the grand novelty, the prime author of the new spiritual

world, of whom all the others are but superficial, transient modifications . . . . What better can you do than vigorously set to the *Kritik der reinen Vernunft*, a very attainable book, and resolutely study it and re-study it till you understand it? You will find it actually capable of being understood, rigorously sequent, like a book of mathematics; labour that pays itself; really one of the best metaphysical studies that I know of. Once master of Kant, you have attained what I reckon most precious, perhaps alone precious in that multifarious business of German philosophy: namely, deliverance from the fatal incubus of Scotch or French philosophy, with its mechanisms and Atheisms . . ."[24]

To Carlyle, Kant was a force for the rehabilitation of the "spiritual world"; and the post-Kantians were but "transient modifications." It is curious, in the light of Carlyle's scanty, indirect, and faulty comprehension of Kant, that he insists on the ease with which the *Kritik* may be read.[25] Natural, however, is his statement that the book is "rigorously sequent"; for the appearance of order and of organic construction left few of Kant's earliest critics aware of what Professor Norman Kemp Smith has fully shown, that his terms undergo slight changes of meaning in different parts of the work, and that later sections do not follow rigorously on some of the preliminary statements in the two prefaces.[26] It will become clear, on the whole, as we examine Carlyle's interpretation of Kant that, for him, the new doctrine, whatever it meant to its originator, amounted merely to a general "deliverance from the fatal incubus of Scotch or French philosophy, with all its mechanisms and Atheisms." The relativity of space and time, the functions of Reason—as Carlyle interpreted them—, meant the refutation of materialism and the vindication of the spiritual realities expounded in the old theologies.

Among Fichte's works, Carlyle was apparently most interested in *Über das Wesen des Gelehrten*. No other work of Fichte is quoted in Carlyle's writings. The *Wissenschafts-*

lehre is mentioned in *Sartor* in a paraphrase of a *Fragment* of Novalis.[27]   Other works, however, contain a number of parallels to Carlyle's teachings, sufficient to make them valuable in an analysis of the known influence from the lectures on the Scholar: the *Grundzüge des gegenwärtigen Zeitalters,* the *Bestimmung des Menschen,* and the *Anweisung zum seligen Leben.*   That he never cited these works—assuming that he read them—may be explained by Carlyle's habit of acknowledging only those sources which he either translated or closely paraphrased.   If he used them it was unconsciously, out of the "float of solution" from which he frequently drew.   Fichte's *Staatslehre,* though included among the sources by Professors Vaughan and Cazamian,[28] cannot be proved to have been an unmistakable source.   In the first place, it was too technical and abstract to appeal to Carlyle; in the next place, it fails to account more adequately than the other and more probable sources for Carlyle's social doctrines.[29]

If Carlyle can be said to have entered into the spirit of any metaphysical system, it was into Fichte's that he penetrated the farthest.   Though he certainly made little attempt to grapple with Fichte's technical problems, he found in the philosophy of the Ego a very congenial body of doctrine. It served the purpose of giving greater intellectual form to the ideas he had found in Goethe.   Unconscious of any illegitimate identification of Goethe's teachings with those of the philosopher, he regarded Fichte and Goethe as two exponents of one general doctrine.   The spiritual nature of all existence, the immanence of the divine in the actual, the symbolic significance of Nature, the outflowering of finite forms from the Infinite, the function of history as revelation, the alternation of periods of belief with those of unbelief, the divine mission of the Hero—as thinker, poet, prophet, king—, the moral significance of action—these elements in Carlyle's philosophy derive, more or less directly, from Fichte; yet are frequently treated by Carlyle in the

figurative language of Goethe. It is not too much to say
that whenever Carlyle momentarily speaks like a philosopher,
it is as a follower of Fichte. Of all the German metaphysicians, Carlyle understood him most naturally and interpreted
him with the least sacrifice of the original meaning.

His knowledge of Schelling, as that of Fichte, was limited
to the popular works, especially to the *Methode des akademischen Studiums.* Mentions of Schelling are frequent enough
to warrant our inferring his intense interest in Schelling's
ideas. That he understood him, however, or read widely in
him, is very doubtful. We gather from his Notebooks that
either at Comely Bank or early at Craigenputtock, he was
pondering "Schelling's *Ideal Realism, Philosophy of Nature
. . . .* usually called the *System of Identity . . .* subject and
object as absolutely identical." The next phrase is expressive
of his incapacity to follow metaphysical argument; he adds:
"to which I can attach next to no meaning."[30] Yet Schelling
had much for Carlyle on the nature of history, symbols, and
the world as an organism; and we shall see that the *Methode
des akademischen Studiums* very probably contributed to the
influence which Goethe and Fichte exerted.

In Novalis, Carlyle read the *Fragmente,* and frequently
returned to certain of the aphorisms as the expression of
the essence of his own convictions. No problems arise as to
his first-hand acquaintance with the *Lehrlinge zu Sais, Die
Christenheit oder Europa, Heinrich von Ofterdingen,* and the
Hymnen an die Nacht.[31] After Goethe and Richter, no
German writer is more often quoted by Carlyle than Novalis.
In this mystic he found a stimulating interpreter of Kant
and Fichte. Novalis's vivid and concise phrasing rendered
abstract ideas less difficult and repugnant to him. And the
German's gentleness of character, his exaltation of *Selbst-
tödtung,* made a strong appeal to Carlyle's nature.

Much less important, but nevertheless noteworthy, were
the influences of Schiller, the Schlegels, Jacobi, Werner, and
Richter. Although Küchler has conclusively shown wherein

Carlyle misunderstood Schiller, and how he drew no definite religious or philosophic principles from him,[32] it will be found that there were indeed very specific borrowings in respect to theories on history, on the nature of the physical world, and on knowledge. Aside from these intellectual influences, there was the example of Schiller's character, which in a measure did for Carlyle what Goethe did. From the Schlegels, Carlyle drew much information concerning the new world of German literature, some degree of confirmation of his view of the *Aufklärung*, a new approach to a critical evaluation of literature, and, in the case of Friedrich Schlegel, some views on the nature of *Phantasie* and on revelation in history. Zacharias Werner, "the most problematic of all the romantic problematic tribe," had, curiously enough, considerable interest for Carlyle, who probably never realized the full extent of the sadistic mysticism underlying Werner's amorphous, phantasmagorical dramas. What struck him was Werner's occasional embracing of the Fichtean ideal of the submergence of the finite ego in the Idea, and the similarity, at times, of his ideas with those of Goethe and Novalis. He is not properly an influence at all; Carlyle's interest in him is always a half-puzzled one. Werner's dissolute life, the diabolical note in his dramas, the Asiatic passivity of his mysticism, and his final flight to Catholicism, all kept him on the periphery of Carlyle's interests.[33]

Richter's influence on Carlyle's intellectual world was somewhat greater than is suggested by those critics concerned with his debt to Richter for style, tone, humor, and the structural side of *Sartor*. Though it is an exaggeration to say, with Dr. Wellek, that "Carlyle . . . is also in his whole thought remarkably close to Jean Paul and not to Fichte, or Kant, or even to Goethe as is usually maintained," it is undeniable, as the author goes on to say, that "Jean Paul, just as Carlyle, saw in the ethical deed, in the practice of life, the whole meaning of life and the whole aim of philosophy."[34] Like Schiller and Goethe, Jean Paul had been confronted with the problem of creating out of his own unhappiness a philosophy of experience. Like Schiller, he had fought with poverty, obscurity, ill health, and religious doubt. It was thus Jean Paul's character, as well as his creative works, which gave him a high place in Carlyle's mind. Intellectually, Richter seemed as striking an analogue to Carlyle's experience as he was morally. He fought the rationalist philosophy of the time, and took, like Carlyle, an essentially negative attitude toward Kant's teachings. For Jean Paul, as for Carlyle, Fichte was "much the most comprehensible and sympathetic philosopher among the great Kantian lineage."[35] Both men were struck by the philosophy of Jacobi, and both were determined to find in the new doctrines a renewal of faith under more acceptable forms. Both were seeking a new approach to history, to ethics, to the meaning of Nature. Richter's occasional reflections on these subjects, in the most irrelevant passages, gave rise to some of the most characteristic phrases in Carlyle's writings. Besides the general intellectual influence, however, Richter filled for Carlyle somewhat the same rôle that Novalis occupied: he supplied the memorable image, the impassioned tone, which was necessary for Carlyle's acceptance of any abstraction.

Among Carlyle's sources, a unique place is occupied by Jacobi. He is quoted but once,[36] and mentioned only three or four times in the essays, yet will later be seen as very probably a source for some of Carlyle's ideas on knowledge and faith. Aside from the parallelism in their thought, there was a remarkable similarity between their aims and their reactions to current doctrines. Both men were dualists, unable to the end of their careers to reconcile the claims of the heart and the head. They ultimately sought escape in a *salto mortale* into faith, and the direct evidence of feeling. To the *Kritik der reinen Vernunft* they both reacted negatively, seeing in it only the destruction of dogmatic philosophy and Scotch skepticism. For both men, Kant was the liberator, by whom life, art, religion, and conduct could again be vindicated by faith. The difficulties involved in their solution of the inevitable dilemmas of faith-philosophy left them both in disharmony with themselves. To call faith by the new Kantian term *Reason,* as both did, was not a satisfactory way out; and Carlyle eventually repudiated it and poured scorn upon Coleridge's attempt to use the term as a divining-rod of truth.[37] It will become evident, as we proceed, that Carlyle owed something to the author of *Allwill.* Their problems were alike, and they attacked them in that peculiar fashion which recalls at times, in an extraordinarily familiar way, the thought-patterns of the late eighteenth century, and yet makes them speak frequently in the terms of the Kantian and post-Kantian world. The influence of Jacobi belongs properly to our inquiry into Carlyle's ideas concerning knowledge, where the work of Coleridge—and the ideas of Jacobi, with which the latter was familiar—will throw light on how much (and how little) Carlyle owed to Kant for his notions of Reason and Understanding.

3. CARLYLE AND THE NEW OUTLOOK

It will perhaps bear stating again that the effect of all these writers and their doctrines upon Carlyle cannot be strictly defined as an influence. Instead of contributing directly to the content of his thought, they provided a stimulus, an atmosphere, and a number of new terms for what he regarded as old ideas. Indeed, he was not seeking a new philosophy or a new creed. Deeply but inarticulately certain of the truth of his home-taught faith, he sought for new champions and fresh expressions of its spirit. It was thus that he fell into paradoxes and inconsistencies between what he thought and what he said. That he never took the trouble to explain how inaccurate were some of his newly-found terms for his fundamentally orthodox position, was probably owing to an assumption that his readers would understand his aims. He was obviously not a philosopher but a wanderer among ideas, seeking here and there an echo of his own convictions. Standing "at the transition from the Christian philosophy of the 18th century to new idealistic theories, he could not avoid using some of the terminology";[38] yet his task was not one of complete assimilation of the new doctrines, but an inevitably eclectic one. Many of the new conceptions he evidently understood in a very limited degree: some of them were plainly repugnant to him; while others were wholly irrelevant. Though his language frequently gives the appearance of community with the aims of Goethe and the Idealists, he never really penetrated to the heart of their most characteristic teachings. His attitude was to the last a wavering one. His roots were in the Reformation; but his early enthusiasms included a shocked admiration for the lucidity and simplicity of the Enlightenment, which turned ultimately to bitter denunciation of its destructive rationalism. Eclectic, contradictory, yet determined to find in the new literature of Germany a deliverance from mechanism and despair, he felt less the direct influence, than the general *spirit,* of German thought. If that spirit at times becomes discernible in specific parallels of thought, the more common term is applicable. In any discussion of Carlyle's German indebtedness, the word "influence" is almost unavoidable; and if it is understood in its larger implications, as suggesting very little conscious borrowing, it will seldom be misleading.

How Carlyle was to adjust the multifarious and conflicting doctrines expressed in an alien philosophy and literature to the essential spirit of his native creed; above all, how he himself was to find a path from negation to affirmation, constituted his chief problem in the years between 1820, when he first read *Faust,* and 1831, when he had finally and comprehensively stated his newly formulated doctrine in *Sartor Resartus.* It was essentially a quest for the Everlasting Yea, which should be capable at once of retrieving his spiritual health and of leading to constructive theories of literature, history, ethics, and religion. It is necessary, therefore, to examine briefly the psychological and biographical background out of which Carlyle's quest emerged.

CHAPTER II

CARLYLE'S PROBLEM

1. WINDS OF DOCTRINE

We need only remember the well-known features of the period in which Carlyle grew to intellectual maturity to realize the sharp discrepancy between the atmosphere of the speculative world and that of his childhood environment. A glance at several representative statements in the current philosophy, psychology, and ethics of the time will suffice to bring that discrepancy to mind.

Carlyle was born into the period which was just emerging from the thralldom of that empirical philosophy which virtually began in the year 1690, with the publication of Locke's *Essay Concerning Human Understanding,* and which promised to end, so far as periods ever end at a particular historical moment, with the publication of Kant's *Critique of Pure Reason* in 1781. The promise of release from the older philosophy had not, when Carlyle went to the University of Edinburgh in 1809, found any measure of fulfillment in England. The school of Locke still reigned, in spite of the devastating power of Hume's skepticism. The dominant spirit of the age was still rationalistic. While it offered to Carlyle the exhilarating knowledge of new achievements of the intellect, it imposed the rigorous duty of recognising its limitations. It said, in substance:

"Let us not concern ourselves with idle speculation in reference to things which the mind of man can never compass and understand. Why busy ourselves concerning the deeper significance and purpose of nature which our thought is utterly incapable of penetrating? While we may observe and classify the phenomena of nature, and formulate the laws of their behavior, we can never hope to comprehend their inner meaning, forever veiled and obscure.   Nature, which seems so near—of which, indeed, we ourselves are a part—nevertheless lies far beyond our ken.   And the being and nature of God, who must be regarded as dwelling in a sphere far out and beyond the outermost bounds of nature, must remain still more incomprehensible.   If we cannot understand the inscrutable mysteries of the world which we have seen, much less the mystery of God whom we have not seen."[1]

Philosophy, therefore, had little aid to offer Carlyle in his quest for "inner meaning."   In the first place, the corrosive skepticism of Hume had placed philosophical speculation in a dilemma.   His theory of causation had undermined the validity of reason, as Berkeley's doctrines had ruined the validity of the senses.   Carlyle early learnt that Hume's chief purpose, in respect to knowledge and faith, was "to make the reader sensible of the truth . . . that all our reasoning concerning causes and effects are derived from nothing but custom; and that belief is more properly an act of the sensitive, than of the cogitative part of our natures . . . ."   Our ideas of necessity and causation arise entirely from the uniformity observable in the operations of nature, where similar objects are constantly conjoined together, and the mind is "determined by custom to infer the one from the appearance of the other."[2]   This *reductio ad absurdum* of the empirical philosophy left everyone convinced that Locke had overlooked an essential factor in his account of the sources of knowledge; "our Scotch Metaphysicians," Carlyle noted, "had a dim notion that much of this was wrong; but they knew not how to right it."[3]   As yet the opposite stream of tendency, the Continental rationalism as represented in the tradition of thought from Descartes to Spinoza and Leibnitz, had received no effective introduction into England.   In the absence of their influence, native philosophical effort had proved naïve and fruitless.   Carlyle could see that the Scotch "commonsense school" had striven in vain to shake Hume's position:

"Dr. Reid's grand triumph over the Sceptics is as good as no triumph whatever."[4]   Philosophy was virtually dead. Dugald Stewart, "its last amiable cultivator," merely "encompasses it with fences, invites cultivators, and drives away intruders; often (fallen on evil days) he is reduced to long arguments with passers-by, to prove that it *is* a field . . . ."[5] For Carlyle, the period preceding his own had been one of "Dogmatical or Constructive Metaphysics, when the mind constructively endeavors to scheme out and assert for itself an actual Theorem of the Universe, and therewith for a time [to] rest satisfied."   The "second or sick stage might be called that of Sceptical or Inquisitory Metaphysics; when the mind having widened its sphere of vision, the existing Theorem of the Universe no longer answers the phenomena, no longer yields contentment, but must be torn in pieces, and certainty anew sought for in the endless realms of denial."[6] He noted the irony in the fact that it had been "Locke, himself a clear, humble-minded, patient, reverent, nay, religious man [who] had paved the way for banishing religion from the world."[7]   Thus in the early years, before Carlyle had clearly reached his own philosophical conclusions, the prevailing temper in speculative thought indicated only the "wide-wasting Whirlwind of a departing Era . . . . Not Godhead, but an iron, ignoble circle of Necessity embraces all things."[8]

In the dominant theories attempting to explain human motive and conduct, he found a similar attitude.   He had only to study Hartley's physiological psychology to discover how thought and will arise from "vibrations" which begin in the senses and pass through the nerves to "the white medullary substance of the brain," so that "simple ideas will run into complex ones, by means of association."[9]   Hume had already defined association as the "mechanism" by which complex ideas (relations, modes, substance, etc.) arise from simpler ones, the "necessity," apparent in the process, being but the effect of "custom."[10]   Whatever Carlyle thought of "Hartley's vibrations and vibranticles," he objected to the soul's being reduced to a mass of sensations and ideas, operating like a mechanism, with association as the only unifying agent; and he commented with amused indignation upon Cabanis's notion that "as the liver secretes bile, so does the brain secrete thought."[11]

Applied to morality, this conception of human nature led naturally to an egoistic and utilitarian ethic. The whole field of ethics became a "mechanic of pleasure and pain," in which pleasant experiences promoted right conduct and unpleasant experiences deterred the individual from transgressing the laws of society. Carlyle found the hedonistic calculus expressed most elaborately, of course, in the writings of Bentham: "A man's moral sensibility," said the Utilitarian, "may be said to be strong when the pains and pleasures of the moral sanctions shew greater in his eyes in comparison with other pleasures and pains (and consequently exert a stronger influence) than in the eyes of the persons he is compared with..."[12] In opposition to—or in neglect of—the old ethical doctrine that pain and sorrow have a disciplinary and spiritual value in themselves, Bentham maintained that "pain is in itself an evil; and indeed, without exception the only evil."[13] To the Calvinist, the whole attempt to simplify and "mechanise" the elements in man's nature was a lamentable error:

> "Goodness, which was a rule to itself," Carlyle wrote later, "must now appeal to Precept, and seek strength from Sanctions; the Freewill no longer reigns unquestioned and by divine right, but like a mere earthly sovereign, by expediency, by Rewards and Punishments ... now that mysterious Self-impulse of the whole man, heaven-inspired, and in all senses partaking of the Infinite, ... is conceived as non-extant, and only the outward Mechanism of it remains acknowledged: of Volition, except as the synonym of Desire, we hear nothing; of 'Motives', without any Mover, more than enough."[14]

Such a doctrine had radical implications when employed as
a basis for a theory of man in society. While Carlyle was
still seeking to believe that "a mystic miraculous unfathomable union establishes itself" among men in society,[15] the
Utilitarians were viewing society atomistically, as made up
of individuals consistently pursuing their own private ends.
Left to itself, the enlightened ego would readily find the
moral solutions to its problems and further the good of
society. To speak of altruism was, for the new thinkers, to
take refuge in obscurantism; altruism was nothing but one
of the subtler forms of egoism. The aim of society—of the
mass of "spiritual atoms"—should be the compromise of all
individual desires in the effective achievement of happiness
for the greatest number. The aim of government should be
"to promote the happiness of . . . society, by punishing and
rewarding."[16] Otherwise it should observe the principle of
laissez faire, and permit the natural adjustments of individual
desires in furthering the social, economic, and ethical harmony of society. In these current theories Carlyle, of course,
missed those ideas and assumptions which he had at one time
regarded as profound and unquestionable: the deeply
dynamic nature of man, of society, of the world itself; the
old relationships of loyalty, reverence, and obedience on the
part of the servant, and responsibility on the part of the
master; the performance of duty as the end of life, and
happiness as the uncertain by-product which it was ignoble
to pursue; and government as the effort of the wise and
the strong to insure the peace and wholesomeness of the many.
Looking back in 1851, Carlyle ruminated bitterly upon the
temper of that period:

> "All Science had become mechanical; the science not
> of men, but of a kind of human beavers. Churches
> themselves had died away into a godless mechanical
> condition; and stood there as mere Cases of Articles,
> mere Forms of Churches; like the dried carcasses of
> once-swift camels, which you find left withering in the

thirst of the universal desert. . . Men's souls were blinded, hebetated, and sunk under the influence of Atheism and Materialism, and Hume and Voltaire: the world for the present was as an extinct world, deserted of God, and incapable of welldoing till it changed its heart and spirit."[17]

How the spirit of the reigning doctrines contrasted with his temperament and his early religious training may now be inquired, sufficiently at least to throw light on his independent treatment of the opposing ideas emanating from Germany. His pride, independence, and stoicism, as much as certain Calvinistic doctrines, predisposed him to his peculiarly original approach to many of the ideas dominant in the alien literature and philosophy.

2. THE TEMPER OF CARLYLE'S MIND

In the development of independence and stoicism in the character of Carlyle, the example of his parents was, of course, the great moulding influence. In spite of their poverty—and partly because of it—these traits were perhaps inordinately prized by the Carlyles as a family. In Carlyle himself they fostered a habit of abstraction, and an aloofness in speech which, as Masson quotes him, was "like talk from an upper window to people passing in the streets."[18] All of the Carlyles had a profound belief in the rightness of their convictions, an unquestioned assumption of their self-sufficiency. Whatever was new or novel could be assimilated only if it left their essential position undisturbed. It should not be surprising, therefore, if when Carlyle began to think for himself and fell into skepticism, he should be sharply eclectic and fundamentally true to his underlying Calvinism. In seeking to retrieve his faith, he would naturally appropriate—from German thought or elsewhere—only those terms and ideas which would leave him still in possession of a fundamentally Calvinistic point of view. His independence, his self-sufficiency, his aloofness explain in some degree why his ultimate philosophy bears only a deceptive resemblance to many of the German doctrines which he championed.

His stoicism, likewise, is not to be forgotten. As the son of a stern puritan father, he soon learned to exult in stoical endurance. He learned to look upon suffering with the grim sadness of one who has conceived life as largely a noble struggle against the tremendous and ignoble powers of evil. "A root of bitterness [is at] the bottom of our cup," he wrote to a friend; "happy he who learns to drink it without wincing; . . . there is medicine for the soul in it . . ." He was fond of reminding his friends that "Man is born unto trouble, unto toil, as the sparks fly upwards."[19] A deep constitutional melancholy is traceable in these and similar utterances. It is safe to say, however, that it is not always present: frequently they are examples of that puritan understatement with which the Carlyles sometimes fended off a mood of satisfaction in the pleasure of being alive. Yet Carlyle's deeply rooted, almost Mohammedan stoicism is never to be questioned. "To be resigned to God . . . to know that we know nothing . . . Denial of Self," this, says Carlyle, "is the soul of Islam; it is properly the soul of Christianity."[20] And, like his puritan self-sufficiency, that spirit in Carlyle was a factor in his choice and treatment of any new idea.

The religious creed of the little sect of "Burghers" in which he was brought up was such that these elements in Carlyle's nature were enormously strengthened. It was not a creed for cowards or weaklings. According to its articles, life was a hard, ungracious bargain between man and his Maker, the great Taskmaster. As a partial expression of the struggle of the Scotch with a meager soil, and of their centuries of oppression under Church and State, the creed naturally exalted labor and suffering as the chief realities of life. There was little place for Love and the other tenderer elements of Christianity. If the Maker drives a hard bargain,

men will be likely to do the same with each other: they will
not be inclined to give or accept mercy. Endurance becomes
an ideal; one strives to achieve a fierce joy in measuring up
to austere standards; and the guiding spirit of one's conduct
is a patient, sad stoicism which is to substitute for the "peace
which passeth understanding." In thus laboring and enduring, man finds himself, according to this creed, surrounded at
every moment with eternal issues; he is the focal point of a
struggle between the powers of good and evil for the possession of a human soul. Man's freedom makes his choice
of tremendous significance. Though the battle in each man's
life is, comparatively, but for a moment, the decision is for
eternity. Misfortune, suffering, and sorrow were therefore
regarded by the Carlyles from the "long view," and as
trifling in comparison with error, which, from the same view,
took on staggering dimensions by the perspective of eternity.
The creed of the "Burghers" was an off-shoot of Calvinism,
and the first word of Calvinism is God, immanent and
transcendent. God was believed to be terribly present everywhere at every moment, testing, judging, rewarding, punishing. To many a Calvinist, however, God's immanence was
not so much cause for comfort as the ground for a constant
shuddering awareness of being observed, while God's transcendence gave reason not so much to adore his exalted, if
remote, perfection as to hate mankind for its moral short-
comings. Much of the gloom in Calvinism arises here. On
the other hand, this consciousness of man's depravity leads to
the moral strenuousness which characterises Carlyle's point
of view: since all Creation is guided by the secret inspiration
of the Almighty, and men are either saved or damned, according to the predestined course of events, nothing in life is so
important for a man as his sense of which side of the eternal
conflict he is on. According to this creed, the only important
fact about a man is his moral state.[21]

It is possible now to see, perhaps more clearly than otherwise, how the religious atmosphere of Carlyle's early years

may throw light on his later encounters with philosophical ideas. In the creed we find some of the grounds for that gloom and melancholy which his dyspepsia fails largely to explain. As a Puritan, Carlyle expected much from man, and was disappointed. The creed also nourished his tendency to aloofness and independence. The relation between the individual and his God was of such a magnitude that merely human relationships, particularly as expressed in the distinctions of title and worldly power, could have little to impress him. All outward distinctions were, after all, adventitious wrappings, "clothes," under which men were really equal before eternal judgment. The great problem of man was his moral state: only if that were satisfactorily answered could the "garment" have any significance. Not the external multiplicity of things could properly be man's real interest, but the one indwelling divinity. And that divinity, both in the objects around man and in man himself, must not slumber unexpressed, but be glorified in activity, in righteous labor. Idleness was the unpardonable sin.

Not only in matters of conduct, but also perhaps much more in concept and conviction did the creed predispose Carlyle to several notions which he regarded as elaborated in the new German point of view. The Calvinist's belief in an immanent God, working ceaselessly throughout all nature and in all of man's actions, *i.e.*, in history, led very readily, in Carlyle's mind, to the comprehension of Fichte, Goethe, and Schelling. He likewise felt prepared for Goethe's doctrine of self-development through work. Novalis's doctrine of *Selbsttödtung* came to him as only another expression for obedient, "self-annihilating" devotion to duty. History had shown him numerous examples of such devotion, and his admiration of strong character and vivid personality needed only a little of Fichte's treatment to suggest to him the doctrine of heroes. His observation that great deeds grew out of silent allegiance to ideals, and matured less through discussion than through a quiet and often unconscious effecting of good, harmonized with his puritan distrust of impressive talk. Akin to that distrust was another: a distrust of man's reason in dealing with reality. He naturally saw man as related closely to God, whose ways were "past finding out." The presumptions of reason, therefore, regarding either God or man, were likely, in Carlyle's opinion, to be either impertinent or blasphemous. To the questions which intruded upon him, there was but one answer: faith. Indeed, a great element of mystery Carlyle acknowledged at the outset; like Teufelsdröckh, he was a "wonder-loving and wonder-seeking man."[22] Before a universe which sublimely flouted man's attempts at comprehension, the only proper attitude was one of reverence. Thus if Carlyle felt at home with the Kantian doctrine of Reason, he felt an even greater familiarity with Goethe's ideal of "reverence." Mystery and wonder, central in Carlyle's point of view, lead us to what for Carlyle was the greatest mystery of all: suffering. A creed not made for weaklings could hardly be expected to deny the highest value to suffering and sorrow. As Carlyle later came to see, in his study of Goethe, religion for him was nothing if not a "worship of sorrow." In all these convictions, however, there was nothing dreamy or visionary. On the contrary, they derived their reality from a sense for *fact*. Labor, self-denial, faith, reverence for good and for suffering, all needed a realistic spirit for their full development. For the Calvinist, the world was not the truth, but it was real; the fact that it was dominated largely by the forces of evil prevented him from thinking, for any length of time, that it was unreal. Again, Goethe seemed to offer the congenial thought: for Carlyle, as for Meister, the world was man's "seedfield."

It was no doubt with a feeling of meeting old and familiar doctrines under new and provocative names that Carlyle began in the early half of the second decade of the new century to seek a reply to the materialistic theories everywhere about him. Throughout his pilgrimage among German

ideas, he was harassed by the spirit of doubt which he had
caught from the *Aufklärung*. This early period was marked
by two psychological events: the crisis of 1822, and the
quiet "conversion" of 1826.

3. A NOT UNBLESSED PILGRIMAGE: TO THE CRISIS OF 1822

There was little evidence, in Carlyle's intellectual development at the University of Edinburgh (1809-1813), that his
mind had other than a mathematical and scientific turn.
Though he read widely—in literature, history, travel—he
showed the readiest assimilation in Professor Leslie's "1st
Mathematics Class." Yet his interests were not speculative or philosophical. Though his list of books for 1810-
1811 included Locke's *Essay* and Reid's *Inquiry*, that fact
can be accounted for by his membership in the Logic Class.
Indeed, Carlyle's earliest resistance to the analysis of mind
or spirit manifests itself in these first Edinburgh years. His
attendance at the brilliant lectures of Thomas Brown, which
James and John Stuart Mill regarded as an introduction to
much that was best in British philosophy, left him irritated
at having his mind subjected to systematic analysis. But
if he rejected the validity of rational inquiry into certain
ultimate questions, he nevertheless pursued a course of reading or thinking which led him to skepticism. We have no
record of his readings for his third and fourth session, but
it is safe to say that the period of doubt which culminated
in the "Everlasting No" had its beginnings in his student
years.[23]

In his old age, when he was seventy-two, he remembered
that in 1810, when he was a young student of fifteen years,
he grieved his mother by a very blunt question: "Did God
Almighty come down and make wheelbarrows in a shop?"
This habit of questioning the faith of his fathers "went on,"
he remembered, "for about ten years," or until about 1819-

1820, when he began the study of German.[24]   It would seem that the habit of doubt had established itself by the time Carlyle left the University and began a four-year period of schoolmastering, first at Annan and then in Kirkaldy. His slow and uncertain intellectual development, the beginnings of ill health, his distaste for teaching, and the increasingly confused state of his beliefs, all marked this early period as one of the unhappiest in Carlyle's life. Unable to find a stable pause in any conviction, he was similarly unable to make a decision on his life-work. He renounced the teaching profession, and along with it the divinity studies which he had been pursuing through the device of "partial sessions." In his preparation for the Kirk he had gone so far as to deliver two trial discourses: the first, delivered in the winter of 1814, was on the text, "Before I was afflicted I went astray: but now I have kept thy word" (Psalm cxix. 67); the second, in Latin, and delivered in the winter of 1815, was entitled, "Num detur Religio Naturalis?"   (Is a Natural Religion Possible?)   Though both discourses satisfied the requirements of the authorities, he gave up the Kirk in 1818, and began the study of law. Then, in a mood of restlessness and despair, he abandoned the law, likewise, and entered upon a still unhappier period of hack work for Brewster's *Encyclopaedia*, along with desultory tutoring, feverish reading, and agonised self-doubting. Among his miscellaneous occupations, only the Buller tutorship, from 1822 to 1824, gave him any pleasure in the period which extended from 1814 to 1826. By 1821, however, two momentous things had happened to him: he had met the attractive and baffling personality of Jane Welsh, and he had read *Faust* and *Wilhelm Meisters Lehrjahre*. For the next five years he combined his work as a tutor with his labors as a translator.[25]

Carlyle's inner development during this turbulent, gloomy period is partially recorded in his correspondence, in his *Reminiscences*, and in the published fragments of his conversation in later years. We find him, in the Kirkaldy

period, and especially in 1815, writing to his friends about
his application to philosophical problems, of his "wrestling
with Berkeley," and of his distaste for "the thick darkness
of metaphysics."[26]   Having read Dugald Stewart's *Elements
of the Philosophy of the Human Mind*, he writes,

> "I cannot help thinking that the perusal of his book
> has done me hurt.   Perpetually talking about analysing
> perceptions, and retiring within one's self, and mighty
> improvements that we are to make—no one knows
> how,—I believe he will generally leave the mind of his
> reader crowded with disjointed notions and nondescript
> ideas—which the sooner he gets rid of, the better!"[27]

Though working with his *Exegesis*, he is also "wrestling
with lexicons, chemical experiments, Scotch philosophy, and
Berkeleian Metaphysics," reading the *Essays* of Hume and
of Dugald Stewart, and studying Simson's *Fluxions*.   Such
miscellaneous and often recalcitrant studies fill these early
years.   And through it all, in spite of his persistent reading
in philosophical works, his distrust of metaphysics makes
frequent appearance.   Thus in the following year (1816) he
again expresses his exasperation with Dugald Stewart:

> "I return always to the study of Physics with more
> pleasure after trying the 'Philosophy of Mind!' . . .
> When *will* there arise a man who will do for the science
> of Mind what Newton did for that of Matter—establish
> its fundamental laws on the firm basis of induction—
> and discard forever those absurd theories that so many
> dreamers have devised?   I believe this is a foolish ques-
> tion,—for its answer is—never.   I am led to talk in this
> manner by having lately read Stewart's *History of
> Philosophy* in the Supplement to the *Encyclopaedia
> Britannica*. . . . I must say that I do not recollect of ever
> having bestowed as much attention with so little effect
> upon any author as upon Professor Stewart.   Let me
> study his writings as I like, my mind seems only to turn
> on its axis,—but without progressive or retrograde
> motion at all."[28]

It is worth quoting Carlyle at this length because his criticism of Stewart reveals a significant fact about his present habit of thinking. Apparently his admiration for the precision and order of scientific knowledge has led him to desire the same qualities to emerge from his inquiries into moral and spiritual problems. He is evidently seeking in the analyses of Berkeley and Stewart a means of buttressing his faith; and he is naïvely desiring to apply to the nature of mind and soul that mechanical and inductive analysis which will lead him to the abyss of despair, and concerning which a critic has said, "Pity he had to go so far to learn so little."[29] In short, his scientific studies have—perhaps unobtrusively—supplanted any other criteria than the observable, the objective, and the inductive. If he resists Stewart's arguments, and scorns the "thick darkness" of Berkeley, it is largely because of his pugnacious independence and his inability to think systematically. But if straightforward argument fails to convince him, his studies in science have subtly altered his standards of truth. He wants done for mind what Newton did for matter: the establishment of the laws of mind on "the firm basis of induction." At present his distrust of philosophical speculation is not, as in later years, the conviction that it constitutes the "disease of metaphysics," but that so far it has failed to do its work well enough. It will not be long, therefore, before Carlyle will see to his dismay that he can believe nothing that cannot be demonstrated and inductively proved, and that only matter and mechanism seem real. The universe will then indeed be like a "dead, immeasurable Steam-engine," threatening "to grind him limb from limb."[30]

Stewart's works, it may be said here, probably supplied more assistance to Carlyle than he realized; certainly he seems more indebted to the "History of Philosophy" than has hitherto been supposed. That work, under its proper title of *Dissertation on the Progress of Metaphysical, Ethical, and Political Philosophy,* had been for Carlyle a source of

information on philosophy from the Renaissance to Kant and
the Scotch "Common-sense School."[31] It supplied him with
a lucid, though biased and incomplete, history of modern
thought. As one of the sources of Carlyle's earliest acquaintance with philosophy, whether historically or analytically, it
requires a brief indication of its contents, its point of view,
and of the passages which were probably of interest to him.
In respect to passages of more or less speculative importance
for Carlyle, we shall see later in what degree Stewart possibly
contributed to his notions of Reason and Understanding, and
to his consideration of Kant's doctrine of the relative unreality of matter as in no important way different from other
and more definitely "spiritual" philosophies. On the whole,
however, Stewart's *Dissertation* must have had, to a large
extent, only the value of a text-book. Certainly Carlyle
must have objected to the author's exaltation of Locke; and
it is equally certain that he discounted Stewart's estimate of
Kant and the post-Kantians, since that estimate was entirely
opposite to the one he himself ultimately made. Yet he
read the *Dissertation* twice within two years,[32] and later consulted one of the chief authorities on German philosophy
which Stewart recommends: Madame de Staël's *De l'Allemagne*. Even if Stewart's account of the new German
doctrines is prejudiced and uninformed, it is nevertheless
interesting to examine it as one of the earliest works which
Carlyle consulted on German thought.

"Part I" brings the history of modern philosophy down
to the time of Locke, at which point the author's own speculative position is revealed in his assurance to the reader that
"we scent the morning air of the coming day." After setting
forth the chief doctrines of French philosophy in the seventeenth century—in Descartes, Gassendi, Malebranche—,
Stewart holds up Locke and Leibnitz as heralds of a new
age. In "Part II" he surveys the thought of the eighteenth
century—in the works of Locke, Leibnitz, Berkeley, Spinoza,
Hartley, Condillac—, and adds a short discussion on the

new and puzzling doctrines coming out of Germany. The spirit of this last section is curiously irritable. Stewart "cannot make anything" of Fichte's *Ich* or of Schelling's "identity;" and he deplores the numerous conversions to the Roman Catholic faith which seem to be among the consequences of Kantian and post-Kantian teachings. His knowledge of Kant is entirely second-hand. Having vainly tried to read him in the Latin, Stewart depends, for his knowledge of Kant's theories, upon expositions by Willich, Degerando, Madame de Staël, Reinhold, Buhle, and Nitsch.[33] According to the author, Kant is needlessly obscure; he is presumptuous and intellectually arrogant; and his *Critique of Pure Reason* is not the reply to Hume's *Treatise* which the world has been taught to believe it to be. Indeed Kant's reach exceeded his grasp; "the probability is," Stewart surmises "that he began with a serious wish to refute the doctrines of Hume; and that, in the progress of his inquiries, he met with obstacles of which he was not aware. It was to remove these obstacles that he had recourse to practical reason; an idea which has every appearance of being an *afterthought*. . . ." But not only did Kant fail to fulfill his original ambitions; he has not even the merit of originality: his distinction between the reason and the understanding was anticipated by the doctrines of Cudworth and the Cambridge Platonists. We shall have occasion, later, to see that Stewart's last criticism is not wholly without foundation. His treatment of Kant's work as a whole, however, is hardly even a caricature of the original; his serious lack of first-hand knowledge gives his discussion an air of unreality to the reader of to-day. And the dismissal of Kant as presumptuous and obscure is rendered quaint by the condescension in his apology for including Kant in a history of philosophy at all:

> "After all, the metaphysics of Kant is well entitled to attention as an article of Philosophical History. If it has thrown no new light on the laws of the intellectual

world, the unbounded popularity which it enjoyed for
some years in Germany has placed in a new and striking
point of view one of the most extraordinary varieties
of national character which Europe exhibited in the
eighteenth century; and, while it is kept in remembrance, will preserve to posterity a more perfect idea of
the *heads* of its admirers than all the craniological
researches of Gall and Spurzheim."[34]

In the discussion of the post-Kantians, Fichte receives
about four hundred words, Schelling about three hundred
and fifty. If Fichte's *Ich* puzzles Stewart, much more does
his philosophy of history—with its three epochs, of Chance,
Will, and God—and Fichte's famous jest: "Tomorrow,
gentlemen, I shall create God." He is repelled likewise by
the "vein of transcendental mysticism" in Schelling, who is,
according to Degerando, an "extension" of Fichte. The
effort to present these theories in outline, however, proves
too irksome to the author, and he concludes his discussion
on a mildly mournful note: ". . . it is painful to contemplate
these sad aberrations of human reason; nor would I have
dwelt so long as I have done, had I not been anxious to
convey to my readers a general, but I trust not unfaithful,
idea of the style and spirit of a philosophy, which, within
the short period of our recollection, rose, flourished, and
fell . . ."[35] His own delight, he adds, has been in such
thinkers as Herder, Jacobi, and Meiners; but he is ashamed
to say that in Great Britain the only name extolled is that
of Kant. He turns with evident relief to the final section
of "Part II," which is devoted to Scotch Philosophy, and to
"Part III," "The Progress of Ethical and Political Philosophy of the 18th Century."

It may be wondered what profit Carlyle could have found
in such a distorted presentation of the outlines of German
philosophy. It must be admitted, of course, that he has
given us no proof that Stewart's account in any way conditioned his own. Yet we can infer this, in that he mentions
Stewart's name with admiration as late as 1827. In a foot-

note to the *State of German Literature,* he acknowledges that
name as "venerable to all Europe, and to none more dear
and venerable than to ourselves," and ends with a recom-
mendation apparently based on his own experience: "We
regard the assiduous study of his Works as the best preparation for studying those of Kant." He is conscious, he
says, that "Mr. Stewart has written warmly against Kant;
but it would surprise him to find how much of a Kantist he
himself essentially is." On just how far Dugald Stewart
could be considered a Kantist, Carlyle is silent beyond stating that the philosopher's theories on "Philosophic Language" constitute a "sufficient and final answer to Hartley's
and Darwin's, and all other possible forms of Materialism,"
and that Stewart seeks, without apparently realizing it, to
reconcile Reason and Understanding.[36] We may have here
an example of Carlyle's loose and careless manner of thinking. Evidently he interprets Stewart's position according to
a standard peculiarly his own. At any rate, in spite of his
complaints that Stewart merely charts rather than tills the
field of philosophy, the philosopher had more importance,
undefined and highly individual as it is, for Carlyle's early
approach to philosophy than has been generally recognized.
It may partly account for Carlyle's treatment of the new
theories as merely a new statement of old points of view.
Certainly this must have been the case in regard to Stewart's
citation of Cudworth and the Cambridge Platonists as having
anticipated some of Kant's epistemological distinctions.[37]

In 1820, before Carlyle could have made any direct study
of German philosophy, he juxtaposes the names of philosophers in such a way as to suggest that he was more familiar
with the historical outlines of philosophy than with the doctrines discussed: "Plato obscured the fame of Pythagoras,
Cudworth and Kant of Plato: the Stagirite and his idle
spawn have been swept away by Lord Bacon, himself to be
swept away in his turn."[38] This connecting of names recalls
Stewart's linking of Cudworth, Kant, and Plato's *Theaetetus*
in his criticism of Kant's originality. A little later, Carlyle

writes again critically of Stewart and the other Scotch
thinkers, this time in relation to the Germans: he assures his
brother that he will not lead him into the "mazes of Kantism," and adds that,

> "as to Kant, and Schelling and Fichte and all those
> worthies, I confess myself but an exoteric after all;
> and whoever can imagine that Stewart and Hume, with
> Reid and Brown to help them, have sounded all the
> depths of our nature, or, which is better, can contrive to
> overlook those mysteries entirely,—is too fortunate a
> gentleman for me to intermeddle with."[39]

In none of these remarks do we discern any indication of
how much, or how little, Carlyle was reading in the philosophers, nor how great a part was played by interpreters such
as Dugald Stewart. As yet his interest seems to be even
more desultory than in the period after 1826 when he made
as great an effort as he was able in the comprehension of
Kant, Fichte, Schelling, and Jacobi.

In the meantime, and shortly before he began the study
of German, he had his memorable experience with Gibbon.
In 1809-1810, when he opened the first volume of Gibbon's
history at the University, he was apparently too immature
to appreciate completely its full significance. But eight years
later, by February, 1818, Gibbon was to have a fateful
influence. Carlyle read Edward Irving's copy of the *Decline
and Fall of the Roman Empire* with what he called a "greedy
velocity," until he had finished the twelve volumes in as
many days.

> "It was, of all the books," he said later, "perhaps the
> most impressive on me in my then stage of investigation
> and state of mind. I by no means completely admired
> Gibbon, perhaps not more than I now do; but his
> winged sarcasms, so quiet, and yet so conclusively trans-
> piercing, and killing dead, were often admirably potent
> and illuminative to me."[40]

Of this same period he also remembered having "studied the *Evidences of Christianity* for several years, with the greatest desire to be convinced, but in vain. I read Gibbon, and then first clearly saw that Christianity was not true."[41] His experience with Gibbon was obviously like many of the other intellectual adventures of Carlyle: he was convinced by an oblique attack on his point of view. It was not the force of an argument that convinced him, for in Gibbon there was nothing so open and avowed; it was the indirect persuasion of that "grave and temperate irony, even on subjects of ecclesiastical solemnity" which Gibbon said he had learned from Pascal's *Provincial Letters*, and which the British law prohibiting any attack on Christianity had prompted him to employ with the greatest subtlety and effect.[42] Carlyle was led to think he saw the truth for himself. He was probably most struck by Chapters XV and XVI of the first volume, in which occurs the famous account of the early Christians and the grounds on which they conquered imperial opposition. His enthusiasm for Gibbon never entirely waned; he read the *Decline and Fall* in his last years with something of the old pleasure. It is extremely interesting, and indicative of Carlyle's mental recalcitrance, that what had made Gibbon so powerfully persuasive of skepticism was precisely the indirect, unargumentative manner which enabled Goethe, a little later, to release him from the spell. "Goethe . . . taught me that the true things in Christianity survived and were eternally true; pointed out to me the real nature of life and things—*not that he did this directly; but incidentally and let me see it rather than told me.*"[43]

How he came to read Goethe, and thus to be eventually directed to his fundamental belief, has been variously recorded. There is little basis for the generally accepted notion that he began the study of German in order to find a solution to his spiritual problems. While it is true, as he told Emerson, that a friend had intimated to him that he

would find what he wanted in German writers, it is not clear
whether what he wanted was not simply to read Werner's
Mineralogy in the original.   Possibly because he had noted
Dugald Stewart's dependence upon Madame de Staël, he
desired to know more about the German literature and
philosophy of which she had given a revelatory account in
De l'Allemagne.[44]   Whatever the reason—or combination of
reasons—, Carlyle began the reading of Kotzebue by March,
1819, and soon followed it with a history of Frederick the
Great.   By October, 1820, he had read Klopstock's *Messias*,
and was "living riotously with Schiller, Goethe, and the
rest."[45]

His first enthusiasm was in German literature, as we have
noted, rather than in German philosophy.   In 1820-1821 his
chief interest seems to have been in Schiller's plays; as yet
Goethe's *Faust* and *Wilhelm Meister* had only a subordinate,
though growing, significance for him.   As late as 1827
Carlyle's preoccupation with Schiller manifests itself in his
offer to Longman's of a translated portion of *The Thirty
Years' War*.   That Goethe was gradually rising to greater
importance for Carlyle, however, is perhaps evident in the
fact that as early as 1820, Carlyle sent Irving an estimate of
Faust.   In the following year, there began a period in which
Carlyle and Jane Welsh read the plays of both Schiller and
Goethe, and studied numerous German works, partly under
the guidance of *De l'Allemagne*.   In his *Reminiscences*
Carlyle permits us to surmise that even in 1821 he had dimly
perceived the potential significance, in his own experience, of
the practical ethics expressed in *Wilhelm Meister*: "I had
at length, after some repulsions, got into the heart of *Wilhelm
Meister*, and eagerly read it through;—my sally out, after
finishing, along the vacant streets of Edinburgh (a windless,
Scotch-misty Sunday night) is still vivid to me: 'Grand,
surely, harmoniously built together, far-seeing, wise and true:
when, for many years, or almost in my life before, have I
read such a Book?' "[46]   By January of the next year, he

finished his essay on *Faust* for the *New Edinburgh Review*, a work which he regarded as ambitious, bombastic, and jejune. Awkward and tentative as it is, given wholly to formal criticism, and hardly prophetic of his later comprehension of Goethe, it nevertheless indicates Carlyle's growing consciousness of Goethe's preëminence. Though he now began his *Life of Schiller*, Goethe haunted him until, in the midst of his labors, he began the translation of *Wilhelm Meisters Lehrjahre*. His fascination in the characters of Wallenstein, Thekla, Moor, and Tell began to wane before the moral and philosophic significance of the *Lehrjahre* and *Faust*.[47] Throughout this study of Schiller, Goethe, and other German authors, Carlyle's work as a tutor had been more or less continuous; his health had in no way improved; and his inner conflict was nearing a crisis. By the summer of 1822 the crisis, a combination of moral, physical, and intellectual tumults, reached its apex.

The subject of Carlyle's "conversion" has been somewhat perplexed both by his critics and biographers and by his own statements. In the first place, in an early letter to Goethe he evidently attributes to *Faust*, which he read in 1820, the effects of a revelation or "conversion" which were really made by *Wilhelm Meister* not earlier than 1821, and certainly not fully until 1825-1826.[48] In the second place, his account in *Sartor* of Teufelsdröckh's experience in the "Rue Saint-Thomas de l'Enfer" led Froude to date Carlyle's conversion in Leith Walk at June, 1821, and to designate it as a "spiritual new birth" in which Carlyle "achieved finally the convictions, positive and negative, by which the whole of his later life was governed."[49] There is nothing, however, in Carlyle's letters or works to indicate that any such complete change occurred. A realization of Froude's blunder has led some critics to deny that any but physical distress was troubling Carlyle at this time, and to declare, as does Professor Roe, that "it is a mistake to fix upon this period as the crisis of the revolution and to maintain that the chief cause, or any really determining cause, of his distress was a questioning of the truth of revelation or of the existence of a moral Providence in the universe."[50] What was tormenting Carlyle was lack of congenial work, failure to attain his goal and to express himself. "The unbroken progress of the next few years add to the evidence that his religious life underwent no convulsive transformation."[51] Three elements in the problem of Carlyle's conversion are readily seen: the part played by German ideas; the date of the conversion; and, if it was indeed a conversion, its precise nature. It is perhaps best to inquire, first, into what really happened to Carlyle in Leith Walk.

Though, as we shall see, the conversion had probably no theological or metaphysical content, it is difficult to believe that Carlyle was suffering only from frustrated hopes of successful work, or merely from ill health. It is hard to believe that his violent inner experience was little more than "a moral wrestle with himself as to whether he would continue the fight to make a living by literature in spite of the nearly overwhelming defeats of the past months."[52] It was this, of course, but certainly it was much more. If it was a moral struggle at all, it involved more than the decision to continue or to abandon literature as a vocation. Otherwise Carlyle would hardly have written of it as he does in the *Reminiscences*: though he writes that Teufelsdröckh's experience is "symbolical myth all," he nevertheless goes on to say: "the incident . . . occurred quite literally to myself . . . . I remember it well and could go straight to the place."[53] There is reason to believe, as Professor Leopold has ably shown, that Carlyle's experience was neither a "conversion" nor a moment of important practical decision, but an *awakening*.[54] It was profoundly moral and psychological. It was evidently an awakening of his whole manhood against despair, a sudden realization of great inner resources with which to front a mechanical and hostile world. While no new concepts or clearly-defined convictions emerged from the experience, he nevertheless discovered in the depths of his will a force which shook "base fear" from him, and which revealed him as free and distinct from the mechanical forces of nature which his scientific studies had gradually led him to assume to be more real than his own soul. With a passionate will to believe, he was still harassed by the disparity between the clear and demonstrable facts of science and the elusive and unprovable spiritual realities which he felt to be supreme but which he was powerless to defend. Even if he granted a spiritual element in the world, how was he, in the absence of all conventional modes of approach to it, to answer the questions involved in its assumption? What was one to conclude as to the possibility of "knowing" the world of spirit, as to man's relation to such a world, as to the meaning of the world, of death, of the future, and not least, as to the destiny and duty of Thomas Carlyle? It is clear from the account of Teufelsdröckh that Carlyle was sufficiently subtle and spiritually discerning to see that these questions could find their solution only through the efforts of a changing will. And it is noteworthy that in Teufelsdröckh's progress toward the "Everlasting Yea," every advance is made not through a flood of intellectual light but through a stirring of the roots of conscience and will. "Teufelsdröckh's mental progress out of the mood of the 'Everlasting No,'" says Masson, "is a succession of *practical determinations as to the conduct of his own spirit*, each determination coming as an inspired effort of the will . . . bringing him into a final condition of freedom and self-mastery."[55] Thus in the Leith Walk incident, in the midst of intellectual and moral confusion, Carlyle's sudden experience was the emancipation from self-doubt, the awakening of his ego, the discovery of his *self*. In this discovery there was, for him, the implicit rediscovery of God; the struggle of the will to believe in its own freedom and power was potentially also a struggle for faith. The articles of that faith were as yet undefined; but that Carlyle's ultimate faith should have begun in a psychological

experience, in the will's assertion of freedom, is fitting and
proper in the experience of a man who was to base his
philosophy on personality and character. Carlyle's awakening had nothing Pauline or apocalyptic in it. Nor does he
apply the term "conversion" to it, as he does to that experience which occurred very quietly four years later at Hoddam
Hill. Contrary to Garnett's interpretation, it cannot "be
paralleled from the experiences of St. Paul, Mahomet,
Luther."[56] Nor was it, as Hensel says, "der Krystallisations-
punkt einer neuen Weltanschauung."[57] It was only the
beginning of a state of mind and spirit, from which a new
path of action and a new world would have to be slowly and
painfully constructed.

Mr. Alexander Carlyle has shown conclusively that the
incident occurred in the late summer or early autumn of 1822.
The validity of this date is borne out by the burst of activity
which followed. Carlyle made numerous plans: before the
end of the year, he sought to engage with Boyd for the
writing of a book on Milton; he translated *Faust's Curse*;
he wrote and published the short narrative, *Cruthers and
Jonson*; and in the early months of 1823, he began the
writing of his *Life of Schiller*, prosecuted with renewed
energy his study of German literature, and discovered with
increasing delight the moral depths of Goethe's genius.[58]

Yet it is probable that in this first crisis of his life, the
works of Schiller and Goethe played no part whatever. It has
been profitable to consider the crisis at this length, however,
since we thus have before us, more clearly than otherwise, the
elements of the situation in which German ideas were to be
productive of a new assurance and a stable point of view.
The principles which he found in Goethe and Schiller were
thus in the background of his experience. As M. Carré aptly
observes, Goethe was not for Carlyle a point of departure,
but a *point d'arrivée*.[59] He had still to pass through the
"Center of Indifference." As for the effect which Schiller
and Goethe had upon his ideas, nothing definite emerges.
The *Lehrjahre* had struck him, to be sure, as harmoniously

constructed, "far-seeing, wise and true"; but as yet he found in it little of the illumination which he later, in 1824-1825, discovered on translating it. The conviction that man's moral wholesomeness demands action rather than reflection, which had come vividly home to him in his crisis, had been present to him many years before. In 1819 he had written to a friend: "Till not very long ago, I imagined my whole duty to consist in thinking and endeavoring. It now appears that I ought not only to suffer but to act."[60] Stoical passivity had once seemed the highest moral aim; now he admits that it is "impossible to attain the solitary happiness of the stoic—and hurtful if it were possible."[61] This conviction, maturing through several years, had come to him with releasing power in Leith Walk. It is impossible to say that his recent German studies had anything to do with it.

It is true, of course, that in his first letter to Goethe he virtually attributes his renewed faith in Christianity to the reading of Goethe's works. Writing in 1827, he again mentions their effect upon him:

> "Your works have been a mirror to me; unasked and unhoped-for, your wisdom has counselled me; and so peace and health of Soul have visited me from afar. For I was once an Unbeliever, not in Religion only, but in all the Mercy and Beauty of which it is the Symbol; storm-tossed in my own imaginations; a man divided from men; exasperated, wretched, driven almost to despair; so that Faust's wild *curse* seemed the only fit greeting for human life; and his passionate *Fluch vor allen der Geduld*! was spoken from my very inmost heart. But now, thank Heaven, all this is altered. . . ."[62]

The earliest precise date, however, to which we can assign the influence of Goethe is 1823-24. By that time, his marriage to Miss Welsh was becoming more certain, and his peace and health seemed assured. Within a year the ethical revelation in *Wilhelm Meisters Wanderjahre* brought him the peaceful interlude of Hoddam Hill.

4. Peace at Hoddam Hill: The Conversion of 1826

In the early months of 1823, while at Kinnaird House with the Bullers, Carlyle kept Jane Welsh informed of his progress with *Wilhelm Meisters Lehrjahre*. In his letters to Miss Welsh, he alternates between enthusiasm and disgust. He admires the "ethereal genius" of Goethe, which is "the strangest and in many points the greatest now extant." Yet he feels nothing but disgust for the "libidinous actresses" in the story, and judges Wilhelm "one of the greatest *ganaches* that ever was created by quill and ink." At times the "immorality" of the book makes him attack his work with "the ferocity of a hyena." He feels divided between falling "down [to] worship" Goethe, and deciding to "kick him out of the room."[63] In January, 1824, however, the *Life of Schiller* is finished, and *Meister* is taking on a new meaning. By the end of the year, he decides against writing the "fierce preface" disclaiming all concern with the literary or moral worth of the novel. Instead he writes a preface which, while it admits that "the hero is a milksop," and that the novel "contains much that should have been suppressed entirely," points out nevertheless that the reader will doubtless admire

> "the philosophical discussions it contains, its keen glances into life and art . . . [and the] light airy sketch of the development of man in all his endowments and faculties, gradually proceeding from the first rude exhibitions of puppets and mountebanks, through the perfection of poetic and dramatic art, up to the unfolding of the principle of religion, and the greatest of all arts, the art of life." For most readers, "it will be pleasing and profitable to see the horizon of their certainties widened."[64]

We find here, two years before Carlyle's final comprehension of Goethe's fullest meaning for him, a hint of the ultimate nature of its influence.

The winter of 1824-1825 he spent in London, in company with the Bullers. In December he resigned his tutorship, and spent much time in London's literary circles, developing a distaste for the new art of "puffing," or advertising, and seeking to measure the stature of the reigning literary figures. He had evidently hoped to find among them something of the high, moral, and prophetic passion which, now that he had tasted Goethe, had begun to mount into his spirit. He was disappointed. His reaction to Coleridge, Lamb, Campbell, Rogers, De Quincey is too well known to need recounting. It is enough to remember his futile pilgrimage to Highgate, and the gospel of theosophic flight which he heard there expounded. To Carlyle, here was no eternal affirmation, but an incoherent attempt to reconstruct the old orthodoxy out of the new materials of German transcendentalism, to reconcile dogma and pure reason, only to sink in endless seas of terminology and abstraction. This was not the direction in which Meister had set out. Instead of quitting life for the labyrinths of metaphysics, Goethe's hero had discovered the dynamic and productive value of simple things, of common life, of daily hours and minutes. He had embraced the actual, and had discovered the curative and creative power of action.

Carlyle returned to Scotland, his outlook deepened, his "Center of Indifference" trembling away from Negation. When he settled down at Hoddam Hill to translate *German Romance,* and decided to include the *Wanderjahre* instead of *Werther*, he had already achieved the "Everlasting Yea." He had seen the great world; and now the simple and routine duties—the "nearest" duties—of translating German fiction seemed at once a refuge and a fulfillment. It was the translation of the *Wanderjahre* which crowned the long spiritual pilgrimage with victory. He had been "in the very midst of Wertherism, the blackness and darkness of death."[65] But at Hoddam Hill he found "a constant inward happiness," and a renewed sense of physical vitality. "I call that year *idyllic,"* he later wrote, "in spite of its russet coat." In his "pious musings, communings, silent and spontaneous with Fact and Nature . . . in [those] poor Annandale localities," he listened to the peal of the Hoddam kirk-bell, which sounded touchingly "like the departing voice of eighteen hundred years."[66] It was here that his "conversion" actually took place, a quiet progressive development of the awakened need for action which he had felt in Leith Walk four years before, but now richly filled with the reality of ethical and spiritual principles. From the life-history of Goethe, and from Goethe's teachings, he had achieved his new faith and a definite body of doctrine.

> "This year I found that I had conquered all my scepticisms, agonising doubtings, fearful wrestlings with the foul and vile and soul-murdering Mud-gods of my Epoch . . . and was emerging, free in spirit, into the eternal blue of ether . . . I, poor, obscure, without outlook, almost without worldly hope, had became independent of the world . . . I understood well what the old Christian people meant by their 'Conversion,' by God's Infinite Mercy to them . . . I then felt, and still feel, endlessly indebted to *Goethe* in the business; he, in his fashion, I perceived, had travelled the steep rocky road before me,—the first of the moderns."[67]

Just as the incident of 1822 had stimulated him to a more intense study of German literature, so the present "conversion" impelled him to an investigation of the philosophic background of Schiller and Goethe. Perhaps the speculative thinkers could supply the wider implications, or further confirm and fill-in the "horizon of his certainties." "I read Richter and Jacobi," he wrote to Jane Welsh; "I ride, and hoe cabbages, and . . . am 'a lover of all quiet things.' "[68] The long and curious courtship was now to end in their marriage in October, 1826, and Carlyle was to pursue his German studies at Comley Bank, Edinburgh. As their wedding day drew near, he attempted to fathom the *Critique of Pure Reason,* and read as far as the hundred and fiftieth page, when the argument, "getting rather abstruse," and puzzling him "in one or two points," caused him to lay the work aside in the realization that, under the circumstances, "One of Scott's Novels would suit me much better."[69]

In 1820 he had discovered German literature, and its moral revelation in Goethe, Schiller, and Richter.   Now, in 1827, as he prepared himself for writing an essay on *The State of German Literature,* he discovered German philosophy, and its intellectual revelation in the doctrines of Kant, Fichte, Jacobi, Schelling.[70]   In both the creative and the speculative writers, however, he had found a "new Heaven and a new Earth."[71]

CHAPTER III

THE NEW HEAVEN AND NEW EARTH

By 1827, when Carlyle began to show, in a series of essays, his wide reading in German thought, he had already been familiar for a number of years with several interpreters of the "new evangel." As early as 1817 he had read *De l'Allemagne*, though without deriving any particular inspiration from it.[1] But by 1819, Madame de Staël's varied experience in European affairs, and her talent for lucid—if superficial—exposition, made her valuable for Carlyle as one of the two non-German sources for fact and stimulus concerning Germany and its thought and literature. The other source, though less frequently mentioned and less effective for him in scope if not in content, was Coleridge. Neither of these sources, of course, was in any major degree satisfactory to Carlyle, and they are considered here only as factors in the general background of knowledge and stimulus in which he attempted to understand the new doctrines.

1. CARLYLE AND COLERIDGE

Though no specific influence can be traced from Coleridge to Carlyle, there are several reasons for inferring a general one.[2] Carlyle could hardly have returned from Highgate without at least a more lively sense of the meaning and significance of some of Kant's doctrines. Much as he rebelled against the Coleridgean application of them to bolster up a tottering system of dogma, he certainly left Coleridge with a keener realization of what Kant might do in the reconstruction of his own point of view, and with the intention of making a careful study of Kant's principles. Traces of Coleridgean thought—or of German thought in Coleridge's terms—are at times strikingly evident, even though Carlyle spoke disparagingly of the poet's philosophical efforts from comparatively early years, and never acknowledged any indebtedness to him for either ideas or method. We shall see later that their views on Reason and Understanding are almost identical, and that they both cite the English thinkers of the seventeenth century as anticipating much that seemed novel in "Kantism."[3]   A comparison of their doctrines will show, furthermore, that they are akin in their purposes in employing German ideas to solve their moral and intellectual problems, and that they view the *Aufklärung* with similar repugnance and reject English associationism—such as Hartley's—with equal decision. Though there are profound differences in their principles and in their temperaments, one cannot overlook a very close contact between them at certain points.

Much that has been written on Coleridge in relation to the new age might, with equal truth, have been written of Carlyle. Mr. J. H. Muirhead, for example, has noted Coleridge's conviction that of the forms of experience everywhere emerging, the popular philosophy as represented by Locke, Hume, and Hartley was wholly unable to give any intelligible account. "Owing to the narrowness of its foundations and the defects of its method it failed to represent what was best in philosophical tradition." Coleridge, like Carlyle, "had the insight . . . to perceive that it was from Germany that the chief light on the problem as set by his own time was coming." Yet it was the experience of Coleridge—as it was also to be that of Carlyle—"that, profound and in some respects decisive as were the contributions of German philosophy, particularly of Kant, to its solution, there was as little finality in them as in those of his own country."[4]   It is interesting to remember, from Carlyle's account of Kant's philosophy in his *Life of Schiller*, and in the *State of German Literature*—in which he seems partly indebted to Coleridge—that for Carlyle, too, "the Philosophy of Kant is probably combined with errors to its very core,"[5] and that "Kantism"

is "at best only the beginning of better things."[6]   With
Coleridge, he felt the new needs of the epoch and yet refused
to accept wholly the German answer.   It is not impossible
that Coleridge framed, at first, the general view which Carlyle
took of the whole subject.

The references to Coleridge in Carlyle's works and correspondence, however, indicate little beyond an acquaintance
with the poet's writings and a characteristic habit of alternating between praise and disparagement.   His tendency to
ally himself with the "mystics" in the years between 1820
and 1834 is at variance with his reference to Coleridge, in a
letter of 1823, as "very great but rather mystical, sometimes
absurd."[7]   Much more significant, perhaps, is his later reference in *The Life of Schiller* to Coleridge as prompting the
British public to expect some helpful exposition of Kantian
doctrine: "Are our hopes from Mr. Coleridge always to
be fruitless?"[8]   Clearly Carlyle had at one time felt the
almost universal respect for Coleridge's philosophical capacities.   That he read him much earlier than 1823 is evident
from his remark in the *Reminiscences* that, "We were all
taught at that time [1816-1817], by Coleridge, etc., that
the old English Dramatists, Divines, Philosophers, judicious
Hooker, Milton, Sir Thomas Browne, were the genuine
exemplars" of prose style.[9]   In the *Notebooks*—where the
dating is unfortunately vague—he ruminates on several of
Coleridge's philosophical notions.   But he is unable to comprehend the nature of "an *Idea*" as not being "a conception
or Image" but "infinite" and defying to "be painted."   In
another entry he is irritated by Coleridge's distinction
between "talent" and "genius," and dismisses it as "completely *blarney*."[10]   His impatience with Coleridge's ideas is
perhaps owing less to a disagreement with the ideas themselves than to an exasperation with their incompleteness and
obscurity.   Thus in the essay on *Novalis*, he considers
Coleridge's *The Friend* and the *Biographia Literaria*, in comparison with the mystic's *Schriften*, to be "but a slight busi-

ness . . . little more than the Alphabet." Yet, in his characteristic championing of anything promoting a knowledge of
German ideas, he upbraids the British reviews for having
"triumphantly condemned" Coleridge as "clearly unintel-
ligible."[11] Little consistent evidence emerges, therefore, to
point to any definite agreement with the Coleridge's philosophical principles.

If Coleridge and Carlyle were akin in their consciousness
of the new needs of the time, and in their realization of the
limitations of German doctrines in meeting those needs, they
had little in common in their approach to the new doctrines.
Coleridge was, to some extent, a metaphysician; and if his
"fundamental lack of real philosophical individuality"[12] prevented him ever attaining the status of philosopher, he
certainly surpassed Carlyle in his wide range of purely
philosophic vision, in a passionate willingness to use the
philosopher's tools to get at the philosopher's "truth", to seek
philosophic answers to problems in science, logic, metaphysics, education, law, politics. We know how violent was
Carlyle's skepticism of logic, and how averse he was to a
systematic philosophy of politics, science, law, or morals.
If Coleridge ultimately fell away from his earlier and more
austere inquiries, and took refuge in "a theosophic refabrica-
tion out of the wrecks of the forsaken orthodoxy,"[13] it may
be said that Carlyle, in spite of the metaphysical content in
his point of view, never even made the attempt to re-think
the newer German doctrines in the spirit of a philosopher.
It is true that they both started with a conviction of the unity
of experience as a whole, but for Carlyle that unity had far
less an intellectual and far more a mystical nature than for
Coleridge. And if they both endeavored to promote the "self-
recognition of that spiritual life of the world which fulfills
itself in many ways but most completely in religion," they
were far from agreeing on the most effective means.[14]
"Action," the key-word in Carlyle's doctrine, contrasts diametrically with Coleridge's faith in the mind's eventual vic-

tory over the intractable and bewilderingly involved nature of its own processes.   The further we compare the two men, the more natural it seems that Carlyle seldom mentions Coleridge's name, and that he fails to do so even when, in discussing Reason and Understanding, he employs Coleridge's very terminology.   The borrowing—if indeed there was one—was largely unconscious, the residue of very early reading, both in and concerning Coleridge's works.   It was largely an influence through sympathy in spirit, through an inevitably similar reaction to what they must reject and to what they needed in the solution of similar problems.   Carlyle's final knowledge of the Germans might therefore have been substantially what it was had he never encountered Coleridge's exposition and teachings.

The further Carlyle moved away from his early German interests the greater grew his disdain for the epistemological distinctions on which Coleridge had shed a certain light. He said less and less about Reason, Understanding, faith, and intuition; more and more about action, heroism, right.   Later, when he wrote his *Life of Sterling*, he naturally exaggerated the impression early made upon him by Coleridge's "high seas of theosophic philosophy" and the "hazy infinitude of Kantian transcendentalism."   The "sublime secret of believing by 'the Reason' what 'the Understanding' had been obliged to fling out as incredible" seemed more and more an absurd and pernicious delusion.[15]   And the distance which, in 1851, he had traversed since he once sat at the feet of Coleridge at Highgate, when Kant's distinctions were still prophetic of great renewals of faith and insight, is a reminder of the limits of Carlyle's interest in German thought, both in respect to the number of years he devoted to it, and in regard to the quality of its influence.   In the history of Carlyle's mind, Coleridge occupies a curious place, as a vague but once powerful force in aiding his first gropings toward the truth in an alien philosophy.   It was one of many quasi-anonymous but fertilizing agencies in Carlyle's intellectual development between 1816 and 1830.

2. MADAME DE STAËL

Carlyle's opinion of Madame de Staël seems from the first to have been more favorable than was frequently customary with him in approaching a newly prominent writer. Together with Jane Welsh he pursued a course of reading, during the early years of their courtship, in both Madame de Staël's expository and creative works. Writing to Jane in 1821 regarding *De l'Allemagne* and its author, he admits that "she is misty and inconsistent here and there . . . . but if a brilliant imagination, a magnificent intellect, a noble heart, can yield you any delight, then here is for you!"[16] The eulogistic exaggeration present here is lacking in a later reference to her *De l'Allemagne*. Though he encourages Jane to study the work, he adds a warning that "those latter volumes of the *Allemagne* will perplex you, I fear. The third in particular is very mysterious; now and then quite absurd . . . ."[17] A year later, he refers again to Madame de Staël's character, and with the former exaggerated praise: "the Miltons, the de Staëls—these *are* the very salt of the Earth; they derive their 'patents of nobility direct from Almighty God,' and live in the bosoms of all true men to all ages."[18] Whatever may have been the vagaries of Carlyle's conception of Madame de Staël's character, there is no doubt that her account of German life, literature, and thought was a revelation to him. That it was "mysterious" in some respects may well have been the case, but that he actually found it "absurd" is rather to be doubted. It is worthwhile, at any rate, to look into the nature of *De l'Allemagne*, and to become acquainted with one of Carlyle's earliest sources on German writers.

The general purpose and tone of *De l'Allemagne* were such as to commend the work to a reader in Carlyle's state of mind. Madame de Staël was, to some extent, seeking in German literature and philosophy the expression of a religious ideal. For this she found, of course, different grounds from those which Carlyle later was to discover. Guided by

sentiment—rather than by the moral need which actuated
Carlyle—she found a religious ideal in the True and the
Beautiful. Where Carlyle was to find spiritual sustenance
in the classical elements of the new literature and in the
moral challenge of the new philosophy, Madame de Staël found
a divine vindication of things earthly in a romanticism which
pointed toward a Catholic-mystical *Weltanschauung*. She
approached the new Germany as a civilized alien pointing with
pleased surprise to the unexpected cultural riches in what
had seemed a barbarous nation.   Carlyle looked to the
Germans as a humble student, willing to listen, ready to
accept the acceptable, and determined to understand whatever was relevant to his moral plight. Thus while Madame
de Staël turned to Germany as a romantic, Carlyle turned to
the new doctrines as a man passionately in search of a
Lebensführer. Yet *De l'Allemagne*, in spite of its author's
aesthetic and distorting perspective, had a certain value for
Carlyle. It mapped for him, as it were, the *terra incognita*;
it provided him with suggestions for a profitable journey;
and while it was designed primarily for French minds, it
inevitably touched upon details which would be of the utmost
value to any traveller among strange and yet peculiarly
familiar ideas.[19]

The contents of the work attempted to cover the whole
of German civilization.   In Part I, Carlyle read short
and lucid chapters on German geography, climate, society,
women, cities, universities, the French spirit in Germany,
the German language, German poetry and taste, the Romantic
and the Classic, and six of the chief German writers:
Wieland, Klopstock, Lessing, Winckelmann, Goethe, and
Schiller. More definitely literary is Part II, in which are
chapters on comedy, declamation, novels, historians, the fine
arts, and separate treatments of the greater writers. Here
we note Madame de Staël's exaggeration of Schiller, in
which Carlyle was to follow her, as he was to follow her
exaggeration of Werner. It is interesting to compare the

relative numbers of pages devoted to the three "major" authors. Schiller, being accorded the place of honor, receives four chapters, or 106 pages. Goethe, next in rank, is discussed in three chapters, or 88 pages. Zacharias Werner is given one chapter, or 23 pages. These chapters consist, for the most part, of the narration of plots and the facile commentary on style and character which could have had little more effect on Carlyle than to stimulate his curiosity. The superficial character of the analyses, however, was undoubtedly off-set for him by the author's enthusiasm, her stimulating questions, her skill in quoting enough of the most significant passages to arouse a desire to read the original. The "mysterious"—and perhaps "absurd"—Part III deals wholly with German philosophy, science, and religion. We are probably justified in supposing that this section of the work had the greatest interest for Carlyle when he had finally righted his judgment of the relative merits of Goethe and Schiller and sought to understand their contemporary philosophic background. Yet he must have been considerably disappointed. The early chapters sketch the course of English and French philosophy of the time to Kant, to whom is accorded 28 pages of popular exposition. The author's chief concern with Kant centers in his ethical doctrines; there is virtually nothing on Kant's epistemological inquiries. There follow chapters on the influence of Kant upon the German mind and upon literature, art, science, and morals. It is indicative of Madame de Staël's religious preoccupations in connection with German thought that Jacobi is given two chapters—or 11 pages—of sympathetic analysis, and that there are all together twelve chapters on religion, religious sects, and mysticism.

There is every reason to believe that Carlyle realized the shortcomings of Madame de Staël's account. He no doubt agreed with Henry Crabb Robinson that "she is absolutely incapable of thinking a philosophical thought—her philosophy is only a map of observations connected together by a loose logic . . . of course, she cannot properly understand a syllable of the new philosophy."[20]   He seems to have been more acutely aware of the incompleteness of her account than conscious of its unreliable and erroneous nature. This, of course, is quite in keeping with his neglect of the specific meaning of a doctrine if he felt he had grasped its general outlines. He is at least grateful that "Madame de Staël's book has done away with" much of the current misunderstanding and undervaluing of German writers. But while she has demonstrated that there is something deeply valuable in their works, "what that something is, indeed, is still undecided; for this gifted lady's *Allemagne,* in doing much to excite curiosity, has still done little to satisfy or even direct it."[21]   His admiration for the work, however, and his consciousness of a debt to it, is now and then clearly evident: "There are few of our readers," he writes in 1830, "but have read and partially admired Madame de Staël's *Germany;* the work, indeed, which, with all its vagueness and manifold shortcomings, must be regarded as the precursor, if not parent, of whatever acquaintance with German literature exists among us."[22]

His own knowledge of German literature shows at times a direct dependence upon her treatment of it. He devotes an entire essay to Werner, whom she discusses immediately after Schiller and Goethe. He views the philosophy of Kant more or less as she does, seeing in it the forces for spiritual re-birth.[23]   He is concerned, like her, with religious problems, and comprehends the new movement less in terms of literature or metaphysics than in terms of the unification of poetry, religion, and knowledge.[24]   He quotes some of the passages which appear in her work, as, for example, Richter's vision of the dead Christ.[25]   Madame de Staël wrote of Goethe as "a man of universal mind," and Carlyle, came to see him as "the clearest, most universal man" of his time.[26]   Again, we possibly find a parallel between them in their conception of Mephistopheles. In Carlyle's now little-read essay on *Faust,* he conceives Mephistopheles as strikingly like a "French philosophe," intellectual, given to mockery, the product of civilization. So also does Madame de Staël: "The Mephistopheles of Goethe," she says, "is a civilized Devil. He handles with dexterity that ridicule, so trifling in appearance, which is nevertheless often found to consist with a profundity of malice."[27]

However little Madame de Staël may have contributed to the content of Carlyle's ideas regarding German writers, it is certain that she played a real part in directing them. She confirmed his sense of the latent power in German literature and philosophy, and turned it in a general way to the most conspicuous sources. She provided him with a frame-work of preliminary judgment, with a vague but suggestive background, and with a tentative perspective. Her spirit, in so far as it was actuated by religious desires, was akin to his own: like him, she was weary of the brilliant void of the *Aufklärung,* and sought, among other things, to find a spiritual revelation in Germany.

3. The German Attitude Toward the Enlightenment

In the new school of writers in Germany, Carlyle found not only a number of solutions for old problems, but also an analysis of the spiritual dilemmas bequeathed by the previous age. More than the rest of Europe, Germany was conscious that the eighteenth century had robbed life of dynamic promise and of moral freedom, that while it had sought to release man from many of his political and religious fetters, eighteenth century thought had at the same time impoverished his moral powers by dwelling excessively on the rational and mechanical side of human nature. The age of reason was sufficiently recent, however, in the years when the Kantian and post-Kantian influence was at its height, for one to realize the degree in which the new writers and thinkers had their roots in the *Aufklärung,* and to see that their analysis of that period, as well as their reaction against it, owed something to their legacy from a rationalistic and inquiring generation. Perhaps this is why Carlyle was evidently as frequently repelled as attracted by them. Certainly in the new German doctrines there was much that persisted from the age of reason. We find the spirit of the eighteenth century present in the rigor with which Kant studied the formal side of reason, and in the austerity with which he enunciated the categorical imperative.[28] We find it again in Fichte's dogma of progress, in his purely rational deduction of the individual ego, in his statement that "Pure Thought is itself the Divine Existence."[29] If the newer thinkers were alive to the fallacies of Hume, it was because they were acquainted with the atmosphere in which his theories matured, and could fight with his own weapons. If they chafed under the hampering grip of reason misapplied, it was partly because they knew the circumstances which led to the imprisonment. And if they sought a way out, if they analysed the previous epoch, they had to their credit a realization of the full significance of its achievements and its failures. Carlyle, himself partly a child of the late *Aufklärung*, at least through his early reading, was thus able to find in their writings an analysis of that period which met his own.[30]

His dissatisfaction with the fruits of the Enlightment found expression in various passages in Fichte, Goethe, Richter, Kant, Novalis, Friedrich Schlegel, Schiller, and Schelling. It will be illuminating to note a number of such passages as they affected Carlyle, either as they appear in his actual translation, or as considered in comparison with his own point of view.

"Something . . . must have decayed in our age," wrote Richter, lamenting the fall of religious faith before the triumph of reason and the ideal of pleasure:

> "The spirit of Eternity, which judges the heart of the world, strongly declares what spirit is wanting to the present men inspired by the senses, to these fire-

worshippers of the passions,—the holy one of Him who
is above the earth. The ruins of His temple sink lower
and lower into the present earth. Prayer is thought to
draw along its false lights of fanaticism. The apprehension and belief in what is beyond the world . . .
bears no fruits in our pure thin air. If, formerly, religion was in war, there is now no war in religion—
there has grown for us out of the world a mighty
edifice, out of the ether a cloud, out of God a mere
power, out of heaven a coffin![31] . . . . This century lies
upon a sick-bed . . . . and those who suffer from the
mental falling-sickness of the French philosophy have,
like bodily epileptics, no consciousness of their malady,
but only pride in their strength . . . . Our present age
is indeed a criticising and a critical one, wavering
between the desire and the inability to believe,—a chaos
of times struggling against one another . . . ."[32]

We find in passages such as these the expression of Carlyle's
own reaction to the previous age. Richter's lines became for
him a sort of refrain when he viewed the triumphs of the
age of Voltaire.

In Schiller, likewise, he found utterances of a sharp repugnance for the ideals and limitations of that period, particularly in its mechanistic and egoistic philosophy:

"Many of our thinkers," wrote Schiller, "have made
it their business to laugh this heavenly instinct [of moral
freedom] out of the human soul, to efface the impress
of Deity, and to extinguish the energy of noble enthusiasm, in the cold and killing vapor of heartless indifference. Fettered by the consciousness of their own
degradation, they have hit upon [self-]interest, this
dangerous enemy of benevolence, in order to account
for a phenomenon which was too divine for their con-
tracted hearts. They have spun their desolate doctrine
out of the cobwebs of a starving egotism, and have made
their own small measure the standard of their Creator,
like degenerate slaves decrying freedom amidst the
the clangor of their chains."

Yet for Schiller, as later for Carlyle, the age of unbelief
and despair has much that is prophetic of a new and positive

order: "Skepticism is but the fever-paroxysms of the human spirit," added Schiller, in phrases which Carlyle was eventually to quote, "the more dazzling and seductive the error, the greater the triumph of Truth . . . To propose doubt and error was indeed necessary; the knowledge of the malady must precede the return to health."[33]   In Schiller, as in Goethe, there was the optimistic doctrine that a negative age tends ever to produce its opposite.

A comparatively full account of the shortcomings of the *Aufklärung* was available to Carlyle in Fichte's *Characteristics of the Present Age*.   In the five-fold division into which Fichte declared world history to fall, the eighteenth century, or the "Third Age," represented nothing less than a state of "completed sinfulness."   As an "Epoch of Liberation" from external authority, the Enlightenment had rebelled against authority as a principle, and had achieved only an "empty freedom."   For Fichte, the Enlightenment meant the triumph of the Understanding over the Reason, the exaltation of Common Sense as the standard of truth, and of "ridicule" as a convenient touchstone.   Only what was "clearly comprehensible" received attention and acceptance.   In morality, individual self-interest was the sole ethical standard, and happiness the only end of man.   Utilitarianism, "experience" as the test of values, was inevitable in an age dominated by these cognate doctrines.   Much of the weariness and vacuity of the period, manifested in the Sentimentalists and in the *Sorrows of Werther*, struck Fichte as the natural result of exclusive preoccupation with the merely useful, the egoistic, the purely logical.   In his philosophy of history, the "Third Age" touched the nadir of human achievement in "the life according to reason."   Previous epochs, though poor in various respects, nevertheless honored Reason in the form of blind instinct or in the form of external authority; the Enlightenment, however, had turned upon its instincts with an unwholesome self-consciousness, had overturned external authority, and remained without higher guidance than the cunning of logic and the impulse of individual desire.[34]

In Schelling's *Method of Academical Study*, which Carlyle read in preparation for his essay on *The State of German Literature*, it is principally the narrowness and falseness of French rationalism which receives the harshest judgment. "That absence of ideas (*Ideenleerheit*) which has been called the *Aufklärung*," wrote Schelling dryly, "is most opposite to philosophy proper." No nation has elevated the Understanding, or the merely logical faculty, to a greater or more blighting eminence than has the French.[35] With them philosophy has indeed abdicated its true functions and is at present concerned only with exercising its instrumental powers, in the sphere of political and social amelioration. Even in these restricted fields the reign of the sophists and *raisonneurs* is supreme. Neither the old rationalism of the tradition of Descartes nor the newer philosophy of opportunism can avail in the great work of the coming age, *i.e.* the revelation of the world as the union of the real and the ideal. The old effort to account for things by referring only to the real—to the actual and the material—has betrayed itself into hopeless skepticism, licentiousness, and ignoble despair.[36]

Friedrich Schlegel offered still further criticism of the age of reason. In his *History of Ancient and Modern Literature*, from which Carlyle quotes a significant passage, Schlegel condemns the whole historical and philosophical outlook of the eighteenth century as a denial of nature and of history as "a means, an instrument, a visible Word of Life." The error of the older writers, following in the footsteps of Bacon, Locke, Berkeley, and Hume, had been the neglect of a *Vernunfthypothese*. The philosophy of sensation, leaving no place for spirit, freedom, Reason (*Vernunft*), had produced the malady of the age: "The English philosophy may be likened to a man having a hale and healthy look whilst the germs of some fatal malady lie within him, which, being checked by palliatives in the first instance, has been only driven back into the system." The only promising forces in France, Schlegel concludes, are to be found in the Platonic Christianity in the doctrines of Bonald, Count de Maistre, and St. Martin "the unknown philosopher." Among English thinkers with a similar spiritual outlook, Schlegel is able to think only of Sir William Jones. Indeed, "British philosophy since the time of Hume," says Schlegel in the passage quoted by Carlyle, "appears . . . nothing more than a 'laborious and unsuccessful striving to build dike after dike in front of our Churches and Judgment-halls, and so turn back from them the deluge of Scepticism, with which that extraordinary writer overflowed us, and still threatens to destroy whatever we value most.' "[37]

Novalis, adept at reflecting other men's ideas in vivid phrases, ranks the Enlightenment historically as an age in which "Nature . . . remains . . . ever a frightful Machine of Death," and man's intercourse with it an increasing mechanization of his own nature. Man's "striving to fathom that gigantic Mechanism is already a draught towards the Deep." Only through "Moral Action" can he once again envisage Nature as "a sport of the Mind, a waste fantasy of [his] dream . . . Till then let man honor Nature as the Emblem of his own Spirit." Rather than trust wholly to scientific experiment, let him remember that virtuous action is the "only Experiment, in which all riddles of the most manifold appearance explain themselves. Who so understands it, and in rigid sequence of Thought can lay it open, is forever Master of Nature."[38] Such was Novalis's answer to those who philosophised over-hastily on the basis of Newton or Laplace. *Christianity or Europe*, with which Carlyle was familiar, contains still other criticism of the age of Mechanism. While Carlyle certainly rejected Novalis's argument that all the ills of the Enlightenment flowed from the Reformation, he undoubtedly read with sympathetic comprehension the mystic's account of the rise of that rationalistic fervor which culminated in "hatred for the Bible, for Christian belief, and finally for Religion itself." He understood Novalis's indictment of that movement which undermined the dynamic in ethics, art, and human nature, placing man "in the domain of natural objects, encircled with Necessity, and making the infinite creative Music of the Universe merely the monotonous din of a huge Mill . . . a Mill *an sich*, without Millwright or Miller . . . ."[39]

In Kant himself, in the great seminal influence of the thought of the day, it was possible to see an effort to right the balance so disastrously disturbed by the old school. In his endeavor to disclose the laws of cognition, to reveal their narrow limits, was there not an attack, as it were, on the age of Reason in its very stronghold? Kant plainly avowed his intention of striking a blow at "the root of materialism, fatalism, atheism, free-thinking, fanaticism, and superstition . . ."[40] Among the aims of the *Critique of Pure Reason* was that of destroying the old dogmatism which had somewhat arrogantly boasted the attainment of what it called "knowledge." To reveal the hollowness of much of that "knowledge," Kant decided to "deny *knowledge*, in order to make room for *faith*."[41] Whatever may have been the technical significance of Kant's promise, Carlyle must have welcomed, if he read Kant's prefaces, what he thought was a demonstration, by one of the final glories of the *Aufklärung*, of the possibility of substituting for the dry twigs of rationalist "knowledge" a knowledge which should answer his whole being.

It would be an error, of course, to assume that what Carlyle learned from scattered passages in the writers he was now studying, was a true or complete picture of the Enlightenment. What was most significant for him—and what is most significant in any study of his reaction to the new writers—was the fact that in their occasional allusions to the previous age, and in the common grounds of their criticisms, he found both an indication of the great needs

of the present time and an optimistic promise, especially in
Jean Paul, Fichte, and Novalis, of the ultimate deliverance
of his own generation.   It was the first entrance into the
"new heaven and new earth," a clearing away of the old and
obstructive results of a former period.   Some of its promises,
of course, he could scarcely accept.   Fichte and Novalis were
both preaching a philosophy of progress, and it may be
doubted if Carlyle ever looked with favor upon the *a priori*
method by which Fichte arrived at his philosophy of history.
But he was manifestly impressed and inspirited by Goethe's
notion that an age of creative faith always succeeds an age
of unbelief.   And he was fond of remembering Jean Paul's
reassurance in a sonorous passage from his Preface to
Hesperus:

> "But there will come another era, when it shall be
> light, and man will awaken from his lofty dreams, and
> find—his dreams still there, and that nothing has gone
> save his sleep . . . .
> Infinite Providence, Thou wilt cause the day to dawn.
> But as yet struggles the twelfth-hour of the Night:
> nocturnal birds of prey are on the wing, spectres uproar,
> the dead walk, the living dream."[42]

4. THE NEW EVANGEL: IDEAS AND PERSONALITIES

If the German attitude toward the Enlightenment, as expressed in the newer literature and philosophy, had provided
Carlyle with an introductory, though negative, view of the
new world of thought and belief, there was yet that greater,
positive revelation which he found in the personalities of
such men as Schiller, Goethe, and Fichte, and in the great
body of doctrine which he loosely denominated "the Critical
Philosophy," "Kantism," or "German Metaphysics," according to his desire, and which included, in one way or another,
all of the new point of view, from Kant's theories of space
and time or Novalis's mystical notions, to Goethe's most
practical maxim on the conduct of life.[43]   What gave all that

multifarious complex of doctrines and personalities a supreme
unity for Carlyle was his interpretation of it as the ultimate
and positive product of the Reformation. The negative
product, arising from a depraved and egoistic worship of
reason, had been the French Revolution. Germany had
escaped the scourge of revolution, he argued, because she
had remained true to the essential spirit of the age of Luther.
It was now her task to reaffirm for the world the essence of
Christianity. And he sought to find—and in his eclectic way
did find—such a reaffirmation; it was implicit, he thought,
in Kant's doctrines of the subjective nature of time and
space, it was explicit in much of Goethe, Fichte, Novalis,
Schelling. Whether in the field of metaphysics or of ethics,
literature, or art, he thought he found a single and more or
less coördinated movement which affirmed once more the
Calvinistic belief that the world is a snare and a delusion.

More specifically regarded, the Critical Philosophy appeared to him to be the life-giving foundation of the new
literature and thought. It made for a "noble system of
morality," a "purer theology" and "lofty views of man's
nature." He found the reason for these rather vague
promises in the fact that "the Kantist, in direct contradiction to Locke and all his followers, both of the French and
English or Scotch School, commences from within and proceeds outwards," interpreting the external world as in itself
illusory but nevertheless as dynamically expressive of an
inner reality. The implications of this reversal of the older
method of reasoning struck Carlyle as of wide significance. "No writer of any importance" in Germany, "be he
acquainted or not with the Critical Philosophy, but breathes
a spirit of devoutness and elevation more or less directly
drawn from it." This philosophy had infused a "higher tone
into the literature of Germany."[44] How far this explanation
falls short of accounting for Goethe, Schiller, Werner, Tieck,
or Hoffman, is of little relevance here; it is sufficient to
note that in Carlyle's wayward and wishful interpretation,

we find the explanation of much of his attitude toward the
new doctrines.   He felt that they had definitely discredited
the old dispensation, in which "simplicity of heart was gone,"
and when "earnest emotions must no longer be expressed in
earnest symbols . . . . [and] devoutness of character be
replaced by shrewdness and *persiflage*."[45]   In the light of
their promises, perhaps the nineteenth century would no
longer stand before him "in all its contradiction and per-
plexity, barren, mean, and baleful."[46]

It was natural that Carlyle, for whom character was the
most indisputable reality, should lay great stress on the
importance of character in the formation and success of the
new doctrines.   If Germany was now turning away from
the spiritual dryness of the Enlightenment, it was in no
small degree because a "quiet, vigilant, clear-sighted man . . .
characterised by the distinctness of his perceptions, and the
iron strictness with which he reasoned," had discerned the
hidden error of eighteenth century reason.   It was Kant's
"cool judgment, and determinate energetic character," as
much as any of his ideas that made him for Carlyle the
great regenerating force in contemporary thought.   Though
Carlyle obviously knew but little of the philosopher's teachings, he was certain that Kant was far from being the
"Necromancer and Black-artist in Metaphysics" which England in 1827 had alleged.[47]   Carlyle's idealised and distorted
conception of the philosopher makes one wonder what he
would have said of Novalis's reference to "Kant's Advo-
katengeist."[48]   On the whole, Kant meant to Carlyle the
heroic striving with materialism, the struggle of a "determinate energetic character" with the perversity of the age of
unbelief.   "I began with Hume and Diderot," Carlyle said in
later years, "and as long as I was with them I ran at Atheism,
at blackness, at materialism of all kinds.   If I read Kant, I
arrived at precisely opposite conclusions, that all the world
was spirit namely, that there was nothing material at all
anywhere . . ."[49]   In this highly individual conception of

Kant as the slayer of materialism and the exponent of "spiritualism," Carlyle's reverence for what he considered Kant's heroic character was no negligible factor.

The dominant place which Goethe's character occupied in Carlyle's Goethe-worship is well known. To what extent Goethe's work was entirely independent of the Critical Philosophy Carlyle seems never to have inquired. He writes in the *Life of Schiller*, of course, that during the controversy over Kant's doctrines, "Goethe alone seemed altogether to retain his wonted composure; he was clear for allowing the Kantian scheme to 'have its day, as all things have.' "[50] Carlyle was content to observe that Goethe's deepest influence was undeniably aided by the newer and more spiritual outlook suggested by the Kantians. Independently of Kant, however, Goethe had travelled his own way from the despair of *Werther*, through the "wild apocalypse" of *Faust*, to the "melodious reverence" and the serenity of his final period as manifested in the *Wanderjahre* and the *West-Oestlicher Divan*.

Many elements in Goethe's complex character, Carlyle was of course unable to understand or appreciate. Though this fact has long since become common knowledge, it is worthwhile to consider once more just what it was in Goethe that Carlyle never truly saw. In the first place, he maintains a significant silence on the pagan side of Goethe, on the haughty, patrician reserve, the pride and distinction which went with Goethe's unyielding objectivity. The clear eye, the bright and sunny glance, the aesthetic joy in nature, the exaltation of beauty for its own sake, the sheer virtuosity in living, the Greek repose and delicacy, the deliberate shaping of his life as a work of art—these elements in Goethe's experience, appearing in various forms and at various times but always expressive of something profound in his genius, were almost entirely lost on Carlyle. He does indeed mention Goethe's "majestic Calmness," his "perfect clearness of vision," his "antique nobleness";[51] but none of these features of Goethe's genius are expressed in the crucial passages in which Carlyle found a gospel for his times. He naturally says little or nothing about Goethe's refusal to gaze on the darker side of Christianity, of his alleged repugnance for the sight of a crucifix, of his repudiation of pietism, original sin, and predestination. Carlyle's Goethe was but one of several that united to form a man more complex and complete than Carlyle seems to have suspected.[52] It was Goethe the moralist, the sage, before whom Carlyle bowed. And in Carlyle's interpretation of his hero, the "melodious wisdom" and "majestic calmness" had been achieved through a heroic struggle with himself and his times.

Again we note that at the bottom of the congenial doctrine there lay the qualities of character which Carlyle admired. He reverenced, above all, Goethe "the Uniter and victorious Reconciler," and Goethe's "giant strength of character."[53] According to Carlyle, there had been for Goethe the depths of unbelief and sorrow which he himself had known, and Goethe had emerged triumphant. We can discern in Carlyle's attitude toward that struggle three fairly distinct stages. When, in 1825-1826, Carlyle was inserting the *Wanderjahre* into the volume later called *German Romance*, Goethe appeared to him as that unusual man who is capable of directing his own life. Later, in the *State of German Literature*, perhaps under the influence of Fichte's doctrine of the hero, Goethe is the seer, the hero sent among men, for whom "the world lies all translucent . . . encircled with Wonder, the Natural in reality the Supernatural."[54] And finally, in 1832, when he wrote the essay on *Goethe's Works*, Goethe has become the supreme revelation of time and eternity in the present age.[55] Thus Carlyle evidently shifted his point of view in regard to Goethe at various times in his own progressive development. Much more indubitably Carlylean, however, is his interpretation of Goethe's three periods in the struggle with despair and unbelief. Whether Goethe's development was as violent and as religious as Carlyle maintains may be open to question. The interpretation of Goethe's life-history in terms of its epochal events has become fair game for any critic with sufficient audacity. No one point of view regarding its successive changes has thus far proved final. And among the various interpretations of Goethe's development from his early *Werther* period to the "neo-Christianism" of his old age, Carlyle's attempt deserves considerable respect. It may be said that whereas one school of critics, drawn largely to Goethe's paganism, declares that he never underwent the violent changes described by the opposite school,[56] Carlyle and his adherents are so struck by the dynamic and "demonic" element in Goethe that they account for his final serenity by pointing to a long inward struggle originating in doubt and pessimism. Thus it is that Carlyle regarded Goethe's *Werther, Faust,* and *Wilhelm Meister* as milestones in Goethe's long and desperate struggle with himself. To the end, Carlyle saw Goethe as battling with spiritual demons. And it was in the magnificent triumph, in the classic calm of Goethe's old age, that Carlyle found his own justification for seeing in Goethe the sage who has passed through his purgation and had now the authentic message of experience.[57]

It has long been a convention among critics of Carlyle to dwell upon his exaggeration of what many Goetheans regard as a very subordinate element in Goethe's nature: the didactic element.[58] For the reader who has adequately scanned the whole of Goethe, it may seem a work of supererogation to point out that the moralist in him represents one of the most fundamental sides of his genius. In his two greatest works, *Faust* and *Meister,* need one point to the fact that Goethe reveals the thinker in him before the end? Both works begin with the concrete, the aesthetic, with the imaginative beauty of pure works of art. But, as is clear to anyone acquainted with those works, the ending in each case exalts an ideal of practical ethics. The final salvation of Faust is found in specific social duties; and Meister finds his problems solved through the practical organization of his powers toward definite service to the world.   In both cases, what began as an aesthetic problem of character as opposed to circumstances and involved in inward conflict, develops at length toward a didactic climax.   It cannot fairly be said, therefore, that Carlyle did Goethe an injustice in stressing the ethical element in Goethe's work.   It was obviously a real element; and Carlyle never pretended to present his hero "in the round." Though he had some appreciation of the purely artistic nature of parts of *Meister* and *Faust*, he chose, inevitably in accordance with his nature and creed, to value their philosophical and ethical teachings.   He was drawn to Goethe as the serene philosopher of life, preaching the religion of the deed, the infinite nature of work—of work as its own progressively enriching reward, of reverence for all that is around, above, and below us.   It is true that even here Carlyle interpreted Goethe after his own puritan fashion, and that these ethical ideals become in the *Miscellaneous Essays* and in *Sartor* something very different from what they were in Goethe's philosophy as a whole.   Yet, Carlyle was conscious of a very real element in Goethe's nature, and realized with the clairvoyance of a sympathetic mind that Goethe was, as Seely later said, "the greatest moralist, the most pregnant thinker among poets."[59]   Goethe had given him the clue to a vitalizing conception of life: he had bidden him to see it as the reflex of the eternal, to re-think it not as a philosopher seeking abstract principles but as a man determined to find the meaning in it through action.

If Goethe, through his character no less than through his teachings, strengthened Carlyle's faith in himself and the world, it was Fichte who in a similar fashion presented a conceptual framework for the new point of view and at the same time manifested the qualities of character which Carlyle demanded.   From about 1826 Carlyle had been reading Horn, Fichte, and Schelling.   In Fichte especially he was impressed by what to him was "the cold, colossal, adamantine spirit, standing erect and clear, like a Cato Major among degenerate men; fit to have been the teacher of the Stoa, and to have

discoursed of Beauty and Virtue in the groves of Academe!"
He was convinced that "so robust an intellect, a soul so calm,
so lofty, massive and immovable [had] not mingled in
philosophical discussion since the time of Luther.... The man
rises before us, amid contradiction and debate, like a granite
mountain amid clouds and wind."[60]   Whatever may be the
truth or falsity of Fichte's doctrines, Carlyle is certain that
"his character, as a thinker, can be slightly valued only by
such as know it ill; and [that] as a man, approved by action
and suffering, in his life and in his death, he ranks with a
class of men who were common only in better ages than
ours."[61]   In Horn he had read of Fichte's early struggles
with poverty, of his heroically laborious formulation of a
constructive philosophy upon the ground-work of Kant's criticism of reason, of his stormy period at Jena when the charge
of atheism was hurled at him by reactionaries.   Throughout those turbulent years, says Horn, Fichte was "ein der
ersten Heroen der neueren Zeit."[62]   In Fichte's character,
Carlyle saw a dynamic force sweeping before it all the
utilitarianism, the external morality, and the unbelief of the
Aufklärung.   And this without recourse to the stale rationalistic sophistries of the eighteenth century, but through an
austere thinking-out of the fundamental postulates of a philosophy of the self.   This thinker, authenticated as "a man
approved by action and suffering," appeared to Carlyle as
embracing the great intellectual movement of the time: Fichte
agreed with Kant that the categories of science fail to catch
the elusive living quality of the whole; with Goethe, that
the universe is an organic unity, a unity in diversity; with
Jacobi, that only in intuition, in the inner living experience of
man, in the act of duty, in the sense of freedom, can man
truly apprehend the nature of reality.   Conscious of the
achievements of the Enlightenment, Fichte opposed arbitrary
authority and worn-out tradition, and sought his solutions in
a new employment of reason.   Yet, while advocating the
rights of man, he abandoned many of the associated doctrines,
and once more made mind or spirit the central reality, con-

ceiving existence as a dynamic process of evolution guided by a moral purpose.[63] These aims in Fichte's thought gained, for Carlyle, in a manifold degree by the fact that Fichte appeared to him as a man of "adamantine spirit," robust, calm, lofty, massive, erect, and clear.

In the works of the purely literary men, such as Richter and Schiller, and in the mysticism of Novalis, the evidence of character again was of decisive importance. In both Schiller and Richter he perceived the heroism of their struggle with poverty, misunderstanding, and inward conflict, which gave to so much of German thought its pragmatically verified character. In a sense they indeed embodied the ideal of work as the creator of character and personality. Novalis never ceased to be, as Garnet says, "an oracle, too enigmatic for him, a poet too ethereal, a personality too little known."[64] Yet Carlyle recognized in him a congenial spirit, of "that class of persons who do not recognize the 'syllogistic method' as the chief organ for investigating truth."[65] He interpreted Novalis's *Selbsttödtung* as virtually identical with Goethe's *Entsagen*, and was gratified by the mystic's adherence to Christianity. Likening him to Pascal, Carlyle admires his "high, fine, discursive intellect," his "purest, most affectionate moral nature"; and notes that "he many times expresses, or implies, a zealous, heart-felt belief in the Christian system."[66] On the whole, however, it cannot be said that he ever understood the subtle and roving mind of Novalis, though he sensed the mystic's genius in penetrating into the most recondite things of the spirit.

Of the two great aspects of the new movement in which Carlyle was now finding a new heaven and a new earth, in the Critical Philosophy with its accompanying doctrines and in the personalities of the German poets and thinkers, much of the former or more intellectual aspect failed to retain for him a permanent vitality. Except for the ethical teachings of Goethe, and a few isolated passages from Kant, Fichte, and Novalis, the intellectual movement as a whole, especially as it manifested itself in metaphysical works, seemed to him "a disease expelling a disease." Adopting a different figure, Carlyle regarded it merely as a means whereby man could "shift [his body] out of a laming posture, and get to stand in a free one. Such a service have German Metaphysics done for man's mind. The second sickness of Speculation has abolished both itself and the first." Friedrich Schlegel had struck a responsive chord in Carlyle when he lamented the "fruitlessness, the tumult and transiency of German as of all Metaphysics."[67] Schlegel's own speculations, Carlyle noted with "a solemn mournful feeling," had ended abruptly in the middle of a sentence, his death bringing him to a sudden stop at the very significant word, *aber*.[68] The stream of metaphysical doctrine "in that wide-spreading, deep-whirling vortex of Kantism" impressed Carlyle more and more as an effort to lift oneself by one's bootstraps. The Critical Philosophy, once so bright and promising, was soon "metamorphosed into Fichteism, Schellingism, and then [into] Hegelism and Cousinism." The chief benefit of the whole endeavor had been that "a faith in Religion had again become possible and inevitable for the scientific mind." The mere possibility, however, was fully validated, and in some respects realized, for Carlyle, in German literature: "In the higher Literature of Germany, there already lies, for him that can read it, the beginning of a new revelation of the Godlike. . . . This age also is not wholly without its Prophets."[69]

What the new prophets were uttering on the nature of the universe was of capital importance to Carlyle when he settled at Comley Bank in 1826. He noted that they were reaffirming the old world of spirit, and that to them matter had ceased to have its ancient grip of "iron necessity." To express the nature of the new world which they presented to him they had had recourse to an old and yet ever-useful term. The world was no longer a mechanism; it was an exfoliation, a growth, a process of eternally unfolding divine revelation. The key-word in the new evangel was *Offenbarung*.

CHAPTER IV

CARLYLE'S UNIVERSE

1. REVELATION: *"So ist die Welt in der That eine Offenbarung."*[1]

According to the creed of Ecclefechan, the visible world was but a shadow of realities which transcended any earthly grandeur. In comparison with the eternal world, common earthly life was hardly more than a dream. For the stern "Burgher," both the glamour of life and its enigmatic pain were but transient things; and since the suffering was no more abiding than the joy, life had at best a strange unreality. So it seems prophetic of much in Carlyle's life and thought that at the early age of eleven he saw some verses on a bust of Shakespeare among the wares of an image-seller in the streets of Ecclefechan.[2] For the verses were to become a text. A neighbor read the lines to the boy:

> We are such stuff
> As dreams are made on, and our little life
> Is rounded with a sleep.

The thought of the dream-like nature of the world haunted Carlyle all his life. In his early reading he found expressions of the idea by various thinkers. In Dugald Stewart's essay *On the Idealism of Berkeley*, the conception of life as a dream was shown to be common to Plato, Voltaire, Leibnitz, D'Alembert, Malebranche, Boscovich, the Hindoos. Stewart quoted in a footnote the very lines from the *Tempest* which had been indelibly printed on Carlyle's mind.[3] Later, in German writers, he found that another and far more kindred spirit than Stewart, namely Jean Paul, had been struck by Shakespeare's lines. In the *Wahrheit aus Jean Pauls Leben*, which he reviewed in his second essay on Richter (1830), he learned that the lines as spoken "in

Plattner's mouth, created whole books" in the German humorist.[4] The passage became one of the central themes in Carlyle's work, and provided the climax for the culminating chapter in *Sartor Resartus*. As late as 1876, he said of the lines that he could recollect "nothing so profound out of the Bible, or in it."[5]

This life-long emphasis on an almost literal interpretation of Shakespeare's passage throws a significant light on the character of Carlyle's universe. Whatever realism we may find in his point of view, especially in the face of mere theory, it is important to remember the fundamental idealism bred in him by his Calvinist environment. From that early puritan point of view, as much as from Goethe or Fichte, sprang his inspiration to view all material forms as clothing of something invisible and abiding. Having its basis in the puritan certainty that man moves among shadows, it readily adapted itself to the notion that the visible is but a vesture. In this connection Carlyle could of course remember Biblical verses describing the world as "waxing old like a garment."[6] In literature, likewise, he found the idea expanded in various ways by Sir Thomas Browne, Swift, Pascal, Richter.[7] At last he came to employ the notion of the unreality of appearances as the touchstone for determining the merit of a thinker's general doctrine. He was fortified in finding that the "brave old Northmen" had seen "what Meditation has taught all men in all ages, That this world is after all but a show,—a phenomenon or appearance, no real thing. All deep souls see into that,—the Hindoo Mythologist, the German Philosopher,—the Shakespeare, the earnest Thinker . . ."[8] One notes that for Carlyle the terms "dream," "phenomenon," and "appearance" are all synonymous. That is to say, he is not tempted into pure subjectivism; the visible world is not *merely* a dream. It is also a curtain for the real, or, to adopt a different phrase, the dynamic expression of reality. The precise nature of phenomena as media for the real did not stir his curiosity. His aim was merely to see what he called "the great Fact of the Universe," *i.e.*, that absolute truth and reality lay behind the world of time and space, and yet lay openly revealed to the eye which could recognize appearances for what they were. His universe may be described in terms of what in medieval theology was technically known as a "mystery," *i.e.*, "that which is everywhere revealed, but is not understood of those who have not right judgment."[9] This, for Carlyle, in the words of Goethe, was "the Open Secret."[10]

In reformulating for himself a conception of the external world as the dynamic expression of the divine, Carlyle was of course establishing himself in a very old tradition. "The conception of the cosmos as the mechanism of self-expression for the infinite has flowed through all ages of thought like a subterranean stream."[11] And he himself realized the continuity of that tradition in a series of great minds, from the "Hindoo Mythologist" to German Idealism.

As he gradually—and perhaps half-unconsciously—fashioned his conception of the universe on the lines suggested by Goethe, Kant, Fichte, and other German writers, he accorded chief place to the notion of *Offenbarung*. We shall see that, once he had grasped and accepted Goethe's picture of a God behind the garment of material things, as musically expressed in the Song of the Earth Spirit in *Faust*, he applied Fichte's conception of the Divine Idea (*die göttliche Idee*), and welcomed the interpretation of the "garment" as also in some way a check and a means for the moral development of the Divine Ego in the world. Kant's doctrine of the ideality of time and space fell readily into Carlyle's bold and unmetaphysical attempt to make several philosophies not only harmonize with one another but be inter-explanatory. In his more pantheistic moods he added elements of Schelling's philosophy of identity, his concept of "organism," and his notion of symbol. Two other doctrines were sufficiently cognate to be incorporated into Carlyle's "ground plan of the Universe": the doctrine of palingenesia—the "phoenix doctrine" which appears in *Sartor*—, and the Fichtean doctrine of "becoming," which had expression, in one form or another, in Goethe, Schelling, and Schiller. The result of this eclectic assembling of doctrines into a rough unity of thought is that Carlyle's general *Weltanschauung* is lacking in internal cohesion, symmetry, clarity, logical structure. Its only philosophical unity rests on the informing conception of *Offenbarung,* or dynamic revelation.

2. THE GARMENT OF THE DIVINE: *"Der Gottheit lebendiges Kleid."*[12]

It is appropriate and intelligible that the germ of Carlyle's whole point of view may be found in a figure of speech. The essentially imaginative character of his thinking, his antipathy to systematic thought, and his impulse to seize at truth through immediate vision, are nowhere better revealed than in the degree to which he imaged a vivid pictorial cosmogony from a few lines in one of the subordinate lyrics in *Faust.* The passage is so familiar as hardly to bear repeating, but because of its profoundly organic place in Carlyle's philosophy it must be given here. The Earth-Spirit sings of all nature as the vesture of God:[13]

> In Lebensfluten, in Tatensturm
> Wall' ich auf und ab,
> Webe hin und her!
> Geburt und Grab,
> Ein ewiges Meer,
> Ein wechselnd Weben,
> Ein glühend Leben,
> So schaff' ich am sausenden Webstuhl der Zeit
> Und wirke der Gottheit lebendiges Kleid.

> In Being's floods, in Action's storm,
> I walk and work, above, beneath,
> Work and weave in endless motion!
> >   Birth and Death,
> >   An infinite ocean;
> >   A seizing and giving
> >   The fire of Living:
> 'Tis thus at the roaring Loom of Time I ply,
> And weave for God the Garment thou seest Him by.[14]

Though Carlyle was undoubtedly content, on the whole, to rest with the thought embodied in these lines, there were numerous expressions of the same idea in Goethe's other works and in the works of other writers. In prose and verse, and under various terminology, Goethe frequently touches on the notion that nature reveals God. In the *Sprüche*, with which Carlyle was familiar, we find that "he who would deny Nature as an instrument of the Divine, will also deny all revelation (*Offenbarung*)."[15] "Would you penetrate into the Infinite? Then you must turn to the Finite everywhere about you."[16] "Truth is like God: it does not shine forth directly (*unmittelbar*); we must divine it from its manifestations."[17] At times Goethe employs the term "Idea" in a way which must have reminded Carlyle of Fichte:

> "The Idea is one and eternal; nor is it proper that we should use the word in the plural. All the things of which we become cognizant and are able to speak, are but manifestations of the Idea. We give expression to concepts, and to this extent the Idea is itself a concept. . . . To live in the Idea means treating the impossible as though it were possible. . . . Napoleon, who lived altogether in the Idea, was nevertheless unable consciously to grasp it; he utterly disavowed all ideals and denied them the smallest particle of reality, the while he was zealously striving to realize them. . . He considered the Idea as a thing of the mind which has no actual reality. . . This may to us appear a decidedly perverse and material view, yet . . . he readily admitted that life produces life, and that a fruitful act is effective for all time."[18]

Either as pictured in the Earth-spirit's song or as stated in more intellectual terms, the theme of nature as the expression of God remained the keystone in Carlyle's world-view. To him it was the great common bond between thinkers as unlike, in other respects, as Kant and Fichte and Goethe.

The pantheism, implicit or expressed, which Carlyle read into in such a view of nature left him in a more or less wavering position. Obviously there was little he could accept in Goethe's view of mind and matter as two aspects of one Reality. For Goethe, matter was not the illusion which it was for Carlyle; it belonged to the realm of multiplicity, determination, and actuality, just as mind belonged to the sphere of essence, intelligence, and ideas. Carlyle could never have understood how mind and matter could be regarded as one and the same God under different forms. Indeed, any consistent doctrine of pantheism was, for Carlyle, the first step toward atheism. While to Goethe's poetic faith the pantheistic conception of nature lent the visible world a constant gleam of divinity inseparable from the divine Source itself, it had no such steady significance for Carlyle. He always wavered between a love of nature as suffused with deity, and a rejection of her as a cloud on the otherwise dazzling face of Truth. In his more optimistic moments, when he felt sure of the nearness of God, he pantheistically praised nature's beauty and justice, and sensed God as resident in all grades of being from "the seraph [to] the glow-worm."[19] When, however, he was oppressed by man's short-comings and nature's darkness and blindness, he reverted to his puritan theism, and saw the divine as remote and transcendent. The Garment no longer looked divine; the world was then a miserable "dog-hutch." Yet Goethe's figure retained its grip on him, since it permitted helpful application in either mood. Whatever the mood, it was natural for Carlyle to be more inclined than Goethe to think only of the God behind the vesture.

As he elaborated on the original Goethean image, and the doctrine suggested by it, he tended more and more to disparage the world of appearances, and to seek refuge from "this worthless sham of an existence"[20] in an emphasis on its essential unreality. It will be seen later that we have here no real contradiction of his high estimate of "fact." Fact, at its best, was but a symbol, an appearance. The aim should be to find true symbols, to recognize the message in appearances. It comforted him, in any case, to conceive of the world as a place of shadows, in the fashion of Novalis: "Die Aussenwelt ist die Schattenwelt."[21]   Even in Fichte, for whom Appearance was indeed more than mere illusion, he found occasional emphasis on the Idea as the sole reality: "alles übrige . . . ist Traum, Schatten, Nichts."[22]   Goethe's language, however, is never very far away, when Carlyle deals with abstract notions. Thus when we read his discussion of the Fichtean element in Novalis's *Fragmente*, we are struck by the skilful use of some lines from *Faust*. Novalis's creed

> "appears everywhere in its essential lineaments synony-
> mous with what little we understand of Fichte's . . .
> For him the material Creation is but an Appearance, a
> typical shadow in which the Deity manifests himself
> to man. Not only has the unseen world a reality, but
> the only reality: the rest being not metaphorically, but
> literally and in scientific strictness, 'a show;' in the
> words of the Poet, '*Schall und Rauch umnebelnd
> Himmels Gluth*, Sound and Smoke overclouding the
> Splendour of Heaven.' "[23]

While the poetic basis of Carlyle's universe is but a few lines in Goethe, the speculative basis, so far as he ever accepted one, is to be found in a few passages in Fichte's *Nature of the Scholar*. Though his references to this work, and to certain chief doctrines in it, might lead one to suppose him comparatively familiar with it, it is probable that he never read the whole of the work, and that he was most impressed by single passages, especially certain statements in the first Lecture ("General Plan"). There he learned that

> "The whole material world, with all its adaptations and
> ends, and in particular the life of man in this world, are
> by no means, in themselves and in deed and truth, that
> which they seem to be to the uncultivated and natural
> sense of man; but there is something higher, which lies
> concealed behind all natural appearance. This concealed

foundation of all appearance may, in its greatest universality, be aptly named *the Divine Idea*."[24]

We shall note later Carlyle's principle of selection in his quotation from this first Lecture; it will be seen that he is interested both in *die göttliche Idee* and in the "perpetual priesthood" appointed by it to lead humanity. Passing over Fichte's discussion of the "hodmen" (*Handlangern*) and the "bungler" (*Stümper*), we come to a passage which contains the words which became memorable for Carlyle:

> "Thus I can suppose . . . some Finished Scholar *according to appearance*, under whose eye, perhaps, these thoughts may come—approaching them, and, puzzled and doubtful, at last thoughtfully exclaiming:—*The Idea—the Divine Idea,—that which lies at the bottom of all appearance,*—what may this mean?"[25]

Strictly speaking, these words constitute the Fichtean basis of Carlyle's universe so far as Fichte's actual terminology determined it. They stated in a less figurative way the view which Carlyle found in Goethe. For a fuller appreciation of what Fichte was offering Carlyle, however, we must glance into the second Lecture, "Closer Definition of the Meaning of the *Divine Idea*," which expands upon the first of four propositions given in the "General Plan," *i.e.*, that the material world is an "appearance" or manifestation of the Divine Idea. In a series of ten *Sätze*, Fichte outlines the nature and operation of the Idea. It is necessary to note only a few sentences from numbers four, five, and ten, since the first three merely lay down Fichte's postulates of Being as "living and essentially active," as self-existent and "entirely . . . resident within itself":

> "Now this Divine Life discloses itself, appears, becomes visible, manifests itself as such—as the Divine Life: and this its Manifestation, presence, or outward existence, is the World: . . . [the Idea] is only in part revealed and in part remains concealed . . .

"[The Idea] continues in this manifestation, as we said, to be life. Life cannot be manifested in death, for these two are altogether opposed to each other; and hence, as Absolute Being alone is life, so the only true Manifestation of that Being is living existence, and death has neither an absolute, nor, in the highest sense of the word, has it even a relative existence. This living and visible Manifestation we call the human race . . . Existence in Time, or the Manifestation of that Divine Life, constitute the whole united life of mankind. . . . Thus, in its Manifestation the Divine Life becomes a continually progressive existence, unfolding in perpetual growth. . . . The Manifestation of Life in Time, unlike the Divine Life, is limited at every point of its existence,—*i.e.*, it is in part not living, not yet interpenetrated by life, but in so far—dead. These limitations it shall gradually break through, lay aside, and transform into life, in its onward progress.

"In this view of the limitations which surround Existence in Time, we have . . . the conception of the objective and material world, or what we call Nature. This is not living and capable of infinite growth like Reason; but dead,—a rigid, self-inclosed existence. It is this which, arresting and hemming in the Time-Life [prevents that attainment] which would otherwise burst forth at once, a perfect and complete life. Further, in the development of spiritual existence, Nature itself is gradually interpenetrated by life; and it is thus both the obstacle to, and the sphere of, that activity. . . . Nature also has its foundation in God . . . but only as the means and condition of another being,—of the Living Being in man. . . .

"And thus it is sufficiently explained for our present purpose how the Divine Idea lies at the foundation of the visible world, and how, and how far, this Idea, hidden from the common eye, may become conceivable and attainable by cultivated thought, and necessarily appear to it as that which man by his free activity *ought* to manifest in the world.

"And thus, as the Life of Man is the only immediate implement and organ of the Divine Idea in the visible

world, so is it also the first and immediate object of
its activity.   The progressive Culture of the human race
is the object of the Divine Idea, and of those in whom
that Idea dwells."[26]

In these passages Carlyle found a clear enunciation of several doctrines involved in the notion of *Offenbarung*: the
conception of the world as a symbolic revelation, partly dis-
closing and partly concealing Reality; of death as unreal
in a universe of immanent life-energy; of time as arresting
and hemming-in (*anhaltend und hemmend*) the life of spirit,
yet providing the sphere of activity for the realization of
that life; of the progressive unfolding of the Idea through
the cultivation of humanity; of man as the *unmittelbares
Werkzeug und Organ* of spirit; of the progressive development of the moral essence of humanity, as the aim of the
Divine Idea and of the "heroes" "in whom that Idea dwells."
As we take up these notions, and discern in what degree
Carlyle approximated their true meaning, we shall see that
there was indeed in these popular lectures of Fichte sufficient
embroidery upon the germinal idea lying in Carlyle's mind
to account for the individual applications and developments
which he gave them in his subsequent writings.   This central
doctrine of the dynamic revelation of a moral principle active
in spite of, and by means of, time and matter will be seen
determining his conception of time, nature, history, heroes,
labor, society, ethics.   For the moment it is necessary only
to bear in mind the general nature of Fichte's ethical idealism,
and how for Carlyle it evidently threw light upon the God
behind the "Garment" in Goethe's lines and at the same
time imparted to the vesture a morally expressive function
in a reinterpretation of nature.

It has frequently been noted that Carlyle's God bears little
resemblance to Goethe's, and that his universe, idealistic as it
is in many respects, has little similarity to Fichte's.   We
have already observed wherein Carlyle could not follow
Goethe's realistic attitude toward matter.   Though it would

take us too far afield to inquire fully into all the technical divergences between Carlyle and Fichte, it is necessary to glance at some of them if we are to draw a clear line around some of the quasi-Fichtean features of his teachings.

We observe, in the first place, that Carlyle cared little about the metaphysical steps whereby Fichte arrived at his conclusion that nature is physical in appearance and spiritual in significance and reality. While they both adopt a spiritual interpretation of the essence and development of the world, and regard it as a harmonious unity because it expresses spiritual force and is guided by eternal and immutable law, Carlyle could not have agreed with Fichte that the only reality is thought. He seems never to have inquired into the Fichtean teaching that being means being conscious, that the universe really is an *idea*—the product of consciousness. He was always inclined to think of the Divine Idea as a "great First Cause," lurking behind the illusion of the senses, somewhat after the fashion of Berkeley's "Spirit." He failed to grasp Fichte's point that the Divine Idea, though it "lies at the bottom of Appearances," is yet the goal of finite activity, only partially attained at any time, and is infinite only in its directing of an ever-approximating realization of spiritual order. It is not a perfect Being controlling and directing the visible world like an anthropomorphic God; in fact, it may be doubted if it is a God at all, as Fichte's accusers realized in the famous controversy over his alleged "atheism." Certainly it fell below the requirements of Carlyle's ideal conception of deity. Yet, while Carlyle never analysed Fichte's doctrine in any detail, he no doubt appreciated the stimulus of its very vagueness and realized the challenge in its call to ethical action.

Both Goethe and Fichte had delivered him from materialism. Writing in 1830, he records in his Journal his final victory:

> "I think I have got rid of materialism: Matter no longer seems to me so ancient, so unsubduable, so *certain* and palpable as Mind. *I* am Mind: whether matter or

not I know not—and care not. Mighty glimpses into the spiritual Universe I have some times had (about the true nature of Religion, the possibility, after all, of 'super-natural' (really natural) influences, etc., etc.): would they could but stay with me, and ripen into a perfect view !"[27]

The "perfect view" never came; but the certainty of the God behind the Garment remained with him. The "glimpses into the spiritual Universe" never took on any great degree of order, and Carlyle's God became less and less "the Divine Idea" and more and more the Hebraic deity, in whose mind, however, man and the world lay as an "idea." The Fichtean conception of God as an infinite Ego seeking in finite forms its own self-expression, the whole world of Ego and Non-Ego being but the process of intellect achieving an eternally progressive moral order—this conception came to mean almost nothing for him. But in his new philosophy of *Offenbarung* he found in Fichte's "Divine Idea" a step whereon he could pause in his re-affirmation of deity; it helped him to re-comprehend the doctrine of immanence, one of the early steps in many a "convert's" re-discovery of God. Thus it released him from the tyranny of "ancient" matter; it confirmed his belief in the God behind the vesture of the external.

The problems of time, space, and matter, all the questions involved in his acceptance of the new universe, now invited his attention. At Comley Bank and in the early years at Craigenputtock, he made an effort to understand Kant's doctrine of the ideality of space and time, and Fichte's philosophy of the Ego and the Non-Ego.

3. Time and Space: *"Deepest of all illusory Appearances."*[28]

As we have already noted, Carlyle's object in studying Kant's treatment of space and time was evidently to establish for himself the unreality of matter. Unaware of distorting Kant's theory, he viewed the doctrine almost entirely from its negative side, concerning himself chiefly with the degree in which it opposed dogmatism, skepticism, and materialism.   Since it is impossible to point out, as in Goethe and Fichte, a number of lines or passages which unmistakably contributed to Carlyle's thought,[29] it is necessary to enter into a somewhat technical statement of Kant's aims and achievements, and to note the manner in which Carlyle's interpretation succeeded and failed to reflect the original doctrine.

Kant may be said to consider space and time from two points of view: according to their nature as modes of sense perception, and according to their ideality.   It was the latter approach to them which was most significant to Carlyle. His own interpretation of them according to the former view, however, merits attention and should be examined first, in comparison with Kant's argument.   "Space," says Kant, "is nothing but the form of all appearances of outer sense,"[30] the subjective mode under which alone any perception of the external world is possible.   It thus does not belong, as a form or property, to outward objects.   Kant concludes that "objects in themselves are quite unknown to us, and that what we call outer objects are nothing but mere representations of our sensibility, the form of which is space."[31]   As space is the form of our perception of external objects, so time is nothing else than the immediate condition of internal sense (*des innern Sinnes*), and the mediate condition of external phenomena.   Having nothing to do with shape or position, if it is taken independently of the mind or subject, "time is nothing but the form of inner sense, that is, of the intuition of ourselves and of our inner state."[32]   No object can ever be presented to us in experience except under the conditions of time, which, like space, is but a mode of our perception.   Summing up the doctrine under the heading, "General Observations on Transcendental Aesthetic," Kant concludes that "if the subject, or even only the subjective constitution of the senses in general, be removed, the whole constitution and all the relations of objects in space and time, nay space and time themselves, would vanish."[33]

In order to make his explanation vividly concrete, Kant gives in a later passage the following example:

> "The rainbow in a sunny shower may be called a mere appearance, and the rain the thing in itself. This is correct, if the latter concept be taken in a merely physical sense. Rain will then be viewed only as that which, in all experience and in all its various positions relative to the senses, is determined thus, and not otherwise, in our intuition. But if we take this empirical object in its general character, and ask, without considering whether or not it is the same for all human sense, whether it represents an object in itself (and by that we cannot mean the drops of rain, for these are already, as appearances, empirical objects), the question as to the relation of the representation to the object at once becomes transcendental. We then realize that not only are the drops of rain mere appearances, but that even their round shape, nay even the space in which they fall, are nothing in themselves, but merely modifications or fundamental forms of our sensible intuition, and that the transcendental object remains unknown to us."[34]

It is hard to believe that Carlyle failed to appreciate the appeal which this passage makes to the imaginative mind. It is possible that such a passage tempted him to the conclusion which distorts his exposition of Kant's theory, namely, that time and space are thus nothing but illusion. This was an inference which Kant of course expressly opposed: "It would be my own fault," he said, "if out of that which I ought to reckon as appearance, I made mere illusion."[35] It is important here, however, to observe what Carlyle made of this doctrine of time and space as forms of sense experience.

In the essay on *Novalis*, he attempts an exposition in popular terms. His brief discussion—amounting to a few general statements—reveals how little of the technical side of the theory he had absorbed, and how persistent is his habit of thinking in terms which merely approximate or suggest his meaning.

> "Time and Space," he says, "are not external but internal entities: they have no outward existence, there is no Time and no Space *out* of the mind; they are mere *forms* of man's spiritual being, *laws* under which his thinking nature is constituted to act. This seems the hardest conclusion of all; but it is an important one with Kant; and is not given forth as a dogma; but carefully deduced in his *Critik der Reinen Vernunft* with great precision, and strictest form of argument."[36]

This passage is the only one in which Carlyle states his conception of time and space as modes of sense. And its avowedly "loose and popular manner,"[37] for which he apologises, should withhold us from any rigorous measuring of his interpretation with Kant's original doctrine were it not that his exposition is sometimes regarded as roughly true.[38] It is necessary, however, to point out that in his vague and ambiguous expressions—"man's spiritual being," "not external but internal entities"—and in his references to time and space as forms, not of sense, but of the "mind,"[39] he shows that he has never penetrated very far into the *Critique* and has only a very hazy notion of what it seeks to demonstrate. What has struck him is that time and space have no objective existence, that the outer world is now seen to be dependent, in some manner, upon the activity of man's mind. This, he notes, is diametrically opposite to the Scotch "Common Sense" faith in the "ancient, unsubduable, *certain*, palpable" status of matter. It is "the hardest conclusion of all," not only because Kant's argument is a strain upon one's capacity for close reasoning, but also because it runs counter to all that he has read since his early childhood. He admires the strict form of Kant's argument, but there is no reason for believing that he understood it or even followed it very far. He is satisfied that it is not mere dogma—indeed he is reading Kant to free himself from dogma—and its dialectical garb, though opaque, for the most part, to his understanding, commends itself to him as an inspired and wholesomely rational demonstration. It is evident, however, from the inadequacy of his exposition, that the *formal* nature of space and time made little clear impression on him.

On the other hand, the *ideality* of time and space made a lasting impression and became—especially as regards time—one of the chief elements in Carlyle's world-view. It goes without saying that he was unable, or unwilling, to adhere to Kant's meaning. We observe this best by noting first how Kant deals with this side of his problem. His aim was to limit our knowledge to the knowable, to show space and time as real when applied to phenomena (which we know) and unreal when applied to noumena, or things in themselves (which we cannot know). He did not expect his reader to over-stress, as Carlyle and Jacobi did, the negative or ideal side of his theory, but to keep thought within the bounds of the empirically real. Underlying his doctrine of space and time, therefore, we find a dualistic conception of reality. He maintained the "empirical reality" of space in regard to external experiences, but otherwise admitted its "transcendental ideality." In regard to time, he held it to be real for subjective experience: "Empirical reality has to be allowed to time, as the condition of all our experiences; on our theory, it is only its absolute reality that has to be denied. It is nothing but the form of our inner intuition."[40] Carlyle, however, used the ideality of space and time, not to limit him to the empirically real, but to conclude that phenomena have not even an empirical reality. Apparently *because* time and space are forms of sense dealing with appearance, they are for Carlyle related only to illusion, and betray the essential unreality of the whole objective world. It is true that Carlyle also speaks of the phenomenal world as the arena of man's moral struggle toward the Good, and thus admits a certain reality to it; but it was not the phenomenal reality maintained in the *Critique of Pure Reason*. Time as man's "seedfield"[41] has not the reality which Kant insists is the indispensable condition of man's experience. Even when admonishing us to work in our seedfield of time, Carlyle is always conscious that "Deepest of all illusory Appearances are your two grand fundamental world-enveloping Appearances, Space and Time." He bids us "sweep away the Illusion of Time; glance from the near moving-cause to its far-distant Mover."[42] No admonition, of course, could be further from Kant's standpoint. For him the empirical world, profoundly real for us, is in part the creation of the human mind; for Carlyle, that world is a veil between us and reality—a trick, as it were, to deceive us, in which we are too often parties to the deception. Whereas in Kant's doctrine, man is free and creating, in Carlyle's he is borne along on "the aether of Deity" which is timeless and spaceless,[43] the illusions of the senses and the mind being the barrier to the recognition of his true position.

We may better observe how Carlyle employed the ideality of space and time, if we turn to the dualism in Kant's attitude toward reality. We note first that Kant's attitude toward time and space rested on their objectivity as proved by the universality of their scope and their validity within the limits of human thought. According to man's nature, the world of ordinary experience will always remain real for him. Any glimpses of a higher world, of things in themselves, of reality behind the appearance, will come through a consciousness of his moral freedom rather than through his thought. Thus from his conception of man as a duality of physical and moral elements, Kant arrived at a reality that was likewise dual. For Carlyle, however, the nature of space and time was determined by his conception that "Nature is one, a living and indivisible whole."[44] His reality behind appearances is not Kant's "things in themselves," unknowable, and predicable only on the basis of moral freedom. Carlyle's monism demanded that reality be a spiritual force active in all things, manifesting itself to us under the forms of space and time as an external world. Time and space are thus merely evidences of man's finitude, by which wholeness is divided by his incomplete vision: "Nature is the Time-vesture of God, and reveals Him to the wise, hides Him from the foolish; for Matter is spirit, the manifestation of spirit."[45] For Carlyle what Kant calls the world of things in themselves, unknowable to man, does not exist. Reality can be known, if not to the mass of men, then at least to the Seer: "Know of a truth that only the Time-shadows have perished, or are perishable; that the real Being of whatever was, and whatever is, and whatever will be, *is* even now and forever" as a reality which is readily discerned by the Seer, but which "to the mass of men, for the most part, lies hidden, the Celestial Everywhere and Forever."[46] Thus, agreeing with Kant that space and time are ideal, that they have no absolute reality, Carlyle goes further and denies them any reality whatsoever. Morover, if they are unreal, then Eternity and Infinity are the only realities.

This was precisely the conclusion at which Carlyle wished to arrive. He seems to have been influenced almost exclusively by Kant's remarks about the purely relative value of time and space, and to have inferred finally that, since they are ideal, they could have no reality in his scheme of things. If Carlyle reasoned at all on the problem, it must have been somewhat in the following fashion: "If time and space are unreal for noumena, they should also be unreal for phenomena, themselves already unreal; thus, if time, space, and phenomena are all unreal, only noumena are real, and we partake of their reality, knowing it and living in it." Bewildering as this statement may be, this at least was what his final position amounted to. Just what passages in the *Critique* could have led to this manner of argument, it is impossible to say. Perhaps none of them did. We may glance, however, at one of the most concise statements of Kant's point of view on this subject:

> "What we are maintaining is, therefore, the *empirical reality* of time, that is, its objective validity in respect of all objects which allow of ever being given to our senses. And since our intuition is always sensible, no object can ever be given to us in experience which does not conform to the condition of time. On the other hand, we deny to time all claim to absolute reality; that is to say, we deny that it belongs to things absolutely, as their condition or property, independently of any reference to the form of our sensible intuition; properties that belong to things in themselves can never be given to us through the senses. This, then, is what constitutes the *transcendental ideality* of time. . . ."[47]

From passages such as this Carlyle proceeded to a very free and arbitrary interpretation of them in the interests of morality and religion.

> "If Time and Space," he concluded in his essay on *Novalis,* "have no absolute existence, no existence out of our minds [if, in short, they are *ideal*], it removes a stumbling block from the very threshold of our Theology. For on this ground, when we say that the Deity is omnipresent and eternal, that with Him it is a universal Here and Now, we say nothing wonderful; nothing but that He also created Time and Space, that Time and Space are not laws of His being, but only of ours . . . the old hostility of Matter is at an end, for Matter itself is annihilated; and the black Spectre, Atheism, 'with all its sickly dews,' melts into nothingness forever."[48]

It was these notions of time and space, as he thought he found them treated in Kant, which he applied to the *Garment* of Goethe's Deity, or to the material world by which Fichte's *Divine Idea* achieved its purposes. Prompted by no interests

in Kant's unknowable world of "noumena," Carlyle was content with a few negative suggestions about the nature of
space and time. Unlike Kant's "noumena," Goethe's "Eternal" and Fichte's "Divine Idea" were far from being unknowable. Indeed it is the duty of man as a participant in the
divine weaving of the phantasmagoria of the external world,
to see that "this so solid-seeming World, after all, [is] but
an air-image, [and] our Me the only reality: and Nature,
with its thousandfold production and destruction, but the
reflex of our own inward Force . . . *the living visible Garment
of God.*"[49]   Neither for man, the microcosm, nor for the
Macrocosm itself, are time and space real; in the degree to
which man rejects them as only greater illusions than the
minor illusions of the senses will man come into his own as
a child of freedom, "the epitome of the Infinite."[50]   Thus
Kant's demonstration of the ideality of space and time performed for Carlyle a curious service: it convinced him that
matter had been "annihilated," that space and time had been
"created" as laws of our experience, that God resided behind
the curtain of illusion in a "universal Here [and] an everlasting Now."[51]   It is hardly necessary to say that Kant
would have repudiated the whole of Carlyle's interpretation
and application of the doctrine. And that Carlyle derived
from "Kantism," ostensibly from the severe epistemological
problems of Kant, a lever for "removing a stumbling block
from the very threshold of Theology," is one of the ironies in
the history of ideas.

4. NATURE: *"Ich bestimme die Welt. . . ."*[52]

It will be interesting, before leaving Carlyle on the subject
of time, space, and matter, to examine for a moment the only
passage in which he definitely attempts to account for the
material world in the new terms, with references to "these
Kantian systems," especially to Fichte's teachings. We must
turn to the essay on *Novalis*, to the paragraph preceding that

one in which he sets forth time and space as "internal entities." Apparently Carlyle believed the transcendental account of matter to be less difficult of apprehension, possibly because he had been prepared for it by his study of Berkeley, of whose theory indeed the exposition is more reminiscent than of Fichte's.

If it were not for the mention of Fichte's "far-famed *Ich* and *Nicht-Ich*," we should at once regard the paragraph as a paraphrase from Berkeley's *Principles of Human Knowledge.*

> "To a Transcendentalist," says Carlyle, "Matter has an existence, but only as a Phenomenon: were *we* not there, neither would it be there; it is a mere Relation, or rather the result of a Relation between our living Souls and the great First Cause; and depends for its apparent qualities on *our* bodily and mental organs; having itself *no* intrinsic qualities; being, in the common sense of that word, Nothing. The tree is green and hard, not of its own natural virtue, but simply because my eye and my hand are fashioned so as to discern such and such appearances under such and such conditions. Nay, as an Idealist might say, even on the most popular grounds, *must* it not be so? Bring a sentient Being, with eyes a little different, with fingers ten times harder than mine; and to him that Thing which I call Tree shall be yellow and soft, as truly as to me it is green and hard. Form his Nervous-structure in all points the *reverse* of mine, and this same Tree shall not be combustible or heat-producing, but dissoluble and cold-producing, not high and convex, but deep and concave; shall simply have *all* properties exactly the reverse of those I attribute to it."[53]

So far, Carlyle's exposition of the ideality of matter appears as a good popular account of Berkeley's doctrine. For though Fichte, too, has a tree-passage in his *Vocation of Man*, it deals with the "tree in general,"[54] and cannot compare in appositeness with the following passage from the *Principles of Human Knowledge.* Berkeley's argument, in this instance, to be sure, relates not to the deception of the senses, as in Car'yle's discussion, but to the fact that an object, *e.g.*, a tree, cannot be conceived to exist apart from some one to conceive it—as Carlyle puts it, "were *we* not there, neither would it be there." The external world is thus not self-existent, but depends upon a knower. The underlying principle is the same in both discussions. Berkeley says:

> "But, say you, surely there is nothing easier than for me to imagine trees, for instance, in a park, or books existing in a closet, and nobody by to perceive them. I answer, you may so, there is no difficulty in it. What is all this, I beseech you, more than framing in your mind certain ideas which you call *books* and *trees*, at the same time omitting to frame the idea of any one that may perceive them? But do not you yourself perceive or think of them all the while? This therefore is nothing to the purpose: it only shews you have the power of imagining, or forming ideas in your mind; but it does not shew that you can conceive it possible the objects of your thought may exist without the mind. To make out this, it is necessary that you conceive them existing unconceived, or unthought of; which is a manifest repugnancy. When we do our uttermost to conceive the existence of external bodies, we are all the while only contemplating our own ideas. But the mind, taking no notion of itself, is deluded to think it can and does conceive bodies existing unthought of, or without the mind, though at the same time they are apprehended by, or exist, in itself. A little attention will discover to anyone the truth and evidence of what is here said, and make it unnecessary to insist on any other proofs against the existence of *material substance*."[55]

Another representative passage in Berkeley, which might well have been in the back of Carlyle's mind when he mentioned the "great first Cause," occurs in the *Three Dialogues*. Hylas has made a similar effort to "conceive a tree as existing unperceived or unthought of," and is forced by the argument of Philonous to admit that "I may indeed conceive in my own thoughts the idea of a tree . . ., but that is all. And that is far from proving that I can conceive them *existing out of the minds of all Spirits.*"[56]   The "Spirit" which holds all objects in existence, even when no finite spirit is present to perceive them, appears to have been more congenial to Carlyle, as a concept, than the Fichtean Ego, which, unlike Berkeley's "Spirit," is present in and through the object, employing it as a means of self-expression.   Carlyle's next sentences, however, attribute his "Berkeleyan" notions to Fichte :

> "There is, in fact, says Fichte, no Tree there ; but only a Manifestation of Power from something which is *not I.*   The same is true of material Nature at large, of the whole visible Universe, with all its movements, figures, accidents and qualities ; all are Impressions produced on *me* by something *different from me.*"

Berkeleyan as these sentences sound, they do not, however, indicate any thorough-going adoption of such idealism. From Carlyle's point of view, nature is not, as for Berkeley, the creation by a Spirit *for* created spirits, but is the illusory fabric spun by our notions of time and space.   Carlyle apparently never made any greater effort to penetrate to the heart of Berkeley's philosophy than he did to grasp the true nature of Kant or Fichte.   All that we can say of his interpretation of Fichteism is that it might well have been an interpretation of Berkeley, and that he betrays his usual vagueness regarding the origin and differences of various doctrines when he concludes, "This, we suppose, may be the foundation of what Fichte means by his far-famed *Ich* and *Nicht-Ich* (I and Not-I)."

For we remember that Fichte's *Ich*, or Ego, is Intelligence, which is, for him, the sole reality.   It is not the individual ego of man—the subject apprehending the tree—but the universal, absolute, pure Ego, from which we must dis-

tinguish man's individual, finite, empirical ego. The absolute
Ego is present everywhere as pure activity, finding its true
being in freedom. Man's finite ego, however, is rooted in
nature, bound by necessity, from which point of view it is one
of the innumerable limited expressions of the pure Ego in
the material world. Man's ego is also partly free; as a
thinking moral agent, as also a pure ego, he partakes of the
divine, and is thus, as Carlyle was fond of saying, a conflux
of necessity and freedom, of time and eternity. Originally,
according to the Fichtean conception, all things were one,
abiding in a primal unity. Now the goal of all moral
endeavor is to recapture that unity, to seek increasingly to
free the pure spirit in man from the shackles of his individual,
empirical ego. This is to be done by concentrating our
effort on what is universal, free, and moral in man's being.
Pure freedom, however, can never be attained by man; that
is possible only for the absolute, self-determining, divine Ego.
Our only means of approaching the state of complete freedom
is through moral action, by means of our material body,
which, however, as an object of nature, keeps such a goal
ideally unrealizable. If we were able wholly to deny our
individual ego, and pass from it to the pure universal, absolute freedom of the Divine Idea, we should become that Idea,
be "made one with God." The mystic believes such a union
to be possible. For Fichte, however, this act is forever
impossible to man as man. His real duty is so to act that at
every moment the empirical ego is kept subordinate to the
moral claims of the pure-ego, and thus to ally himself with
the eternal struggle of the Absolute Ego to spiritualize the
world. To perform this duty means living true to one's highest native capacities, achieving one's vocation in the life of
the spirit. Thus, Fichte's exhortation: "Erfülle jedesmal
Deine Bestimmung."[57]   It is important to remember, of
course, that when Carlyle was not attempting a paraphrase
of Fichte's statements concerning the Divine Idea, but was
merely uttering Fichtean doctrine in his own idiom, he

came very much nearer to the original. Throughout Carlyle's teaching there is the insistence on the universal presence and activity of the divine, whether as an "Idea" or as the "law" of the old Hebraic deity; there is the distinction between the lower, happiness-hungry self and the higher "celestial ME"; and there is the doctrine—better known as the "gospel of work"—that man's primary duty is to aid the Divine Ego in its spiritualization of the world, to "make the will of God prevail," by finding and fulfilling his vocation in the world of fact. Thus Carlyle's grasp of Fichte's doctrine of the Ego amounted, in the long run, to practical comprehension.

On the other hand, he shows little evidence of such comprehension of the Non-Ego. It is worthwhile stating, in the words of one of Fichte's expositors, just what is meant by this doctrine.

> "Fichte holds that, as there can be no knowing without an object, the Ego, or Intellect, in order to insure its continued existence, must create an object of its activity. Therefore it produces—or in Fichte's terminology, posits—itself as its object; but in order to know this self, it must find in it distinguishing features, it must differentiate it from something else. The original Ego, then, in order to create a sphere of activity and to acquire a knowledge of itself and of the laws of its activity, posits a Non-Ego. This Non-Ego, or limiting object of an active intelligence, is the world of physical nature. By a successful resolution of the implicit contradiction, the mutually-determining Ego and Non-Ego together realize the original Ego."[58]

Now from Carlyle's paragraph on the tree, it can be seen that he has no real grasp of the significance of the *Nicht-Ich*. That it is "something which is different from me," a "Manifestation of Power from something which is *not I*" is inadequate and misleading. It leaves unstated, for example, the fact that the *Nicht-Ich* is after all a part of the original *Ich*.

Matter as a manifestation of a Power is, of course, a Fichtean principle; but, unlike Carlyle, Fichte holds it to be not essentially an illusion but "a contradiction of thought by thought, or the opposing element of an essentially self-contrasting intelligence."[59]

We have perhaps gone further than necessary into the technical divergence between the thought of the two men, especially in view of the almost negligible ingredient of technical Fichteanism in Carlyle's conception of matter. But it is important to see clearly the relationship between their concepts. Otherwise it is difficult to understand the relationship between Carlyle and Novalis, or to realize that, at moments, Carlyle indeed approximates the original doctrine. Through Novalis he came to interpret Fichte's philosophy more definitely as a refutation of the substantiality of matter, as a demonstration that man's spirit is primary, that the outer world is derivative, or, in the words of Novalis's *Lehrlinge,* "eine wüste Phantasie ihres Traumes."[60] It sufficed for Carlyle that the visible world was somehow determined by the operation of his "Me," and that man was in turn determined, as the laborer is by his tools, by the "Not-Me." Novalis had said: "There must be a Not-Me, in order for me to be able to posit myself as a Me . . . I determine [or posit, *bestimme*] the world, in that I determine myself, . . . and *vice versa.*"[61] Moreover, Carlyle found in Novalis the Fichtean notion of man as a "reflex of the All,"[62] stated with greater definiteness; "According to Fichte," said Novalis, "the Me is, as it were, the result (*Resultat*) of the Universe. I must presuppose the whole Universe, in order to assume the conscious *Ich*; just as, on the other hand, the absolute positing (*Setzung*) of the *Ich* is nothing else than the positing of the All (*Universums*)."[63] In words less metaphysical, and more in harmony with Carlyle's fundamental theistic tendencies, Novalis touches further on this theme: "God is just as personal and individual as we are—for our so-called *Ich* is not our true *Ich*, but only its reflection."[64] How our

real selves may be distinguished from our illusory or empirical selves becomes clearer in Novalis's paraphrase of Fichte's
remarks about the Non-Ego: "Nothing becomes evident
except through representation. One most easily understands
a thing when one sees it represented. Thus one understands
the *Ich* only in so far as it is represented by the *Nicht-Ich*.
The *Nicht-Ich* is the symbol of the *Ich*, and serves only for
the ego's knowledge of itself. . . ."[65] That Carlyle did indeed
grasp the significance of this, especially in its practical and
ethical relations, is evident from a short passage in *Sartor*.
Teufelsdröckh, we remember, pauses in the "Center of Indifference," and seeks to regain his moral equilibrium by turning from the torture of self-contemplation to the tangible
world about him: "In a word, he clutches round him outwardly on the NOT-ME for wholesomer food."[66] His
achievement of the "Everlasting Yea" was little more than the
realization that the seemingly hostile world of matter was
indeed a symbol of the spirit of which he was a partaker,
and that his salvation lay through an active, creative seizing
of the Not-Me in an effort to know himself: "Hence . . . the
folly of that impossible Precept, *Know thyself*, till it be
translated into this partially possible one, *Know what thou
canst work at*."[67] Other passages in *Sartor* suggest that
Carlyle toyed even with the Fichtean doctrine of the two
egos in man: "das reine Ich," which becomes Carlyle's
"celestial Me," or the "divine Me"; and "das empirische
Ich," to which Carlyle refers simply as "the self."[68] Little,
however, came of this momentary employment of ideas so
foreign to Carlyle's simple attitude toward the soul.

We may say, in summary, that on the whole, the significance for Carlyle of the ideas of Kant, Fichte, and Novalis on
the nature of the external world—on time, space, matter—
amounted to little more than a denial of its absolute existence.
His interest in the subject, as treated by these thinkers,
apparently followed his adoption of Goethe's "Garment philosophy." In Fichte's *Nicht-Ich*, in Kant's demonstration

of the subjectivity of time and space, he thought he saw a justification for regarding matter as fundamentally spiritual. We have seen that he apparently saw little difference between the arguments of Fichte and the arguments of Berkeley, and it seems certain that he was unaware of Kant's careful attempt to refute Idealism in the *Critique of Pure Reason*.[69] His sole purpose was to escape the materialism of men like Hartley and the skepticism of thinkers like Hume.   He agreed with the "transcendentalists" that matter had a relative existence, and great practical value in the realization of spirit; but in the writings of his early period the physical world had little glamor or substantiality in comparison with the newly discovered Infinite. The value of the natural world was chiefly symbolical. Far more important than learning the mechanical laws of its operation was the need for a sharp divinatory instinct for interpreting the symbolism in "that God-written Apocalypse."[70]

5. SYMBOLISM: *"Alles Vergängliche ist nur ein Gleichniss."*[71]

Of central importance in Carlyle's attitude toward the world was the power of the symbol to convey a sense of the inexpressible.   It explains in part his disdain for natural science, in spite of his early love of science and mathematics. His conviction of the transcendent importance of moral truth over knowledge of physical nature led him at times to emphasize the symbolical interpretation of nature at the expense of analytical knowledge. From his point of view, man needed the spiritual deliverance of a symbolism well interpreted rather than a mass of classified facts about nature, of which he could know nothing ultimate.   His natural tendency to think in terms of images and symbols, and his high estimate of their efficacy and significance, was no doubt greatly strengthened by what he read in Goethe, Schelling,

Novalis, and Schiller. We turn first to Carlyle's remarks on
the subject:

> "In the Symbol proper . . . there is ever, more or less
> distinctly and directly, some embodiment and revelation
> of the Infinite; the Infinite is made to blend itself with
> the Finite, to stand visible, and as it were, attainable
> there. By Symbols, accordingly, is man guided and
> commanded, made happy, made wretched. He every-
> where finds himself encompassed with Symbols, recog-
> nized as such or not recognized: the Universe is but one
> vast Symbol of God; . . . what is man himself but a
> Symbol of God; is not all that he does symbolical; a
> revelation to Sense of the mystic god-given force that
> is in him; a 'Gospel of Freedom,' which he, the 'Messias
> of Nature,' preaches, as he can, by act and word? Not
> a Hut he builds but is the visible embodiment of a
> Thought; but bears visible record of invisible things;
> but is, in the transcendental sense, symbolical as well as
> real."[72]

It is possible that much of the element of symbolism in
Carlyle came from Schelling, in whose "philosophy of
identity" it naturally had a major position. The forms of
matter in the outer world, Schelling maintained, are symbolic
in that they are analogous, step by step, with the processes of
the inner life. The proper study of nature, he held, was the
tracing of likenesses between the inner life and the nature of
magnets, crystals, solar systems, living creatures, the whole
physical world.[73] The outer world is but the thought of God
visible to our eyes; the inner world is God's thought become
conscious of itself: the former is the symbol of thought or
spirit. In nature, itself a vast symbol, we see the unity,
the *identity*, of the ideal (or thought), with the real (or
matter). The symbol thus becomes both extrinsically and
intrinsically significant, both a mere symbol and, in part, the
truth it symbolizes. "In all things," he says, "there is but
one life, but one power, the same fusion through ideas. In
nature there is no purely corporeal existence, but everywhere

soul symbolically transformed into body, and only in appearance a predominance of the one over the other."[74]

But we find Schelling's phrasing most strikingly similar to Carlyle's in another passage of the *Method of Academical Study*. The discussion relates to the symbolic value of history, and especially of the church, and of their revealing the union of the finite and the infinite. Schelling holds that any conception of religion which is to show the infinite in the finite must be principally expressed in the forms of nature, in natural objects taken symbolically as they stand. The opposite conception of religion calls for arbitrary symbols and revelation only through action.

> "The true symbol," Schelling continues, "with every manifestation of God in it, is history. But history is indeterminate, incommensurable. It should thus be represented by a manifestation at once finite and infinite, not itself real, like the State, but ideal, representing everything in the universal spirit in spite of the division of its parts. This symbolic conception is the Church, as a living work of art."[75]

Here we have, without regard to the religious subject, a passage in Schelling which parallels Carlyle's statement that "in the symbol . . . . the Infinite is made to blend itself with the Finite." For Carlyle, as for Schelling, the highest symbols were "religious symbols," and the Church, when it was a vital symbol, appeared to him, as to Schelling, the greatest symbol of all.[76]

Another interesting parallel, however, appears in Goethe's remarks that,

> "Symbolism transforms the phenomenon into an idea, the idea into an image, in such a way that in the image the idea still remains unattainable and forever effective, and though it be expressed in all languages, yet remains inexpressible. . . . That is true Symbolism in which the particular represents the universal, not as a dream or a shadow, but as a living, instantaneous revelation of the Inscrutable."[77]

Translated into Fichtean language, Novalis gives us the same notion: "One comprehends the *Nicht-Ich* . . . only in so far as it is represented by the *Ich*, and this [the *Nicht-Ich*] becomes its symbol."[78]

Carlyle's doctrine that nature is "the realized thought of God" has frequently been attributed to Schelling's influence. While there is no reason to doubt such an influence, we need also to remember that Carlyle found the same thought expressed in Schiller's *Philosophical Letters*: "The universe is God's thought expressed . . . Thus I recognize but one phenomenon in Nature, the thinking being. The great combination which we call Universe excites my interest only in so far as it is designed to furnish symbolic representations of the varied manifestations of this being."[79]

For Carlyle, as for the Germans, the comprehension of the significance of the world as a great symbol was possible chiefly because man and all his actions constituted symbols in themselves. According to Novalis, "Man has ever expressed some symbolical Philosophy of his Being in his Works and Conduct; he announces himself and his Gospel of Nature; he is the Messiah of Nature."[80] Himself a symbol, man's aim should be the interpretation of the hieroglyph of the Idea in the visible objects of the world: "We speak of the Volume of Nature," says Carlyle, "and truly a Volume it is,— whose Author is God . . . Dost thou, does man, so much as well know the Alphabet thereof? . . . It is a Volume written in celestial hieroglyphs."[81] For Novalis, man's former ability to read the cypher of Creation has long since been lost: "Die Bedeutung der Hieroglyphe fehlt."[82] But, according to Carlyle, Goethe, Schelling, and Schiller, the task remains: "Nature," says Schelling, "is for us a primeval author, who has written in hieroglyphs, and whose pages are colossal";[83]

> "Everything," says Schiller, "within and without me, is the hieroglyphical expression of a power analogous to my own being. The laws of Nature are figures which

a thinking being combines for the purpose of rendering
itself intelligible to other thinking beings, the alphabet
by means of which all spirits hold intercourse with the
most perfect One."[84]

Thus nature, according to this view, is to be explained by
man, not man by nature. Man's moral and spiritual being
partakes of the reality of which nature is the "systematic
Index or Plan." The aim should be, not to understand the
essence of nature, for it has no reality in itself, and is but
a means of reference, but to understand man and his destiny
as indicated in the handwriting of nature: "What is
Nature?" asks Novalis, in a passage which Carlyle quotes.
"[It is] an encyclopedical, systematic Index or Plan of our
Spirit. Why will we content us with the mere catalogue
of our Treasures? Let us contemplate them ourselves, and
in all ways elaborate and use them."[85]

It is evident that there is here a great community of
thought between Carlyle on the one hand and Goethe,
Schelling, Schiller, and Novalis, on the other, in respect to
conceiving natural objects as symbols, as hieroglyphs, and
in regard to man's obligation to decipher the message written
in the language of nature in an attempt to know himself
and to discover his destiny. The writings of the German
thinkers and poets obviously supplied a richer content to
his natural tendency to think in images and to conceive of
nature as primarily symbolical. Indeed, the symbolical element in Carlyle's thought can hardly be over-stressed. As
we study its relation to the similar elements in Goethe and
Fichte, we become aware of how sharply Carlyle diverges
from their general point of view. The symbolism underlying his whole philosophy explains to a large extent why he
wavered on Fichte's doctrine of the dynamic nature of the
Ego, and saw matter as more illusory than in Fichte's theory.
It reminds us that Carlyle took Goethe's figure of the Garment more literally than did Goethe, and made it a philo-

sophical tenet.[86]   Though he never developed the idea of symbolism in any detail, it conditioned his whole *Weltan-schauung*, and determined much of his attitude toward history, society, political theory, and ethics.

Another aspect of his philosophy shows a still further interest in the nature and purpose of the world of transient objects. Carlyle never ceased to wonder at the phenomenon of change, especially as presented in the enigma of time. The world of "becoming" was susceptible to two interpretations, as being either the arena of death or the scene of universal growth, re-birth, eternal revelation of life. It is necessary to examine briefly the German background from which much of his notion of *das Werdende* emanated.

6. "The Thing that is A-being": *das Werdende*.

In a letter to Abraham Hayward, the translator of *Faust*, Carlyle gave a concise and adequate exposition of one of the speeches in "The Prologue in Heaven." We thus have direct evidence that he comprehended the general significance of the doctrine of "becoming." In the "Prologue," the Lord admits to Mephistopheles that man will err, that indeed he requires opposition, struggle, the Devil himself, to spur him on:

> *The Lord.* Aye, show thy face, succeeds thy trial,
> Freely. Thy likes Mine hatred ne'er have won.
> Of all the Spirits of Denial,
> Irks Me the least the mischievous buffoon.
> Man's efforts lightly flag, and seek too low a level.
> Soon doth he pine for all-untrammelled sloth.
> Wherefore a mate I give him, nothing loth,
> Who spurs, and shapes and must create though Devil.

Then follow the lines which Carlyle explains:

> But ye, God's sons in love and duty,
> Rejoice ye in the living wealth of beauty.
> Eternal Growth (*das Werdende*), that works and faileth
> not,

Within Love's golden bars ever enfold you.
In wavering apparition what doth float,
Bodied in thought unperishing uphold you.[87]

Carlyle's explanation:

"The Lord has just remarked, that man (poor fellow!)
needs a devil, as travelling companion, to spur him on
by means of Denial; whereupon, turning round (to the
Angels and other perfect characters), he adds, 'But ye,
the genuine sons of Heaven, joy ye in the living fullness
of the beautiful (not the logical, practical, contradictory,
wherein man toils imprisoned); let Being (or Existence), which is everywhere a glorious birth into higher
Being, as it for ever works and lives, encircle you with
the soft ties of Love; and whatsoever wavers in the
doubtful empire of appearance (as all earthly things
do); that do ye by enduring thought make firm.' Thus
would *Das Werdende* (the thing that is—a being) mean
no less than the universe (the visible universe) itself;
and I here phrase it by 'Existence,' which is every where
a birth into higher existence (or in some such way), and
make a comfortable enough kind of sense out of that
quatrain."[88]

Here we are again reminded that for Carlyle the problem
of the external world was twofold. We have already seen
that he regarded all matter as unreal. But in his exposition
of Goethe's lines, he interprets "existence"—the "logical,
practical, contradictory [realm] wherein man toils imprisoned"—as the material for achieving "higher Being." In
the light of Divine Reality, matter has unreality; but as a
gradus ad Deum, the material world is the indispensable
medium for the realization of the spirit. Indeed when
viewed from its ethical side, this doctrine in Carlyle's teachings cannot be considered as of secondary importance. Underlying his gospel of work, it becomes one of the major
elements in his point of view. It is only when we ask if
he speculated about its metaphysical basis that we relegate
it to a subordinate plane.

In Fichte, as we have noted earlier, Carlyle found abundant statement of the progressive unfolding of the Idea in the physical world. It is not difficult to imagine how readily the Fichtean version confirmed for him the lessons in practical ethics as set forth in *Wilhelm Meister*. For Fichte, the significance of the realm of change is that a moral order is ceaselessly and progressively establishing itself in the world:

> "God has conceived of the whole world, not only *as it now is*, but also *as it shall become* by its own spontaneous growth; moreover, *what it now is* lies in the original Divine Thought as the germ of an endless development,—and that a development proceeding from the *highest* that exists in it, namely, from the rational beings, by means of their own freedom."[89]

In such a passage we see the basis, so far as Fichte offered it, for one of Carlyle's two views of evil, and for whatever optimism crept into his temperamental melancholy. If he was at times oppressed by the " 'Time element' wherein man's soul here below lives imprisoned,"[90] he could at least regard the fetters of time, space, matter, and evil itself, as "the dark, disordered material" of our duty.[91] In the world of ceaseless change, time became his "seedfield." And Carlyle's Calvinism was at times so overpowered by this conception that his tendency to think of man's ingrained depravity gave way to the belief that man's baseness is his "Environment," not his "*Me.*"[92]

Yet the German background for Carlyle's belief in this interpretation of phenomena was also, in spite of definite passages in Goethe and Fichte, a very general one. The conception of change as growth from lower and simpler levels to higher and richer levels of spiritual life is present, of course, in Herder, Schiller, and Schelling. Carlyle was acquainted with Schiller's dictum that truth "immer wird, nie ist." In the general atmosphere produced by the works of Carlyle's German thinkers, the doctrine of "becoming" was a natural element. He apparently made no effort to isolate any one expression of it, but, as with many other contemporary doctrines, found it congenial to his point of view. Yet, sympathetic as he was toward such a doctrine, and definitely as he placed it in his own teachings, he never maintained the steadiness of Goethe or Fichte toward it as a satisfying truth. Too theistic, even in this early period, for such a view, he oscillated between his Calvinistic conviction of "original sin," and his desire to adopt the Goethean optimism toward human nature, the poet's serene acceptance of the world, his belief in the fundamentally divine nature of man. Beneath his intermittent espousal of the Fichtean belief in the moral progress of the world, in the inevitable and divinely decreed development of man to high spiritual attainments by means of man's indwelling divinity, Carlyle never quite lost his ascetic pessimism, the hatred of evil, the need of expiation, of renunciation.[93]

But the idea that through grappling with the transient objects round us we can approach reality, never ceased to fortify him. "Time . . . stern, wide-devouring,"[94] could not hide from him the inspiriting spectacle of universal re-birth. The doctrine of *Palingenesia*,[95] of the world as a Phoenix ever renewing itself by a resurrection from the ashes of time's destruction, became a very important element in Carlyle's later social thinking. Like the doctrine of *das Werdende* it has both a general and specific place in Carlyle's German background. His references to the Norse and to Sir Thomas Browne, and the fact that we find the same idea touched upon by writers as widely separated as Tacitus, Milton, and Vico, make it improbable that the German versions were other than contributory. It is perhaps enough to note that in Goethe—ethically in *Wilhelm Meister* and philosophically in *Faust*—he found the world of change a "glorious birth into higher Being."[96] In Fichte, too, was the assurance that nature opposes us, not "[in] the agonies of Death, but [in] the pangs of a New Birth,"[97] that "all Death in Nature is Birth, and in Death itself appears visibly the exaltation of Life."[98]   It was the ethical, the practical, the problem-solving treatment of *das Werdende*, however, which, as we shall later see, made the doctrine of capital importance to Carlyle.

It is probable, too, that this view was more easily made tenable by Goethe's conception of nature and by Schelling's doctrine of "organism." Ethical imperatives always gain by the conviction that the entire fabric of the moral as well as of the physical world is an organic unity, in which any disturbance or activity of a part is immediately transferred to the whole. Though Carlyle's theism forbade him ever really believing that God and nature are one and co-extensive, he had moods in which nature seemed so expressive of divine justice or sublimity that he momentarily identified nature with God. The least which the doctrine of "organism" could do for him was to deepen his native tendency to think of all things as related, a notion which he best expressed in the chapter on "Organic Filaments" in *Sartor Resartus*. At one time, it seems, he was strongly attracted by Schelling's treatment of the subject in the *Method of Academical Study*.

7. ORGANISM : *"The immeasurable, universal World-tissue."*[99]

So far we have seen that Carlyle conceives Nature from two points of view: as entirely illusory and dream-like, and as the obstacle and means of moral realization. The first view is a reflection of Goethe's Garment passage, and of such *pensées* of Novalis as the epigram about the *Schattenwelt*. We might also add the lines from *Faust* describing the physical world, for Carlyle, as "Schall und Rauch umnebelnd Himmels Gluth." The other view derives from Fichte's ethical idealism as much as from Goethe's ethical doctrine of self-realization through right use of material means. Carlyle regarded the two points of view as readily reconcilable, as they were also regarded by Novalis, who held that the outer world, though relatively a shadow, was a means of *Selbstverständnis*.[100] The particular steps in the logic of such a reconciliation did not trouble the primarily intuitive thinking of Novalis and Carlyle.

What may be considered as a third attitude toward nature appears in Carlyle's version of the deeply Germanic conception of "organism." This doctrine, we may say, has been as fundamental to the German genius of speculation as have rationalism and empiricism been fundamental, respectively, to French and English thought. In falling under its influence, Carlyle was merely experiencing the essence of the German point of view. And in it he readily saw a way of retrieving the old ideals of Christian faith, of altruism, and of unselfish devotion to duty through work, superior to any conception in the traditions of Descartes or Bacon. According to the German conception, the moral imperative had the authority of both the real and the unreal, of both the ideal and the actual. Since both may be regarded as one, since nature is both the symbol and presence of God, finding life in the Whole, or the Ideal, is the first step to finding it in the particular, or the actual, and *vice versa*.[101]

When, as in certain passages in *Sartor*, Carlyle is not regarding nature as the adventitious and illusion-bearing garment of man, and God as the Reality apart from any physical vestment, he is inclined to conceive of Nature as the presence of God himself. In the former case, Carlyle follows Berkeley and attributes the doctrine to Fichte;[102] in the latter, he follows Goethe and Schelling, as in the following lines:

> "Or what is Nature? Ha! why do I not name thee God? Art thou not the 'Living Garment of God?' O Heavens, is it, in very deed, He, then, that ever speaks through thee; that lives and loves in thee, that lives and loves in me?"[103]

Here nature is, as it were, identified with God, worthy of
reverence and worship; and man becomes a speck in the
"All," a light-sparkle "floating in the aether of Deity."[104]

No such figurative description, of course, occurs in Schelling. Though Schelling indulged in metaphors often more
vivid than philosophically helpful, his *Naturphilosophie* he
himself defined as "speculative physics."[105] By the time
Carlyle was reading the *Method of Academical Study* he
had long since lost his early interest in either physics or
speculation. But in Schelling's popular little book Carlyle
must have found some stimulating doctrine. He read, for
instance, that Nature contains all the essence of the divine,
under the form of the real, and that man, as both an epitome
and a "complement of the universe," finds his proper vocation
in completing "the totality of the manifestation of God":

> "Now everything which proceeds immediately out of
> the Absolute as its source, is itself absolute; and thus
> has no end outside itself, but is its own end. Science,
> in its universality, is one of the absolute manifestations
> of universal being, the real world, or nature, being its
> other term. In the domain of the real, the finite domi-
> nates; in that of the ideal, the infinite. The former is
> what it is by virtue of necessity; the latter, by virtue
> of freedom. Man, primarily a rational being, is destined
> to be a complement of the universe. Through him,
> through his activity, there should develop whatever is
> lacking in the totality of the manifestation of God, since
> nature contains, to be sure, all the essence of the divine,
> but only under the form of the real. The reasonable
> being [man] must express the idea of that divine nature
> itself, as it is in itself, and thus in the form of the
> ideal."[106]

On another page, and in similarly abstract language, Schelling mentions the identity of the real and the ideal:

> "But this datum (*Voraussetzung*) of all the sciences,
> this essential unity of the absolutely ideal and the abso-
> lutely real, is possible only inasmuch as the identical

being (*das Dasselbe*), which is one of the two terms, is also at the same time the other. Now, this is the idea of the Absolute; that with regard to itself, it is also being. The Absolute is thus at once this fundamental basis of science and the first science itself."[107]

Schelling urges the concept of organism as a curative for the metaphysical maladies following upon the rationalism of the eighteenth century. As another way of expressing "die Einheit des Realen und Idealen," he holds that the only escape from the *cul-de-sac* of materialism lies through the comprehension of the organic unity of the potential and the actual: "The purely relative and finite point of view," he says, "wholly destroys the idea of organism, in order to substitute simple, mechanical succession (*Reihe des Mechanismus*), just as it substitutes rational explanation for philosophic construction."[108] The affinity between these ideas and some of those which Carlyle preached is obvious: the absolute value of human action, man as a microcosm, human life as the conflux of two orders of reality, the finite and the infinite, work as the "discerning of the Infinite in the Finite, of the Idea made Real."[109]

Yet, in spite of the echoes of Schelling's *Naturphilosophie* in Carlyle's thought, the relation between their ideas is very tenuous. Much in Carlyle on which Schelling appears explanatory is more definitely illuminated by a few lines from Goethe. Nature for Carlyle could never assume the self-contained character, even if somehow divine, which it could for Schelling. Like Fichte, Carlyle looked on the uncritical divinizing of nature as another way of arriving at atheism and materialism.[110] He was probably interested in Schelling chiefly in so far as the philosopher showed nature to be far from merely mechanical, to be indeed mysterious, creative, dynamic, the embodiment of the divine. No doubt Schelling encouraged his reverence for that "Force" by which "that smithy-fire . . . (primarily) kindled at the Sun, is fed by air that circulates from before Noah's Deluge, from beyond the Dogstar."[111]   Schelling's influence is perhaps discernible—among other influences—in his doctrine that "Nature is one, and a living indivisible whole."[112]   But here Carlyle stopped: Nature is God, true enough; but God is more than Nature.   Organic filaments are indeed discernible everywhere, binding all nature and all men into one organic unity. But for Carlyle, the unshaken Calvinist, as for Goethe, the many-sided thinker,[113] the Ideal is not exhausted in the Real: "Nature is good," says Carlyle in *Sartor*; "but she is not the best."[114]

As a third way by which Carlyle viewed nature—"why do I not name thee God?"—the Schellingian doctrine of identity served to elaborate his conviction of the clear revelation of the divine in the material, to deepen the recognition of what he was fond of calling the Open Secret.

8. THE OPEN SECRET: *Das offenbare Geheimniss.*[115]

At the heart of Carlyle's faith lay the certainty that the enigma of the divine was no enigma at all, that however transcendent the divine may be, it is also immanent in the world.   "That seeking for a God *there*, and not *here*," he wrote, "begins to get wearisome."   Against that "faint possible theism" to which English skepticism had pushed the average believer, Carlyle urged the belief of Goethe:

> Was wär ein Gott, der nur von aussen stiesse,
> Im Kreis das All am Finger laufen liesse!

" 'Think ye,' says Goethe, 'that God made the Universe, and then let it run around his finger?' "[116]   It was the reverse of this view, says Carlyle, which made the heroes of the past:

> "They have penetrated . . . into the sacred mystery of the Universe; what Goethe calls 'the open secret' . . . open to all, seen by almost none!   That divine mystery, which lies everywhere in all Beings, 'the Divine Idea of

the World, that which lies at the bottom of Appearance,'
as Fichte styles it; of which all Appearance, from the
starry sky to the grass of the field, but especially the
Appearance of Man and his work, is but the *vesture,*
the embodiment that renders it visible . . . The Universe
[is]definable always in one or the other dialect, as the
realised Thought of God. . . ."[117]

Several observations on these lines should be made before
we summarize the German element in Carlyle's "world-plan."
In the first place, we note that the "open secret" is a sacred
mystery, probably in a double sense: as beyond fathoming
by human reason, and as lying undiscerned to the mass of
mankind. This, as we have already said, has not necessarily
any specific German background.[118] We notice also that
Carlyle identifies the open secret, as a Goethean doctrine,
with Fichte's Divine Idea lying at the bottom of Appearances,
a fusion of ideas which neither Goethe nor Fichte would
have accepted without heavy qualifications. Goethe's God,
resident equally in both mind and matter, had little in common with a dynamic ego underlying and yet pressing forward, through struggle in the world of "becoming," toward
an ever-unattained goal, in which process the physical world
is seen as wholly derived. Goethe was by nature too realistic
to conceive of the external world as merely the derivative of
Intellect. Yet the emphasis of both Fichte and Goethe upon
the Eternal and the Infinite was sufficient for Carlyle's
impatient mind to see a large measure of identity between
the poet and the philosopher. In fact, Carlyle's God does not
develop like Fichte's, and as Carlyle grew older his conception of deity became more and more Hebraic and Miltonic.
In the next place, we note that Carlyle uses *vesture* and
embodiment as synonymous. Ordinarily, according to the
first term, only God is real; according to the second, the
Real and the Apparent are one, so far as the latter may
contain the former. To merge the two meanings, Carlyle
has recourse to the word *mystery.* If he ever undertook to

account for the identification, he possibly argued that, when we think primarily of God, all nature is merely a garment; when, however, we think chiefly of nature and her wonders, we see her as the embodiment of God—of a Being, however, whose nature is not exhausted in its manifestations. Nature, according to Carlyle, thus embodies the Ideal only in so far as man is capable of receiving a revelation and in the degree in which matter is capable of expressing it. As such, Nature is the "realized thought of God."

It is possible thus to explain Carlyle's very rough and seemingly uncritical fusion of different philosophies. Seeking a basis for what may be called a *panentheistic* point of view,[119] according to which God is both immanent and transcendent, he sought to reconcile the pantheistic element in Goethe with Fichte's doctrine of the Idea as alone real and of matter as subjective. Kant's doctrine of space and time was lifted from its epistemological context, and employed as an elaboration upon the relative unreality of matter. The current statements of symbolism were also brought in to give matter, in so far as it had reality and a function, a symbolical value, to expand further the notion of matter as both a mere vesture and an actual embodiment—up to a certain point—of divine significance. From this point of view, man's knowledge of himself and his proper vocation was revealed as a seizing of the concrete manifestations of God—whereby God himself partly fulfilled his Being—and as a realization of man's approximation to the divine. The gospel of work, and Carlyle's love for *fact*, now take on fresh meaning. As work and fact are God's own means of self-expression, and as man is a "reflex of the Eternal," the divinity of labor and the infinite value of fact become at once of cardinal importance in Carlyle's philosophy.

On its more pictorial side, Carlyle's thought is obviously indebted to Goethe. But, in spite of the differences in doctrines, Carlyle saw Goethe and Fichte as two prophets of the same religion: their ideas, though deeply divergent, struck him as merely two forms of the same general point of view, one imaginative and the other abstract.   His originality, as M. Cazamian has well said, lies not so much in the discovery of ideas as in their imaginative transposition and interpretation.[120]   In all his dealings with them, as we have seen, he remained thoroughly himself, a monist when he reflected, a pluralist, even a Manichæan, when he acted and felt.[121]   Throughout all his study of Goethe and Fichte, he retained a sense of Puritan realities—of sin, punishment, humility before "the great Taskmaster."   Yet it was just here that the "open secret" promised a more encouraging and enlightened revelation.   The world and the flesh, when rightly viewed and handled, were mysteriously God himself, and the whole realm of flux and "becoming" lifted him from a native pessimism to periods of optimism and serenity.

The possibility of penetrating to the heart of that "secret" was indeed as newly revealed to him as the "secret" itself. German thinkers had reinterpreted the old accesses to truth, and now held out a number of doctrines purporting to show how, without risking the deadening effect of rationalism, man could again believe himself equipped to know reality. In the distinction between the Reason and the Understanding, Carlyle found more or less direct aid in German philosophy.

Chapter V

UNDERSTANDING, REASON, PHANTASY

1. Carlyle and Knowledge

Though the distinction between Reason and Understanding had no persistent place in Carlyle's thought, he at one time regarded it as the "grand characteristic" of Kantian metaphysics,[1] and devoted considerable attention in his early essays, and to some extent in *Sartor*, to what he believed to be their respective provinces. Even when, in later years, he had lost all interest in epistemological problems, and had repudiated the very terms themselves as a snare to the mind, he retained his conviction of the possibility of supersensible knowledge which his early preoccupation with Reason and Understanding had greatly strengthened. It has indeed been considered the basis of much of the mystical in Carlyle's teachings, *i.e.*, "that the deepest of all truths are known otherwise than by reasoning."[2] He had no doubt worked his own way to a very similar distinction before he found it set forth in the *Critique of Pure Reason* and in more popular forms. From his earliest reflections on the capacities of the intellect he had been inclined, as in 1819, to ask the disdainful question, "What logic can withstand Experience?"[3] Though he had as yet found no name for the faculty which he believed to be superior to Understanding, he was evidently very certain of its existence. For him, Reason was to become a faculty of spiritual discernment, an organ of knowledge whereby the essence of reality which lies behind Appearance may be, at least by glimpses, unmistakably apprehended. Not content, however, with what he learned about Reason, he was to give occasional evidence of his interest in Phantasy, another and perhaps more vivid instrument for apprehending the significance of the symbolical world of nature.

The conventional explanation of Carlyle's adoption of the threefold nature of our knowledge as being definitely traceable to Kant, and to such additional sources as Fichte and Novalis, proves on examination to be inadequate. Carlyle's debt here is also to Richter, Friedrich Schlegel, and Jacobi. Among the probable English sources are Dugald Stewart, Coleridge, and the English divines of the seventeenth century.[4]

2. THE ENGLISH BACKGROUND

Dugald Stewart's *Philosophy of the Human Mind* contains, as I have already said, an account of Reason and Understanding sufficiently similar to Kant's, in a rough approximation, to induce a mind such as Carlyle's to conclude that "the assiduous study of his Works [are] the best preparation for studying those of Kant."[5] Stewart believed that Reason originally meant more than it has meant since the rise of Hume's influence. In support of his belief that it formerly was considered as a moral faculty for gaining truth, he quotes Locke: "Reason is natural Revelation, whereby the eternal Father of Light, and fountain of all knowledge, communicates to mankind that portion of truth which he had laid within the reach of their natural faculties."[6] It was Hume, says Stewart, who disastrously restricted Reason within narrow bounds, and made it merely an organ for distinguishing between the true and the false, between taste and deformity. "Another ambiguity," he continues, ". . . . leads us to confound our rational powers in general with that particular branch of them, known among logicians by the name of the *Discursive Faculty.*" But the discursive faculty alone can not "obtain a notion of either the good or the beautiful."[7] On the next page, Stewart quotes Hooker in defense of his position: "Reason is the director of man's will, discovering in action what is good; for the laws of well-doing are the

dictates of right reason."[8]   Milton likewise is brought forth
as an authority on this principle:

> . . . . Whence the soul
> Reason receives; and Reason is her Being—
> Discursive or intuitive.
>   (*Paradise Lost*, V, 486.)[9]

Nowhere in Stewart is Reason given the high powers which
Carlyle assigns to it.   But while it is restricted to "distinguish truth from falsehood," it is not denied the power to
distinguish right from wrong, and is clearly placed above
Understanding, which is merely the "intellectual faculty," as
will is the active faculty.[10]

The quotation from Hooker reminds us that Carlyle, in
discussing "Kantism," occasionally refers to "our own Puritan Divines."[11]   It is safe to assume that he was acquainted
with that train of thought which goes back beyond the
seventeenth century, to Plato, for whom there were different
functions assigned to νοῦς and διάνοια.   In Plato we find a
contrast between *discourse* of reason and the intuitive exercise
of that faculty.[12]   Understanding is the "faculty of judging
according to sense," of generalizing from the data of sense
experience, and of drawing inferences from them according
to formal laws.   On the other hand, Reason apprehends
"truths above sense and having their evidence in themselves,"
among them the law of non-contradiction.   It has been
remarked that this distinction, with the inevitable variations
in phrasing, emphasis, and meaning, may be found in a
number of English writers—Locke, Milton, Bacon, the
Cambridge Platonists, Shakespeare.[13]   And although it is by
no means the elaborate and severely formal distinction
drawn up by Kant, it no doubt struck Carlyle as substantially
the same distinction as set forth in the *Critique of Pure
Reason*.   Cudworth's reply to the skepticism of Hobbes has

points of resemblance to Kant's reply to Hume; there is the attempt, curiously similar to Kant's later effort, to construct a transcendental epistemology, which should base universal truths, not on experience, which is incomplete, but upon the very laws of reason itself as it determines experience.[14]

More specifically in Coleridge, Carlyle must have noted that Reason had become something more than it was in Kant, that, as Henry More maintained, it is a "part of the image of God in us,"[15]—virtually what Hooker held, adopting the words of the Fourth Evangelist: "the true Light, which lighteth every man that cometh into the world."[16] "This Law [of Reason]," says Hooker, ". . . comprehendeth all those things which men by the light of their natural understanding evidently know, or at least wise men know, to be becoming or unbecoming, virtuous or vicious, good or evil for them to do."[17] The distinction between this higher organ of knowledge and man's ordinary intellectual reasoning became of momentous importance in Coleridge's philosophy: "He seems," says Howard, "almost obsessed with the distinction."[18] Announcing that he had "cautiously discriminated the terms, the reason and the understanding, encouraged and confirmed by the authority of our genuine divines and philosophers before the revolution," he welcomed Hooker's standpoint: "Goodness is seeing with the eye of the understanding. And the light of that eye, is reason."[19] Though in Hooker the boundaries of the provinces of Reason and Understanding are frequently blurred, the conception of Reason as the divine light, as an organ receiving essential truth, appealed to Coleridge, whose practical application of it to spiritual problems was in some ways remarkably similar to Carlyle's.

The distinction between these two modes of knowing, as set forth by Coleridge, throws an interesting light on Carlyle's sentences in the essays on *Novalis* and the *State of German Literature*.[20] The most poetical and, for Carlyle, probably the most striking passage on Reason occurs in the apostrophe in *The Friend*:

> "Reason! best and holiest gift of God and bond of union with the giver,—the high title by which the majesty of man claims precedence above all other living creatures;—mysterious faculty, the mother of conscience, of language, of tears, and of smiles;—calm and incorruptible legislator of the soul, without whom all its other powers would 'meet in mere oppugnancy';—sole principle of permanence amid endless change . . . To thee, who being one art the same in all, we owe the privilege, that of all we can become one, a living whole,—that we have a country."[21]

Less rhetorical is the following statement of the natures of Reason and Understanding:

> "Reason is pre-eminently spiritual, and a spirit, even our spirit, through an effulgence of the same grace by which we are privileged to say, Our Father!
> On the other hand, the judgments of the Understanding are binding only in relation to the objects of our senses . . . . as Leighton rightly defines it, 'the faculty of judging according to sense.' . . . There neither is nor can be but one reason, one and the same; even the light that lighteth every man's individual understanding (*discursus*), and thus maketh it a reasonable understanding, discourse of reason. . . ."[22]

Other and more representative passages will serve to show, as we shall see, that Carlyle's version of Kant is substantially the transformation wrought by Coleridge: Understanding will be burdened by the same slight, in comparison with Reason, which will have lost all its Kantian meaning and will have become an organ of faith. In both cases, however, the unKantian element present in Jacobi's influence will explain much of their individual interpretation of Kant's doctrines. "I have no objection," wrote Coleridge in *The Friend*, "to define Reason with Jacobi. . ."[23] Carlyle could have made the same statement, for virtually the same reasons.

3. JACOBI: *"Denken und Fühlen . . . Kopf und Herz."*[24]

Carlyle's references to Jacobi are singularly rare; those in the essays indicate that he confused him—as the "elder Jacobi"—with Jacobi's older brother, the poet, Johann Georg.[25] But a close and unmistakable affinity between Jacobi and Carlyle is evident from even a cursory comparison of their ideas.

Both men saw that the older philosophy—the dogmatism which Kant opposed—sought to deduce life from some fundamental concept, after the fashion of mathematics.[26] They held, on the contrary, that action does not spring from one's philosophy, but one's philosophy from one's action. The former course may lead to materialism, or, as both Jacobi and Carlyle styled it, to a "mud-philosophy" (*Kothphilosophie*).[27] Such an approach to one's problems repelled their deeply mystical sense of the supersensuous.[28] Their early religious background, remarkably similar in many ways, made it impossible for them to accept any doctrine fundamentally at variance with their puritan convictions, *i.e.*, with Jacobi's pietism and Carlyle's Calvinism.[29] It was the individual, and the individual's spiritual experience, which determined their attitude toward any doctrine. They resisted any but a dynamical account of human nature, and of its position in the world of freedom and necessity.[30] That the soul should be treated scientifically struck them alike as at once futile and sacrilegious. By temperament more a philosopher than Carlyle, Jacobi was able, however, to accept the possibility of a rigidly scientific account of nature, and thus sought to reconcile—almost wholly in vain—the science of the *Aufklärung* and of the Sensationalists with a philosophy of faith or feeling.[31] The dualism in Jacobi, between the intuitions of his heart and the workings of his intellect, left whole ranges of his view untenable for Carlyle. But the fact that Jacobi ruled out man's speculative faculty from any real attainment of spiritual truth provided abundant common ground between their points of view.

Jacobi had seen, with Kant, that pure speculative reason can never demonstrate divine things, that only pure practical reason, moral freedom, can point to their reality. For him, as for Carlyle, this became a positive doctrine. If the supersensible cannot be proved, then our certainty of it, grounded in our awareness of moral freedom, can be one only of faith,—yet not merely of blind unreasoning faith, but of Reason itself. Following Kant, he agreed that Understanding in no way deals with reality directly, but depends upon perception for the materials of its thought. He differed from Kant, however, in holding, further, that reason (now transformed into faith-reason) furnishes material for our knowledge of noumena, of absolute truth, beauty, goodness, God himself. The whole contention of Jacobi's philosophy, says Crawford, is ultimately the insistence that reason is as much a faculty of intuition as is sense.[32] It becomes for Jacobi, as for Carlyle and Coleridge, a divinatory instinct penetrating to realms of truth shut off from ordinary intellectual effort.[33] What he had earlier called *Glaube*, he came in time to call *Vernunft*.

Carlyle found in Jacobi that emphasis on the negative and subjective side of Kant which he himself came to adopt. And throughout Jacobi's works he must have noted the author's profound conviction that philosophy is self-devouring,[34] that the more consistent it becomes the more it shows that it cannot come at truth, that the relentless dilemma of subjectivity shuts us off forever from any complete speculative knowledge of the world. Perception was a miracle for Jacobi, as much as fact was for Carlyle; and in many ways there is not much difference between the two standpoints. For both men, man must accept both nature and God on faith, believe where he cannot understand. And for them both there was never a complete reconciliation between the claims of the head and the heart, between reason and faith.[35] They admired intellectual precision, yet feared to admit it into the realm of values and ends.

Carlyle's individual rendering of Reason and Understanding owed no little, we may be sure, to Jacobi's brilliant but somewhat unstable arguments.

4. UNDERSTANDING: *"The talent of the Beaver."*[36]

In the *Critique of Pure Reason,* Kant's starting point is an inquiry into how our world of experience is built up, how we attain certainty in our knowledge of the principles underlying the mathematical and physical sciences, and how, at the same time, we arrive at the validity of our moral postulates, which we cannot justify by the same operations of the mind. The solution of this problem was found to lie in the assumption of a fundamental duality, in which understanding provides knowledge of the sense-world, and Reason attains certain Ideas which, if not realizable in experience, at least point to God, freedom, and immortality, and leave the "proof" of their reality to be supplied by the *practical* reason. Since, as we have seen, Carlyle does not postulate any such dualism, his differentiation between Understanding and Reason will be largely his own. He will differ from Kant in maintaining that Reason and Understanding work upon the same materials, and find separate provinces only by virtue of their relative scope, certainty, and depth of penetration. How he interprets Understanding may best be seen by first looking into Kant's exposition.[37]

It is by the Understanding that the intelligible world of phenomena is built up for us—and by us. Upon data provided by the senses, "imagination" imposes a synthesis under the forms of time and space, giving rise, in a further step, by the operation of the Understanding, to the formation of conceptions, under the categories of quantity, quality, relation, and modality. Besides the perceptions of individual objects, and the concepts fashioned from them, the general field of experience is rendered a whole by the transcendental unity of apperception—by the unity imposed upon them by the single conscious *self*. Understanding thus creates our ordinary world of sound, color, figure, and all our ideas based upon them, from what is at bottom sense-experience. Any other method, says Kant, would result in either emptiness or unintelligibility: "Thoughts without content are empty, intuitions without concepts are blind."[38] The distinguishing function of Understanding is the ordering, relating, and unifying of the data of sense according to its own laws, producing thereby the only possible knowledge we have of the world, a knowledge of "appearances" or phenomena. Its validity is unimpeachable so long as it is empirical, or limited to the sphere of experience; it is not transcendental, however, and has no validity when applied to objects beyond experience, *e.g.*, to God or immortality:

> "From all this it undeniably follows [says Kant] that the pure concepts of understanding can *never* admit of *transcendental* but *always* only of *empirical* employment, and that the principles of pure understanding can apply only to objects of the senses under the universal conditions of a possible experience, never to things in general without regard to the mode in which we are able to intuit them.
>
> ". . . The most the understanding can achieve *a priori* is to anticipate the form of a possible experience in general. And since that which is not appearance cannot be an object of experience, the understanding can never transcend those limits of sensibility within which alone objects can be given to us. Its principles are merely rules for the exposition of appearances; and the proud name of an Ontology that presumptuously claims to supply, in systematic doctrinal form, synthetic *a priori* knowledge of things in general (for instance, the principle of causality) must, therefore, give place to the modest title of a mere Analytic of pure understanding.
>
> ". . . .The merely transcendental employment of the categories is, therefore, really no employment at all, and has no determinate object, not even one that is determinable in its mere form."[39]

Of course all of this technical treatment of the act of knowing meant little to Carlyle. In what degree it meant anything at all, we may see by turning to certain of his passages on Kant, in which, with the aid of Kant's own statements, we may discern Carlyle's divergence from the original doctrine. We turn first to *Wotton Reinfred,* and note that for Carlyle there is more than one kind of truth, and that Understanding does not attain the highest:

> "Demonstrability is not the test of truth; logic is for what the understanding *sees* . . . There is a truth of the market-place, . . . a truth of the laboratory, and a truth of the soul. The first two are of things seen and their relations, they are practical or physically scientific, and belong to the understanding . . . Laplace's *Mécanique Céleste,* Adam Smith's *Wealth of Nations* are full of understanding, . . . but of reason there is hardly any trace in either. . . . Understanding perceives and judges of images and measures of things; . . . reason perceives and judges of what has no measure or image. The latter only is unchangeable and everlasting in its decisions, the results of the former change from age to age . . . these comparatively are not worth the name of truth, they are not truth, but only ephemeral garments of truth."[40]

In *The State of German Literature* this interpretation is expanded:

> "Both Understanding and Reason are organs, or rather, we should say, modes of operation, by which the mind discovers truth; but . . . their manner of proceeding is essentially different; . . . their provinces are separable and distinguishable, . . . it is of the last importance to separate and distinguish them. . . . Understanding discerns only *relations,* and cannot decide without *if.* The proper province of Understanding is all, strictly speaking, *real* practical and material knowledge, Mathematics, Physics, Political Economy, the adaptation of means to ends in the whole business of life. In this province it is the strength and universal implement of

the mind: an indispensable servant . . . Let it not step
beyond this province, however; not usurp the province
of Reason, which it is appointed to obey, and cannot rule
without ruin to the whole spiritual man. Should Understanding [step beyond its province], it ends . . . in
Atheism, or a faint possible Theism . . . in *Utility* . . .
[in] everlasting paradoxes on Necessity and the Freedom of the Will; [in] ominous silence on the end and
meaning of man, and the enigma which, under such
inspection, the whole purport of existence becomes . . .
The French are of all European nations the most gifted
with Understanding, and the most destitute of Reason."[41]

The essay on *Novalis* contains further sentences on the
subject:

"But farther, if it be, as Kant maintains, that the logical mechanism of the mind is arbitrary, so to speak,
and might have been made different, it will follow, that
all inductive conclusions, all conclusions of the Understanding, have only a relative truth, are true only for *us*,
and *if* some other thing be true.

"Thus far Hume and Kant go together . . . but . . . all
Poetry, Virtue, Religion [are] things which are properly beyond the province of the Understanding, of which
the Understanding *can* take no cognizance, except a
false one. The elder Jacobi, who indeed is no Kantist,
says once, we remember: 'It is the instinct of Understanding to *contradict* Reason.' . . . The aim of Novalis's
whole philosophy . . . is to preach and establish the
majesty of Reason . . . to . . . reduce its vassal, Understanding, into fealty, the right and only useful relation
for it. . . . . ."[42]

Now there are several observations to be made on these
three passages as we have them before us. Four statements
concerning the nature and function of Understanding are
clearly unKantian. (1) That the results of Understanding
"change from age to age." It is significant that Carlyle
nowhere mentions the "categories" in the Kantian sense. If
he had clearly comprehended Kant's treatment of them, he

would have understood that the "results" of the Understanding, in the sense of conceptual forms, are universal and
unchanging; otherwise the Understanding itself would have
no foundation or character. It is evident that Carlyle is not
concerned with the formal side of Kant's distinction, but
solely with the *existence* of a distinction. The content of
concepts certainly change from age to age; but what would
Carlyle have said to the reply that the content of the Ideas
of Kant's "Reason"—for example the Ideas of God and
immortality—likewise "change" according to the character
of an age? Clearly the significance of both Understanding
and Reason has become wholly alien to Kant's meaning.
Here Carlyle echoes Coleridge, for whom, as we have seen,
Reason is the "sole principle of permanence amid endless
change."[43]

(2) The products of Understanding are also said to be
but the garments of truth, not truth itself in the deeper
sense. As we have noted, in connection with Carlyle's understanding of Kant's doctrine of time, space, and phenomena,
Kant refused to regard the world of Appearance as mere
illusion; in the same manner, and for the same reasons,
Kant refuses to consider Understanding as dealing only
with the husks of truth. But as Carlyle had inferred the
unreality of matter from the phenomenal unreality of time
and space, he naturally reasons at times as if Understanding,
which deals only with time, space, and matter, must be productive only of illusion. For Kant, however, if there is no
empirical reality for man in Appearance, there is no reality
attainable by him at all; the whole of life rests on our
belief that *empirically* the Understanding delivers us real
knowledge. But Carlyle was evidently dazzled by what he
saw in Reason, and although he conceded the validity of
Understanding in the work-a-day affairs of this "somnam-
bulism of uneasy souls," he exalted Reason as alone yielding
us substantial knowledge. Again Coleridge appears to share
with Carlyle this unKantian emphasis on one side of the

doctrine. This is nowhere more evident than in their striking parallelism on the subject of *names*. Coleridge declares:
"It is words or names, that are the only and exclusive subjects of understanding. In no instance do we understand
a thing in itself; but only the name to which it is referred."[44]
Carlyle's consciousness of the significance of the name as a
garment needs little emphasis: "Science, Poetry itself is no
other . . . than a right *Naming* . . . The Name is the earliest
garment you wrap round the earth-visiting Me."[45]   That
Understanding should thus deal with the mere husks of truth
and reality seemed to Carlyle only the logical purport of
Kant's conception of the faculty.   And in the light of
Carlyle's exaltation of Reason to an unKantian eminence,
it was only natural that Understanding, also transformed,
should be relegated to an unKantian subordination.

(3) The subordination is also a subserviency.   Understanding is to obey, to occupy a position of "fealty" to
Reason.   Admitting that here Carlyle's language may be
merely figurative, it is worth noting that Kant's duality
would make any question of "fealty" irrelevant. "The isolation of the two worlds and of the independent, unrelated
powers of the two faculties, would make it impossible for
him to hold that the understanding is appointed to 'obey'
the reason."[46]   But in both Jacobi and Coleridge, such a
treatment of the faculties apparently presented no difficulty.
For Jacobi, Reason "als königlicher Name" rules "als unbedingte Autorität über dem Verstand."[47]   Coleridge goes further, and inveighs against using Understanding in the service of divine truth, pointing to Atheism as a possible consequence of such use: "An insight into the proper functions
and subaltern rank of the understanding . . . will deprive
[one] of the only rational pretext for having recourse to
tools so liable to abuse . . ."[48]

(4) Understanding "cannot decide without *if*." Just what
meaning Carlyle intends to convey here is difficult to determine.   For Kant, the Understanding attains truths of mathe-

matics which hold good universally within the limits of possible experience, and, under such circumstances, require no "if."

"To be sure," notes Miss Storrs, commenting on this point in Carlyle's exposition, "even these truths are contingent in the sense that they are significant only in application to phenomena, and it may be that Carlyle refers to such a contingency by his '*if*'; but it is more probable that he has in mind such judgments of the understanding which predict results of given sets of conditions: 'if this be given that will follow.' At any rate, his meaning is not clear, and his words justify a suspicion that he does not do full justice to Kant's conception of the understanding."[49]

It is possible, of course, that he was half-consciously remembering the second item in Coleridge's parallel between Understanding and Reason:[50]

2. The Understanding in all its judgments refers to some other faculty as its ultimate authority.	2. The Reason in all its decisions appeals to itself as the ground and *substance* of their truth. (*Heb.* vi. 13.)

It is possible, too, that Carlyle had in mind something of Kant's doctrine of the categories, though the word "relations" would properly touch upon only one of the four groups.[51] On the whole, he seems to be referring to the *logical* nature of the Understanding.

Indeed, it is as a "logical" organ that Understanding always appeared to Carlyle, as an organ dealing in a mechanical and uncreative way with Appearance. He is conscious of the paradoxical behavior of Understanding on final problems, and while he shows no acquaintance with Kant's "antinomies," he is keenly aware that "logic-chopping" "circulates and must circulate in endless vortices; creating, swallowing—itself," being essentially "the attempt of the mind to rise above the mind."[52] Like Kant, he realizes that Understanding is the uninspired, pedestrian, practical element of the mind, and leads to skepticism if permitted to deal with religious problems. He is nearer Coleridge and Jacobi, however, in insisting that Understanding is the enemy of wonder, which is the beginning of philosophy, religion, and art, as it is the enemy also of virtue, as Fichte observed.[53] At its best, and working in Carlyle's fundamentally spiritual world, it cannot penetrate to the deeper spiritual law, but must be content with half truth. The monism suggested here does not contradict his statement that the "provinces [of Reason and Understanding] are separable and distinguishable"; for though Understanding deals only with the "Garment of the Unseen," we have observed that essentially for Carlyle "Matter is Spirit," and Understanding begins what Reason is able to complete, namely, the deeper knowledge of the heart of a reality which is one.[54]

"Understanding is to Reason," he wrote in his Journal, "as the talent of a Beaver . . . to the genius of a Prophet and Poet . . ."[55] What part Kant's doctrines played in the production of this view of Understanding it is impossible to say. It is certain, however, that the influence was wholly indirect. Equally certain is the undefined but shaping influence of Dugald Stewart's distinction between Reason and Understanding, the Platonic tradition in the thought of the English divines of the seventeenth century, the general treatment of their notions of Reason and Understanding in Coleridge, and, finally, the criticism of Kant's epistemology as set forth by Jacobi. Fichte and Novalis, though provocative on the subject of Reason, have much less to say of Understanding. On the whole, the evidence is sufficient to point to Carlyle's debt to Germany. The general attitude of a number of her writers towards the ravages of triumphant Understanding was expressed, for Carlyle, in Jean Paul's prophecy: "Of the World will be made a World-Machine, of the Aether a Gas, of God a Force, and of the Second World—a Coffin."[56]

5. REASON: *"The pure, ultimate light of our nature."*[57]

Even more important than his departure from Kant's
notion of the Understanding is Carlyle's departure from the
Kantian doctrine of the Reason. And, just as in the case
of the former faculty, the works of Jacobi and Coleridge
explain in a large measure the unKantian nature and function of Reason as Carlyle understood it. For him, Reason
is little else than a mystical penetration to spiritual truth,
an organ able to

> "discover what the Germans call the *Urwahr*, the Primi-
> tive Truth, the necessarily, absolutely and eternally
> *True*. . . . They deny [Hume's] first principle, that
> Sense is the only inlet of Knowledge, that Experience
> is the primary ground of Belief. Their Primitive
> Truth, however, they seek . . . by intuition, in the deep-
> est and purest nature of Man. . . . God *is*, nay alone *is*
> . . . . This is the Absolute, the Primitively True, which
> the philosopher seeks . . . To open the inward eye to the
> sight of this Primitively True; or rather we might call
> it, to clear off the Obscurations of Sense . . .
>
> ". . . We state what to ourselves has long appeared
> the grand characteristic of Kant's Philosophy, when we
> mention his distinction, seldom perhaps expressed so
> broadly, but uniformly implied, between Understanding
> and Reason (*Verstand* and *Vernunft*). . . . Reason,
> the Kantists say, is of a higher nature than Under-
> standing; it works by more subtle methods, on higher
> objects, and requires a far finer culture for its develop-
> ment, indeed in many men it is never developed at all:
> but its results are no less certain, nay, rather, they are
> much more so; for Reason discerns Truth itself, the
> absolutely and primitively *True*. . . . To discern these
> truths [of religion, morality, art] is the province of
> Reason, which therefore is to be cultivated as the high-
> est faculty in man. Not by logic and argument does it
> work; yet surely and clearly may it be taught to work:
> and its domain lies in that higher region whither logic
> and argument cannot reach; in that holier region, where
> Poetry, and Virtue and Divinity abide, in whose pres-

ence Understanding wavers and recoils, dazzled into utter darkness by that 'sea of light,' at once the fountain and the termination of all true knowledge. . . .

"We allude [further] to the recognition, by these Transcendentalists, of a higher faculty in man than Understanding: of Reason (*Vernunft*), the pure, ultimate light of our nature; wherein, as they assert, lies the foundation of all Poetry, Virtue, Religion; things which are properly beyond the province of the Understanding . . . observing only farther, that the *Teologia Mistica*, so much venerated by Tasso in his philosophical writings; the 'Mysticism' alluded to by Novalis; and generally all true Christian Faith and Devotion, appear, so far as we can see, more or less included in this doctrine of the Transcendentalists; under their several shapes, the essence of them all being what is here designated by the name Reason, and set forth as the true sovereign of man's mind. . . . Thus, to live in that light of Reason, to have, even while here and encircled with this Vision of Existence, our abode in that Eternal City, is the highest and sole duty of man."[58]

In this merging of Kant's "pure reason" with religious faith, devotion, moral sensing of truth, and the mystic's "sea of light," we observe in brief just what Carlyle sought in appropriating Reason to his own purposes. In the passage given above there is scarcely a single Kantian thought. Indeed, the references are to "these Transcendentalists," "the Kantists," "the Germans," only once to Kant's philosophy, and that to the mere fact of the distinction. But before we turn to other and more probable sources for Carlyle's individual treatment of Reason, it is only proper, in order to get a right perspective, to remember what the term included and excluded in the *Critique of Pure Reason*.

In Kant's doctrine, both Understanding and Reason are concerned with thought; Reason is no more able than Understanding to penetrate with any empirical validity to the "holier regions" of Virtue and Religion. Both are limited to experience. Yet thought is not limited to the creation of knowledge; it may exercise a unifying power independently of all data, and produce Ideas which can never be objectified in experience. Under such circumstances they are the product of Reason. Understanding may, for example, produce the concept of power, as an attribute of a strong man; then Reason may produce, from combined concepts of various kinds and examples of power, the Idea of unlimited Power as a thing in itself. The purpose of the Idea is not to lead one to expect to encounter absolute Power in experience, or even to conclude, on the basis of Reason, that it exists, but to stimulate the Understanding to seek constantly a more complete unity of knowledge of powerful objects. In this sense, Ideas have a purely "regulative" function, never a "constitutive" one:

> "I accordingly maintain [says Kant] that transcendental ideas never allow of any constitutive employment. . . . On the other hand, they have an excellent, and indeed indispensably necessary, regulative employment, namely, that of directing the understanding towards a certain goal upon which the routes marked out by all its rules converge, as upon their point of intersection."[59]

An illusion may arise, however, which induces us to believe that these lines of regulative reason proceed from an object lying outside the sphere of empirical cognition, just as objects reflected in a mirror appear to be behind it; but Kant is at pains to insist that it *is* an illusion, and that Absolute Power, or Absolute Goodness, must not be taken in a Platonic sense, as self-existent.[60]

Now, although Carlyle seems to have had little interest in the technical discussion in the *Critique of Practical Reason*,[61] it is noteworthy that in that work he would have found an extension upon the concept of Reason which would have offered a substantial basis for precisely what he sought:

the grounds for the determination of man's freedom and of his moral will. If, says Kant, we cannot "know" the realm of things in themselves, there is yet a "practical Reason" which rehabilitates our world of moral values. Kant sought to show that the Ideas of Reason, though they can never be "known," have a certain validity. This is because of the position he assigns to Reason in respect to Will: "since, to deduce action from laws, reason is required, it follows that will is nothing else than practical reason."[62]   To the objection that the possibility of freedom remains totally incomprehensible, Kant replies that, though as an Idea of Reason it remains of doubtful objectivity, it is nevertheless of infinite *practical* importance.[63]   Our consciousness of the moral law is "an ultimate fact of reason," and Reason is "spontaneously practical, and gives that universal law (to man) which is called the moral law."[64]   As such, "the moral law expresses . . . nothing else than just the autonomy of reason, *i.e.* of a man's freedom or spontaneity."[65]   It may be said, in other words, that as Understanding deals only with the objects of the cognitive faculty, Reason is concerned with the grounds of the determination of the will: the field of the former is nature, that of the latter is freedom.[66] Seeking to assign objective causality to freedom, without reference to anything outside itself as the grounds of its causality, seeking, in short, "the *a priori* spring of the will,"[67] Kant finds such a principle in the "practical Reason." Man's recognition of the command of *duty*, as the great fact of his very nature, involves the further recognition that he can *do* it, and so assures him of the objective reality of his transcendental freedom which he can never perceive or "know" through experience. Except for the command of the moral law, the Idea of freedom is a purely rational deduction. But though Kant's pure practical reason is a form of pure thought, as is his pure speculative reason, and works by the same methods of logical deduction, it yet works in the realm of noumena, of the transcendental, and attains a valid basis for action.[68] To realize and fulfill the moral law is thus to realize the Ideas of Reason. Though they do not admit of a *full* realization in the natural world, they are indispensable, both as satisfying our consciousness of freedom and as providing the self, which is a unity, with the aim of making the world itself a unity by man's moral acts. Though we can never empirically know the Idea of freedom, we strive ceaselessly to realize it in our moral experience.[69]

We have seen nothing, however, in the passages from Carlyle which would indicate that he ever made conscious use of Kant's theory of the practical reason. To be sure, he speaks occasionally of the transcendental nature of duty,[70] but it is probably more in the sense that duty cannot be argued about, that it belongs with those realities about which a Carlylean "Silence" is to be preserved. Kant's categorical imperative—"So act that thy maxims of will might become law in a system of universal moral legislation"[71]—has little resemblance to Carlyle's, which resembles the Mosaic law. For Kant, the moral law is not a law solely because it is God's will, but because it is the law of pure reason; for Carlyle, moral law is the will of God imposed on man, with a specific content. Again, for Kant the practical reason, though of the noumenal world, can never deliver us constitutive knowledge of that world, since such knowledge—if it may be so called—comes not through insight but through action. On the other hand, Carlyle's "Reason" is the instrument which, in the hands of the Seer, gives direct vision into eternal truths. It is but one of the two great gifts of the Hero: the other is, as Kant would agree, *action*. Finally, we note that while, in Kant's theory, the moral law is regarded as wholly independent of phenomena, in Carlyle's teachings, it is present in the Garment as well as in the Reality behind it.[72] Thus we may see that Kant's "practical reason," though it could have suggested to Carlyle the grounds for the freedom of the will and for a certain indisputable knowledge of the Real, had apparently little effect upon his thought.

It is possible now to return to Carlyle's exposition of Reason, and to observe wherein it adheres to, and wherein it departs from, the original theory, and to what other sources it is evidently indebted.

(1) Reason, says Carlyle, is to seek, "by intuition," the *Urwahr*, or Primitive truth. The question of the origin of Carlyle's use of the term *Urwahr* has caused some speculation among Carlyle's critics.[73]   But his use of the term is another reminder of the importance of Madame de Staël in his introduction to German ideas.   "Dante," she writes in her *De l'Allemagne*, "has expressed a grand philosophical thought by this verse:

A guisa del ver primo che l'uom crede."

Her translation of this line, as it appeared in the English version of 1813, was as follows:

"It is thus that man believes in primitive truth."[74]

Later, in pointing out Kant's services in freeing Europe from materialism, from "the empire of external objects, and . . . personal interest," the author declares that "Kant wished to re-establish *primitive truths* and spontaneous activity in the soul, conscience in morals, and *the ideal* in the arts."[75]   It is needless to point out that for Kant there was no *Urwahr* in Carlyle's sense, and that Reason performed in no such mystical fashion to gain knowledge of the spiritual world.   Carlyle is much nearer Jacobi, for whom Reason provided "the power . . . of ascending (*steigen*) to the Supersensuous."[76]   He is nearer Coleridge, who quotes Hooker as holding that Reason is "a direct aspect of truth."[77]   Clearly the domain of Reason is not, as in Kant, the regulation of concepts so as to limit man's cognition within strictly empirical boundaries.   It penetrates to the supersensible, as in

Fichte: "the true law of reason in itself is the practical law, the law of the super-sensual world, or of that sublime will."[78]

(2) Reason is of "a higher nature . . . works by more subtle methods, on higher objects . . . [and] in many men it is never developed." The first part of this sentence is true to Kant in that Reason regulates the highest concepts and provides a rational ground for the moral will. But, though it has a certain supremacy over Understanding, it does not differ from it in being more dynamical, more capable of soaring into the realm of noumena. It is no more sacred for Kant than is the Understanding; for him only the moral will may be properly so called: "There is nothing in the world which can be termed absolutely and altogether good, a good will alone excepted."[79] Carlyle would have been nearer Kant's position, had he conceived Understanding as dealing with the physical world, and Reason with the world of moral ideas. The next point of difference is also noteworthy: Kant's "Reason" does not work "by more subtle methods." Both Understanding and Reason work by *a priori* principles. If the Ideas of the Reason are more subtle, it is because they are extensions of concepts beyond experience. But this subtlety is just the kind that would be repugnant to Carlyle, as "logic chopping." As for Reason requiring a finer culture, and failing to appear in many human beings, Kant believed that the moral imperative—and therefore Reason, by which it is determined—is resident in every one: ". . . all ethical ideas have their origin and seat altogether *a priori* in reason (in the reason of the unlettered, of course, as much as in that of the most finished sage)."[80] Individual opposition to the universal law is to be found, says Kant, only in pathological cases.[81] Without the Ideas of Reason, not only would the intellectual ground for morality disappear; the very possibility of understanding the world would disappear as well, since cognition depends upon the Ideas as stimulating

and unifying principles.[82]   The cultivation of Reason is, in Kant's doctrine, neither rarer nor more difficult than the deduction of theoretical principles from the *a priori* concepts of the Understanding.

We have already seen that Jacobi and Coleridge relegate Understanding to a "subaltern" position to Reason.   Once Carlyle identifies Reason with "faith" and "devotion," it is not difficult to see that, unlike Understanding, it will require cultivating, and will be found virtually wanting in many men. The "sea of light" will be inaccessible to many.   For Coleridge, as for Jacobi and Carlyle, "faith is the interpenetration of the Reason and the Will,"[83] and has little to do with Kantian "Ideas" and the regulation of concepts.   For all three, Reason is spiritual discernment, a rare endowment. The "higher objects" are obviously those involved in what Coleridge calls "a quickening communion with the Divine Spirit."[84]   They are for Carlyle what they were for Jacobi: "Gott, Freiheit, und Tugend . . . das Wahre, Schoene, und Gute,"[85] the "holier region, where Poetry, and Virtue and Divinity abide."[86]

(3) As "the pure, ultimate light of our nature," Reason has for Carlyle a mystical significance.   That he regards it as inclusive of the mysticism of Novalis, and of the mystical knowledge of the Pseudo-Dionysius (whose mystical Theology, was "so much venerated by Tasso"), is proof that Carlyle's Reason is not Kant's.   Even Kant's "practical reason" has no relevancy here to the "Vision of Existence," and the "Eternal City."   Reason is now "the fresh gaze of the child" (*der frische Blick des Kindes*), which Novalis said was of richer significance than the foresight of the most indubitable Seer.[87]   It is, according to Jacobi, "a spiritual eye for spiritual objects . . . a power directly from God."[88]   It is indistinguishable from what Coleridge said was the "best and holiest gift of God and bond of union with the giver . . . the mother of conscience, of language, of tears, of smiles . . . [the] calm and incorruptible legislator of the soul . . . :

"It is an organ identical with its appropriate objects. Thus God, the soul, eternal truth, etc., are the objects of reason; but they are themselves reason. We name God the Supreme Reason . . . Reason . . . may be safely defined the organ of the supersensuous . . ."[89]

(4) Thus, interpreted not from Kant's point of view but from that of several distinctly unKantian sources, Reason can easily be identified by Carlyle with "all true Christian Faith and Devotion." It clearly became that for Coleridge. As for Jacobi, it is faith alone which makes the objects of reason certain, so that Reason appears under the name of *Glaubenskraft*.[90] In Fichte and Novalis, also, Carlyle had precedent for assigning a faith content to Reason:

"I have found the organ [says Fichte] by which to apprehend this reality, and, with this, probably all other reality. Knowledge is not this organ. . . . It is Faith. . . a resolution of the will to admit the validity of knowledge . . . All my conviction is but faith . . . Conscience alone is the root of all truth . . . Self-active reason is will. The law of the super-sensual world must, therefore, be a will."[91]

Novalis is likewise convinced that conceptual knowledge does not exhaust man's contact with reality:[92]

Knowledge (*Wissenschaft*) is only a half; Faith is the other half . . . in all Knowledge (*Wissen*) there is faith.

It sufficed for Carlyle that Reason, or moral will, should be, as it was for Coleridge, "the spirit of regenerated man," a force active within him for the attainment of spiritual good. "Von dem Willen, nicht von dem Verstand," said Fichte,[93] can come the virtuous act. "Let the free, reasonable Will," said Carlyle, ". . . be indeed free, and obeyed like a Divinity."[94] If belief and conviction, as evidences of this moral will, seemed incomprehensible or miraculous, he observed that Novalis had already boldly faced that fact:

> "All Faith is wondrous and wonder-working . . . Can Miracles work Conviction? Or is not real Conviction, this highest function of our soul and personality, the only true God-announcing Miracle?"[95]

It is evident now that what Carlyle was seeking was a dynamic instrument of knowledge. He agreed with Novalis that "our thinking was hitherto either merely mechanical, discursive, atomistic, or merely intuitive, dynamic." Carlyle was apparently interested in Novalis's distinction, for he quotes the mystic at length in his essay:

> "Common Logic is the Grammar of the higher Speech, that is, of Thought; it examines merely the *relations* of ideas one to another, the *Mechanics* of Thought, the pure Physiology of ideas. Now logical ideas stand related to one another, like words without thoughts. Logic occupies itself with the mere dead Body of the Science of Thinking.—Metaphysics, again, is the *Dynamics* of Thought; treats of the primary *Powers* of Thought; occupies itself with the mere Soul of the Science of Thinking. . . ."[96]

There was clearly an appeal, in such a passage, to Carlyle's desire to think of ordinary metaphysics as dealing with the "dead body" of thought, to hope for a dynamic approach to thinking. It was this possibility of dynamically interpreting Reason that permitted Carlyle a wide application of it, as including more, indeed, than Kant, Jacobi, or Coleridge meant by it. In accordance with the underlying Garment philosophy, he regarded Reason as the means for piercing behind the "Garment of the Unseen," through "the material Creation [which] is but a reflex shadowed on the mirror of the Infinite."[97] At times, in speaking of the Hero, he identifies Reason with the ability to see the permanent beneath diversity and change.[98] Again, although not employing the term itself, he writes as if Reason were synonymous with "sympathetic understanding"—"to have an open loving heart" is "the beginning of all Knowledge."[99] Considering its field to be Virtue and Religion, it may be said also that Reason enables one to gain spiritual knowledge through the realization of "the *transcendental,* immeasurable character of Duty . . . the essence of all Religion."[100] Thus it involves not only the intellect but also the heart. True knowledge, for Carlyle, combines intellectual intuition, mystical communion, and moral revelation. It is sometimes little more than conscience illuminated by an act of sharp intellectual insight, rendered religious by a sense of other-worldliness. It yields knowledge not only of the world of appearances but also— for most men in fitting glimpses—of the world of noumena, which is fundamentally, for Carlyle, the world of divine law manifesting itself through nature and the law of right.

Carlyle's "Reason" thus includes Kant's "Reason" and transcends it, extending its domain even beyond the combined fields of Reason and Understanding as Kant conceived them, and including sympathetic insight or sensitivity of soul. Its content is far less rational than Kant's pure practical reason, and its province is the whole experience of man. Being less rational in content, its "Primitive Truth" is not merely the practical certainty of freedom and moral responsibility, which it was for Kant, but a mystical consciousness of the reality to which they lead. The very fact that we cannot, and that Carlyle cannot, precisely state just what that reality is, shows the essentially non-rational interpretation which he gave to Reason and to the "Truth" which it gains.

Nor has Carlyle's Reason very much similarity to the term as used by Fichte and Schelling. In both philosophers it is far too metaphysical, both in its nature and in the way it is deduced, for Carlyle's comprehension and acceptance. He apparently knew nothing of the manner in which Fichte transformed Reason into the active principle of the Ego, into

Intelligence as such, or universal reason, prior logically to the personal, empirical ego, and yet the condition or logical ground of that ego. At times, Reason is used by Fichte to mean something like the "life-force" or soul of men collectively, or universal humanity.[101] Since humanity, for Fichte, is a high revelation of the Divine Idea, Reason may be regarded as a manifestation of the Idea in man. As such it possibly appealed to Carlyle as a spark of the divine in man's nature, the point at which the human faculties may rise to a real glimpse of supersensuous things. Equally limited for Carlyle's purposes was Schelling's "intellectual intuition" (*intellektuelle Anschauung*) which apprehended the union of the real and the ideal, multiplicity and oneness. It was a faculty for seizing immediately the fundamental Knowledge (*Urwissen*), the perfect Total, or Absolute. Such a faculty, so put forth, could have but slight significance for Carlyle.[102]

We may say in conclusion that for the distinction between Understanding and Reason Carlyle was obviously indebted, directly or indirectly, to Kant; but that for their nature and function he shows a greater debt to Coleridge and Jacobi, with perhaps half-conscious memories of the English divines of the seventeenth century and the Platonic tradition in English thought. It is impossible to point out specific details of indebtedness beyond those we have seen. The paucity of references to Jacobi and Coleridge suggests that for Carlyle they merely represented a wide-spread tendency of the time to interpret Kant's Reason as loosely as individual desires required. It is possible that he was also aware of the numerous and ambiguous, but generally religious, paraphrases of Kant's arguments in Bouterwek, Richter, Horn, and various minor writers of the period. In all of them the severely formal character of Reason had more or less given way to attributes of spiritual insight. In the end, Carlyle arrived at the position from which he started: "It is the 'inspiration of the Almighty that giveth us understanding.' "[103]

In Novalis, with whom Reason had occasionally become synonymous with Phantasy or Imagination, Carlyle found a still further elaboration upon the problem of knowledge. It appears that he dallied with the notion of Phantasy for a short time, and although it quickly disappeared from his writings after *Sartor Resartus,* the place it occupied in his early thought should be stated.

6. PHANTASY: *"Das Organ des Menschen für die Gottheit."*[104]

"Phantasy," says Carlyle, ". . . superadds itself to sight," and is "the true Heaven-gate and Hell-gate of man," capable alike of "either true or false, either seraphic or demoniac, Inspiration or Insanity."[105]   At its best, and working with symbols, it permits the "sheen . . . . of Inspiration" to "gleam-in from the circumambient Eternity," and to color "with its own hues our little islet of Time."   As an organ of knowledge it has some resemblance to Carlyle's conception of Reason: "Not our Logical, Mensurative faculty, but our Imaginative one is King over us . . . The Understanding is indeed thy window . . .; Fantasy is thy eye, with its color-giving retina . . . Fantasy [is] . . . the organ of the God-like."[106]

It has been suggested that Carlyle is here attempting to introduce into Fichte's world the duality of good and evil, and of Phantasy as the double-natured organ in man for admitting or rejecting the good or the bad.[107]   There is little in his German sources to support his individual treatment of Phantasy, and so little definite agreement among the German writers on the nature and function of Phantasy that Carlyle would seem to have received from them only a very general notion of the term.   Both Richter and Novalis occasionally treated it as unwholesome or treacherous.[108] Though Richter loves to think of his *Joditzer Idyllen,* of his mother and his early home, through "das Mondlicht der Phantasie," yet he writes elsewhere as if reflection and phantasy were the "day and night elements" in his nature.[109] Neither Schiller's doctrine of the aesthetic education of man, nor Schelling's "Imagination" (*Einbildungskraft*) has anything vitally to do with Carlyle's notion.[110]   Nor had he probably given any thought to Imagination as the principle of continuity in Fichte's "Ego."[111]   As for possible English sources, while he probably knew that for Dugald Stewart, Imagination and "Phantasia" are the same and deal not with "visible things," but with the "objects of poetry," he could have had little interest either in Stewart's theories or in those of Coleridge as patterned after Jean Paul and Schelling.[112]

Carlyle had little definitely to say on Phantasy, and seems to have turned it over in his mind for a moment and let it pass.   For him it represented the power to receive intimations from the supersensible, probably in so far as the free play of imagination recapitulates in its creativeness the creative power behind the "Garment of Nature."   For a moment he tried to see in it another instrument for access to the world of spirit, and, with Friedrich Schlegel, called it the "organ of the God-like."[113]

7. KNOWLEDGE: *"Die Worte sind gut, sie sind aber nicht das Beste."*[114]

Carlyle's interest in Reason and Understanding, as we have already noted, was short-lived.   As the practical side of Goethe's teachings became uppermost in his mind, he felt more and more that "quietly to revere the unfathomable"[115] was a primary duty.   Goethe's famous line in *Faust* became a motto for him on all questions relating to Reality or God: *Wer darf ihn nennen?*[116]   He seems to have become increasingly conscious, with Novalis, that certain questions are "dumme Fragen."[117]   In this attitude he had other notable examples in Fichte, Jean Paul, Jacobi, and Kant.[118]

Both the English and the German writers strengthened in him a tendency to regard comprehensible things with disdain, and later to write: "Nothing that is wholly seen through has other than a trivial character."[119]   For him, as for Mephistopheles:

> "Ein Kerl, der spekuliert,
> Ist wie ein Tier, auf dürrer Heide
> Von einem bösen Geist im Kreis herumgeführt,
> Und ringsumher liegt schöne grüne Weide."[120]

Goethe's call was: "Gedenke zu leben!"[121]   Carlyle's was equally urgent.   Instead of speculating on one's origin and destiny, one was to act, to turn the speculative mystery into an active reality.   "Man begins in darkness [and] ends in darkness; mystery is everywhere around us and in us, under our feet, among our hands . . . . What is all working, what is all knowing, but a faint interpreting, and a faint showing forth of that same *Mystery of Life?*"[122]   At length the only knowledge was regarded as coming through work; and the old distinctions between Understanding and Reason seemed grotesque and futile.   Coleridge's solution, he said later, was "attending to the 'reason' of man . . . and duly chaining up the 'understanding' of man: the *Vernunft* (Reason) and *Verstand* (Understanding) of the Germans; it all turned upon these, if you could well understand them,—which you couldn't."[123]   Disdainful as these words sound, they should not, however, be taken as expressive of his early attitude toward the Kantian doctrine.   Until he had completed his "ground plan" in *Sartor*, Carlyle was vitally concerned in levying upon almost any doctrine for the reconstruction of his faith.   And in that reconstruction, the distinction between Reason and Understanding played no small part.

As he moved away from the technical aspects of German theories, and grew indifferent to specific developments of the notion of revelation in nature and in Reason, he found increasing interest in history. More vividly than in nature, and more authoritatively than in the individual's knowledge, there was significant revelation in the history of man. In Carlyle's treatment of this doctrine, German ideas influenced both his theory and his practice.

CHAPTER VI

CARLYLE AND HISTORY

1. THE HISTORICAL TRIUMVIRATE

Carlyle's evaluation of history as equal, or even superior, to other forms of literary art may be said to represent the survival of a prevalent feeling in the eighteenth century concerning history in general and the proper manner of setting forth historical fact. The reading of history was indeed one of the prominent features of the culture of the period.

> "In all probability," says a present-day critic of history, "there has never been a period when history was so much in demand among the reading public in all European countries as the latter part of the eighteenth century. It would be no exaggeration to say that the vogue of historical books between 1750 and the outbreak of the French Revolution was as great as the vogue of poetical literature in the age of Shakespeare or of the novel in the age of Scott."[1]

The extraordinary success of Voltaire's *Charles XII*, the fact that Gibbon's *Decline and Fall* "sold like a threepenny pamphlet on the affairs of the day," the remarkable popularity of Robertson's *Scotland,* and the fondness of the Empress Catherine of Russia for Robertson's *Charles V* as a companion on her long journeys, are all evidences of the singular eminence accorded to historical works in the last years of the Age of Reason. And they take on a special significance for us when we remember that Carlyle was, after all, one of the youngest inheritors of the *Aufklärung*, and that the early reading which moulded his taste and directed his intellectual tendencies was largely in the literature of the neo-Classic period. He read history partly because in Scotland it was still a major department in one's reading. That two of the great British triumvirate of historians were Scotchmen was probably another reason for his study of history, especially of Robertson and Hume.

It is possible that his disdain for Dryasdust had no slight foundation in the historical tradition of the previous generation. If the theory on which Gibbon, Robertson, and Hume based their historical procedure was not explicitly hostile to the mere annalist, at least their practice was that of the man of wide and generous culture, for whom a considerable mastery in literary art had become almost second-nature. Their books were the culmination of their entire mental growth, rather than the researches of the few years that often went into their production. They were not historical artisans, engaged in laboriously accumulating facts. Indeed they entered upon their careers as historians only after they had won distinction in other fields. Hume had won fame as an essayist, an economist, and a philosopher. Gibbon had attempted literary criticism, and had distinguished himself as a classical scholar. What they brought to their histories from their storehouse of general knowledge is often as interesting as their narrative; and their interpretation of facts by their point of view, matured not only by books but by an active contact with the world, is one of the chief elements in their continuing vitality. They were primarily men of letters, appealing to their public on the ground of their broad humanistic culture rather than upon their mastery of the technical problems of the "scientific" historian. To them, as to their public, history was a combination of literature, learning, philosophy, and practical wisdom.[2] Now, it is noteworthy that Carlyle, though dissatisfied with their method and their achievement, shows a certain degree of similarity to his predecessors. His first historical work, *The French Revolution*, was the product of his mature manhood; it came at the end of his stormy quest for philosophical and religious certainty. Moreover, it represents not the uninspired "annalist," but the man of letters. As such, Carlyle had achieved distinction in criticism, and in the introduction of German literature and thought into England. His history is thus a work of art, the re-creation of the past through the author's mind, personality, and point of view. It is documented, like Gibbon's, and it holds us not merely by its vivid array of illuminating detail, but also by the interpretation imparted by Carlyle's general philosophy and learning.

This conception of history as closely related to philosophy reveals Carlyle as akin to the eighteenth century historians on another point: their impatience with "history for history's sake." In very much the manner of Hume, though of course for wholly different reasons, Carlyle turned to history for the embodiment of his doctrines, and to his doctrines for the interpretation of his facts. Though the result in his case, as in Hume's and in Gibbon's, was a combination of surprising illumination and curious distortion, it was seldom pedantic or unprofitable. For all three, history was the record of man's effort to discover truth: it was indeed, as Bolingbroke had said,[3] the spectacle of truth being taught by examples.

The question of just what truth it was that history taught, and what was the best method of revealing it, was of course the point at which Carlyle parted company from Gibbon and Hume. Their method alone would have repelled him before long. He found the polished periods of Gibbon irksome; and felt that to exclude any word or phrase of an *outré* character was to strangle his inspiration and corrupt his sincerity. The "logical terseness of a Hume or Robertson"[4] left his dynamic nature dissatisfied. The exaltation of *le bon sens naturel*, the observance of *goût, esprit, élégance*, all the reigning powers in French historiography, struck the Annandale peasant as unworthy of the historian, for whom history should be an awful apocalypse. Nor could the traditional limitation of history to conquests, court intrigues, or political machinations adequately meet Carlyle's insistent

curiosity about the lives of common men, about modest-look-
ing but epoch-making inventions, about the moral and spiritual conflict underlying the warp and woof of historical
event.   The whole pragmatic and rationalistic postulate
behind eighteenth century historical procedure, its hostility
to all metaphysical, idealistic, or religious interpretation of
the human record, was diametrically at variance with Carlyle's
sense of the significance of history.

Thus, while Carlyle exhibits a certain kinship with the
spirit of Gibbon and Hume, partly in his general equipment,
his philosophical approach, his enthusiasm, he has on the
other hand some very evident and well-known differences.
We may note them briefly.   In the first place, Carlyle was
repelled by Hume's mechanical psychology.   Character was
more, he held, than an assemblage of virtues and vices; it
was not an aggregate in the sense that an object is the sum
of its qualities.   The springs of historical acts were deeper,
more mysterious, more spiritual than the mechanical causes
which Hume adduced in explaining that all history is merely
the history of human culture, the record of man's progressive conquest over nature.   Again, Hume's inability to understand religious principles as anything else than "sick men's
dreams," or the "whimsies of monkeys in human shape,"
was a part of the same skeptical tradition exemplified in
Gibbon's ironic treatment of the rise of Christianity.   We
need only to remember Hume's account of the Reformation,
as a battle between two false religions, between Catholic
superstition and Protestant fanaticism, or Robertson's
mechanical and deeply skeptical treatment of the same
upheaval, to realize how foreign and repellent their attitude
was to Carlyle.[5]   In Gibbon there was no philosophical principle to irritate Carlyle, but on the other hand, the occasional
moralizing on the tragi-comedy of history, the pitiless irony
directed alike at the good and the bad, and the general under-
mining of one's belief in the significance of the pageant, all
must have seemed like nothing but brilliant blasphemy.

In Germany another and a quite different attitude toward history was developing: the record of man's life was being regarded as the dynamic revelation of a divine principle. Friedrich Schlegel, harshly criticising the British historians for their irreligious interpretation of history, charged them with being blind to the phenomenon of *development,* and with seeing man as merely an item in nature, growing from the earth like a mushroom. Schiller was not only theorizing about history but was embodying his ideas in great historical works. Indeed, one of the chief characteristics of the new German movement was its sense for history, and its readiness to apply to all problems the historical point of view. In that movement, Carlyle's Calvinism found a very congenial atmosphere. It reinforced his belief in a present God active in human affairs, a God of law and justice; in the establishment of "God's Will" on earth as the true end of all historical progress; in the inevitable paralysis of a nation's energies in an age of unbelief. German writers supplied here, as elsewhere, the new terms and the new concepts for a reinterpretation of history which should also be a justification of the old Puritan ideal of a theocracy.

2. NEW THEORIES IN GERMANY

Carlyle has curiously little to say of much of the new conception of history as put forth by Lessing, Herder, or Kant. He seems never to have studied the development of such a conception as peculiar to German Idealism. It is noteworthy, however, that the doctrine of *Offenbarung* as applied to history had a comparatively late development in German thought. Neither the Orthodox nor Rationalistic traditions of the *Aufklärung* had a truly historical outlook. As yet the alternatives in speculation were Reason and Nature on the one hand, or Biblical revelation on the other. The significance of history, in this notorious dead-lock, had little importance for the antagonists. History as revelation is a conception which belongs properly to the Jews. And if the *Aufklärung* failed to seek a philosophy of history in the concept of "revelation," it was largely owing to the contemporary eclipse of the Augustinian tradition, in which history was interpreted teleologically, as having its end in "the kingdom of God." This interpretation had been kept alive by the Württemberg theologians, who saw historical events as revealing an ascending series of being, a gradual unfolding of divine purpose. Thus it was that when the new Idealists turned to the past for a non-mechanical and dynamic conception of history, they found a distinctly religious one. It was opposed, on almost every point, to the principles which underlay the work of Voltaire, Gibbon, and Hume.[6]

The theories which were soon to attract Carlyle had their most significant beginnings in Lessing and Herder. As one of the fathers of German Idealism, Lessing first applied to history the concept of development. While his philosophy of history remains throughout a religious or theological doctrine, it nevertheless exercised the greatest influence on the tendency of the time to seek in history the philosophic basis of a doctrine of *Offenbarung*. According to Lessing, the education of the human race (*Erziehung des Menschengeschlechts* [1780]) is itself a revelation, a manifestation of continuously developing Reason (*Vernunft*) in the life of man. World-history is the school in which man learns ultimate truth.[7] It is to the race what ordinary education is to the individual; world-history, or the past experience of mankind, enables man to learn faster. The likeness of this point of view to that of Natural Religion is very strong; the difference, after all, is one of form only. At any rate, in regard to anything relevant to Carlyle's needs, its want of something more spiritually dynamic than the mere schooling of man into more rational existence must have left the doctrine comparatively barren for him. He undoubtedly saw that in Lessing's theory, revelation is not the *plan* of

history, as it should be in a Carlylean universe, but merely
the means of further advances to truth.[8] Perhaps in only
two respects did the doctrine appeal to Carlyle: that history
teaches by examples, and that man outgrows the forms of
religion and seeks newer and more adequate expressions of
his spirit.

Nor did Carlyle find any definite illumination in Herder.
Though Herder sought God in history, so far as reason and
nature can reveal Him, though he attempted to outline a
plan of history, his *Ideen zur Philosophie der Geschichte der
Menschheit* (1784-91) does not state unequivocally a spiritual
point of view. Though it repudiated materialism, it never
rose beyond defending spirit as other than organic power,
external and bodily organization. This is why Carlyle's
admiration for Herder's work is so heavily qualified; it is
"an extraordinary book," he writes in his Journal,

> "yet one which by no means wholly pleaseth me. If
> Herder were not known as a devout man and clerk, his
> book would be reckoned atheistical. Everything is the
> effect of circumstances and organisation: *Er war was
> er seyn konnte!* The breath of life is but a higher
> intensation of Light and Electricity! This is surely
> very dubious, to say no worse of it. Theories of this
> and kindred sorts deform his whole work here and
> there.—Immortality not *shewn* us, but left us to be
> hoped for, as believed by Faith. Yet this world, as he
> thinks, sufficiently explainable without reference to
> another: *Humanität* the great object of Nature in all
> her arrangements of society. . . . *How* true is this? At
> least this ought to be *our* object. . . . Strange ideas about
> the Bible and Religion; passing strange we think them
> for a clergyman. . . ."[9]

In Schiller, we come to the first real influence upon Carlyle's theory and practice of history. It is true that Schiller
exalts to a very prominent place the theory of "perfectability"
and the *Humanitätsideal*, toward which Carlyle's Calvinism

was always cool. But, following Kant's theological treatment of History in the *Idee zu einer allgemeinen Geschichte in weltbürgerlicher Absicht* (1784), Schiller adopts a theory and practice which manifestly affected Carlyle's subsequent attitude. Though little systematic doctrine was offered, Schiller's introductory lecture at Jena (*Was Heisst und zu welchem Ende Studiert Man Universalgeschichte?*) contained several points which later appear in Carlyle's theory: that great blanks in history can never be filled; that history is at best only a collection of fragments; that only the Infinite Spirit can survey its entirety; that teleology, the theory of an inner and active purpose in history, can alone make history intelligible; that only the philosophical historian, and never the routine or uninspired fact-gatherer, can hope to seize and re-create the past.[10] In spite of several highly theoretical and *a priori* elements in Schiller's philosophy of history, Carlyle had extravagant praise for Schiller's lectures: "there perhaps has never been in Europe another course of history sketched out on principles so magnificent and philosophical."[11]

It is clear, however, from all that we know of Schiller and Carlyle, that what contributed most substantially to Carlyle's philosophy of history was Schiller's practice. Our best source here is Carlyle's own account of Schiller's preparation for his *Geschichte des Abfalls der vereinigten Niederlande von der spanischen Regierung* (1791-93). It will be noted that what Carlyle says of Schiller's method can with equal truth be said of his own. This is true of Schiller's reasons for turning to history, in his Dresden period, as a relief from tales of horror such as the *Geisterseher*. What drew Schiller to history, says Carlyle, was the fact that "it was grounded on reality"; that "the commanding characters that figure in it would present him with things great and moving"; that, "as recording the past transactions, and indicating the prospects of nations, it could not fail to be delightful to one, for whom .... human nature was a matter of most fascinating speculation." It is not impossible that in Schiller's practice, Carlyle saw the expression of his own passion for "reality"—for *fact*—his own love of "things great and moving," his own desire to narrate and interpret human nature as "a matter of most fascinating speculation."[12]

A further similarity is to be seen in their approach to historical data: Schiller was as dissatisfied with Watson's history of Spain under Philip II as Carlyle was with Robertson's history of Scotland, and for the same reason: the earlier work, in both cases, was "clear but shallow." Both Schiller and Carlyle turned to "the original sources of information." Carlyle proceeds with Schiller:

> "He resolved to explore the minutest circumstance of [the] rise and progress [of the Revolt of the Netherlands]; to arrange the materials he might collect, in a more philosophical order; to interweave with them the general opinions he had formed, or was forming, on many points of polity, and national or individual character; and, if possible, to animate the whole with that warm sympathy, which, in a lover of Freedom, this most glorious of her triumphs naturally called forth. . . . This History . . . he looked upon but as one branch of the great subject . . . History at large, in all its bearings, was now his final aim."

The principles involved here are precisely those involved in Carlyle's *French Revolution* as manifested in the following features: the emphasis on concrete circumstances; the "philosophical order" of the materials; the interweaving of the author's general opinions; his warm sympathy, as "a lover of Freedom," in narrating "this most glorious of her triumphs"; and the general impression that the Revolution is but a branch of a greater historical process, indeed of a cosmic process, in which moral ideals are seeking realization.[13]

But what, in Carlyle's estimation, secured for Schiller "a distinguished rank among historians, of the class denominated philosophical," was Schiller's view of history in general. Carlyle noted that

> "In his view, the business of history is not merely to record, but to interpret; it involves not only a clear conception and a lively exposition of events and characters, but a sound, enlightened theory of individual and national morality, a general philosophy of human life, whereby to judge of them, and measure their effects. The historian now stands on higher ground, takes a wider range than those that went before him; he can now survey vast tracts of human action, and deduce its laws from an experience extending over many climes and ages. With his ideas, moreover, his feelings ought to be enlarged: he should regard the interests not of any sect or state, but of mankind. . . . His narrative, in short, should be moulded according to the science, and impregnated with the liberal spirit of his time. . . . Voltaire . . . applied the ideas of the eighteenth century to the subject; but in this there was nothing radically new. In the hands of a thinking writer history has always been 'philosophy teaching by experience'; that is, such philosophy as the age of the historian has afforded."[14]

We observe here some of the elements of the background from which Carlyle's own practice as a historian undoubtedly emerged. We recognize the position of the historian as standing "on higher ground," equipped with "a general philosophy of human life," imbued with "the liberal spirit of his time," and endeavoring to show history as "philosophy teaching by experience."

If, however, Schiller irritated Carlyle by his "over-tendency to generalization," and by his "extreme attention to the philosophical aspects of the period," what must have been his reaction to Fichte's *Characteristics of the Present Age* (*Grundzüge des gegenwärtigen Zeitalters*)? As the *Höhepunkt* of Idealistic *Geschichtsphilosophie*, it exalted Reason above all historical change, proceeded to interpret the past by the *a priori* method, and thus predicted man's course in the future. History, according to this doctrine, is the *Erscheinung* or symbol of the Divine Idea. Since history is the externalization of a rational Idea, then the deduction of primary and necessary principles inherent in historical processes becomes the business of the historian. For Fichte, it is obviously easy and inevitable for the *a priori* historian to foresee, on the basis of dialectic, what must be the future course of history. Needless to say, Fichte's metaphysical treatment of history was almost wholly lost on Carlyle. Yet there were valid elements in Fichte's doctrine, as we shall later see,[15] which Carlyle could appropriate with considerable profit. The conception of history as the revelation of the Divine Idea was in itself susceptible to Carlylean transformations.

According to Friedrich Schlegel, the writing of history had had a very evident importance: it had embodied the reigning philosophy of past epochs, and had inculcated the writer's doctrines with far greater power than could a direct appeal to the reader's mind:

> "In no other department of human knowledge was the philosophy of the last century able to establish its influence, or root itself so deeply and so extensively as in history, in which false motives are likely to be less apparent to the reader who does not examine for himself, than when they openly court attention in the shape of philosophic doctrines and opinions."[16]

It was thus of capital importance just what the philosophy involved. Schlegel averred that the declining fame of the British historians was due in no small degree to the negative character of the philosophic doctrines underlying their work, and to certain disagreeable qualities in their attitude: the "leaning to paradox"; the "Voltairean spirit of mockery"; the hatred of the clergy and "of religion generally." But, above all, what the British historians lacked was an "animat-

ing principle of philosophy" which should unify and
illuminate the otherwise chaotic data of history:

> "One of the causes of the declension is perhaps the
> want of a fixed and satisfactory system of philosophy:
> this is sensibly felt to have operated even in the case of
> those three historical models.   Without some definite
> perception of the moral existence of man, his origin
> and his destination, the historian is hardly competent to
> decide, or even clearly understand, all the circumstances
> relative to national events, developments, and fortunes.
> Upon the whole, History and Philosophy ought ever to
> be as closely united as possible. . . . . Without the ani-
> mating principle of philosophy, history is but a sense-
> less heap of waste materials, destitute of inner unity,
> fixity of purpose, or definite result. . . . . The spurious
> history of mankind, which characteristically proceeded
> from the corrupt sensual material philosophy prevalent
> in the eighteenth century, is based upon a belief that
> man grew out of the ground like a mushroom,
> but with the additional properties of locomotion and
> consciousness."[17]

Here again, as in the case of Schiller, we find the insistence
upon the historian's need of a consistent philosophy of life.
For Schlegel, as for Schiller, it was "history in all its bearings" which formed the field of the historian's interests.
And the primary need in the historian is that "spiritual perception," that discernment of the forces in history which
alone can reveal man's "origin and his destination . . .
his actual nature."   This, says Schlegel, will involve
"religion and philosophy," and a "fundamental philosophy of
revelation."

In Schelling, likewise, Carlyle found a number of congenial ideas on history and the historian, as set forth in the
Method of Academical Study.   In this work Schelling surveys the whole academic field, as it then lay open to him, in
an encyclopedic view of science from the standpoint of

identity and idealism.   In the eighth and ninth lectures, history is regarded as the higher, *potential* revelation of the Absolute, as Nature is the lower, *actual* manifestation. Schelling, like Kant, Fichte, and Schiller, proceeds, however, to a characteristic emphasis on history as the realization of the ideal State, of the harmony of freedom and necessity, spirit and matter.   In man's historical acts, these two phases of the Absolute are ceaselessly engaged in a struggle for higher synthesis, so that in history, properly interpreted, we have, says Schelling, the most eloquent testimony of the Divine Will.   Historical art becomes the most perfect revelation of the Absolute in human life.   In all this, Carlyle undoubtedly got but a few profitable glimpses of truth.   Yet we can safely assume that the general spirit, in spite of the emphasis on the ideal State, aided Carlyle in conceiving history as the immense spectacle of mind struggling with matter, of good battling with evil.   To this extent the general tenor of Schelling's teachings blended with Carlyle's postulates.

In all these theories of history, the common element of an *Offenbarungsbegriff* was sufficiently dominant to render their divergences of relatively little importance for Carlyle. His point of view, though more narrowly religious than that of the German thinkers, contained enough intellectual curiosity to lend their various utterances on history an especial cogency.   Now that he had lost his belief in the Biblical revelation, as maintained in the old theological tradition, he sought a revelation in the record of man's past.   The secondary principles which were brought forth by the Germans in offering this new revelation, passed off his mind as extraneous.   Only four conceptions found a place in his final philosophy of history: the first we have already noted—the general doctrine of revelation; the second was the idea of alternating periods of positive and negative faith; the third related to time; the fourth was a new view of the historian and his method.

3. History as Revelation : *"denn die ganze Geschichte
    ist Evangelium."*[18]

Though the commonly cited source here is Fichte's
Grundzüge,[19] it is clear by now that the thought of many
writers went to the making of Carlyle's theory. In Novalis
alone we are able to find abundant expression of his doctrine.
But among the generally overlooked sources, we shall first
note a passage from Richter's *Wahrheit aus Jean Pauls
Leben*. It sums up the idea of history in language which is
almost identical with Carlyle's. The passage appears, in
Carlyle's translation, in a footnote in his second essay on
Richter:

> " 'All History,' thus he writes in his thirty-second
> year, " 'in so far as it is an affair of memory, can only be
> reckoned a sapless heartless thistle for pedantic chaf-
> finches;—but, on the other hand, like Nature, it has
> highest value, in as far as we, by means of it, as by
> means of Nature, can divine and read the Infinite Spirit,
> who, with Nature and History, as with letters, legibly
> writes to us. He who finds a God in the physical world
> will also find one in the moral, which is History.
> Nature forces on our heart a Creator; History a
> Providence.' "[20]

On the same subject, Richter elsewhere pronounces similarly: if, he says, one is not pessimistically determined to
make history a record of man's errors, a "biography of the
Devil," it may be regarded as veritably a third Bible, Nature
being the second: "Die Geschichte ist—wenn ihr sie nicht
zur Biographie des Teufels machen wollt—die dritte Bibel;
denn das Buch der Natur ist die zweite . . ."[21] Another
little-known source for Carlyle's notions on history is, as we
have already noted, Friedrich Schlegel, who emphasized
the apocalyptic nature of history, and sought illustrations of
Schiller's famous line, "Die Weltgeschichte ist das Welt-
gericht."[22] We note, finally, that in Goethe, too, there occur

memorable passages in this same direction. In the well-known passage in *Wilhelm Meister,* in which the three religions are set forth, we find that the spirit of the history of man is identical with that of the "Ethnic" religion which founds itself on "reverence for what is above us." Revelation from above is thus possible through the acted history of humanity: "The spirit of it," says Goethe, "is to be sought for in the history of the world; its outward form, in the events of that history . . ."[23]

For a wider background for Carlyle's theory of history as revelation we must go to Fichte, Novalis, and Schelling. In Fichte, Carlyle found an attempt at a complete philosophy of history. His own idea that God is revealed in the history of institutions, like the Church and the State,[24] finds an antecedent in Fichte's doctrine that the Divine Idea manifests itself in the progressive culture of the human race, as expressed in law, religion, science, art.[25] For Fichte, this means that the stream of history in time is the progressive externalization of the timeless Idea, of Reason; so that "the End of the Life of Mankind on Earth is . . . that [men] may order all their relations with Freedom according to Reason."[26] This Reason embraces the "One Life, which manifests itself as the Life of the Race."[27] Fichte's division of historical time into periods, and his views on the ideal aims of the historian, we reserve for discussion in another place. It is noteworthy, therefore, that when we have thus stated Fichte's doctrine of revelation in history, as set forth in the *Grundzüge,* we have exhausted Fichte as a source for Carlyle's ideas on the subject. Fichte's contribution here is evidently confined to the very general concept of *Offenbarung.* It is worthwhile asking why this is so.

Carlyle of course had no patience with the "high *priori* road,"[28] and thus had little use for Fichte's strictly logical deduction of the course of history, in the past, present, and future, independently of all historical evidence. Though he occasionally speaks as if he believed in some sort of cosmic progress, he is always more likely to think of progress as the accumulation of all the good in every age, fructifying and spreading throughout time. Since he never adopted Fichte's doctrine of the Ego in its original form, he never accepted Fichte's conception of history as the necessary progress toward a final realization of the absolute Ego in the "One Life of the Spirit," in which all individuality is lost. Historical development becomes for Carlyle the development of a created cosmos in accordance with God's eternal laws; and history becomes the record of humanity's grappling with those laws in an attempt to get into harmony with a Creator.[29]

Yet he could agree with Fichte that history presents an open book in which the discerning may read the Divine Will, and may see right eventually triumphing as might. More specifically, he agreed that "every Society, every Polity has a spiritual principle; is the embodiment, tentative and more or less complete, of an Idea."[30]   In Fichte this doctrine is expressed as follows:

> "The Philosopher who should propose to himself the task of such a description [of the present Age], would, independently of all experience, seek out an Idea of the Age (which indeed in its own form,—*as Idea,*—cannot be apparent in experience), and exhibit the mode in which this Idea would reveal itself under the forms of the necessary phenomena of the Age . . . Every particular Epoch of time . . . is the fundamental Idea of a particular Age. . . ."[31]

These two doctrines—history as manifestation of divine law, and each age as informed with an Idea peculiar to its constitution and destiny—undoubtedly determined in some measure his treatment of historical fact. The French Revolution, which had very early struck him as a divine judgment on the "age of the *philosophes*," must have taken on added meaning when viewed in the light of these two Fichtean doc-

trines. According to the first, it was a revelation; on the
basis of the second, it was an organic process, manifesting
the peculiar and deeply-working spirit of the age, the spirit
of negation and all the historical phenomena consequent on
its triumph. The debacle of the *ancien régime* was, to Carlyle, the historical proof that "of all Bibles the frightfullest
to disbelieve in is this 'Bible of Universal History.' "[32]

For phrasing resembling Carlyle's, however, we must go
to Novalis. Carlyle's statement that "Man's history, and
Men's history, [is] a perpetual Evangel" echoes very distinctly one of Novalis's most striking *Fragmente*: "The Historian must often become an orator (*Redner*) in his manner
of delivery. He propounds a gospel, for the whole of history is an Evangel."[33] Again, Carlyle's consciousness of the
mystery of human life, and of its relative solution in the
study of biography as the essence of history, also is reminiscent of Novalis: "The greatest mystery (*Geheimnis*) is
man himself. The solution of this infinite problem is indeed
the history of the world."[34] Like Carlyle, Novalis had
sought for revelation outside the traditional sources: "Is it
not possible to consider the composition of a greater Evangel?
Can it not but be historical? . . . Not also an Evangel of the
future?"[35] These questions concerning the further revelation of man's nature and destiny remind us that for Carlyle
life was at bottom without a solution. Only in world history could man glimpse the lineaments of his true character
and end: "What shapes a man," asks Novalis, "if it be not
his life-history? And so the great man is formed by nothing
else than the history of the world."[36]

On this subject, less direct relationship can be established
between Carlyle and Schelling. Yet in the *Methode*, Carlyle
found the ideal historian to be one who rejects the common
interpretation of events as accidentally or mechanically determined. "History . . .," says Schelling, "proceeds from the
eternal Unity, and has its root in the Absolute just as Nature
has." Events are dynamic. True history rests upon the

dynamic synthesis of the actual and the potential, the real and the ideal. In any particular instance it deals immediately with *real* data, but only in so far as they disclose the realization of the ideal latent in historical processes. The historian is thus guided by a sense of development, of general and informing *themes* pervading events. Without departing from factual veracity, he should represent facts, like the dramatist, "in a fullness (*Vollendung*) and Oneness (*Einheit*). . . whereby they become the expression (*Ausdruck*) of the highest Ideas." In history, more than anywhere else, one may observe, as we have noted elsewhere, the significant conflict between freedom and necessity, moral will and matter. Man's effort to order his life according to the conditions of physical nature and the potentialities of his spirit constitutes what Schelling regarded as universal history.[37] Here, again, the abstract form of the doctrine must have left Carlyle with only the most general impression. But, whether he was affected by Schelling's ideas or not, it is certain that Carlyle's historical practice embodied in an interesting measure some of the principles here enunciated. History, for Carlyle, was indeed the effort of man to bring order out of chaos, good out of evil, right out of wrong, the ideal out of the actual. And while, as a historian, he dealt constantly with the most concrete data he could assemble, he employed it always to point out the pervading themes of right, of the value of great leaders, of the Divine Idea working behind and through the events he narrated. Nor was he forgetful of the aesthetic requirements of his subject; he marshalled his historical figures and events so as to produce the very *Einheit* and *Vollendung* which Schelling's theory required. In what degree he was indebted—if at all—to the ideas in the *Methode*, we shall probably never know. But it is difficult to overlook the fact that many of the ideas in Schelling's lectures paralleled a number of Schiller's, and that Carlyle, who had read the *Methode*, could readily have felt their influence.[38]

4. TIME: *"Vielleicht überhaupt Nichts, ein leerer
Schimmer . . .?"*[39]

As involved in his attitude toward history, time seems to
have appeared to Carlyle in somewhat the same fashion as it
did to Fichte in the *Grundzüge*. Behind and through earthly
time, stands universal time; human history transpires through
"necessary epochs" of the "One Time" and of the "One
Eternal Life." Above all ages, that is, there is "the One
Unchanging Time" as the source of all epochs; or, in Carlyle's phraseology, Eternity stands behind Time. Let us
turn to Fichte's words:

> "The Life of Mankind *on this Earth* stands here in
> place of the *One Universal Life*, and *Earthly Time* in
> place of *Universal Time* . . . . for . . . . Human Life on
> Earth, and Earthly Time itself, are but necessary Epochs
> of the One Time and of the One Eternal Life . . . Science
> raises itself above all Ages and all Times, embracing
> and apprehending the One Unchanging Time as the
> higher source of all Ages and Epochs . . ."[40]

Carlyle's interest in *Unendlichkeit* (unending time) rather
than in *Ewigkeit* (eternity, or timelessness),[41] may possibly be
traced from such a passage as the above. For him, universal
time (*die gesamte Zeit*) was simply the sum total of past,
present, and future, without any metaphysical implications.
History, as the sum of finite *times*, was the garment of the
timelessness of God. There are occasions, however, when
Carlyle speaks of time in almost Fichte's words: in *Diderot*,
for example, he wishes to judge "philosophism," not by the
standards of any one age or "time," but by "Time at large":
"If we rise with this matter [of 'Philosophism']," he says,
". . . into the proper region of Universal History, and look
on it with the eye not of this time or of that time, but of
Time at large, perhaps the prediction might stand here, That
intrinsically, essentially little lies in it."[42] This passage,
however, is perhaps the only one in which Carlyle approaches

Fichte's actual words.   And even here we are not safe in inferring an influence.   Yet it can be said that Carlyle's conception of earthly time as symbolical of infinite time, as the garment of "divine time," finds a more relevant background in Fichte than in any other German writer with the exception of Kant.

The oneness, implied in this doctrine, between eternal time and its vesture, gave Carlyle the comfort of believing that "no Truth or Goodness realized by man ever dies, or can die."[43]   In this belief, he had Fichte's words to support him:

> "Thus, I said, does the One, Eternal, Self-comprehensive, Self-existent Idea roll forth in the undivided Stream of Time.   And, I add, that in every individual moment of this Time-stream it comprehends and pervades itself, being throughout all Time, eternally present to itself.   What takes place in it at any moment of time, *is* now, only because the Past *has been*, and because the Future Eternity *shall be*.   Nothing in this system is lost. . . .   Nothing really good is lost in the stream of Time:—how long soever it may lie defamed, misunderstood, and disregarded, the day at length arrives when it throws off its disguises and comes forth into light . . ."[44]

Carlyle had also the stimulating corollary that, as we are part of the "One, Eternal Idea," we have a share in the ceaseless striving of Earthly time to produce the ideal out of the actual.   We are "based on Time, and built on Time," he says; "[our life] is wholly a Movement, a Time-impulse . . . Hence also our Whole Duty, which is to move, to work."[45]   For both Carlyle and Fichte, we are Phenomena of time; Fichte goes on to say:

> "In the view of Religion, all the Phenomena of Time, without exception, are regarded as necessary and progressive developments of the One, Ever-blessed, Orig-

inal Divine Life, and hence each individual Phenomenon is regarded as the necessary condition of a Higher and more Perfect Life in Time, which shall arise from it."[46]

It is obvious that Carlyle's treatment of time in relation to history is necessarily, like his treatment of history itself, a part of his Clothes Philosophy. Time remained for him an insoluble riddle; the nearest approach to a solution was to call it an Appearance, a Vesture, or at best the arena of our moral activity in the service of the Idea.[47] Moreover, as indicating the hopefulness of the future and the pathos of the past, it held a primary place in Carlyle's philosophy of history. Like Novalis, he believed the past to be sacred, and in a measure he illustrated Novalis's penetrating epigram: "Many men live better with the past and the future than with the present."[48]

5. PERIODICITY: *"der Konflikt des Unglaubens und Glaubens."*

Convinced that "this wondrous Mankind is advancing somewhither,"[49] Carlyle appears to have given occasional thought to the phenomenon of historical rhythm. True to his characteristic aversion to interpreting facts by an elaborate doctrine, such as Fichte's, he never advanced very far, in this regard, beyond the rudiments of a point of view. It was not, however, for the want of conspicuous German models of speculation. In Schiller, Fichte, Novalis, Friedrich Schlegel, and Schelling, he could have found abundant effort at charting the past course of man's history according to some principle which marked off and interpreted a series of epochs. Though it was Goethe, rather than any of the philosophers, who contributed most to Carlyle's notion of the rhythm of history, it is necessary to note wherein the more ambitious and systematic attempts at formulating such a notion possibly affected Carlyle's attitude. We shall see that here he follows not only Goethe but also, to some extent, Fichte and Novalis.

Fichte discerns in the evolution of man as an agent in the unfolding of the Divine Idea, a "World-plan" whereby he is able to deduce *a priori* the principles of free active Reason in man's past, present, and future,—"to describe Time as a whole, and all its possible epoch."[50] The complete realization of the Divine Idea, through universal time, is accomplished in five stages or world-epochs. In the first age, Reason is active as blind instinct, as "consciousness without insight." In the second age, "there arises an intermediate condition," between "the dominion of Reason through mere Instinct, and the dominion of the same Reason through Freedom"—the "Consciousness or Science of Reason." Here Reason is but half-conscious of the laws of its activity, and refers the feeling of compulsion to something outside itself, to authoritarian and dogmatic systems. In the third age, however, the knowledge of the arbitrary character of much external authority becomes dominant, and Reason as instinct is liberated. Having now become self-conscious, Reason rebels against all external control, and individualism becomes rife. This third age is the "age of completed sinfulness," of empty freedom, "common sense," utilitarianism, wit and ridicule, "mysticism" and sham spiritualisms. In the fourth age, however, Reason discovers that the laws of its own nature are universal and not individual laws, reasoned for universal ends. This is the epoch of Reason as Science (or Knowledge). The fifth, and last, age is that of "completed justification," in which Humanity builds, with a more unerring hand and on the rational ends perceived in the previous age, the art of life. Reason as art is the feature of this final period.[51]

Before we note in detail the surprising agreement between Carlyle and Fichte on "the Third Age," or the "age of the Philosophes," it is necessary to note first that Fichte's five-fold historical plan is fundamentally two-fold.[52] Fichte's five-fold classification is but an elaboration upon the shorter statement which precedes the full discussion. The shorter passage is as follows:

". . . The Life of Mankind on Earth divides itself,
according to the fundamental Idea which we have laid
down, into two principal Epochs or Ages:—the one, in
which the Race exists and lives without as yet having
ordered its relations with Freedom according to Reason;
and the other, in which this Voluntary and Reasonable
arrangement has been brought about." [*i.e.*, Ages 1-3
and 4-5.][53]

It is evident that Carlyle's two-fold plan corresponds roughly
with the first three ages of Fichte's five-fold division; and
that for Carlyle the rhythm of history was not, as for Fichte,
between blind instinct and supremely ordered and self-direct-
ing Reason, but between Fichte's first period and his third.
Carlyle's second period, the epoch of unbelief, is lost between
the two poles of Fichte's two-fold division. Here, again, is
evidence that, in so far as he studied the *Grundzüge*, he
practiced his usual eclecticism. It is sufficient to note here
that Carlyle's general notion of the rhythm of history may
very reasonably have had a Fichtean background.

In Novalis, something of the same scheme is formulated
in terms of the history of thought. Carlyle quotes the passage at length in his essay.[54] According to Novalis, "the
rude intuitive Poet," as distinguished from the "rude discursive Thinker, . . . hates rules and fixed form . . . all is
animate, no law; wilfulness and wonder everywhere. He
is merely dynamical." In the second stage, however, the
extremes of thought in the first stage conflict, and "misunderstanding begins." The result is the rise of "Eclectic Philosophers." The most popular philosophy is that which is
the most limited, the most concrete, that which "occupies itself
wholly with the actual, present world, in the strictest sense."
The philosophers of this age look, as did Voltaire and Hume,
with condescension upon the "visionary enthusiasm" of the
earlier thinkers, "which they say is absurd, even to insanity."
This is Fichte's "Third Age," the *Aufklärung*, the age of

Reason, which disdained most previous ages as "barbarous"
and "dark." Novalis now contrasts the thinkers of the two
epochs:

> "The early philosophers 'set out from the Absolute;
> whilst the Eclectic and limited sort are essentially at
> variance; and agree only in what is deduced.   The
> former are infinite but uniform, the latter bounded but
> multiform; the former have genius, the latter talent;
> those have Ideas, these have knacks (*Handgriffe*); those
> are heads without hands, these hands without heads.' "

The third and final stage, in Novalis's scheme, is that of the
Artist, "who can be at once implement and genius," who can
unite the conflicting elements in some common principle.
For Carlyle, who confessed to "wringing a significance out
of these mysterious words,"[55] this interpretation seems to
have shed a certain amount of light. If he could not follow
Novalis's intricate, vague, and ambiguous account, he could
at least discern, he thought, the lineaments of the first and
second ages of English thought as extending "from Duns
Scotus to Dugald Stewart." He was also apparently struck
with the need of reconciliation between undirected dynamic
thought and unbridled mechanical thought. Of the two,
however, the first was the closer to reality. We have noted
Novalis's outline here at some length to provide a view of
the background of Carlyle's belief about positive and negative epochs. Aside from Goethe's doctrine, we thus find a
number of other attempts which must have familiarized
Carlyle with the act of thinking of history in terms of periodical rhythm.

The well-known passage in Goethe, which supplied Carlyle
with both the doctrine and the terms, is one which, like others
which Carlyle admired and appropriated, occurs in a relatively
obscure place—in one of the *Notes* to the *West-Oestlicher
Divan*. Carlyle quotes the passage in *Diderot*, in connection
with his statement that "French Philosophism will dwindle

into the thinnest of fractions, or vanish into nonentity," when
viewed from "Time at large":

> " 'The special, sole and deepest theme of the World's
> and Man's History,' says the Thinker of our time,
> 'whereto all other themes are subordinated, remains the
> Conflict of Unbelief and Belief. All epochs wherein
> Belief prevails, under what form it may, are splendid,
> heart-elevating, fruitful for contemporaries and pos-
> terity. All epochs, on the contrary, wherein Unbelief,
> under what form soever, maintains its sorry victory,
> should they even for a moment glitter with a sham
> splendour, vanish from the eyes of posterity; because
> no one chooses to burden himself with study of the
> unfruitful.' "[56]

Goethe's words are as follows:

> "Das eigentliche einzige und tiefste Thema der Welt-
> und Menschengeschichte, dem alle übrigen unter-
> geordnet sind, bleibt *der Konflikt des Unglaubens und
> Glaubens*. Alle Epochen, in welchen der Glaube
> herrscht, unter welcher Gestalt er auch wolle, sind
> glänzend, herzerheben und fruchtbar für Mitwelt und
> Nachwelt. All Epochen dagegen, in welchen der
> Unglaube, in welcher Form es sei, einen kümmerlichen
> Sieg behauptet, und wenn sie auch einen Augenblick mit
> einem Scheinglanze prahlen sollten, verschwinden vor
> der Nachwelt, weil sich niemand gern mit Erkenntnis
> des Unfruchtbaren abquälen mag."[57]

Goethe's idea in this passage was, of course, of a piece with
the general point of view which he offered Carlyle; just as
he offered a dynamic interpretation of Nature, he also presented a dynamic view of history. For them both, the faith
which makes an epoch great and productive is faith taken
in its widest sense: it is the deep, unconscious, creative
energy in man which, taken at its bloom, best expresses itself
in religious forms. Thus history takes on a less profane, and
a more sacred, significance: "as in long-drawn systole and
long-drawn diastole, must the period of Faith alternate with

the period of Denial; must the vernal growth, the summer luxuriance of all Opinions, Spiritual Representations and Creations, be followed by, and again follow, the autumnal decay, the winter dissolution."[58]

In all these theories, there is the thought, expressed or implied, that whatever survives in the historical ordeal is good, that nothing good is ever lost. It is here, in these general conceptions of history rather than in any more specific sources, that we find the German background for Carlyle's doctrine that Might makes Right. It is not necessary to assume that such works as Fichte's *Staatslehre* or the *Geschlossene Handelsstaat* provided, in their treatment of specific social and political ideas, a basis for the doctrine which, in its unfortunate ambiguity, gave such a sinister turn to much of Carlyle's social philosophy. That the test of a historical phenomenon was its ability to survive, is of course implied in Schiller's remark that the world's history is the world's judgment.[59]   Goethe himself maintained that "at the judgment-seat of the God of Nations, it is not asked, Whether this is the best, the most excellent nation, but whether it lasts, whether it has continued."[60]   It is assumed, however, that what has enabled a nation to survive is the good it embodies; it is thus that nothing good is ever lost.[61] The common notion that Carlyle believed Might to be Right by virtue merely of its triumph neglects to take into account the fact that Carlyle made the reservation that Might must first be Right in order to "*make*" Right.[62]   At any rate, the conception does not have for Carlyle, so far as can be determined, any more specific German source than that which we have indicated.

6. THE HISTORIAN: *"Glück ist der divinatorische Instinkt."*[63]

If Carlyle was unable to follow Fichte in an *a priori* interpretation of history, he had less difficulty, we may be sure, in agreeing with several of Novalis's remarks about the equipment of the historian. Like Schiller, Novalis demanded that the historian be also something of a philosopher, since history itself has "a philosophical side," and is at bottom "applied morality and religion (*angewandte Moral und Religion*)."[64] In the narration and interpretation of historical event, the historian, says Novalis, must employ "the human, prophetic gaze (*der menschlich prophetische Blick*)" and the "divinatory instinct (*der divinatorische Instinkt*)."[65] There is little fundamental difference, as one can readily see, between history as "applied morality and religion" and history as "philosophy teaching by experience." Nor does Carlyle's practice as a historian fall far below Novalis's ideal of "prophetic" and "divinatory" insight. How far Carlyle actually attempted to fulfill these requirements, and how far his historical method was simply his own, it is impossible to say; but certainly no knowledge of his work as a historian is complete without a realization that in Novalis, for whom Carlyle had the greatest admiration, he could have found a number of *pensées* illuminative of the field to which he was to devote so many years of his life.[66]

Nor could he have been wholly unaware, in his early years of German reading, that there were suggestive passages on the art of history in Schelling's *Methode des akademischen Studiums*. He very probably observed that Schelling, like Schiller, regarded history as properly resembling tragedy.[67] The materials of history, according to Schelling, should be handled like the materials of art, that is, as the record of man's realization of the ideal through the proper employment of the actual.[68] While there should be no sacrifice of factual truth, the aim of the historian should be the revelation of events organically developing out of each other, and of the totality as forming a unity, synthesized ideally according to some philosophic principle: "In such a presentation history cannot fail to produce the impression of the greatest and most amazing Drama, which only an infinite Spirit could

compose."[69]   Thus history is placed in the same rank as art;
it represents, like tragedy, the identity of necessity and
freedom—the working of a free will with the materials which
symbolize its activity, the *union of freedom and destiny*.
Schelling goes further, however, and points out that since
this may also be said of philosophy and religion, another
and more differentiating feature must be found.   One should
seek, he maintains, such a union of freedom and destiny as
will give, not the ideal appearance of religious truth, but the
appearance of concrete actuality.   To do this, the historian
must conceive the great fact of identity, not as an object of
Reason—ideal and perfect—but as an immediate and visible
object of the senses, in short, as clearly perceptible destiny.
In other words, in so far as history deals with what has
actually happened, it is the business of the historian to
present facts as the embodiment of what happened of necessity.   His task is to show us the union of freedom and
destiny from the point of view of the latter, in that historical
events present to our view the accomplished expression of
the workings of the "pervading themes"[70] in historical
phenomena.

Schelling further points out some of the qualifications of
the historian.   He should be rich in experience, and learned
in the affairs of the world.   His style may justly follow, in
some degree, the great models of antiquity, and may borrow
effects from epic and tragedy.[71]   He is not to waste his
energies on the unknown or obscure dawn of history, but
is to shape the known materials according a "concentric
method": "Events should gravitate around a common central
point."[72]   This is essentially Schiller's doctrine: that the
historian should stand high above his data, surveying his
field, interpreting his materials according to a central philosophy of history, and setting forth his results in a style
recalling the sublimities of the epic or tragedy.

How far all these theories concerning history throw light
upon Carlyle may be judged by anyone who has examined

Carlyle's actual practice. What Professor Lehman has called "the epic temper of Carlyle's mind"[73] found a congenial atmosphere in the theories of Fichte, Schiller, and Schelling. In them Carlyle found history conceived on a grand—a cosmic—scale, as the indubitable manifestation of God; they suggested the progressive unfolding of a divine plan in a series of epochs of varying degrees of faith; they exalted the artist-philosopher-prophet-historian above the artisan-scholar-chronicler of events, and declared the superiority of insight and imagination over the uninspired veracity of Dryasdust; they stressed the dynamic, believing, and creative character of great ages of the past, in contrast with the mechanical, unbelieving, uncreative, and frivolous character of recent epochs; they demanded a historical style in keeping with the exalted point of view which their historian should maintain, a style capable of sublimity, and characterised by concreteness, vivid suggestion, philosophical depth, and artistic flexibility; they viewed history as the grand spectacle of man's grappling with opposing matter, as the union of his free act and his inevitable destiny, as a vast cosmic drama in which the moral realities involved found their ultimate expression and justification. Though these elements in the German philosophies of history should not be pushed too far in an attempt to prove a specific influence, it is impossible to conclude that their expression in the books with which Carlyle was familiar cannot have had some effect upon his attitude toward history.

Among the writers whom we have just studied, Fichte and Novalis developed one phase of their theory which had a strong appeal for Carlyle: they both believed in the transcendent significance of the great man. In Fichte's *Über das Wesen des Gelehrten*, in the *Grundzüge des gegenwärtigen Zeitalters*, and in certain of Novalis's *Fragmente*, Carlyle found the essential elements for a theory of the Hero.

CHAPTER VII

CARLYLE AND HEROES

1. THE QUESTION OF SOURCES

Any discussion of Carlyle's theory of the hero must take into account the fact that hero-worship was a native element in Carlyle's nature. Long before he had read any German account of the "genius" or the *Gelehrter*, he had projected a work which, had it ever been written, might have manifested the same fundamental attitude as that expressed in *Heroes and Hero-Worship*. In 1822 he wrote to his brother Alick that he was planning a book to be entitled "Essay on the Civil Wars [and] the Commonwealth of England." It was not to be a history of that period, he adds, but rather an attempt

> "to exhibit, if I can, some features of the national character as it was then displayed, supporting my remarks by mental portraits, drawn with my best ability, of Cromwell, Laud, George Fox, Milton, Hyde, etc., the most distinguished of the actors in that great scene. I may, of course, intersperse the work of delineation with all the ideas which I can gather from any point of the universe."[1]

These sentences, like many others in Carlyle's works and correspondence, remind us of how largely his interest in history was biographical. He brought to his study of German ideas on great men an already developing point of view, a readiness to exalt men above forces, the leader above the mass, excellence above mediocrity. They point also to Carlyle's early interest in history in terms of "the most distinguished actors" as interpreted by a set of ideas gathered "from any point of the universe." Great men and their significance in world-history, elucidated by applying a kind of philosophy of history—this subject had already been before Carlyle's mind when he encountered the German doctrines which were to shape and define his task. What he found in those doctrines was, again, as it was in the domain of religious and philosophical ideas, not so much a body of thought as a form for the thought which he had already in an inarticulate fashion arrived at, himself.

Besides the sources of the hero-theory which lay in Carlyle himself, we must remember the importance and extent of certain other sources: the "original genius" of the eighteenth century; Hume's theory of the deification of "mortals, superior in power, courage, or understanding"; the Romantic Rebels glorified in the work and the characters of Shelley and Byron. Those who are interested in the relative claims of these sources may turn to Professor Lehman's able study of the subject as a whole.[2] We are concerned here with the German background of the theory, so far as it related to Carlyle's purposes.

As was true of Carlyle's relation to the Germans regarding ideas on history, his treatment of the hero takes us to more than one writer. That Fichte contributed most to Carlyle's theory is too well known to need repeating. Yet it must not be forgotten that Carlyle no doubt was considerably influenced in his theory by the example of Goethe as a hero in modern times. We shall note later, in addition, that Goethe supplied, in the *Epigramme aus Venedig*, a brief but striking statement of certain elements of the theory; and that Schiller, too, had pertinent things to say to Carlyle. If Fichte spoke most persuasively to Carlyle, it was because he presented a deliberate and definitely stated theory. Carlyle had become conscious of the significance of the literary man in the modern world, of the vital need of creative men of action, of the great rôle played by the spiritual leaders of the past. All great men seemed to him to be made of the same stuff, to be called from the same sphere of Reality, and to be commissioned in the service of man. Goethe embodied this thought; Fichte conceptualized it; Novalis and Schiller added illuminating phrases; and Carlyle himself, with his wide knowledge of history, his eagerness to discern revelation in the world of fact, and his natural reverence for greatness, rounded out a doctrine which became the most popular of his teachings.

2. THE HERO AS REVELATION: *"So ist er denn die unmittelbarste Erscheinung Gottes in der Welt."*[3]

The two works of Fichte which presented Carlyle with virtually all the ingredients for a theory of the hero are, of course, *Über das Wesen des Gelehrten* and *Die Grundzüge des gegenwärtigen Zeitalters.* In the latter work, the great man is given almost precisely the position and significance assigned to him by Carlyle: he is the only bearer of good to men; or, as Carlyle would say, "the history of what man has accomplished in this world is at bottom the History of the Great Men who have worked here."[4] This exclusive attribution of man's progress to the efforts of great men is paralleled most strikingly in the following passage from Fichte:

> "Everything great and good upon which our present existence rests, from which it has proceeded, and on the supposition of which alone our Age can order itself in the way it actually does, has an existence only because noble and powerful men have resigned all the enjoyments of life for the sake of Ideas . . . They subdued to their Idea of what *ought to be,* races by whom they were on that account hated and feared . . . It was Heroes, who had left their Age far behind them, giants among surrounding men in material and spiritual power . . ."[5]

It is noteworthy that in the context to this passage, Fichte uses *Heroen* and *Helden* interchangeably, and in much the same fashion as Carlyle, namely, as designating not adventurers and exploiters but leaders and benefactors of the race. They are the champions in whom the spirit of the Time has most gloriously revealed itself :

> "Who rules in this camp, and leads on its armies [in pursuit of "True Knowledge"] ?—'Clearly,' it will be answered, 'the Heroes of the Age; the champions in whom the Spirit of the Time has most gloriously revealed itself.' "[6]

A clearer and more adequate expression of the Hero as the revelation of the Divine Idea occurs in *Das Wesen des Gelehrten*.   It is from this work that Carlyle quotes long passages in *The State of German Literature* and in *Heroes*. His favorite passage is one in Fichte's first Lecture, *Plan des Ganzen*.   The author has maintained that there are among men some individuals who have wholly or in part attained, through the "Learned Culture" of the age, to the possession of a portion of the "Divine Idea of the World," and that it is upon them that the progressive development of the Idea devolves, through the communication of that knowledge to others.   There are, however, two different notions of the Scholar : according to appearance or mere intention, and according to truth.   Fichte elaborates this distinction : either the Scholar has "actually laid hold of the whole Divine Idea in so far as it is attainable by man," and is thus a Finished Scholar, or he as yet succeeds only in attaining knowledge of a portion of the Idea, and is thus a Progressive Scholar. If, however, he should strive only after the outward form, as does the average person, then he is a Bungler (*ein Stümper*).   If, again, he makes no effort whatever, he is, properly speaking, Nothing (*gar Nichts*).[7] The only positive men, says Fichte, are those who seek to reveal the Idea : they are the Heroes, the Leaders, the Sages,[8] who bring order out of chaos, establish right and justice, exalt the ideals of religion and morality.

Such a revelation, in any specific age, must await the "God-inspired man"; otherwise the Idea will fail to manifest itself. This doctrine, so well known as set forth by Carlyle, namely, that it is our duty to find ourselves a hero, appears briefly suggested by Fichte in the following sentence: "The original Divine Idea of any particular point of time remains for the most part unexpressed, until the God-inspired man appears and declares it."[9] His genius is nothing more than the effort of the Idea to assume a definite form: "Das natürliche Talent, oder das Genie ist ja nichts weiter, als der Trieb der Idee, sich zu gestalten."[10] His work is thus "the most direct manifestation of God in the world":

> "In the life of the Divine Men the Godhead is manifest in the flesh, reveals itself to immediate vision, and is perceptible even to outward sense. In their life the unchangeableness of God manifests itself in the firmness and intrepidity of human will which no power can force from its destined path. In it the essential light of the Divinity manifests itself in human comprehension of all finite things in the One which endures forever. In it the energy of God reveals itself, not in directly surrounding the Human Race with happiness—which is not its object—but in ordering, elevating, and ennobling it. A God-like life is the most decisive proof which man can give of the being of a God."[11]

For Fichte, then, the Scholar is the man who has so mastered the Learned Culture of his age that he can disclose the Divine Idea to mankind, either through direct teaching or through action and leadership. In him the Idea "lives and loves itself" . . . "This man loves the Idea, and lives in the Idea . . . and his person is but the sensible manifestation of this existence of the Idea . . . . In the True Scholar the Idea has acquired a personal existence which has entirely superseded his own . . ."[12]

On the whole, in Fichte's *Das Wesen des Gelehrten,* and in a lesser degree in *Die Grundzüge,* we have a good deal of

the general background for Carlyle's theory. For him, as
for Fichte, the history of the world is the history of great
men:

> "They were the leaders of men . . . the modellers,
> patterns, and in a wide sense creators, of whatsoever
> the general mass of men contrived to do or to attain . . .
> The great man [is a] free force direct out of God's own
> hand . . . actually sent down from the skies with a God's-
> message to us . . . A messenger he, sent from the Infinite
> Unknown with tidings to us . . . [He] penetrates into
> the sacred mystery of the Universe . . . [into] 'the
> Divine Idea of the World.' "[13]

3. THE QUALITIES OF THE HERO: *"Was der göttliche Mensch thut, das ist göttlich."*[14]

Carlyle was certain that all types of great men are fundamentally of the same superior material, that "at bottom, the
Great Man . . . . is ever the same kind of thing: Odin,
Luther, Johnson, Burns . . . I have no notion of a truly
great man that could not be *all* sorts of men."[15] The first
quality, therefore, which goes to the making of a hero is
what has been called "the mutability of the hero stuff."[16]
In Fichte the notion is phrased in various ways. The Idea
struggles irresistibly onward to direct activity, extinguishing
the Hero's personal life in that of the Idea as it seeks the
most effective embodiment at a particular time. Thus, says
Fichte, in *Die Grundzüge*, he becomes Artist or Hero, Man
of Science or Prophet.[17] Or again, as in *Das Wesen des
Gelehrten*, Fichte may declare:

> "The impulse which shows itself in man and urges
> him onward, will always exhibit itself as an impulse
> towards some particular side of the one indivisible Idea;
> or, as we may express it, after the investigations of our
> last lecture, without fear of being misunderstood,—as
> an impulse towards one particular idea in the sphere
> of all possible ideas; or if we give to this impulse the

name of Genius, then Genius will always appear as a *specific* Genius, for philosophy, poetry, natural science, legislation, or the like . . ."[18]

The specific manifestation of the Hero's powers will thus be determined by the needs of the age, by the materials offered him in the individualization of what at bottom is his general and infinitely elastic nature. In Fichte's general doctrine, as we shall have occasion to note, the Hero's individuality is even less stressed than in Carlyle's treatment.

More important, perhaps, are the other and less general characteristics of the Great Man. Primary and all-embracing, say Carlyle and Fichte, is the virtue of Integrity, or what Carlyle means when he writes, "I should say *sincerity*, a deep, great, genuine sincerity, is the first characteristic of all men in any way heroic."[19] Fichte uses the term *Rechtschaffenheit*. This virtue leads to another and highly individual feature of Fichte's Scholar and Carlyle's Hero: Insight. What in the Hero is the "seeing eye," "seeing through the shows of things," is in the Scholar the ability to pierce onward to "the Unknown"—"nach diesem Unbekannten wird er unaufhörlich hingezogen."[20] On the Ruler in particular Fichte is explicit that the Scholar penetrates behind the show of things to the hidden Reality: "The Ruler . . . looks beyond that which [is] *in the actual world*, to that which [is] *in the Divine Idea*—to that which therefore . . . ought to be."[21] Insight, in the minds of both thinkers is *moral* insight,[22] a quality which characterizes the ruler as much as the priest. It obviously defines the goal of the leader as one towards which man's struggles are directed in a moral and religious, rather than in an exclusively political or economic, progress toward a fuller, spiritual life. We have here, in the qualities of sincerity and insight, another intimation of what it was that prevented Carlyle from ranking Napoleon with the highest leaders of the past.[23]

The Hero is also gifted with the "talent for silence";

and since he acts rather than speaks or speculates, he is
relatively unconscious of the extent of his powers, and is at
bottom a mystery to himself. Of the Scholar, Fichte says,
"The Idea alone moves him . . . Until it speaks, he too is
silent,—he has no voice but for it."[24] Any tendency toward
self-contemplation or self-flattery is the "sure sign of the
absence of true Genius; whilst forgetfulness of self in the
object pursued, entire devotion to that object, and inability
to entertain any thought of self in its presence, are the
inseparable accompaniments of true Genius . . . Genius knows
least of all about itself."[25] This conception of genius as
unselfconscious, a "secret to itself," is of course a doctrine
of great antiquity. But it is probable that it was German
writers, rather than any others, who impressed the doctrine
deeply upon Carlyle's mind. He found it elaborated, for
instance, in Schiller, as we note in his biography of that
poet:

> " 'The character of child-like simplicity,' he has him-
> self observed, 'which genius impresses on its works, it
> shows also in its private life and manners. It is bashful,
> for nature is ever so; but it is not prudish, for only
> corruption is prudish. It is clear-sighted, for nature can
> never be the contrary; but it is not cunning, for this
> only art can be. It is faithful to its character and incli-
> nations; but not so much because it is directed by
> principles, as because after all vibrations nature con-
> stantly reverts to her original position, constantly
> renews her primitive demand. It is modest, nay timid,
> for genius is always a secret to itself; but it is not
> anxious, for it knows not the dangers of the way which
> it travels. Of the private habits of the persons who
> have been peculiarly distinguished by their genius, our
> information is small; but the little that has been
> recorded for us of the chief of them,—of Sophocles,
> Archimedes, Hippocrates; and in modern times, of
> Dante and Tasso, of Rafaelle, Albrecht Dürer, Cer-
> vantes, Shakspeare, Fielding, and others,—confirms this
> observation.' Schiller himself confirms it; perhaps

more strongly than most of the examples here adduced. No man ever wore his faculties more meekly, or performed great works with less consciousness of their greatness. Abstracted from the contemplation of himself, his eye was turned upon the objects of his labour, and he pursued them with the eagerness, the entireness, the spontaneous sincerity, of a boy pursuing sport. Hence this 'child-like simplicity,' the last perfection of his other excellencies. His was a mighty spirit unheedful of its might. He walked the earth in calm power: 'the staff of his spear was like a weaver's beam'; but he wielded it like a wand."[26]

Carlyle and Fichte agree also, of course, that the vocation of the great man is *action*: "Even after the manifestation of Genius," writes Fichte, "Industry is requisite . . . . Where Genius is really present, Industry spontaneously appears."[27] "Man shall *be* and *do* something; his temporal life shall leave behind it in the spiritual world an imperishable and eternal result."[28] Whatever may be the impulse whereby the Divine Idea moves the great man, it inevitably issues in a divine Deed: "All his thoughts and impulses will of themselves take the most direct way to this end; whatever he does, prompted by this thought, is good and right, and must assuredly prosper, for it is an immediately *divine* act" (*denn es ist selbst unmittelbar göttliche That*).[29] And this act, since it is a revelation of the Divine Idea and is fundamentally creative, is an act of order; the hero conceives the whole, and seeks ever to realize the steps toward a greater totality. In Carlyle's words, this means that the great man "is here to make what is disorderly, chaotic, into a thing ruled, regular. He is the missionary of Order. Is not all work of man in this world *a making of order*?"[30] For Fichte, the Scholar, and above all the Ruler, "never loses sight of the Whole":

"The Ruler possesses, in the first place, a living and comprehensive Idea of that relation of human life which he undertakes to superintend;—he knows what is its essential nature, meaning, and purpose . . . He knows the Whole of which that form is a part . . . His eye always combines the part with the Whole . . ."[31]

Yet, says Fichte, this divine calling is not to be desecrated by application to base ends. And the safeguard of the Scholar's actions, and of their high character, is the virtue of Reverence; it will redeem from vulgarity and popular appeal the hero's genuine "impulse to action, to sway the minds of men": for "what," asks Fichte, "is more noble than the deepest reverence for the Holy, and disdain and abnegation of everything vulgar and opposed to it?"[32] This is especially true of the Ruler. Since, as we have seen, he looks beyond the actual world to the Divine Idea, and seeks to shape the human race according to what "ought to be,"

> "he is thus filled with reverence for a Race called to so high a destiny. Love is not required of him; nay if you think deeper of it, it is even a kind of arrogance for a Ruler to presume to *love* the whole Human Race, or even his own nation,—to assure it of his love, and as it were, make it dependent on his kindness. A Ruler such as we have described is free from such presumption: his reverence for humanity, as the image and protected child of God, does more than overpower it."[33]

Fichte's elaboration upon the characteristics of the Scholar as Ruler remind us that for Carlyle, too, the "Hero as King" was of transcendent importance: "The commander over men . . . may be reckoned the most important of Great Men. He is practically the summary for us of *all* the various figures of Heroism."[34] It is almost as if Carlyle were thinking, as he wrote these lines, of Fichte's eighth lecture, *Vom Regenten*, which, in a sense, sums up all the virtues of the Scholar as they have appeared in various forms. We have already noted a few of the virtues specifically attributed by Fichte to the Scholar as Ruler: silence, reverence, consciousness of the Whole. Fichte is more emphatic than Carlyle on the superior degree to which the Ruler manifests the divine, as contrasted with the Poet, the Prophet, the Literary Man. The Ruler is indeed "the most direct manifestation of God in the world."[35] It is the business of Rulers "to see that the conviction of the Divine Existence shall never perish and disappear from among men," and to labor unceasingly "as the highest disposers of human affairs."[36] For, says Fichte, carrying his thought to its logical conclusion, "in their works do we see God face to face, and need no other proof :— God is, we will say,—for they are, and He in them."[37] These are, of course, strong words, far stronger than Carlyle, with the thought of Jesus in his mind, was able wholly to accept. Yet on the other virtues of the Ruler there is complete agreement. For both, the ruler is to shun fame and happiness as his ideal, "worin auch das göttliche Wirken nicht besteht," and to "obtain Blessedness" through a religious conception of his mission :

> "Every man needs Religion,—every man may acquire it,—and with it every man may obtain Blessedness ;— most of all, as we have seen above, does the Ruler need it. Unless he clothe his calling in the light of Religion, he can never pursue it with a good conscience."[38]

In the *Grundzüge*, Fichte goes further in his delineation of the ideal leader. The wise, he says in this work, are to govern the foolish; the civilized must rule the barbarous, if Right is to be law. The Greeks realized the profound urgency of this truth, until in Alexander "it became a living flame." It is beside the mark, says Fichte, to point to the thousands who fell around him, or to cite his early death; for after realizing the Idea, what was there greater for him than death?[39] There is certainly enough here to suggest the probable strengthening source for Carlyle's tendency to condone the ruthlessness of the great man—to exonerate Frederick the Great in Silesia, or Cromwell in Ireland. It all depended upon one's judgment as to which side possessed the "wisdom," or whether the unwisdom of the foolish was sufficiently great to warrant the deeds of Cromwell or Frederick. And not a little of the doctrine of "Might makes right," in its more unpopular sense, can be discerned in the implications of Fichte's passage. On the whole, Carlyle and Fichte agree fairly closely on the nature and the mission of the Hero as Ruler.

But that Carlyle was not indebted to Fichte alone for this attitude toward the relative positions of the ruler and the ruled, is evident from his translation, in his essay on *Goethe's Works*, of certain of the *Venetian Epigrams*:[40]

> To this stithy I liken the land, the hammer its ruler,
> And the people that plate, beaten between them that writhes:
> Woe to the plate, when nothing but wilful bruises on bruises
> Hit it at random; and made, cometh no Kettle to view!

Goethe thought of the ruler as in unmistakable authority. On the other hand, the ruler is to be, in a sense, the servant of the mass. In spite of the irony implicit in the following epigram, we note Goethe's ideal of human service as one of the requisites for true kingship:

> No Apostle-of-Liberty much to my heart ever found I;
> License, each for himself, this was at bottom their want.
> Liberator of many! first dare to be Servant of many:
> What a business is that, wouldst thou know it, go try!

On the whole, Carlyle found support in both Fichte and Goethe for his conviction that the Many need rulers rather than liberty.

Turning to the ideal of the Literary Man, we find Carlyle and Fichte again in agreement. For both of them, "Literature ... is an 'apocalypse of Nature,' ... a 'continuous revelation' of the God-like in the Terrestrial and Common."[41] In Fichte this thought occurs as follows: "The Author must embody the Idea: *die Idee muss selber reden, nicht der Schriftsteller.*[42]   To arrive at the concept of "the priesthood" of writers,[43] however, Carlyle seems to have combined Fichte's remarks about the Scholar as Author and the Scholar as Teacher. It is true, of course, that Fichte requires the Teacher to be capable of being also an excellent author.[44] It is of the Teacher, however, that Fichte uses the actual term "priest," in speaking of "ein Priester der Wissenschaft," a priest of what Fichte's translator calls "the sacred things of Knowledge" (*der Heiliges*).[45]   The sacredness of the Literary Man's calling is emphasized by Fichte in holding that the writer "works for eternity."[46]   On other and minor points there is further agreement: on the great writers as constituting a Republic of Letters; on Literary Men as the supreme moulders of an age; on the evils consequent on the invention of printing and the habit of reading; on the abuses of bookselling and of book-reviewing.[47]

These numerous agreements make it clear that Carlyle's acknowledgment was hardly as great as his borrowing. In spite of what we know of Carlyle's early and native interest in great men, it would be interesting to speculate on what his doctrine of Heroes would have been had Fichte never written *Über das Wesen des Gelehrten* and *Die Grundzüge des gegenwärtigen Zeitalters.*

4. Average Men: *"Geborne ordinäre Menschen."*[48]

Though Carlyle never conceived of the average man with quite the severity indulged in occasionally by Fichte, and even by Novalis, we are justified in expecting a German background for his belief that the great mass of mankind owed nothing but obedience and reverence to their true rulers. It was Novalis who spoke of "born average men." For Fichte, the uninspired man—any one without a living conception of the Divine Idea—was a "Hodman," for whom there was nothing but "punctual obedience," the "careful

avoidance of all independent thought," and the confiding of
all direction of his occupations to other and superior men.[49]
Both Fichte and Carlyle declare, as we have seen, that all
that mankind is and enjoys has been the work of a few
"noble and powerful men." Thus absolute obedience to the
righteous ruler is explicitly demanded by Fichte in the
eighth lecture of his *Über das Wesen.* The whole tendency
of Fichte's doctrine of the *Gelehrten,* and as interpreted by
Carlyle, involved a definite and rigid subordination of the
average man to his superior.

On the other hand, Carlyle's conception of the reverence
due to other men, as men, is not Fichtean. The unmistakable source here is the "reverence" passage in the *Wanderjahre.* But the debt is also to Novalis; Carlyle noted the
mystic's words:

> "There is but one Temple in the World; and that is
> the Body of Man. Nothing is holier than this high
> form. Bending before men is a reverence done to this
> Revelation in the Flesh. We touch Heaven, when we
> lay our hand on a human body."[50]

If, in Carlyle's opinion, the average man lacks the divinatory
instinct of the Hero, he is nevertheless, by his very being,
an evidence of what that instinct sought to attain. It was
only by his willing self-subordination to the leader that
revelation through an average man could be achieved.
What Carlyle wanted left unspoiled, unobliterated, was the
old spiritual bond between master and servant, between the
ruler and the ruled. Fichte had the same sense of the oneness of human relationships, but he never looked at common
men with that mystic appreciation of their spiritual significance which was vouchsafed to Novalis and Carlyle. For
Fichte, mankind was one, because it had originally been
unindividualized, had once been at one with the Divine Idea;
and now the individual was to seek constantly to be reab-
sorbed in the One. Only great men could make this clear;

and the average man was to regard himself as divine only in so far as he partook of that universal struggle for re-absorption into the primal unity of the Idea. Indeed he can do little either to hasten or retard that infinite process:

> "Time rolls on in the steadfast course marked out for it from eternity, and individual effort can neither hasten nor retard its progress. Only the coöperation of all, and especially of the indwelling Eternal Spirit of Ages and of Worlds, may promote it."[51]

For Carlyle the average man was far less a mere instrument in a metaphysical revelation, and far more a free, responsible agent (in the old puritan sense) than for Fichte. He was likewise of greater social importance. Carlyle's divergence from Fichte, in respect to the "born average man," leads us to other points of difference.

5. CARLYLE'S DEPARTURES FROM FICHTE

Carlyle's theory of the Hero was in no sense a systematic doctrine. But its characteristic features will perhaps become clearer if we consider for a moment wherein he departed from Fichte's theory.

It is obvious that Carlyle's Hero is essentially changed to fit the world which he fashioned for himself by means of accommodating certain German theories to his invincible puritanism. Though his Hero, like Fichte's Scholar, looks through Appearance to Reality, he sees an essentially different object. Fichte's Appearance is a developing one, aiming at an ultimate realization of the only reality, the Divine Idea, which is latent in that Appearance. Carlyle's Appearance is not, in this sense, a development; it is a Garment. Though Carlyle at times writes as if nature were travailing to produce the ideal, as if our deeds when sowed in time would be reaped in a fundamentally developing world, he thinks more frequently in terms of God and the Vesture. His Hero thus is simply a man looking with superior spiritual insight through the "show of things" into the underlying realm of spiritual truth. The Hero, therefore, "possesses insight, whereas the Scholar has foresight."[52]   Nor does Carlyle's Hero need the Learned Culture of his Age before he can manifest Reality to less gifted men. His message is not a rational deduction. It is spiritual, and the Hero possesses insight by his very nature.

And this suggests a further difference. Carlyle translates *Gelehrter* as Literary Man, intimating that the whole of Fichte's lectures on the Scholar dealt with the man of letters. Thus Carlyle departs from Fichte when, in *The State of German Literature*, he asserts that "Literary Men are the appointed interpreters of this Divine Idea."[53]   In Fichte, not merely the Scholar as Author but *all* those who have seized the significance of the Idea are so appointed. This "false emphasis on one subdivision of a class and the omission of the larger group which gives it significance" suggests that Carlyle never closely studied the whole of Fichte's book. Thus if limited in his acqaintance with Fichte's doctrine, he would naturally omit some of the forms which the Scholar might take, as set forth by Fichte, and would have nothing to say about the Hero as Teacher, or as Philosopher. On the other hand he would introduce, as he does, Heroes whom Fichte would have rejected: Odin, Mahomet, Luther, and Knox, men who had no vision of a World Plan such as Fichte had deduced. Their vision was more narrowly religious; their insight, that of simple and discerning souls.[54]

Un-Fichtean also is Carlyle's emphasis on the Hero's character and individuality. In the philosophy of the Divine Idea, the personality of the Scholar is completely absorbed in the Idea; the Scholar seeks to transcend his individual self, to make his will unite with the impersonal Reason of world-development. Though Fichte said that all that men are is the result of the labors of great men, he would never have agreed with Carlyle that history is nothing but biography.

The personal and individual life of Fichte's Scholar had little prominence in universal history, which was greater than, and *other* than, any history of persons. Fichte was more concerned with what the Hero achieved than with what he was : the doer is lost in the deed; the spirit achieved is all. Here appears most strikingly Fichte's deeply metaphysical conception of history and great men, as contrasted with Carlyle's pictorial and psychological attitude. "Hero-worship in Carlyle's sense," remarks Miss Storrs, "would be impossible to Fichte, for his attention was fastened on the purer, and in a sense more elevated, vision of the abstract spiritual force discernible most clearly in great men."[55]

These differences, however, cannot blind us to the striking degree in which Carlyle was able, in spite of his aversion to theoretic discourse, to appropriate so much of the form and substance of Fichte's doctrine. The whole problem of Hero and average man involved an ethical philosophy, and in so far as Carlyle was addressing himself to a world of average men, he developed an ethical doctrine which, in some ways, was a counterpart to his theory of the Hero. We are thus led to examine his final teachings, and their German background, in respect to morality and ethics.

CHAPTER VIII

CARLYLE AND THE PROBLEM OF LIFE

1. *"All men make up mankind."*[1]

Carlyle's practical ethics, toward which all his thinking ultimately tended, rests upon his conception of the nature of the individual and of society. It is here that the overwhelming debt to Goethe becomes most evident. From *Wilhelm Meister*—especially from the *Wanderjahre*—he derived an ethic of action which finally absorbed all the influences which he received from other German writers. This is not to say, however, that the result was a closely formulated or symmetrical theory of conduct. Carlyle had nothing which one might call a philosophy of the individual, certainly nothing in any degree approximating a psychology. For a well-rounded doctrine which aimed at explaining man to himself, for the sake of such knowledge, Carlyle had almost no use whatever. His approach to the problem of man and society was, so to speak, spiritually pragmatic: he sought to know what man was, by asking what man was capable of performing in the domain of moral aims. His point of view was neither that of the technical philosopher nor that of the psychologist, but that of the inspired moralist. Definitions irked him: he never closely defined his favorite word, *work*. He relied upon the individual's moral intuition to specify the nature and urgency of the "task that lies nearest." To get behind the action, to analyse the nature and meaning of it, to see it in its larger bearings, to fathom it rationally in any profound degree, these were feats for which he felt man was by nature forever cut off from performing. Instead of probing and thinking, or seeking to understand the aim of our actions, we should rely on our moral sense and our need for expressing it.   Knowledge, he seems to say, will come from that.

Carlyle was thus, in a very profound sense, a skeptic. We can never know what we are, whence we came, whither we are going.   We are surrounded by the mysteries of time, space, eternity, and infinity;   and we ourselves are compounded of outward and inward mysteries: "man begins in darkness, ends in darkness;   mystery is everywhere around us and in us."[2]   And it is this deep sense of the mysterious upon which Carlyle's gospel of action is based.   He found this sense of mystery present in a number of German writers who, like him, felt the solution to rest in the ethical deed.   Jean Paul, who was fond of speaking of his "mysterious Me," wrote in *Flower, Fruit, and Thorn Pieces*:

> "There come to us moments of twilight in which it seems as though day and night were in the act of dividing—as if we were in the very process of being created and annihilated . . . and we look at ourselves . . . and ask, 'What is it that thou art, *now*, my *me*!'   When we thus ask ourselves this, there is, beyond ourselves, nothing of great or of firm—everything has turned to an endless cloud of night. . . . Only high up above the cloud shines a resplendence—and that is God;   and far beneath it a minute speck of light—and that is a human 'Me!' "[3]

How Teufelsdröckh first discovered his "Me" is too well known to need recounting.[4]   Carlyle undoubtedly had a similar experience in his first awareness of his own identity.   At any rate, he was certainly attracted to Jean Paul's account of his discovery in the *Wahrheit aus Jean Pauls Leben*, for he translated the whole passage in his second essay on *Richter*:

> "Never shall I forget that inward occurrence, till now narrated to no mortal, wherein I witnessed the birth of my Self-consciousness, of which I can still give the place and time.   One forenoon, I was standing, a very young child, in the outer door, and looking leftward at the

stack of fuel-wood,—when all at once the internal vision, 'I am a ME (*ich bin ein Ich*),' came like a flash from heaven before me, and in gleaming light ever afterwards continued: then had my ME, for the first time, seen itself, and forever. Deceptions of memory are scarcely conceivable here; for, in regard to an event occurring altogether in the veiled Holy-of-Holies of man, and whose novelty alone has given permanence to such every-day recollections accompanying it, no posterior description from another party would have mingled itself with accompanying circumstances at all."[5]

What is most significant about Carlyle's attitude toward the pure awareness of the self is that for him it leads directly, as it did for Jean Paul, to what he thought was an experience of the divine. Thus while man, as man, may be a mystery to himself, he may yet fall back into pure consciousness of the self and touch the divine. For Carlyle this was something like empirical evidence that man is primarily a finite extension of God; and it harmonized with his belief in the essential unreality and paradox discernible in the material side of man.

And it was but natural that such a notion should be central in Carlyle's ethics. It gave significance to all that he thought man was and did; a significance, indeed, beyond all calculating. The doctrine of man as a revelation of the divine came not only through Goethe and Fichte but also through Novalis. As we have seen, the mystic believed man to be *der Messias der Natur*—the creature who, emerging from the infinite, is to "redeem" nature, in so far as man is a part of that realm.[6] Other *Fragmente* expand upon this concept: "every man's life should be a Bible . . . In every man God can appear to me . . . We must seek God among men. In human events, in human thoughts and perceptions the Spirit of Heaven manifests itself most brightly . . ."[7] The old idea of man as the microcosm is curiously woven into the texture of Carlyle's thought. He sometimes prefers to hold, with Novalis, that every man's life should be a leaf in "the great prophetic manuscript Book of Existence"; but, again, he may say plainly that "every mortal is a microcrosm; to himself a *macrocosm*, or Universe large as Nature."[8] And in this he is, of course, supported by Goethe.[9] Man in himself is a paradox and a mystery, says Carlyle; he gains significance and meaning only when viewed from the standpoint of the Infinite, of which he is a partial revelation and epitome.

Thus, inwardly man is a self; but he is also a two-fold self: an earthy or empirical self, and a "divine Me," part of the Idea.[10] But both inwardly and outwardly he is a dynamic revelation. His material body is but the vehicle—always conditioning and sometimes hindering—by which the spirit achieves its ends. To hold with Hume and the Mechanists that the instrument wholly determines or wholly constitutes the self is to deny that inward certainty which bursts on one in the first discovery of one's identity, or which arises from the consciousness of moral freedom. The greatest certainty, however, arises, says Carlyle, in moments of action. And since man acts most fully in a society of selves, it is important to realize the significance of man in relation to man. Indeed, says Carlyle, employing Goethe's words, and remembering Pope, "man is properly the *only* object that interests man": "der Mensch ist dem Menschen das Interessanteste und sollte ihn vielleicht ganz allein interessiren."[11] To understand him requires that we understand society, for there alone is man able to be himself.

But society, like the individual, is essentially mysterious. Of the unfathomable nature of man in his social relations, Fichte had an extremely sensitive consciousness, and may have strengthened Carlyle in his belief that society was a "mystic unfathomable union." For Fichte, at any rate, it was the supersensual Will alone which united men in a bond which was "the greatest mystery of the invisible world, and its fundamental law":

> "This Will unites me with himself; He also unites me with all finite beings like myself, and is the common

mediator between us all. This is the great mystery of
the invisible world, and its fundamental law . . . *the
union, and direct reciprocal action, of many separate
and independent wills* . . . This mutual recognition and
reciprocal action of free beings in this world is per-
fectly inexplicable by the laws of nature or of thought,
and can be explained only through the One in whom
they are united, although to each other they are separate. . . . Only through the common fountain of our
spiritual being do we know each other . . ."[12]

It is something like this that Carlyle apparently has in mind
when he writes that "Society is the standing wonder of our
existence; a true region of the Supernatural; as it were, a
second all-embracing Life . . . [a] mystic Union, Nature's
highest work with man . . . [a] mysterious brotherhood."[13]
Society becomes for him a mysterious brotherhood of mysterious selves. It shows us that man, though naturally self-
centered, is dependent upon society, and lives at his best
among his fellows. Society fundamentally rests, not upon a
basis of cause and effect, or time and space relations, but
upon such an infinite, mysterious, and religious foundation
as loyalty and altruism. Only in the right social life, where
the individual will is adjusted to a supra-individual Will can
the divine be made manifest. That is why Carlyle insisted
that all men are at bottom one, that as Goethe said, "All
men make up mankind," and that our greatest want is
a growing consciousness that society is a single, spiritual
organism: "Gesellschaft bleibt eines wackern Mannes
höchstes Bedürfnis."[14]

In Novalis, the doctrine as held by Fichte and Goethe, that
all men are one and are bound together by a spiritual tie,
became a definitely religious doctrine: "Religion must be
made and created through the union (*Vereinigung*) of more
men." Carlyle was particularly drawn to his insistence upon
the religious basis of society: "Religion, as Novalis hints, *is*
a social thing . . . The action of mind on mind is mystical,

infinite; Religion, worship can hardly (perhaps not at all)
support itself without this aid."[15] "It is in Society," he says
in *Characteristics*, "that Morality begins . . . Religion arises
[and] acquires certainty, continuance, when it is shared-in
by [man's] brother men."[16] And so, not merely in the individual, nor in the collective history of mankind, is the divine
supremely revealed; it is most highly manifested in the
operations of man in society, especially as he engages in
moral *action*. Whatever solution is available, in the mysteries
of human and supra-human realities, will come through the
ethical deed.

Before we can proceed to the specific details of Carlyle's
ethics, however, it is necessary to glance for a moment into
that work of Goethe's which influenced Carlyle's practical
attitude at almost every point. It is necessary to know the
nature of the story of *Wilhelm Meister* and its relation to
Carlyle's problem.

2. CARLYLE AND *Wilhelm Meister*.

Carlyle discovered Goethe at a time when his own capabilities had not clearly disclosed themselves. He had not yet
found his true vocation, and was still trying his hand at verse
and fiction. At the same time, as we have already seen, he
was by turns applying himself to schoolmastering, to the
law, to divinity. Moreover, he had lost his religion, and, in
losing it, had lost his foothold in the world as he saw it.
Throughout this stormy period, he wasted his energies in
false starts. And, to add to his dilemma, his health began
to fail him. Before he could begin, properly speaking, to live,
he felt the need of answering certain very fundamental questions: What was he to believe? Was it possible to believe
on the basis of his father's unquestioning faith? Was belief
possible at all? Granted that he could eventually work his
way to a kind of belief, what, in the meantime, was he to
work at? Had he any genius for poetry?—for fiction?

Should he choose between a life of contemplation and a life of action? Above all, what *was* he—whither had he come? Should he try first to think through this question, and then act; or act first, and derive a philosophy from his experience? These questions appeared to young Carlyle, as to all introspective and thinking adolescents, to be so important as to require an answer before he could take his place in the affairs of the world. Time was passing swiftly; he was largely dependent as yet upon his poverty-stricken father and mother; he was no longer a boy; he was ill; his life seemed pointless and chaotic. Now, let us ask ourselves what moral inspiration or practical guidance the young Carlyle was to find in the story of *Wilhelm Meister's Apprenticeship,* in the light-hearted perversities of Philina, in the mercenary schemes of Serlo as the stage manager for a group of impecunious and disorderly players, in the weirdly romantic story of Mignon and the old Harper, in the languishing piety of the *schöne Seele,* in the fantastic mummery and symbolism of the *Gesellschaft vom Turm*? Even on the more serious and elevated plane of the novel, how was Carlyle to find any personal inspiration from Wilhelm's disquisition on *Hamlet* and the art of the stage, or from the numerous other theoretical topics tossed up by the characters for a fitful and inconclusive discussion?

The answer is that Carlyle realized that, both in the pervading theme of a well-rounded personal development as the salvation of modern man, and in the numerous scattered sentences in which Goethe suddenly opened his mind on the problem of the good life, the novel had meanings that could be detached from the purely aesthetical elements. He had recognized in *Faust* a mind so rich and broad that no work of its creation should be passed over as wholly irrelevant to his problem. Content to let Goethe be himself, but, determined to extract from him only that message which should most closely solve his own dilemma, he studied isolated passages, here a sentence, there a chapter. And in his search, he found Goethe's doctrine, that man must make himself; that morality is a conquest and a growth, proceeding by stages, and amenable to the individual's control; that salvation comes through working in the present and the actual, thus freeing oneself and at the same time fulfilling one's potentialities. He saw, further, that to find one's vocation, to dispel illusions of great abilities, and to work at something definite, was one of Wilhelm's earliest lessons. On the other hand, as we have seen, Carlyle was conscious of the serious short-comings of the book: to him it was seldom amusing; its moral emerged with little distinctness or steadiness; its style, except for the early chapters, seldom rose above the level of efficient prose; its characters, except for Mignon, the Harper, Lothario, and the Uncle, made little claim upon his interests or affection; there were, for Carlyle, few vivid or memorable scenes, and practically no humor. Thus, aside from his natural eagerness for the didactic, for "musical wisdom," he was impelled, by the very nature of the novel, to study individual passages. In spite of its faults, it contained, for him, numerous hints on the solution of his problem through action, inner growth, and the humble application of his talents to the duty that "lies nearest."[17]

He observed that at bottom, the story of Meister was a study in the art of life, exhibiting a variety of attempts to fashion from individual materials the kind of life which the particular character desired. As in his own case, there were false starts: Wilhelm, for example, believes himself capable of becoming a great actor and producer, whereas in reality he has very mediocre talents in that direction. He runs away from home, however, and joins a group of wandering players, hoping by so doing to develop his nature and to lift himself above the level of the *Bürgerkreis* in which his merchant-father moves. He is soon disillusioned. At the castle of the nobleman for whom the players are to entertain a visiting prince, he first discovers the true character of upper-class life. The nobleman himself is pretentious, pedantic, egotistic—a dilettante. The Baron is stupid and self-centered. The Countess is beautiful and frivolous. Life at the castle is one of self-indulgence, meanness, misdirected energy, chaos. The players arrive on a cold rainy night, and instead of being brought into the castle, they are quartered in an old and virtually empty building in the yard. Philina is the only one fortunate enough to get into the castle, and that is only because the Countess wants her among her maids. Days pass; the new play is held up by the nobleman's pedantic discussions of stage-craft and ornament; the Countess is more interested in Philina than in Wilhelm's manuscript; and Wilhelm notes that one day the players are exhibited to the guests along with the nobleman's horses. By this time, he begins to see that self-culture can never be attained by merely entering another social group, that it can be achieved only from within.

He remembers his boyhood friend, Werner, who stayed at home and applied himself to his work. But work without vision is soon to transform Werner into the complete Philisstine. Meister sees a life of emotion without action exemplified in Mignon and the Harper; Mignon longs for Italy, the Harper longs to undo the past; in neither case is action possible, and the result is decay and death. Opposite Werner, and his work without vision, stands *die schöne Seele*, with vision without work, luxuriating in pious sentimentality, insipid church-songs, morbid self-analysis. On all hands, life is being misused, misdirected, wasted, perverted. Even among the nobler characters, to whom Wilhelm comes after his disillusionment with the players, life fails to flower out in a balance of beauty and power, action and vision. In Therese there is, to be sure, an admirable self-dedication to practical service to others, a poise and a charm that come from finding and fulfilling one's vocation. But only in Natalia does Wilhelm find the ideal, a combination of supreme spiritual vision and the most realistic grappling with the concrete opportunities of life. Among the men whom he has come to know, he finds the highest achievement in Lothario, the young nobleman, and master of the *Gesellschaft vom Turm*. Lothario had participated in the American war for independence, but had returned to his castle with the conviction that, in respect to achieving self-realization through service to man, *Hier oder nirgends ist Amerika*. Behind the more active characters, and emerging only intermittently to deliver a few oracular utterances on the conduct of life, stands "the Uncle," a shadowy figure serving as the mouth-piece, as it were, for Goethe's direct address to the reader.[18] It is among these more effective characters, after Wilhelm has been drawn away from the hilarious and bitter tumult of the players, to Lothario's castle, that he catches a glimpse of the true aim for his life.

Carlyle, like Wilhelm, saw that to these characters the secret of life was the effort to fill the real with the ideal, to apply one's capabilities, once they were truly discovered, to the materials offered by circumstances, and to achieve the expression of mind or spirit. He saw that to give our action a proper psychological basis, a moral orientation, and a social objective, we should act, partly because we are free and responsible beings, and partly because life indicates the field, the direction, and the goal. This was the answer to Byronism and despair. This was the safeguard against an impotent and rebellious clutching at the infinite, as well as a guarantee against a "do-nothing" pessimism. It cannot be said, however, that this doctrine of action in terms of "capabilities," of creating our character and finding our destiny in applying our talents to the nearest opportunity, found a ready incorporation into Carlyle's thought. He tended more and more to stress action itself, and to say less and less of "capabilities" and self-development. It is true, of course, that in *Sartor*, he says, in connection with Teufelsdröckh's early development, that "To each is given a certain inward Talent, a certain outward Environment . . . to each, . . . a certain maximum of Capability . . . To find by study of your-

self, and of the ground you stand on, what your combined
inward and outward Capability especially is . . . [is] the
hardest problem."[19] But while Carlyle, in his early enthusiasm for Goethe, occasionally exalted the ideal of "Capability"
or of self-development (*Bildung*), his puritan nature
demanded less attention to the desires of the individual, to
man's whole development, and required more emphasis on
action for more definitely moral aims. It may be said, therefore, that Goethe's doctrine of *Bildung* aided Carlyle in his
formulation of a gospel of action only in so far as it adjusted
itself to Carlyle's hatred for Byronic negation, self-indulgence, unrealistic visioning of man's capacities.

Far more important for Carlyle than the idea of *Bildung*
was an occasional passage in the *Wanderjahre* on some
specific ethical problem, or on the religious needs of human
nature. When we leave the doctrine of *Bildung*, as set forth
by Goethe in the *Lehrjahre*, and inquire into the question of
what were the greatest principles which Goethe offered Carlyle, we find ourselves at once in the *Wanderjahre*, the work
which followed the first half of the novel after a period of
some thirty years, and which expressed the Goethe of old
age, of renunciation, and of reverence for suffering. We
shall find numerous short passages from the *Lehrjahre*
explanatory of many of Carlyle's sayings, and elaborating
upon his doctrine of work; but for most of the distinctly
religious element in his thought, as derived from Goethe,
we must go to Chapters X and XI of the *Wanderjahre*.
Thus, in addition to the great doctrine on which Aristotle
had anticipated Goethe, namely, that "the end of man is an
action, not a thought,"[20] Carlyle found in Goethe's novel the
ideals of Reverence, of Self-denial (*Entsagen*) rather than
Happiness, and of a spiritual union of man in society. Of
all these notions, Carlyle grasped most successfully the ideal
of Work. We shall see that he gave his own meaning to
Entsagen and to the famous passage on the Three Reverences.
We shall see also that just as he drew from Schiller's

Wallenstein the admonition, "Ernst ist das Leben," and forgot the rest of the sentence, "heiter ist die Kunst,"[21] in the same manner, he forgets the gaiety and color of Wilhelm's story, and remembers only that earnestness makes life eternity: "der Ernst, der heilige, macht allein das Leben zur Ewigkeit."[22]

3. WORK: *"Tätig zu sein, . . . ist des Menschen erste Bestimmung."*[23]

Though the ethical value of work is given a conspicuous expression in Goethe, Carlyle must have known how admirably it was treated also by Schiller, Jean Paul, and Fichte. In the little poem, *Der Sämann*, for example, Schiller expresses the infinite fertility of the deed:[24]

> Siehe, voll Hoffnung vertraust du der Erde den goldenen Samen
> Und erwartest im Lenz fröhlich die keimende Saat.
> Nur in die Furche der Zeit bedenkst du dich Thaten zu streuen,
> Die, von der Weisheit gesät, still für die Ewigkeit blühn?

In Jean Paul's *Briefe*, action is exalted above learning: "O in Thaten liegen mehr hohe Wahrheiten als in Büchern! Thaten nähren den ganzen Menschen von innen, Bücher und Meinungen sind nur ein warmer nahrhafter Umschlag um den Magen."[25] In Fichte's ethical idealism, of course, action has a central place, though involving something different from what Carlyle sought. Some of Fichte's sentences, however, remind us strikingly of Carlyle's. For example, he insists, as we have seen, that man shall *"be* and *do* something" which will leave an imperishable result in the world of spirit: "sein zeitliches Leben soll ein unvergängliches und ewiges Resultat hinterlassen in der Geisterwelt."[26] Indeed, Fichte is remarkably close to Goethe in insisting that we do

"the duty that lies nearest": that "every one, in the station
where he has been placed by necessity, should do all things
which properly belong to that station."[27] In the *Bestimmung
des Menschen*, he is even more explicit: "Not merely to
know, but according to thy knowledge to do, is thy vocation."[28] The world is merely the object and materials of our
duty, awaiting the plastic operation of our wills in action:
"Meine Welt ist—Object und Sphäre meiner Pflichten, und
absolut nichts Andreres."[29] We do not act because we know ;
we know because we are called upon to act.[30]

But the ideal of action, as Carlyle maintained it, takes on a
familiar character only when we turn to *Wilhelm Meister*.
Goethe held that man can know himself only through an active
loyalty to his daily tasks. It was this infusing of a religious
glamor into the nature of daily work which was one of the
major services which Goethe's philosophy performed for
Carlyle. Carlyle had asked himself how he was ever to know
his powers, his nature, his end. Did the answer lie in books,
philosophies, dogmas, institutions? He saw that the old
channels of revelation had closed up. The traditional creeds,
the validity of the Bible, these no longer illuminated his daily
life or suffused this world with an other-worldly glow. The
ordinary world seemed shrunken, de-spiritualized, dead.
Neither self-knowledge nor inspiration could be drawn from
such a barren source. But since the old dogmatic sources
seemed cut off from him, the only alternative was a re-read-
ing of common things. And in this Goethe was the great
helper. In the first place, Goethe seemed to have diagnosed
Carlyle's malady in a way to suggest the expectation of a cure.
Man's unhappiness, said Goethe, comes from there being an
infinite in him. Wilhelm thus confesses to Werner that the
divine wretchedness expressed in his attempts at poetry
merely show "the arms of his spirit grasping at infinity."[31]
Long afterward, in talking with Friedrich, he learns that
Emigration is the false solution of those unconsciously in
quest of the unlimited: "Go where you will, [however,] you

still find yourself in a conditional world."[32]   This recognition
of the source of man's unhappiness is present not only in
Goethe, but also in Novalis: "We seek everywhere for the
unconditioned (*das Unbedingte*), but find only the conditioned (*immer nur Dinge*)."[33]   It is only natural, says
Goethe, that we should be plunged into doubt or despair on
discovering the disparity between our aspirations and our
limitations; but salvation from doubt can be effected "by
nothing but activity": we must remember that "jede Art von
Zweifel nur durch Wirksamkeit gehoben werden kann."[34]
Unlike Fichte, who counsels a philosophic action, Goethe
reassuringly admonishes: "There where thou art, there where
thou remainest, accomplish what thou canst; be busy, be
courteous, and let the present scene delight thee."[35]   As soon
as action is begun, the opposing circumstances, once so for-
bidding, once threatening us with defeat, now become the
buoyant element wherein we may swim and launch out to our
goal.   Carlyle was very fond of this metaphor; in Goethe
it appears in the words addressed to Wilhelm by the Overseer in the Pedagogical Province, when Wilhelm returns to
learn how his son, Felix, has benefited by his discipline: "We
look upon our scholars," says the Overseer, "as so many
swimmers, who, in the element which threatened to swallow
them, feel with astonishment that they are lighter, that it
bears and carries them forward: and so it is with everything
that man undertakes."[36]   Another figure serves the same purpose, in a narrower sense: the glass bell in which one may
think oneself imprisoned: the "fair Saint" recounts in her
Confessions how impossible it seemed that she should break
the bond which attached her to her lover; but, as she continues, "I at once perceived it to be only as a glass bell, which
shut me up in the exhausted airless space: One bold stroke
to break the bell in pieces, and thou art delivered!"[37]   Thus
Goethe demonstrated in the lives of his characters a series of
predicaments analogous to Carlyle's, and provided also a
sovereign solution in practical action, in the willing acceptance

of limitation, in the treatment of opposing circumstances as the element wherein one is to fashion a positive result.

Once our doubt and unrest have been dispelled, continues Goethe, action becomes the great moulder of our destiny. By it, first of all, our capabilities are discovered and expressed: "How can one learn to know oneself? Never through thought, rather through action. Seek to do your duty, and you will then know yourself. But what is your duty? The demands of the day."[38] This, for Carlyle, became the difference between *Know thyself* and *Know what thou canst work at.* "Our Works [our Capabilities] are the mirror wherein the spirit first sees its natural lineaments."[39] A general capability—"vague wavering capability"—is just as offensive to Carlyle as to Goethe; the Abbé in the *Lehrjahre* was equally certain that "there is no vague general capability in men."[40] Too many of us, says Goethe, and Carlyle after him—especially in his early period—waste ourselves in seeking to perfect a talent which we possess in only a slight degree. In the Hall of the Past, where Jarno reads the Roll from which all Apprentices learn the art of living, Wilhelm learns that "we should guard against a talent which we cannot hope to practise in perfection."[41] Yet action should not wait upon thought; the most deleterious effects proceed from having an idea of which the expression is impossible; Carlyle's life-long insistence on the perniciousness of thought without action can be traced, so far as Goethe is concerned, to the words of the "Clergyman" who has taken charge of the unfortunate Harper: "For man there is but one misfortune; when some idea lays hold of him, which exerts no influence upon active life, or still more, which withdraws him from it."[42] On the other hand, once we have engaged ourselves in activity, we must remember that it is not the activity itself which is of most worth, but the spirit in which it is carried on. The whole faith of the nineteenth century, it has been said, speaks in Teufelsdröckh's conclusion that "the Man is the spirit he worked in;

not what he did, but what he became."[43] This is Goethe's conclusion, likewise: "Der Geist, aus dem wir handeln, ist das Höchste."[44]

Of this plastic shaping of ourselves there is more to be said. We have seen that "through action only could we ever be in a condition to inspect and watch ourselves."[45] Goethe is aware that men have little inclination to pursue such a study; like Carlyle, Goethe is oppressed by the average man's "wish to find a sort of recipe for comfort, directions for acquiring riches . . ."[46] But for those who would apprehend reality, circumstance is the quarry from which to draw the materials for the art of living:

> "Man's highest merit [writes Goethe] always is, as much as possible to rule external circumstances, and as little as possible to let himself be ruled by them. Life lies before us, as a huge quarry lies before the architect. . . . All things without us, nay, I may add, all things on us, are mere elements: but deep within us lies the creative force, which out of these can produce what they were meant to be . . . I reverence the individual who understands distinctly what it is he wishes; who unweariedly advances, who knows the means conducive to his object, and can seize and use them."[47]

These words are addressed by the Uncle to the "fair Saint" as an antidote to her merely inward activity, her habits of inactive piety and sentimental musings. It is not difficult to imagine the stimulating effect they must have had upon Carlyle's spirit, heavy with despair and doubt, frustrated by false starts, burdened with the conviction that the world— external circumstance—was merely a machine, and still hoping for evidence that happiness was not an impossible ideal.

Goethe's emphasis on the *nearest* duty, as the dynamic beginning of self-realization, can hardly be over-estimated in its bearing upon Carlyle's problem. It was this simple but illuminating reversal of the usual quest for reality which formed, as Kraeger truly says, the beginning of Carlyle's *vita nuova*.[48] Lothario explains to Wilhelm his attempts in America to find his real self: "In America, I fancied I might accomplish something; over seas, I hoped to become useful and essential . . . How differently do matters now appear! How precious, how important seems the duty which is nearest me, whatever it may be." Whereupon Jarno interrupts: "I recollect the letter which you sent me from the Western world; it contained the words: 'I will return, and in my house, amid my fields, among my people, I will say: *Here or nowhere is America!*'" No doubt these words recalled to Wilhelm the conversation he had had with the "stranger" when he set out for Lothario's castle: Wilhelm had lamented the time he had wasted in the company of the players; to him it now seemed "an endless void; nothing of it has remained with me." To which the "stranger" had replied:

> "Here you are mistaken; everything that happens to us leaves some trace behind it, everything contributes imperceptibly to form us. Yet often it is dangerous to take a strict account of that. For either we grow proud and negligent, or downcast and dispirited; and both are equally injurious in their consequences. The safe plan is, always simply to do the task that lies nearest us; and this in the present case," added he with a smile, "is to hasten to our quarters."[49]

Throughout Goethe's treatment of the proper field of action, it is noteworthy that there is little consideration given to space, but a great deal of importance attached to *time*. Goethe seems to say it does not matter *where* one's duty is performed, but *when*: all action is seed sown in the field of time. Here, of course, occurs Carlyle's favorite thought, as epigrammatically expressed in Goethe's *West-Oestlicher Divan*:

> My inheritance how wide and fair!
> Time is my fair seed-field, of Time I'm heir.[50]

The thought is of course an extremely old one, and Carlyle probably found it in many quarters. In Novalis, it appears in two very brief and simple *Fragmente*: "Alles ist Samenkorn," and "Manche Tat schreit ewig."[51]

We have seen that thus to live by deed requires a recognition of one's limitations, and an effort to actualize whatever potential powers we may have within us. The first is preliminary to the latter: only by renouncing the impossible and the impracticable, says Goethe, can we enter fully into a life of harmonious and creative activity. Goethe's doctrine of *Entsagen* was integrally involved in his doctrine of work. It is to this notion of a rational renunciation of the erring claims of the self, and to the transformation which the doctrine underwent at the hands of Carlyle, that we now turn.

4. RENUNCIATION: *"durch welche der eigentliche Eintritt ins Leben denkbar ist."*[52]

Carlyle desired a concept which would, in all its essentials, correspond to the traditional Christian ideal of self-denial. For this, he went to Goethe and Novalis, and possibly to Fichte. The doctrine which emerged from his adoption and transformation differed in several fundamental ways from the originals. It will be well to take up Fichte's doctrine first.

In Fichte, we find numerous passages which might very easily have suggested the ultimate meaning which Carlyle gave to Goethe's term. These passages suggest, sometimes more clearly than Goethe's, or even Novalis's, the common notion of self-denial as the way to "Eternal Life." In the *Bestimmung des Menschen*, Fichte declares, for instance, that "the faculty by which we lay hold on Eternal Life is to be attained only by actually renouncing [Fichte uses the term *aufgeben*, rather than *entsagen*] the sensuous and its objects, and sacrificing them to that law which takes cognizance of

our will only and not of our actions."[53]   Again, in the
Anweisung zum seligen Leben, he demands that man
"renounce himself as the true negation,—and then he is
wholly absorbed in God.   This self-renunciation is the
entrance into the Higher Life which is wholly opposed to
the lower life . . ."[54]   It is this self-renunciation, this "Love
of God," which, says Fichte, "extirpates personal Self-love."
We have here, in these few sentences, two or three striking
parallels to Carlyle's phrasing: Fichte maintains that renunciation is "the entrance into Higher Life," and that it means
extirpation of the self.   Carlyle, too, maintains that renunciation is the entrance to life, and that it means the "annihilation of self."[55]   Yet Fichte's language is too much that of
traditional Christian ethics to warrant our assuming an influence.   Both Carlyle and Fichte obviously drew from the
same source, hence the parallelism.   Even Goethe seems to
have levied upon the language of the New Testament:
Entsagen is der eigentliche Eintritt ins Leben.   It will
become clear, as we proceed, that Carlyle's doctrine is the
same as Fichte's—self-denial as "the way to the Blessed
Life"—but that his terms are those of Goethe and Novalis.

It is interesting to note that nowhere in the *Wanderjahre*
is *Entsagen* defined or discussed.   We observe that the sub-
title to this part of the novel as a whole is *Die Entsagenden*
(*The Resigned,* or, more literally, *The Resigning*).   At
various times the term is applied to the characters as they
enter a new and purgative experience.   Wilhelm, for example, writes to Natalia, whom he has renounced in order to
complete his preparation for life, that he looks forward to
the time when he can have the "happiness of lying at thy
feet . . . weeping over thy hands for all that I renounce."[56]
As the novel draws to a close, and as Goethe apparently
becomes engrossed in the idea, even to the detriment of the
work as a whole, the term *die Entsagenden* occurs more
frequently.   But the passage which struck Carlyle most
forcibly, and which remained with him as a glowing text for

preachments on the good life, occurs, characteristically, in an unlikely context. It is to be found in a passage interpolated by Goethe into the fourteenth chapter, to account for the growing incoherence of his narrative: "At this point our manuscripts forsake us," he says, and then proceeds to indicate the nature of some of the passages he now introduces, as being "rather in the way of exclamation [*sic*] than of narrative," and as pointing "to the high meaning of Renunciation, by which alone the first real entrance into life is conceivable."[57]

What did Goethe mean by it?

> "The two great fundamental ideas running through *Die Wanderjahre*," says one Goethean, "are work and resignation. Resignation means much. It means limitation, concentration. It is man's duty to limit his striving and to concentrate all his powers on the limited field. Resignation means the conquering of passions, means the giving up of many inherited and earned advantages, rights, and possessions. It transforms the man of impulse into a man of reason, the selfish man into a public-spirited man, the egoist into an altruist. It exerts such a profound influence on man's nature and development that Goethe considered it, next to work, the most important principle of life. Hence he gave the novel, which was to show forth the foundation of a prosperous individual and public life, the sub-title *The Resigned*."[58]

Goethe's whole philosophy of life required the submission of feeling to intelligence, of individual caprice to the reason of the whole, of immediate attainments to the achievement of more remote but majestic ends. At bottom, Goethe's ideal was an aesthetic ideal, the exaltation of the classical attributes of order and balance. It pointed to the harmonious outflowering of all one's energies, the lower subordinated to the higher. *Entsagen* meant for him something closely analogous to the artist's "selecting," ordering, and shaping of his materials. This involves a denial of the artist's momentary impulses, his tendency to yield to the opposing material, to snatch at a quick result. It has no similarity to the ascetic ideal; it is fundamentally a creative act, an effort at a constant envisaging of the whole. It is both a practical and an idealistic effort. And so with *Entsagen* as a rule of life. In it there is no absolute denial of any part of ourselves or of life. The denial is wholly relative; all parts are permitted expression at the proper time. To realize this important fact, we need only remember that Lothario, the ideal man, the embodiment of the principles of work and renunciation, had nothing of the puritan in him; on the contrary, as Wilhelm soon discovered to his bewilderment, Lothario had somehow combined his high ethical will to public service, with unconventional relationships with Aurelia and Lydia. Evidently so long as indulgence toward one side of one's nature did not interfere with the action of the whole, there was, in Goethe's mind, no question of real immorality. *Entsagen* was thus not a puritan subjugation of parts of the self in the interest of other parts, but a relative withholding of such elements as should be active at another time. It was the passive side of that reverence for the unattained Ideal, of which work was the active side. In Goethe himself, we may behold the illustration of this idea; he was ever struggling with the vagaries of his temperament, ever forcing his wayward impulses into some clearly defined course of action. He sought increasingly to limit his field, his movement, his ambitions, in order to achieve, in the actual, something definite and harmonious. The Renunciation, therefore, of which Fichte and Carlyle write, was something almost wholly foreign to the ideal which Goethe desired with all his being—aesthetically, philosophically, religiously. The idea of absolute denial of anything was repulsive to him.

It is significant that Carlyle's great passage on "The Everlasting Yea," on the release of the self from the error of its waywardness, should employ, not Goethe's term, but that which Novalis chose as fittingly expressing Fichte's doctrine of rationally denying the empirical ego in order to attain a conception of the infinite Divine Ego. Let us look first at Teufelsdröckh's words:

> "I seemed to surrender, to renounce utterly, and say: Fly, then, false shadows of Hope; I will chase you no more, I will believe you no more. And ye too, haggard spectres of Fear, I care not for you; ye too are all shadows and a lie. Let me rest here: for I am way-weary and life-weary; I will rest here, were it but to die: to die or to live is alike to me; alike insignificant. . . . Here, then, as I lay in that Centre of Indifference; cast, doubtless by benignant upper Influence, into a healing sleep, the heavy dreams rolled gradually away, and I awoke to a new Heaven and a new Earth. The first preliminary moral Act, Annihilation of Self (*Selbsttödtung*), had been happily accomplished; and my mind's eyes were now unsealed, and its hands ungyved."[59]

Several words and phrases should be noted here before we turn to Novalis. In the first place, Teufelsdröckh has been pursuing "false shadows" and has been pursued by the "spectres of Fear." Whatever relation this may have to Novalis's term, it has little relevancy to Goethe's ideal as preparation for concrete action as a moulder of life and character. Teufelsdröckh's symptoms are those of the "sick soul," seeking a "conversion to God," rather than the marks of a Goethean hero who, like Wilhelm Meister, has wasted his talents in the wrong direction. Moreover, Teufelsdröckh is "way-weary" and "life-weary," indifferent now to life or death. This is hardly the preliminary state for an active and rational limitation of one's field, goal, and will in the interests of a definite course of action. Teufelsdröckh lies passive in the "Centre of Indifference"; whereas Goethe's moral man requires no "healing sleep," from which to awaken to an "Annihilation of Self." Teufelsdröckh's experience is more like the strenuous and turbulent stages which the mystic undergoes immediately before he attains the "illumination" consequent upon an absolute renunciation of the self, rather than like Wilhelm's gradual discovery that he must purify his desires, re-align his objectives, cease to develop talents he does not wholly have, and pursue the cultivation of all his definitely discovered abilities. Finally, let us note again that Carlyle calls this striking experience, in which Teufelsdröckh suddenly regains serenity and poise, by the name of *Selbsttötdtung*, "Annihilation of Self." In contrast to this we have Wilhelm, far from annihilating his individual self, seeking progressively to develop it, convinced that in so far as he develops all his real endowments, he will be promoting the development of the life of the Whole. In the one case, Teufelsdröckh "merges his Me in the Idea," identifies himself, at least for the moment of his experience, completely with the Absolute, annihilates every atom of his individuality. This comes so near to true mystical experience (as near as Carlyle's hero ever came to it) as to remove once and for all any very fundamental agreement between Carlyle's doctrine of the "annihilation of the self" and Goethe's doctrine of *Entsagen*. Carlyle increasingly talked about renunciation, and in proportion as he did so he ceased talking about capabilities and self-culture. *Entsagen* came more and more to mean for him a puritan denial of self, a chastising of natural impulses in order to attain spiritual good.

What Carlyle really wanted, as Ströle has pointed out,[60] was not *Entsagen*, but *Selbstverleugnung, Selbstvernichtung*, literally *Selbsttödtung*,—self-denial, self-annihilation, self-killing. He had read in Novalis that

> "The true philosophical Act is annihilation of self (*Selbsttödtung*) ; this is the real beginning of all Philosophy; all requisites for being a Disciple of Philosophy point hither. This Act alone corresponds to all the conditions and characteristics of transcendental conduct."[61]

He chose to ignore, however, that for Novalis and Fichte, *Selbsttödtung* "is the beginning of all *Philosophy*," is the preliminary rational act of ridding oneself of the purely personal point of view. To be sure, Novalis also says that this act is the condition likewise of all moral conduct. With Carlyle, however, *Selbsttödtung* is conceived as a continuing state of soul. It means the complete acceptance of suffering, *i.e.* the crushing of the self's deep hunger for happiness, and yet an identification of the self, the higher self, with all that is good and creative. This was Carlyle's answer to the problem of evil: the renunciation of the struggling self, the acceptance of suffering and wrong, and the worship of sorrow as the path to reality. His admiration for Novalis was largely owing to the mystic's acceptance of the fact that "earthly fortune is in no instance so sweet and smooth, that it does not by and by teach the great doctrine of *Entsagen*, of 'Renunciation.' " Then Carlyle adds his paraphrase of Goethe: " 'by which alone,' as a wise man . . . has observed, 'can the real entrance on Life be properly said to begin.' "⁶²
This application of Goethe's words to Novalis's belief that life demands an acceptance of suffering is characteristic of Carlyle's treatment of doctrines and terminology. First he interprets Novalis's theory according to his ethical preoccupations; then he identifies the doctrine, thus interpreted, with Goethe's *Entsagen*; finally he applies both terms, *Entsagen* and *Selbsttödtung*, to his own doctrine, which is, strictly speaking, neither Novalis's nor Goethe's.

Indeed it is to Werner, rather than to Goethe or Novalis, that we must go if we are to find a parallel with Carlyle's conception. He maintains that Werner's great significance for us is that he learned

> "the grand secret of Renunciation . . . His fundamental principle of morals we have seen in part already: it does not exclusively or primarily belong to himself; being little more than that high tenet of entire Self-forgetfulness, that 'merging of the *Me* in the *Idea*'; a

principle which reigns both in Stoical and Christian
ethics, and is at this day common, in theory, among all
German philosophers, especially of the Transcendental
class. . . . He will not have Happiness, under any form,
to be the real or chief end of man."[63]

Carlyle takes pains to translate in his essay on Werner
several passages from the poet's dramas which turn upon
this doctrine of "self-annihilation." From the Fifth Act of
Die Kreuzesbrüder he translates the passage in which the
Old Man of Carmel reads the story of Phosphorus, whose
sin of "Prideful Thought of being One and Somewhat" had
brought down divine wrath, which has now shut him up in
a "prison called Life." Phosphorus is tortured, symbolically, with all the adversities and struggling efforts of man
to accommodate his infinite desires to his finite being; but,
while he has the "Salt" of intellectual culture, he is nevertheless in pain and darkness, and is released only by the
"Cup of Fluidness," the "Drops of Sadness and the Drops
of Longing," the "Cup of Faith," and "the long-forgotten
Name, and the Remembrance of his Birthplace." Remembering himself thus as a child of eternity, he sees his error—
the sin of individuation:[64]

> Then fell there as if scales from Phosphor's eyes;
> He left the Thought of being One and Somewhat,
> His nature melted in the mighty All.

Werner goes so far, in his chastising of the self, as to deny
the ethical validity of immortality in true religion. He
holds, at least in the passage quoted by Carlyle, that the
desire for immortality is merely the last, clinging vestige of
the selfish ego soaring to the Infinite. Such a doctrine as
immortality, Werner implies, tends only to pervert religion
and to impair its sacredness. In the *Söhne des Thals*, he
shows Robert d'Heredon finally discovering for himself that

"cripplish Immortality" is not a concept worthy of a truly
spiritual being:

> ROBERT. And Death,—so dawns it on me,—
>   Death perhaps,
> The doom that leaves nought of this *Me* remaining,
> May be perhaps the Symbol of that Self-denial,—
> Perhaps still more,—perhaps,—I have it, friend!—
> That cripplish Immortality,—think'st not?—
> Which but spins forth our paltry *Me*, so thin
> And pitiful, into Infinitude,
> *That* too must *die?*—This shallow Self of ours,
> We are not nail'd to it eternally?
> We can, we must be free of it, and then
> Uncumbered wanton in the Force of All!
>   ADAM [*calling joyfully into the interior of the
>   Cavern*].
> Brethren, he has renounced![65]

Carlyle makes no comment on this passage, though he admits
on the next page that Werner bids fair to "play fantastic
tricks in abundance . . . at least in his religious history . . .
Conversion, not to Popery, but, if it so chanced, to Bramin-
ism, was a thing nowise to be thought impossible."[66] But
he must have welcomed Werner's reference to "our paltry
Me," and he no doubt felt a certain sympathy for Werner's
notion of the self being absolutely and eternally destroyed.
At any rate, it is not too much to say that Carlyle's doctrine
of *Selbsttödtung* is nearer to Werner's renunciation of "the
Me" in the "force of All" than it is to Goethe's doctrine of
Entsagen or to Novalis's notion of the rational act which is
"the real beginning of all Philosophy." What Carlyle
really meant can be definitely seen from an entry in his
Journal: "Deny thyself; whatsoever is *thyself*, consider it
as nothing."[67]   This was Carlyle's transformation of
Entsagen.

That it involved an exaltation of suffering and sorrow as
the highest object of reverence was still another point on

which Carlyle differed from Goethe. To realize this divergence of emphasis, we need only turn again to the chapter
on "The Everlasting Yea," and to observe the relation, in
turn, of *Selbsttödtung* to the "Sanctuary of Sorrow" (or the
"Divine Depth of Sorrow," "the Worship of Sorrow," etc.),
and to the exhortation to "Produce, produce . . . for the
Night cometh wherein no man can work."[68] It is after the
"first preliminary moral Act, Annihilation of Self," that
Teufelsdröckh arrives at a serene and tender consciousness
of the divinity of common things, of Nature as the Living
Garment of God, of the Universe as "not dead and demonia-
cal, a charnel-house with spectres; but godlike, and my
Father's." It is now, too, that he can look on his fellow-
man "with an infinite Love, and infinite Pity," and on "the
poor Earth, with her poor joys, [as] now my needy Mother,
not my cruel Stepdame." Thus he stands "in the porch of
that 'Sanctuary of Sorrow,'" gazing into the "Divine Depth
of Sorrow." The "vain interminable" problem of Evil likewise assumes a different character, and man's unhappiness becomes eradicable by reducing "the Fraction of Life," through
"increasing the numerator and lessening the denominator,"
that is, by self-denial, by renunciation of the claim to happiness and to positive adjustment to every facet of life. It
is here that Carlyle paraphrases Goethe: "It is only with
Renunciation (*Entsagen*) that Life, properly speaking, can
be said to begin." Then comes the un-Goethean question:
"What Act of Legislature was there that *thou* shouldst be
happy?" Now Goethe was no hedonist, and happiness
seemed to him, as to Carlyle, by no means the end of life;
but he was equally sure that life could not be complete
without a positive experiencing of all of it: the end of life
is the joy of creative, harmonious living. Carlyle goes on
to say, however: "Thou canst love the Earth while it
injures thee." Then he takes the next step, familiar to all
deeply religious persons, and adds: ". . . even because it
injures thee . . . Knowest thou that 'Worship of Sorrow'? . . .

Feel it in thy heart, then say whether it is of God! **This is** belief; all else is Opinion." This, says Carlyle, is "applied Christianity"—not the whole duty of man, to be sure, but "the Passive half." The other half, now that the self is purged of all centripetal tendencies, is Action: "Do the Duty which lies nearest thee . . ."[69] Having renounced worldly ease and gain, man is now to accept and to love the world of suffering, and to "work in well-doing."[70]

Extracted thus from *Sartor Resartus,* and re-stated, the doctrine appears as nothing more than what it really is, a part of traditional Christian ethics, with here and there a phrase of Goethe's. That the Bible was the real basis for Carlyle's thought here, is revealed in the quotations from *Ecclesiastes* and the Fourth Gospel, in the last and climactic sentences of the chapter: "Whatsoever thy hand findeth to do, do it with thy whole might. Work while it is called Today; for the Night cometh wherein no man can work."[71]

What relation, then, do Carlyle's ideas have to those of Goethe? To answer this question, we must turn to the eleventh chapter of the *Wanderjahre*, which Carlyle, interpreting according to his point of view, regarded as "the best chapter ever yet written on Christianity."[72] Wilhelm Meister is paying a visit to the Pedagogical Province, to which he has sent his son Felix, and has just learned of the three "Reverences," reverence for what is below us, around us, and above us. The first Reverence is dominant in the Christian religion. But all three Reverences constitute the true Reverence, reverence for oneself as "the best that God and Nature have produced."[73] Wilhelm is led further on, however, into the "Sanctuary," a great hall in which he beholds a series of mural paintings illustrating the three Religions (corresponding to the three Reverences), especially as exemplified in "the Sacred Books of the Israelites." Wilhelm is puzzled to note that the series ends with the Lord's Supper. He is informed, however, that it is thought better to "disjoin that sublime Man's life from its termina-

tion." On being led into the next hall, Wilhelm suddenly
finds, to his dismay, that he is once more at the entrance of
the Sanctuary and has not yet seen the representations of
"the Reverence of what is beneath us." The "Eldest"
explains that,

> "That last Religion which arises from the Reverence
> of what is beneath us; that veneration of the contra-
> dictory, the hated, the avoided, we give each of our
> pupils, in small portions . . . I invite you to return hither
> at the end of a year, to visit our general festival, and
> see how far your son is advanced: then shall you be
> admitted into the Sanctuary of Sorrow."[74]

Before leaving, however, Wilhelm asks one more question:
"Have you likewise selected his sufferings, his death, as a
model of exalted patience?" The answer—which was most
significant to Carlyle—is that it would be a "damnable
audacity" to expose "that torturing Cross" and the sufferings of "the Holy one," or to "take these mysterious secrets,
in which the divine depth of Sorrow lies hid, and play with
them, fondle them, trick them out . . ." The Society of the
Tower thus draws "a veil over those sufferings, even
because we reverence them so highly."

Now the question of how closely—and how remotely—
Carlyle was able to adopt the true meaning of the passage
we have just quoted may best be answered by seeking to
know, as definitely as possible, just what Goethe meant. This
is not easy, since Goethe's passage is hardly less vague than
Carlyle's. Goethe was fond of mystification, of leaving his
ideas incompletely set forth, of presenting several alternative
meanings. This was especially true when he was dealing
with such symbolical material as the subject of the tenth and
eleventh chapters of the *Wanderjahre*. It is possible, therefore, to grant Carlyle a certain freedom in his adjustment of
Goethe's ideas to his own. It should be noted, however,
that Goethe has in mind three religions, of which the rever-

ence for "the contradictory" (for suffering) is but one.
Carlyle apparently found little interest in the other two, as
they are presented in the passage in question. We should
note also that Goethe uses the term "reverence" (*Verehrung*,
Ehrfurcht), and that Carlyle so translates it; the word
"worship," which Carlyle came to prefer, may indeed be
taken as equivalent to *Verehrung*, but the attitude of worship
in the sense of "adoration" or complete subordination of the
self in the contemplation of an Ultimate, is better translated
by the word *Anbetung*, which Goethe does not use. Thus we
have another example, in the present connection, of that
characteristic latitude by which Carlyle transformed the
other and more metaphysical ideas which he drew from
Goethe, Kant, and Fichte.

We next remember that Wilhelm is told that he will later
be admitted to the "Sanctuary of Sorrow," an actual hall in
the greater Sanctuary of the three-fold Religion of Reverence. Carlyle introduces the name of this hall to describe
Teufelsdröckh's state of soul, his sudden vision of all things
in sorrow and travail: "Thus was I standing in the porch of
that 'Sanctuary of Sorrow.' " Carlyle thus adopts the word
figuratively and applies it psychologically. It is possible, of
course, that the "Eldest," also, gave a symbolical or figurative hint to Wilhelm in bidding him to return in a year for
a visit to the Sanctuary of Sorrow; Wilhelm's renunciation
would by that time have prepared him for understanding
both the symbol and the actuality. At any rate, Carlyle
came to think of the whole world as such a Sanctuary, and
of all men, at their best moments, as experiencing the
"Divine Depth of Sorrow." This latter expression, of
course, is applied by Goethe to describe the physical and
spiritual agony of Jesus on the Cross. From that spectacle,
says Goethe, the world itself "hid its face." Carlyle, however, broadens Goethe's description of the experience of
Jesus to signify the state of the religious soul. While
Goethe seems to have had a distinct aversion—amounting

eventually almost to morbidity—to the exhibition of a crucifix, Carlyle had no such antipathy, and would have been
unable to understand Goethe's avoidance of all reminders
of suffering and death. To this extent, therefore, Carlyle's
emphasis upon the "Divine Depth of Sorrow" is out of
keeping with the spirit of Goethe's passage. On the other
hand, he was right in insisting that Goethe had a profound
appreciation of the spirit of Christianity, and in finding it in
such expressions as we have considered.

We have already seen that in "The Everlasting Yea,"
Carlyle sets forth, in a general way, the three steps by which
Teufelsdröckh achieved the affirmative attitude toward the
world: (1) Self-annihilation, (2) the Worship of Sorrow,
and (3) doing the duty which lies nearest. We may throw
into final relief the differences between Carlyle's point of
view and Goethe's by asking: Is this the order, and are
these the steps, by which Wilhelm approaches his goal?
There is obviously little in Carlyle's ethical scheme that can
be paralleled in Goethe. We have already noted that Self-
annihilation was the farthest from Goethe's thought; that
Entsagen meant, for him, the subjugation of indefinite and
conflicting efforts to harmonious and definite endeavor
toward a specific goal. Renunciation, we also observe, is
nowhere mentioned in the chapter on the Reverence for
Sorrow. In Goethe's scheme, sorrow is not to be exchanged
for happiness—as with Carlyle—but is to be regarded as an
inevitable element in life, requiring that we accept it as one
phase of the Infinite, in order to free ourselves from fear
and to release us for action. The deliverance "from a
degrading Fear" is also the aim of the reverence for what
is above us. And the reverence for what is around us and
in us is to insure the spiritual solidarity of the human race,
and the "inspired Communion of Saints, that is, of men in
the highest degree good and wise."[75] Only in so far as
man has attained to these "reverences," and has welded them
into one—into the "Reverence for oneself"—is he acting in

the fullest sense of the term. Thus, though Wilhelm's experience did indeed involve self-denial, acceptance of suffering, and the need for action, it rested on other premises than those with which Carlyle began.

Carlyle's ethics, like his metaphysics—such as it is—is far more definitely spiritual than Goethe's. It is permeated with the Hebraic sense of sin; and it demands the renunciation of whole segments of life in order to attain a heightened vividness of only one. His belief that evil is the material from which good is made was, after all, only a fitful one; when he felt particularly dissatisfied with a pantheistic buttressing of his point of view—and this was a growing attitude with him—evil became for him almost the dominant fact about existence. To live at all in "this dog-hutch of a world" required the radical abandoning of the self and the world. To find any peace in the midst of universal sorrow and evil meant that one must worship sorrow as fundamentally the only reality. "All the *good* I ever got," he wrote to Thomas Erskine, "came to me rather in the shape of sorrow."[76] And so he came to dwell upon the eleventh chapter of the *Wanderjahre*, and to apply to his own spiritual experience the words of Goethe—so inexpressive of Goethe's religion as a whole—that we are

> "not only to be patient with the Earth, and let it lie beneath us, [we] appealing to a higher birthplace; but also to recognize humility and poverty, mockery and despite, disgrace and wretchedness, suffering and death, to recognize these things as divine; nay, even on sin and crime to look not as hindrances, but to honour and love them as furtherances, of what is holy."[77]

This was Goethe's admission that in the full life, the life of balance and harmony, there must be a courageous embrace of the dark and chaotic elements of existence. Reverence for suffering and all that is evil was, for Goethe, an act of release from fear, just as his Renunciation was an act of release from the immediate and unseeing demands of one's ego. For Carlyle, however, as Carré remarks, "le sacrifice... doit être douloureux. La souffrance est un absolu: par elle on atteint Dieu, et le fameux silence de Carlyle n'est au fond que la capacité d'endurance et de douleur."[78] Carlyle's terms are those of Goethe and Novalis; his ideas are those of Fichte and the New Testament. He noted that Novalis had remarked on the infinite sadness of religion: "Die Religion enthält unendliche Wehmut." The mystic further insisted that unhappiness is God's call to man, and that only through sorrow can holiness be attained: "Unglück ist der Beruf zu Gott. Heilig kann man nur durch Unglück werden."[79]

If, then, Carlyle's final attitude is different from Goethe's, in what way, we may ask, did Goethe's passage on *Entsagen* and the Reverence for Sorrow offer any aid? Carlyle, it must be remembered, went to Goethe for a reinterpretation of life: he wanted a new approach to the problem of evil; a new form for his conviction that happiness is not the end of man, that duty, even sorrow, is his more indubitable destiny; and a new, yet unskeptical, attitude toward Christianity. In Goethe he found all that he wanted. In the new terms—*Entsagen*, Worship of Sorrow, Divine Depth of Sorrow—he saw an approximate expression of Christian self-denial and the embrace of suffering as both the path and the essence of reality, which satisfied the requirements of his reawakened belief. But not only did Goethe supply him with certain new and useful terms; the poet also, in spite of his avowed Paganism, championed the spirit and essential truth of Christianity. It was this bold and serene assertion, in Goethe's old age, this evident crown of all his wisdom, that re-imparted to the Christian faith the authentic note which convinced Carlyle: "In a time like ours," he wrote, "it is rare to see, in the writings of cultivated men, any opinion whatever bearing any mark of sincerity on such a subject as this."[80]   Carlyle noted, too, that Goethe was sure not only of Christianity's truth but also of its permanency: "The Christian religion," said "the Three" to Wilhelm, "having once appeared, cannot again vanish; having once assumed its divine shape, can be subject to no dissolution."[81]   Thus, while Carlyle adapted Goethe's treatment of ethics and religion to his own needs, and felt no obligation to adhere to Goethe's meaning or to accept all its implications, he did indeed fathom a "deep, still meaning" in those memorable chapters of the *Wanderjahre.*

5.   SILENCE: *"Das Beste wird nicht deutlich durch Worte."*[82]

As Carlyle uses the word *Silence,* there are at least five possible meanings of the term: (1) the silence accompanying an act which transcends talk—the act of the "unselfconscious genius"; (2) the silence which Carlyle insisted should meet all inconclusive questions, such as those of theology; (3) the silence of stoical endurance; (4) the silence appropriate to the worship of the "Unnamable"; and (5) the two "great silences" of the grave and the stars. The last three "silences" are what concern us here. We have already studied the unselfconscious genius; and Carlyle's well-known reluctance to engage in theological dispute needs no comment.

Aside from Goethe, Carlyle probably found pertinent words on silence in Jean Paul and Fichte. In the *Wahrheit aus Jean Pauls Leben,* he must have read Richter's statement: "Ich thue einiges Böse im Stillen, aber noch weit mehr Gutes im Stillen."[83]   In Fichte, too, it is possible that he read, in *Die Grundzüge,* the sonorous and rhetorical passage at the end of the fourth lecture: "Might there some more gladdening dream from out the Infinite Silence at times refresh the slumberer in the cradle of Eternity!—might there, from time to time, prophetic whispers fall upon his ear, that there *is* a Light and a Day!"[84]   In each case, silence is revered as both the domain in which man's moral acts take root, and as the substance, as it were, of the divine reality, the Abyss to which the mystics refer, and the "Silence of deep Eternities," by which Carlyle sometimes chose to assign to deity a less anthropomorphic name than "God."[85]

On the whole, however, in respect to silence, there are few allusions to German writers. We may note in *Wilhelm Meisters Wanderjahre*, that silence as uncomplaining endurance is given an important place: Wilhelm writes to Natalia, who yet remains remote and unattainable, like an ideal, and whom he has renounced until his preparatory "wanderings" are over: "Yet I must not complain of my destiny, seeing I have promised thee that I will suffer and *be silent,* as thou also hast undertaken."[86]   Indeed all the chief characters in the closing chapters of the *Wanderjahre* find it proper to be cheerfully silent during their period of renunciation.   It is in the "Indenture," however, in the "little roll" which is handed to Wilhelm at the end of his Apprenticeship, that we find Goethe setting forth silence as one of the cardinal virtues of the master of the art of living:

> ". . . It is but a part of art that can be taught; the artist needs it all. Who knows it half, speaks much, and is always wrong; who knows it wholly, inclines to act, and speaks seldom or late. The former have no secrets and no force: the instruction they can give is like baked bread, savoury and satisfying for a single day; but flour cannot be sown and seed-corn ought not to be ground. Words are good, but they are not the best. The best is not to be explained by words. The spirit in which we act is the highest matter. Action can be understood and again represented by the spirit alone, . . ."[87]

There can be little doubt that here is one of the unmistakable sources of Carlyle's doctrine of silence as the circumstance of the deepest and most spontaneous acts.

The silence at the heart of man's destiny was expressed for Carlyle by both Schiller and Goethe. In *Der Geisterseher,*

Carlyle came upon Schiller's sublime passage on the theme of the "undiscovered bourne from which no traveller returns":

> "What went before and what will follow me, I regard as two black impenetrable curtains, which hang down at the two extremities of human life, and which no living man has yet drawn aside. Many hundreds of generations have already stood before them with their torches, guessing anxiously what lies behind. On the curtain of Futurity, many see their own shadows, the forms of their passions enlarged and put in motion; they shrink in terror at this image of themselves. . . . A deep silence reigns behind this curtain; no one once within it will answer those he has left without; all you can hear is a hollow echo of your own question, as if you shouted into a chasm. To the other side of this curtain we are all bound: . . ."[88]

A similar silence is maintained by the God in whom Goethe believed. Both His silence and His transcendence, says Goethe, impose on us the duty of refraining from even naming him: "Wer darf Ihn nennen?" asks Faust, when Margarete presses him for an answer to her question.[89]

But it is in Goethe's *Mason-Lodge* (the *Symbolum*) that Carlyle found the most satisfying expression of the mystery and the silence of destiny. It answered his questions on immortality, earthly duty, the meaning of life. "Man is, properly speaking," said Carlyle, "based upon Hope, he has no other possession but Hope; this world of his is emphatically the Place of Hope."[90] It is his duty to hope in silence that the meaning of the world is somehow linked up with his heart's desire. In Goethe, Carlyle was bidden to "press still thorow":

> The Future hides in it
> Gladness and sorrow;
> We press still thorow,
> Naught that abides in it
> Daunting us,—onward.

> And solemn before us,
> Veiled, the dark Portal,
> Goal of all mortal;
> Stars silent rest o'er us,
> Graves under us silent.

The "Portal" is the same as that described by Schiller; and before it, while man gazes, "comes boding of terror, comes phantasm and error," and the bravest are perplexed "with doubt and misgiving." But the exhortation to act comes as a release from fear, and

> . . . heard are the Voices,—
> Heard are the Sages,
> The Worlds and the Ages:
> "Choose well, your choice is
> Brief and yet endless:

The final bidding of the poem is to "work and despair not," remembering always the "infinite nature of duty," that, finite as man is, his deeds involve the infinite and eternal whole:

> Here eyes do regard you,
> In Eternity's stillness;
> Here is all fulness,
> Ye brave, to reward you;
> Work and despair not."

In this little poem,[91] by no means one of Goethe's greatest achievements, Carlyle succeeds, through his translation, in condensing most of Goethe's wisdom on the art of life, in relation to ultimate ends: his doctrine that reality lies behind the temporal; that man is to act out the eternal in his present daily life; that his spirit creates its own setting; and that, above all, he is to work and hope in silence, himself a part of a greater Silence, moving between the silences of the stars and the graves. In his conception of Silence, Carlyle at times reaches the ethical sublime. From the amalgam of ideas which he fashioned from those of Goethe, Fichte, and Novalis, he arrived at a notion of the indescribable splendor of the pure moral act, an act rooted in the silence of the soul, expanding in the physical world between the upper and nether silences, expressing the infinite silence of the universe, and continuing mysteriously to grow and ramify in the silent world of moral relationships.

On the problem of life Carlyle had singularly few specific things to say; but those things were of major magnitude, and when followed to the limit of their implications, they ultimately involved, in one way or another, all the problems which a more comprehensive and systematic ethic might have included.   Renunciation; the reverence for sorrow; silence; work and duty, rather than happiness, as the end of life,— these were the chief tenets of his practical belief.   For their underlying meaning, their essential substance, Carlyle was indebted to Fichte, Novalis, and his Calvinist background; for their phrasing, for their renewed significance, and for the context which made them of saving practical importance, he was "endlessly indebted to Goethe."

Chapter IX

CONCLUSION

In his handling of German ideas Carlyle touched nothing that he did not alter. From first to last, he was the born Calvinist, seeking to reconstruct, largely from German thought, a belief in the transcendent sovereignty of Right and in a world of immanent divine law. Independent in spirit, groping half-articulately for new forms of concept and faith, innocently wandering among complex systems of thought, and naïvely appropriating a huge segment of one doctrine and uniting it with part of another, he dwelt fundamentally in the steadfast simplicity of an Hebraic point of view. He carried into his religious and philosophic thinking all the characteristics discernible in his daily life: his self-sufficiency, his aloofness, his tortuous indirectness of thought, his spontaneity of choice, his appreciation of character, his exaltation of work, his love of fact, his constant sensing of an other-worldly presence in common things. In the early period of his career, as we have examined it, he was more liberal and inquisitive than he was ever to be again. He attempted at moments, in spite of his temperamental aversion, to penetrate into the abstract region of metaphysics, and somehow to find there the concrete assurances which his dogma-emancipated spirit demanded. That he found as much as he did is not a little strange, and perhaps hardly to be expected. The result of his attempt could scarcely be other than a curiously eclectic philosophy, an unharmonious body of thought which indeed, after 1834, rapidly relegated to the background most of its metaphysical elements, when his interests became centered on history and social ideals. The disharmony thus present in his early formulation of principles persisted throughout his life, and accounts in no small degree, especially in the light of his fragmentary grasp of German ideas, for Carlyle's later outbursts of pessimism.   Though he had partially accepted the "new evangel" presented by Germany, he never parted wholly from some of the thought-forms of dogmatic Christianity: he never made the "exodus from Houndsditch." Though the author of *Sartor Resartus*, he never adequately re-tailored his convictions.   His failure to do so contributed one of the major elements in the "Victorian compromise." And we are now able to glimpse, from a survey of some of the springs of his thought, in what striking degree his eclectic method with German ideas helped to determine the character of the Victorian epoch.

By the time Carlyle began the writing of *Cromwell* (late in 1843), his universe had become considerably simplified. His old preoccupations with space, time, Reason, organism, symbolism, "revelation," had all become merely the background, or the premise, of his more specific concerns.   The physical world remained, indeed, the "Garment of God." The subjectivity of time and space was still, for him, the guarantee of the supreme reality of mind and spirit.   And the ideas of organism, symbolism, and spiritual revelation through matter were constantly integral in his teachings. But God had become less the Divine Idea and more the Maker, less the Being whom Faust dared not name, and more the Jehovah of eternal law and wrath, namable by Carlyle in scores of passages of thundering rhetoric.   And physical fact, in turn, became more palpable, less and less the unreal shadow of an *Ich*. As he increasingly dealt with historical fact, and as he witnessed the facts of social disintegration all about him, it became difficult to think in terms merely of *das Vergängliche*.

Among the early notions which remained unchanged, bright, and dynamic for him, none were more unfailingly vital than the conceptions of moral right as the only reality, of the duty of obedience and "self-annihilation," of the religious nature of work, of the organic unity of all things, and of the reality of heroes.   These are discernible to the end in all his writings, as the theoretic foundation of his historical works from *The French Revolution* to *Frederick the Great,* and as the basis of the dynamic and prophetic note in his social pamphlets.   They explain his hatred of democracy, his advocacy of the organization of labor, his shrill outcries against what he thought were the stupidities and the shallow panaceas of his time.   It is clear at this point, now that we have examined the background and the development of his thought, that without the shaping influence of German doctrines, Carlyle would hardly have attained that prophetic stature which made him so great a force in Victorian life.   Though as a Calvinist shorn of his theology he began, as we have seen, with a definite predisposition toward belief in great men, in a spiritual-material unity, in self-annihilating devotion to work, he was nevertheless, in the ten years preceding his translation of the *Wanderjahre,* without hope, or peace, or any formulae for his general convictions.

On the whole, as M. Cazamian has observed, German literature and thought were influences upon Carlyle second only to those of his parents.   They became for a time the country of his soul.   And they remained, even throughout the later years, part of the sturdy foundation of all that he thought and was.   The essential spirit of the German genius, its idealism and its sense of the organic, fortified his faith in a moral reality beside which all things spatial and temporal were the "stuff that dreams are made on."   It reconciled him to the silence of destiny, when he could no longer believe in immortality as a dogma, and confirmed him in his half-mystical unwillingness to say more than that, after the phantasmagoria of evil and suffering, "our little life is rounded with a sleep."   To the end he was profoundly indebted to Goethe, to German literature as a whole, and to all "that multifarious business of German philosophy."

APPENDIX

CARLYLE'S HANDBOOKS
ON THE HISTORY OF GERMAN LITERATURE

By W. Leopold, Northwestern University

An examination of the sources from which Carlyle drew his knowledge of the history of German literature does not result in taking credit away from him; it shows his originality and the quality of his literary judgment in the brightest light. Up to the time when his first general survey of German literature, his essay on the *State of German Literature*, was published (1827), no adequate history of it had been written; that of Koberstein appeared in the same year, 1827, that of Gervinus in 1835-40, that of Vilmar in 1845, that of Wackernagel in 1848-55. In fact, there was no history of *English* literature other than Warton's fragments in existence in those days. What books there were on German literature strike us today as curiously distorted in many points; many of them were laborious collections of countless details, from which the uninitiated reader could not hope to glean a satisfactory survey of essentials. No wonder, then, that Carlyle's predecessors in England failed to grasp the spirit of German literature, and that the educated public, even including those particularly interested in it, went far astray in their attempts to appreciate it.

It is necessary to examine the situation from these various angles[1] in order to be able to appreciate Carlyle's genius in gaining a view which to this day remains close to the judg-

---

[1] I have tried to do this in the opening chapter of my publication (Werner Leopold: *Die religiöse Wurzel von Carlyles literarischer Wirksamkeit*, Halle, 1922), of which this appendix is essentially a summary.

ment of posterity based on a century's painstaking research and the test of time.

Carlyle is not stingy in giving the sources of his information. Certain handbooks he uses again and again. They are dear companions to him. On various occasions he mentions the Leipzig *Konversationslexikon*, Flögel, Meister, Koch, Eichhorn, Bouterwek, Jördens, Horn.

He refers repeatedly to the Leipzig *Konversationslexikon*; in the first essay on Jean Paul Richter (1827) he gives it among the sources for biographies of German writers. The reference is doubtless to the encyclopedia edited in its first edition by Löbel in Leipzig (1796), which later developed into the well-known Brockhaus encyclopedia. It could help him in details, but hardly contributed to his profound appreciation of the spirit of German literature as a whole.

Karl Friedrich Flögel's *Geschichte der komischen Litteratur* (4 vols., Leipzig, 1784-87) could be of no help to him either for biographical details, which are never given, or for a general survey and evaluation. The work gives data first about the satire, then about the comedy of all nations, volumes three and four dealing with those of the Germans. But it consists of nothing but bibliographical material, accumulated with hopeless industry and learning and with a total absence of ideas and ideals. Carlyle mentions the book repeatedly; it may have called his attention to certain early authors, among them Hans Sachs; but it is not surprising that in the mass of dry material some other significant writers, about whom he might have learned here, escaped his notice. It is certain that of German thought he found nothing in this work; it could serve only as a reference work for statistical details.[1]

Another work which he mentions on several occasions,

---

[1] Flögel's *Geschichte des gegenwärtigen Zustandes der schönen Literatur in Deutschland* (Jauer Schulprogramm, 1771), in spite of its suggestive title, can hardly have been in Carlyle's hands on account of the manner of its publication.

Leonard Meister's *Charakteristik deutscher Dichter* (Zürich, I, 1785; II, 1787), is again of biographical character. In unconnected portraits of poets it leads down to the late eighteenth century, not including Goethe, Schiller, and Herder. Its style is awkward and pedantic. It had a passing importance as one of the earliest treatments of the subject; Coleridge read it in 1799 while studying in Göttingen. No trace of an influence of any kind on Carlyle can be found.

Erduin Julius Koch's *Compendium der deutschen Literaturgeschichte* is another bibliographical and statistical handbook after the order of Flögel's work. As such it retains its value for the investigator; minute accuracy and scrupulous inclusiveness make it a priceless source of information, particularly about minor literary stars which have long since faded out of the sky of German literature. How great the demand was for a survey of German literature is testified by the fact that the first volume (Berlin, 1790) was sold out and re-edited (1795) before the second was published (1798). The work is incomplete. Of the whole plan, embracing all literature in the widest sense, only the part on poetry was finished. The material is subdivided by *genres*, each of which is followed through the whole history of literature, precluding any insight into the spirit of a period. There is no sign of life in the work, nothing which could have stimulated Carlyle's thought.

Johann Gottfried Eichhorn was a man whose erudition and literary energy must cause admiration. He was a professor of oriental languages in Jena and later in Göttingen, where Coleridge studied under him. He wrote outstanding works in all fields of theology and, in addition, many books on the Hebrew and Arabic languages, on history, biography, etc. His widespread research culminated in his *Allgemeine Geschichte der Kultur und Litteratur des neueren Europa* (Göttingen, 1796-99, 2 vols., unfinished). The general demand for works on the history of literature drove him into research in that field. The first volume of his *Litterärgeschichte* (Göttingen,

1797) was sold out in two years and re-edited in 1812. The second volume (1814) had the more accurate title *Litter-ärgeschichte der drey letzten Jahrhunderte.* But the scope is so wide (literature in the widest sense and of all nations of the world) that out of (471 + 1263 =)1734 pages, only 91 pages are allotted to German literature in the narrower sense (vol. I, pp. 394-395 and vol. II, pp. 339-428). Such space allowed no more than a mere enumeration of the most important names. The arrangement is by *genres,* each of which is followed through three centuries. No inspiration could come to Carlyle from such a meagre sketch.

In the meantime Eichhorn's larger work *Geschichte der Litteratur von ihrem Anfang bis auf die neuesten Zeiten* had appeared (Göttingen, 1805-12, 4 vols., in 7 parts). His starting point in each chapter, the general conditions of civilization, could have been very fruitful. But he is satisfied with lifeless enumerations of facts. He deals with all fields of letters and learning in all nations, literature proper being only one field among many in the history of the human mind. Literature is subdivided into minute parcels, each of which is recorded in splendid isolation. Eichhorn stands with both feet in the eighteenth century, against the spirit of which Carlyle fought with such passionate ardor. He has no use for Kant or for Romanticism. He speaks of Goethe and Schiller with reluctant appreciation, but does not recognize their outstanding importance. He includes them in a "tri-umvirate of great genius" (IV^2, p. 990), but the third writer whom he links with them is—Klinger! He is a great admirer of Klinger.

Such lack of perspective is by no means unusual in the writings of contemporary German critics. Our admiration for Carlyle's perspicacity rises in comparing his stand with theirs. It is obvious that Carlyle could draw no vital impulse from a pedantic compilation of facts like Eichhorn's. Nor is he sparing in his use of contemptuous epithets for Eichhorn's "almost frightful laboriousness." In fact, writers like Eichhorn have to bear their share of guilt in the reputation for industrious pedantry which German scholarship acquired, a reproach not at all unjustified at the time of Father Bouhours,[1] but handed down, owing to the force of inertia, even to our days in the face of so much evidence to the contrary.

Friedrich Bouterwek's *Geschichte der Poesie und Beredsamkeit seit dem Ende des dreizehnten Jahrhunderts* (Göttingen, 1801-19, 12 vols.) represented a great step forward; it was the connecting link between the pedantic compilations of the Rationalistic age and the great works which the Romantic period was soon to bring. Bouterwek was also a professor at the University of Göttingen, Eichhorn's colleague.[2] He taught philosophy, wrote in various fields of learning, and is a figure of note in the history of esthetics; he is reputed to have been one of the most popular and inspiring teachers. Himself a poet and a patron of rising poetic talents, he writes in a more lively style, although with the detachment of a scholar, objective even where he feels obliged to antagonize, as he does with regard to the Romantic School. He shows the poets and writers in their age and environment and thus achieves better cultural portraits than Eichhorn with his more ambitious aim. He rejects statistical data and arrives at better cross-sections by eliminating the system of sub-dividing poetic *genres* too nicely. In spite of the title of his work, he begins with the oldest period, drawing on Koch for many facts. The contemporary period is dealt with

[1] Compare "Mr. Carlyle and Père Bouhours," *Catholic World*, vol. 13 (1871), pp. 820-825.

[2] The Americans Everett and Bancroft, while students in Göttingen (1815-17 and 1818-20 respectively), lived in the house where Bouterwek resided (1797-1828), Weender Strasse 8. In the same house, incidentally, I wrote a hundred years later my *Religiöse Wurzel*, not insensible to its illustrious associations. A biography of Bouterwek was published by Gustav Struck: *Friedrich Bouterwek*, Rostock, Carl Hinstorffs Hofbuchdruckerei, in which also Bouterwek's relation to Friedrich Heinrich Jacobi is analyzed.

"summarily"; the survey does not extend much beyond the year 1800. He fully recognizes Goethe's importance. The older period is illustrated by many specimens of literature. His work is the first from which the reader could really gain an impression of German literature. It is not surprising, then, that it was generally used until Koberstein's history appeared (1827); that it influenced even his antagonists of the Romantic School; that it was the source of most English magazine articles during that time when German literature was the vogue in England; and that William Taylor of Norwich, the ardent apostle of German literature in England, called it his "instructor and guide." Carlyle was able to glean many details from it. It did not, however, influence his thought, for Bouterwek's detached scholarly treatment could not and did not inspire him. Bouterwek rejects with some sharpness only two writers: Fichte and Schelling, the Romantic philosophers—exactly those in whose writings Carlyle found the most inspiration.

Karl Heinrich Jördens's *Lexikon der deutschen Dichter und Prosaisten* (6 vols., Leipzig, 1806-11) is frequently mentioned by Carlyle. It is a biographical reference-work in alphabetical order, on which Carlyle (like Bouterwek) drew freely for details on the poets' lives; the Appendix on Schubart in his *Life of Schiller* is based on Jördens. But an influence on his thought or even on his appreciation of German literature is out of the question.

Looking back over this array of works on German literature, we easily come to the conclusion that Carlyle received from them no contributions to the formation of his thought, although they helped him in factual details. Moreover, their very wealth of material was instrumental in giving other English writers a distorted view of German literature. None of them was perfect enough to give a true perspective to anybody unable to sift their offerings with the help of a thorough first-hand knowledge of German literature. Carlyle stands out from other contemporary English, and even German, critics by his remarkable grasp of the vital and the enduring.

One of his guides was on a different level, the one whose books he "pretended reviewing" in his *State of German Literature*: Franz Horn.[1] The two works which Carlyle used over a long period (at least 1826-1845), for reference, and recommended to all students of German literature "as a valuable guide and indicator," were *Umrisse zur Geschichte und Kritik der schönen Literatur Deutschlands während der Jahre 1790-1818* (Berlin, 1819) and *Die Poesie und Beredsamkeit der Deutschen, von Luthers Zeit bis zur Gegenwart* (3 vols., Berlin, 1822-24). Horn, himself a Romantic novelist of great ambition and of temporarily considerable success, writes in a manner strikingly different from the more or less dry enumerations of his Rationalistic predecessors. His style is vivid, enthusiastic, poetic, though it cannot be denied that it frequently degenerates into freakishness and loquacity. His enthusiasm and his gift for amiable chatting sometimes lead to fascinating portrayals of contemporary reactions to the works of great writers. But on the other hand the exaggerated organization of previous works gives way to a total lack of coherence. Unconnected sketches of poets and writers follow each other in chronological order with no attempt at scholarly elucidation of historical developments. His greatest fault is that he likes polemics better than direct criticism. But he always tries to find out the merits of a writer; a warm heart leads his pen where his precursors had exercised their intellects only. He tests the world-view of every writer by comparison with his own convictions, in which religion and patriotism rule. Thus he

---

[1] A competent biography of him has been published by Lisel Grützmacher: *Franz Horn, ein Nachfahre der Romantik*, Universitäts-Verlag, Münster i.W., 1928. Unfortunately, this study fails to notice the important line leading forward from Horn to Carlyle. Compare my review in the *Journal of English and Germanic Philology*, vol. 28 (1929), pp. 452-455.

wants above all to know whether a given work is a genuine manifestation of the Divine Idea, and he has the highest conceptions about a writer's mission.

In this and other respects he is the only historian of German literature who has a basis similar to Carlyle's. They are both idealists; Fichte appeals to both much more than does Kant; Love and the Divine Idea are the touchstones of one as well as the other; poetry, life, and belief are for both one and the same thing; both reject entertainment as the purpose of poetry; both write in the manner of teachers, moralists, preachers, prophets, with warm enthusiasm and constructive zeal; they also have in common a great admiration for Jean Paul. This does not mean, however, that Carlyle is influenced by Horn. The latter is too much inferior to Carlyle to make any considerable contribution to the formation of his thought, which to a certain extent justifies a certain condescension with which Carlyle occasionally speaks of Horn. Yet, in spite of this condescension, Carlyle recognized and acknowledged him as a kindred spirit. It is therefore no accident that Horn's works are alone among his handbooks on German literature which supplied him with some minor accessories for his message— verbal reminiscences not restricted to purely factual information and woven into the very fabric of his thought. I have shown[1] that the significant formulae, "the Everlasting Yea" and "the Everlasting No," in *Sartor*, have to be credited to Horn. I have pointed out[2] that a passage in the *State of German Literature* concerning the denied "blessing of half-sleep" in reading philosophical treatises, and a passage in his diary rejecting the comparison of style with a coat, quite likely go back to Horn; likewise an allegory, also in the *State of German Literature*, about the garment, body, and

---

[1] *Die religiöse Wurzel*, pp. 55-56, and again "Thomas Carlyle and Franz Horn," *Journal of English and Germanic Philology*, vol. 28 (1929), p. 215.

[2] *Journal of English and Germanic Philology*, vol. 28, pp. 216-217.

soul of poetry. I can here add a further resemblance. In the same article, Carlyle has a sentence: "With mere readers for amusement, therefore, this criticism has, and can have, nothing to do." Horn says in *Poesie und Beredsamkeit* (vol. 1, pp. 28-29) that "die herrschenden Ansichten über die Poesie von der Mittelmässigkeit und Seichtheit stammen, und dass es vergeblich ist, Leuten die sich nur amüsiren wollen—das widerliche Wort sagt alles—ein neues oder vielmehr das urälteste Evangelium zu predigen." This sentence furnishes an excellent example of the similarity between Horn and Carlyle: it could well pass for a translation from Carlyle, in its central convictions, its critical attitude, its choice of words, and even its details of style.[1] To be sure, the similarity between the two passages might well be explained from the similarity of their critical attitude alone. But at least it serves to elucidate the fact that Horn was congenial to Carlyle. Even so, all these "influences" touch only the surface of Carlyle's thought, the formulation of fragments of thought rather than its substance. They demonstrate clearly, however, that Horn's books meant much more for Carlyle than his other handbooks, and explain why they were really dear to him.

With these meagre findings we can conclude our survey of the handbooks on German literature which Carlyle used. I have discussed the inferiority of his predecessors in England who tried to give information on German literature in detail,[2] including Madame de Staël, who, in spite of the similarity of her attitude towards German literature, proved to have yielded for Carlyle nothing more than an inspiration for further first-hand study. The literary criticism of the Schlegel brothers, the fathers of modern literary criticism, had a very great influence on French and English Romanticism; Coleridge, though he denies it, is in his *Biographia*

[1] Compare my analysis of Carlyle's style in *Die religiöse Wurzel*, pp. 69-94, particularly pp. 74-76.
[2] *Ibid.*, pp. 15-41.

Literaria largely under their spell. Carlyle knew their writings and referred to them. But Dr. René Wellek has shown
in an able summary[1] how little ground there is for believing
in an influence. Wachler's lectures on *Werden und Wirken
der Literatur* (1819), also a work of good quality, Carlyle
did not know until 1830, when Goethe sent him the book—
just in time to suggest to him the title of Teufelsdröckh's
book,[2] but not much else. After the period discussed,
German literature gradually recedes from the foreground
of his interest, although it never disappeared from his intellectual horizon. It is not likely that the handbooks with
which he later became acquainted contributed to any larger
extent to his thought.[3]

Carlyle thus did use handbooks for information about
facts, but their influence on his thought is negligible. If
the result of this investigation is essentially negative, it at
least throws some light on his first-hand knowledge of
German literature and on the originality and sagacity of his
appreciation. Frequently he succeeds better than the writers
of his handbooks in discovering lasting values. He had a
keen sense for finding manifestations of a spirit which
agreed with his own gospel. But "influence" is too mechanical a term to apply to the discoveries of a mind of such
power as Carlyle's.

[1] *Xenia Pragensia* (1929), pp. 384-387.
[2] *Xenia Pragensia* (1929), p. 377.
[3] Among them Taylor's *Historic Survey of German Poetry*
(1828-30), with which I have dealt at length in *Religiöse Wurzel*,
pp. 20-23.

NOTES

(All Roman numerals in brackets, following the titles of works cited in the Notes, refer to the appropriate volumes in the writer's "collected works." This method of citation makes possible a more specific reference than would the mention of the volume number only, or the title of an essay, chapter, etc. All references to Goethe's *Wilhelm Meisters Wanderjahre* are to the edition of Stuttgart, 1821, which Carlyle used in translating that work; occasional reference is also made to the later, enlarged form of the work, as in Vols. XIX and XX of the "Jubiläums-Ausgabe." The texts of the standard editions of Kant and Fichte were not always accessible during the preparation of this study. The texts which I have used in the one-volume German editions of the *Kritik der reinen Vernunft*, and of Fichte's *Über das Wesen des Gelehrten, Die Bestimmung des Menschen, Die Grundzüge des gegenwärtigen Zeitalters*, and *Die Anweisung zum seligen Leben* have all been collated with the standard texts listed in the Bibliography, and made identical with them except for occasional variations in punctuation and spelling. All references to Carlyle's writings are to the Centenary Edition, edited by H. D. Traill, London, 1896-99, except for *Sartor Resartus* and *On Heroes*, which have been cited in the editions of Archibald MacMechan, Boston, 1896 and 1901, respectively.)

C. F. H.

NOTES TO CHAPTER I

1. David Masson, *Edinburgh Sketches and Memories*, London, 1892, p. 341.
2. Carlyle, "Varnhagen von Ense's Memoirs," *Critical and Miscellaneous Essays*, IV, p. 108.
3. H. L. Stewart, "Carlyle's Conception of Religion," *American Journal of Theology*, XXI (1917), p. 46.
4. *Cf.* B. H. Lehman, *Carlyle's theory of the Hero*, Durham, N. C., 1928, p. 90. Also, J.-M. Carré, *Goethe en Angleterre*, Paris, 1920, p. 102.

Goethe's influence has been exaggerated, more or less, by O. Baumgarten, *Carlyle und Goethe*, Tübingen, 1906: just as the influence of German Idealism has been heavily stressed by M. Boeuf (*Pseud.*

Camille Bos), "Le Kantisme de Carlyle," *Archiv für Geschichte der Philosophie*, XV (1902), pp. 32-41; B. Fehr, "Der deutsche Idealismus in Carlyles Sartor Resartus," *Germanisch-romanische Monatsschrift*, V (1913), pp. 81-101; P. Hensel, *Carlyle*, Stuttgart, 1901; Dilthey, "Thomas Carlyle," *Archiv für Geschichte der Philosophie*, IV (1891), pp. 260-85.

5. *Cf.* H. Kraeger, "Carlyles deutsche Studien und der Wotton Reinfred," *Anglia*, Beiblatt, IX (1898), pp. 193-219; T. Geissendoerfer, "Carlyle and Jean Paul Friedrich Richter," *Journal of English and Germanic Philology*, XXV (1926), pp. 540-53; R. Wellek, "Carlyle and German Romanticism," *Xenia Pragensia,* Sumptibus societatis neophilologorum, 1929, pp. 390-403; Susanne Howe, *Wilhelm Meister and his English Kinsmen*, N. Y., 1930, Chapter V.

6. Carlyle, *Two Notebooks: from the 23d March, 1822, to the 16th May, 1832*, ed. C. E. Norton, N. Y. (Grolier Club), 1898, p. 41. For a less hostile entry, see p. 204.

7. *Cf.* Carré, p. 113.

8. See Carlyle, "Schiller," *Misc. and Crit. Essays*, II, p. 173; Goethe, *Generalbeichte*, 5th stanza; also, Kraeger, "Carlyle's Stellung zur deutschen Sprache und Litteratur," *Anglia*, XXII (1899), p. 124; L. Kellner, *Die Englische Literatur der neuesten Zeit, von Dickens bis Shaw*, Leipzig, 1921, pp. 79-90, especially pp. 88-89.

9. Carlyle's wording in *Sartor Resartus*, ed. MacMechan, Boston, 1896, p. 177. Carlyle's more common translation is that found in his *Wilhelm Meister's Apprenticeship and Travels* (Centenary Ed.), I, p. 386: ". . . doubt of any kind can be removed by nothing but activity." *Cf.* Goethe, *Werke* (Jubiläums-Ausgabe), XVIII, p. 81.

10. *Two Notebooks*, p. 140: "Novalis is an anti-Mechanist; a deep man; the most perfect of modern spirit-seers. I thank him for somewhat."

11. Novalis, *Werke*, ed. H. Friedmann, Berlin, 1908, III, p. 185.

12. Kraeger, "Carlyle's Stellung," etc., p. 141.

13. *Cf.* Wellek, *Immanuel Kant in England*, Princeton, N. J., 1931, pp. 139, 286; see, also, J.-M. Carré, "Quelques lettres inédites de William Taylor, Coleridge, Carlyle à H. C. Robinson sur la littérature allemande," *Revue Germanique*, VIII (1912), p. 40 *et seq.*

14. Carré, pp. 102-03.

15. *Cf.* W. F. Hauhart, *The Reception of Goethe's Faust in England in the First Half of the Nineteenth Century*, N. Y., 1909, Chapter III; W. A. Speck, "New Letters of Carlyle," *Yale Review*, July, 1926, p. 6.

16. Hauhart, pp. 61-62.

17. *Id.*, p. 62.

18. *Cf.* Carlyle, *Two Notebooks*, p. 151. See also C. E. Vaughan, "Carlyle and his German Masters," *Essays and Studies by Members of the English Association*, Oxford, 1910, pp. 168-183. Vaughan's discussion of Goethe's influence on Carlyle is much more reliable than his treatment of Carlyle and Fichte, in the same essay (pp. 186-195). The essay as a whole, however, is insufficiently founded on a study of the actual sources of Carlyle's ideas.

19. According to the *Two Notebooks*, p. 112, by 1827 Carlyle had read only the first hundred pages of the *Critique of Pure Reason*. On the other hand, according to *The Love Letters of T. C.* (ed. A. Carlyle, London, 1909), II, p. 324, he read to the hundred and fiftieth page by September, 1826. Carlyle's copy of the *Critique* which now lies in the Carlyle House at Chelsea (the 6th ed., Leipzig, 1818) bears no marks of ever having been opened. Page 100 of this edition would have taken Carlyle well into Kant's discussion of the Categories; page 150 would have taken him into Chapter II of the Transcendental Analytic, Book II, "Anticipations of Perception." Nowhere does Carlyle mention any of the principles treated in these two sections of the *Critique*.

20. *Cf.* B. Fehr, 82; also, p. 84: "Kants, und Fichtes Einfluss auf Carlyle ist weitgehender als der Einfluss Goethes."

21. *Cf.* Hensel, p. 66; A. Ströle, *Thomas Carlyle's Anschauung vom Fortschritt in der Geschichte*, Gütersloh, 1909, p. 76; W. Leopold, *"Die Religiöse Wurzel von Carlyles Literarischer Wirksamkeit . . .,"* Halle, 1922, pp. 58-59; C. F. Harrold, "Carlyle's Interpretation of Kant," *Philological Quarterly*, VII (1928), 345-57.

22. Knut Hagberg, *Carlyle*, Stockholm, 1925, p. 111; *cf.* Carlyle, *Life of Schiller*, pp. 108 *ff.*

23. The passages on Kant in Carlyle's *Life of Schiller* were added in 1825, when the work appeared in book form after running serially in the *London Magazine* (Oct., 1823–Sept., 1824). Batt is probably in error when he asserts that Carlyle here attempts to suggest the nature of Kant's philosophy through the medium of Schiller's essays. Carlyle himself professed to find scarcely a trace of Kant in Schiller's writings subsequent to his Jena period! Carlyle's remarks on Kantian doctrine are indeed, as Hildebrand says, little more than a caricature. Wilm has shown how little of the metaphysical, and how much of the aesthetic and ethical, Schiller sought in Kant; Carlyle thus found little elucidation of Kant's fundamental metaphysics in the writings of Schiller. . . . *Cf.* Max Batt, "Carlyle's Life of Schiller," *Modern Philology*, I (1903-04), pp. 391-92; A. Hildebrand, *Carlyle und Schiller*, Berlin, 1913, p. 16; Wellek, *Kant in England*,

p. 184; E. C. Wilm, *The Philosophy of Schiller in its Historical Relations*, Boston, 1912, pp. 159-60.

Another medium for Kantian ideas was Reinhold. Carlyle notes: "I begin to see some light through the clouds in Kantism; tho' Reinhold is somewhat of a Will-o'-wisp guide, I fear." Carlyle probably alludes here to C. L. Reinhold's *Briefe über die Kantische Philosophie* (Leipzig, 1786-87), which, however, considered mainly Kant's philosophy in relation to morality and religion, immortality, the existence of God, etc. See *Two Notebooks*, p. 102.

24. Francis Espinasse, *Literary Recollections and Sketches*, London, 1893, p. 59.

25. M. Boeuf exclaims: "Hum! on se demande avec effroi quelles étaient les lectures ordinaires des auditeurs de Carlyle!"—"Le Kantisme de Carlyle," p. 35.

26. N. K. Smith, *A Commentary to Kant's Critique of Pure Reason*, London, 1923, pp. xxiv, 2, 10, etc.

27. *Sartor Resartus*, p. 177.

28. Vaughan, pp. 186, 193, etc.; L. Cazamian, *Carlyle*, Paris, 1913, p. 45. *Cf.* Lehman, pp. 118-119.

29. We shall see, as we proceed, that a number of passages from the *Vocation of Man, Characteristics of the Present Age*, and *The Way to a Blessed Life* are virtually "proof passages" pointing to Carlyle's having been familiar with them.

30. *Two Notebooks*, p. 112.—At this time Carlyle was also reading Bouterwek's "*System of Virtuality*," "Fichte's *Transcendental Idealism*, 'elimination of the object'; that is deducing the not-me from the me?" He mentions "Wagner, Weiller, Hegel, Krug . . . [as] commentators of Kant," and asks if Bardilli's *Rational Realism* is not like the doctrine of Malebranche. He wishes he understood the philosophy of Kant: "Is it a chapter in the history of human folly, or the brightest in the history of human wisdom?" At times Kant reminds him of "father Boscovich." These miscellaneous and unconnected jottings remind us of the highly eclectic and unsystematic nature of Carlyle's readings among the philosophers.—See *Two Notebooks*, pp. 46, 112, etc. I am indebted, however, to Professor Hill Shine's unpublished paper on "Carlyle and the German Philosophy Problem During the Year 1826-27," for a study of the fact that the miscellaneous jottings in the *Two Notebooks* on pp. 112-13 are the results of Carlyle's reading an article by P. A. Stapfer, "Problème de l'esprit humain," *Revue Encyclopedique*, XXXIII (1827), pp. 414-31. Carlyle's notes "were taken almost literally from Stapfer's article." The secondary nature of much of Carlyle's knowledge of German thought is here definitely revealed. That he "can attach next to no meaning" to

Schelling's "System of Identity" as it comes to him indirectly and inadequately through an article in a periodical, is not to be wondered at.

31. *Cf.* Carlyle, *Novalis* [II], pp. 30 *ff.*, 43 *ff.*—Carlyle read *Novalis Schriften*, in the fourth edition, edited by Tieck and Fr. v. Schlegel, Berlin, 1826; and reviewed the work for the *Foreign Review*, July, 1829. Much of Carlyle's knowledge and impression of Novalis was gleaned from Tieck's *Vorrede*, reprinted from the third edition, in which Novalis is said to have zealously studied Fichte's doctrines and to have been encouraged in his mystical tendencies by the works of Fichte, Spinoza, and the Neo-Platonists.

The present writer owns Carlyle's copy of *Novalis Schriften*; no marginal notes or other indication of close study are to be found in the book.

32. Frowahlt Küchler, "Carlyle und Schiller," *Anglia*, XXVI (1903), p. 444; also pp. 69-76. The author here points out Carlyle's obvious neglect of Schiller's primarily *aesthetic* preoccupation in the *Philosophical Letters* and in *The Aesthetic Education of Man*, and his attempt to find in these works a greater ethical and metaphysical content than they possess.

33. *Cf.* Carlyle, *Life and Writings of Werner* [I]; Werner, *Sämmtliche Werke*, Grimma [1840-44] IV, "Die Söhne des Thals," pp. 165-67 (the story of Baffometus, from which Carlyle derived the expression, "Baffometic fire-baptism"), and V, "Die Kreuzenbrüder."— For a fuller indication of Werner's relation to Carlyle's thought, see Chapter VIII, section 4.

We may conveniently note here a number of other minor and somewhat problematical sources.

Verbal loans, though not falling within the scope of the present inquiry, may be seen in connection with Horn and Wachler. For the title of Teufelsdröckh's book, "Die Kleider, ihr Werden und Wirken," Carlyle appears to have drawn upon the title of L. Wachler's *Ueber Werden und Wirken der Literatur* (Breslau, 1819). Carlyle received the work as a gift from Goethe, in August, 1830. *Cf. Correspondence between Goethe and Carlyle*, ed. C. E. Norton, London, 1887, pp. 201-12. In Franz Horn's *Poesie und Beredsamkeit* and in the *Umrisse zur Geschichte und Kritik der Schönen Literatur Deutschlands*, Carlyle found an earlier use of the expressions, "Everlasting Yea" and "Everlasting No," as well as a congenial spirit in which literature was regarded as a revelation of the Divine. Horn, like Carlyle in later years, sought to unite poetry, knowledge, and belief. For further discussion of Horn, see Appendix.

Herder's *Ideen zur Philosophie der Geschichte der Menschheit* repelled Carlyle by its deterministic philosophy. (See *Two Notebooks*, pp. 72-73, and Chapter VI, Sect. 2, of the present work.)   For Lessing Carlyle had great respect, but appears to have thought of him primarily as a brilliant critic and as a man who "deserved to believe." Though Schleiermacher has been suggested as a possible source for many of Carlyle's ideas, there is no evidence supporting the conjectures of Kellner (p. 81), Cazamian (p. 54), or Hagberg (p. 119). Mendelssohn, the author of Phaedon, however, is accorded a long footnote in *The State of German Literature* [I], p. 49, in which the author's arguments on the immortality of the soul are praised in a tone indicating some knowledge of the work. The mere fact that Carlyle mentions these writers—Herder, Lessing, Schleiermacher, Mendelssohn, and yet others—and seems familiar with their ideas and their general significance in the world of German thought, does not warrant an assumption that they played any positive part in the formation of his point of view.

34.   R. Wellek, "Carlyle and German Romanticism," p. 401.

35.   *Id.*, p. 402.

36.   Carlyle, *Novalis* [II], p. 27: "The elder Jacobi, who indeed is no Kantist, says once, we remember: 'It is the instinct of Understanding to *contradict* Reason.' "   I have not been able to trace this wording in any of Jacobi's sentences. The substance of the statement, however, is present in the *Vorrede* of Jacobi's *Werke* (Leipzig, 1812-25), II, pp. 101 ff., in which Understanding is shown as incapable of dealing with the world of Reason. *Cf.*, also, pp. 51-52. For further discussion of Carlyle and Jacobi, see Chapter V, Sect. 3.

37.   Wellek, "Carlyle and German Romanticism," p. 402; A. W. Crawford, *The Philosophy of Jacobi*, N. Y., 1905, pp. 18, 19, 27, 28, 29, 38-39, 40, etc.

38.   Wellek, "Carlyle and German Romanticism," p. 403.

Notes to Chapter II

1.   J. G. Hibben, *The Philosophy of the Enlightenment*, London, 1910, pp. 4-5.

2.   David Hume, *A Treatise of Human Nature*, ed. L. A. Selby-Bigge, Oxford, 1896, p. 183; and *Concerning Human Understanding*, ed. L. A. Selby-Bigge, Oxford, 1894, p. 43.

3.   Carlyle, *Signs of the Times* [II], p. 64.

4.   *Novalis* [II], p. 24.

5. *State of German Literature* [I], p. 79, n.

6. *Characteristics* [III], p. 26.

7. *Goethe* [I], p. 215.

8. *Characteristics* [I], p. 30.

9. David Hartley, *Observations on Man*, London, 1791, I, Chapter I, pp. 3-114, especially Propositions 2, 4, 8-12.

10. Hume, *Concerning Human Understanding*, p. 43.

11. Carlyle, *Signs of the Times* [II], p. 65. Cabanis's famous words, more often remembered in Carlyle's version than in the original, are as follows: "Pour se faire une idée juste des opérations dont résulte la pensée, il faut considérer le cerveau comme un organe particulier destiné spécialement à la produire, de même que l'estomac et les intestins à opérer la digestion, le foie à filtrer la bile, les parotides et les glandes maxillaires et sublinguales à préparer les sucs salivaires." De Cabanis, *Oeuvres*, Paris, 1823-24, III ("Rapports du Physique et du Moral de L'Homme"), pp. 159-60.

12. Jeremy Bentham, *An Introduction to the Principles of Morals and Legislation*, London, 1789, p. xlvii.

13. *Id.*, p. xcviii.

14. Carlyle, *Characteristics* [III], p. 9.

15. *Id.*, p. 11.

16. Bentham, *Int. to the Princ. of Morals and Leg.*, p. lxvii. See, also, Adam Smith, *The Theory of the Moral Sentiments . . .*, London, 1774, pp. 365, 368, 370.

17. Carlyle, *Life of Sterling*, p. 58. *Cf.* Leslie Stephen, *English Thought in the Eighteenth Century*, London, 1876, I, pp. 34-37, 41-43, 50-51, Ch. VI, 446-53; II, pp. 63-76; Ch. IX, sect. VI, Chap. XI, sect. IV, etc.

18. David Masson, *Edinburgh Sketches and Memories*, p. 333.

19. *Letters of Thomas Carlyle*, ed. C. E. Norton, London, 1889, pp. 16, 111.

20. Carlyle, *Heroes*, p. 65.

21. *Cf.* Cazamian, pp. 13-26, etc.; W. S. Craig, *The Making of Carlyle*, London, 1908, pp. 5-20; R. H. Murray, *Studies in the English Social and Political Thinkers of the Nineteenth Century*, Cambridge, 1929, I, pp. 298-299; S. Sagar, *Round by Repentance Tower*, London, 1930, pp. 9-40; and the early Chapters of Froude's *Thomas Carlyle, the First Forty Years of his Life*, and D. A. Wilson's *Carlyle Till Marriage*, etc. . . .

22. *Sartor Resartus*, p. 188.

23. *Cf.* Masson, *Edinburgh Sketches and Memories*, pp. 231 *ff.*

24. William Allingham, *A Diary*, London, 1907, p. 253.

25. *Cf.* Masson, *op. cit.*, and the early chapters of Froude and Wilson.

26. *Early Letters of Thomas Carlyle*, ed. C. E. Norton, London, 1886, I, pp. 51-53, and 81-82.

27. *Id.*, p. 40.

28. *Id.*, pp. 52, 81-82.

29. Wilson, *Carlyle Till Marriage*, p. 222.

30. *Sartor*, p. 151.

31. Stewart's *Dissertation* is now most easily available in his collected *Works*, ed. Sir William Hamilton, Edinburgh, 1854-58, Volume I.

32. Carlyle read this work in the summer of 1816 and in June, 1818. (See the *Early Letters*, I, pp. 81-82 and 159-60.) It is very probable that he consulted it at various times in his Comley Bank and early Craigenputtock period, when he was studying the philosophies of Great Britain and Germany. For example, as late as May 15, 1827, writing to Crabb Robinson relative to applying for the chair of moral philosophy in the projected University of London, Carlyle admits that he will offer "the oddest mixture of Scotch and German, Dugald Stewart and Immanuel Kant." See Edith J. Morley, "Carlyle in the Diary, Reminiscences, and Correspondence of Henry Crabb Robinson," *London Mercury*, VI (1922), p. 617. (Noted by Emery Neff, *Carlyle*, N. Y., 1932, p. 93.)

33. For a full and technical account of Stewart's relation to Kantian doctrines, see Wellek, *Immanuel Kant in England*, pp. 40-49. On the inadequacy of Willich and Nitsch: pp. 7-15.

34. Stewart, *Works*, I, pp. 412-13, 417.

35. *Id.*, pp. 418-20, 421, etc.

36. *State of German Literature* [I], p. 79, n.

37. See Chapter IV, Sect. 1, and Chapter V, Sect. 2.

38. *Early Letters*, I, p. 283.

39. *Id.*, pp. 332-33.

40. Carlyle, *Reminiscences*, ed. C. E. Norton, Everyman ed., London, 1932, p. 187. On Carlyle's first reading of Gibbon, little is known. *Cf.* Masson, *Edinburgh Sketches*, etc., p. 231; also, p. 263.

41. Allingham, *A Diary*, p. 232.

42. Gibbon, *Memoirs of his Life and Writings*, ed. George Birkbeck Hill, London, 1909, p. 97.

43. Allingham, p. 253. (Italics added.)

44. *Cf.* Wilson, *Carlyle Till Marriage*, pp. 165-67, 173-78; Carlyle attributes his study of German to the desire to read Werner, in a letter to Goethe (*Corresp. between Goethe and Carlyle*, pp. 156-157). Carlyle's accounts of his own motives, however, are not always to be trusted, since they frequently betray either a confusion in memory or a care-

lessness in dealing with more than one possibility. His study of German was probably urged by a combination of circumstances: his desire to read Werner, his interest in *De l'Allemagne*, the remark of the "friend" whom he mentioned to Emerson, and the fact that the study of foreign languages was generally in vogue in the Edinburgh of his early years (see J. H. Muirhead, *The Platonic Tradition in Anglo-Saxon Philosophy*, London, 1931, "Carlyle's Transcendental Symbolism," p. 132).

45. Wilson, *Carlyle Till Marriage*, pp. 165, 201-02.

46. *Reminiscences*, p. 241.

47. *Cf.* Carré, pp. 112-114; Leopold, p. 40; Wilson, *Carlyle Till Marriage*, p. 277 *ff*. *Early Letters*, II, pp. 199-200, 219, 223-24, etc.

48. *Corresp. between Goethe and Carlyle*, p. 2.

49. J. A. Froude, *Thomas Carlyle, the First Forty Years*, etc., London, 1882, I, p. 101.

50. F. W. Roe, *Thomas Carlyle as a Critic of Literature*, N. Y., 1910, p. 19.

51. *Id.*, pp. 18-19.

52. *Id.*, p. 19, n.

53. Quoted by Froude, *First Forty Years*, I, p. 101.

54. See Werner Leopold, *Die religiöse Wurzel von Carlyles literarischer Wirksamkeit*, etc., pp. 45-56. This analysis is one of the most cogent treatments of Carlyle's inner development from his student days to 1826.

55. Masson, *Edinburgh Sketches*, etc., p. 299.

56. Garnett, *Thomas Carlyle*, London, 1887, p. 25. Garnett follows Froude in dating the first crisis in 1821.

57. Hensel, p. 35. *Cf.* Carlyle, *Schiller* [II], pp. 206-09 (Moor's victory over himself, in *Die Räuber*. To some extent, like Teufelsdröckh's—an act of the moral will).

58. *The Love Letters of Thomas Carlyle*, ed. A. Carlyle, London, 1909, II, pp. 380-382. The Appendices in this edition of Carlyle's love letters are of great value in the reinterpretation of many phases of Carlyle's early years.

59. Carré, pp. 104-110, especially p. 110.

60. *Early Letters*, I, pp. 206-07.

61. *Ibid.*

62. By "first letter" is meant the first appearing in Norton's edition of the Goethe-Carlyle correspondence, dated June 24, 1824 (*cf.* p. 2). The letter of August 20, 1827, occurs on p. 30 *ff.*; *cf.* p 34.

63. *Early Letters*, II, pp. 219, 223-24, 263, 269.

64. Goethe, *Wilhelm Meister* (Carlyle's translation, Centenary Edition), I, pp. 6-8.

65. Carlyle, *Lectures on Literature*, ed. J. Reay Greene, London, 1892, pp. 201-02.
66. *Reminiscences*, p. 282. (Quotation rearranged.)
67. *Id.*, 281-82.
68. *Love Letters*, II, p. 133.
69. *Id.*, II, p. 324. Carlyle describes himself as "full of projects for instructing my benighted countrymen on the true merits of this sublime system, at some more propitious season."
70. In August, 1827, Carlyle writes to his brother John that he has "been reading Horn, somewhat of Fichte, Schelling, etc. . . ."—*Letters of T. C.*, p. 53.
71. Masson, *Edinburgh Sketches*, p. 283; *cf. Sartor* ("The Everlasting Yea"), p. 169: ". . . the heavy dreams rolled gradually away, and I awoke to a new Heaven and a new Earth."

NOTES TO CHAPTER III

1. *Early Letters*, I, p. 119.
2. *Cf.* Leopold, *Die Religiöse Wurzel*, etc.; pp. 19-20; Hagberg, pp. 103-107. It is generally agreed that Carlyle absorbed a good deal of German doctrine from Coleridge: the world as an organism, the distinction between Reason and Understanding, subjective idealism, etc. But few Carlyleans are willing to point to specific passages in Carlyle as *borrowings*. As we shall see, the influence was one of spirit and attitude. It is necessary, therefore, to reject the long list of parallels drawn up by N. Schanck (*Die sozialpolitischen Anschauungen Coleridges und sein Einfluss auf Carlyle*, Bonn, 1924), as indicating less an influence than a general similarity in point of view. It is easy to do with many writers what Schanck does with Coleridge and Carlyle: enumerate the points of resemblance, and then proceed to infer an influence of one upon the other. In the present case, the error in logic is disastrous.
3. See Chapter V. Evidence of the early impression of Coleridge upon Carlyle's mind may be found in *Wotton Reinfred*, written in 1827, shortly after his marriage, and three years after his first visit with Coleridge at Highgate. Dalbrook, the chief speaker in the novel, pours forth "floods of speech," without "purpose, tendency, or meaning in it," displaying an "imbecility of will," and an inability to "talk with you," only to preach "to you." The germ of all Carlyle's

failure to understand Kant is present in what he makes Dalbrook (Coleridge) say in this unfinished novel. There can be little doubt that Coleridge conditioned his early approach to German ideas. *Cf.* Wellek, *Kant in England*, pp. 185-89; Carlyle, *Wotton Reinfred*, in *Last Words of Thomas Carlyle*, London, 1892, pp. 60-73, 98-99, etc.

4. J. H. Muirhead, *Coleridge as a Philosopher*, London, 1930, pp. 30-31.

5. Carlyle, *Life of Schiller*, p. 114.

6. *State of German Literature* [I], p. 85. On the general nature of German Idealism Carlyle, like Coleridge, had little understanding of the incompatibility between various Idealistic philosophies. Both men were unable to differentiate the technical individualities of Fichte and Schelling, though Coleridge, of course, had much more ability in this respect than Carlyle and was more successful in the attempt.

7. *Early Letters*, II, p. 240.

8. *Life of Schiller*, p. 114, n.

9. *Reminiscences*, p. 195.

10. *Two Notebooks*, pp. 46-47, 78.

11. *Novalis* [II], p. 3.

12. Wellek, *Kant in England*, p. 66.

13. Masson, *Edinburgh Sketches*, p. 277; Muirhead, *Coleridge as Philosopher*, pp. 30-31.

14. Muirhead, p. 30.

15. Carlyle, *Life of Sterling*, pp. 53, 56, 59, 60, etc.

16. *Love Letters*, I, p. 3 *ff.*

17. *Early Letters*, I, p. 355.

18. *Early Letters*, II, p. 107.

19. *Cf.* Leopold, *Die Religiöse Wurzel*, pp. 30-34.

20. *Crabb Robinson in Germany: 1800-1805. Extracts from his Correspondence*, ed. Edith J. Morley, Oxford, 1929, pp. 133-34 (Jan. 30, 1804).

21. *State of German Literature* [I], p. 35.

22. *Jean Paul Friedrich Richter's Review of Madame de Staël's 'Allemagne* [I], p. 476.

23. Madame de Staël, *Germany*, London, 1813, I, p. 224 *ff.*

24. *Id.*, p. 224, etc.

25. Noted by Leopold, *Die Religiöse Wurzel*, etc., p. 33, n. *Cf.* De Staël, *Germany*, II, pp. 345-49; Carlyle, *On Richter Again* [II], pp. 155-58.—Madame de Staël shows further evidence of having possibly contributed to Carlyle's notion of German thought: she uses general terms to indicate German philosophy, rather than specific names for individual doctrines, *e.g.* "doctrines of *Kantism*," which reminds us of Carlyle's "German Metaphysics generally," "Kantism,"

etc.; Cabanis's doctrine that the mind secretes thought as the liver secretes bile is alluded to also; the author likewise asks, like Carlyle, if "Homer, Dante, or Shakespeare knew anything of all this . . . metaphysical reason" or aesthetic theory "to be great writers?" (*Cf. Two Notebooks*, p. 41: "Did Shakespeare know aught of the aesthetic? Did Homer? . . . .") She observed, as Carlyle was later to observe, that Germany was "the country of thought"; that the Germans rejected all pursuit of truth that had a merely utilitarian value; etc. (*Cf. Germany*, I, pp. xiv, 222, 226-27; III, pp. 100, 141; Carlyle, *Signs of the Times* [II], pp. 155-58; *Novalis* [II], pp. 22-29.)

26. *Germany*, I, pp. 269-70; Carlyle, *Goethe's Portrait* [II], p. 371.

27. *Id.*, II, p. 184; Carlyle, "Goethe's Faust," *New Edinburgh Review*, II (1822), pp. 326-27.

28. W. Lütgert, *Die Religion des deutschen Idealismus und ihr Ende*, Erster Teil, Gütersloh, 1923, pp. 8-13, 21, etc.

29. Fichte, *The Doctrine of Religion*, transl. W. Smith, London, 1873, p. 406; Fichte, *Werke*, V, pp. 418-19.

30. Lütgert, pp. 10, 33, 77, etc.—It was not meant here, of course, that Carlyle was in sympathy with the spirit and the methods of the *Aufklärung*. He was, however, a "child" of the period inasmuch as his early enthusiasm for eighteenth-century writers conditioned his development. They aided him in a more immediate understanding of the period than would probably have been possible had he been born twenty-five years later. It is necessary to remember his early fondness for Gibbon, Hume, Smollett, *Hudibras*, Sterne, Johnson, and other eighteenth-century writers for us to realize the degree in which German criticisms of neo-classical rationalism, conventionalism, and skepticism struck home to his convictions. His admiration for Johnson's religious faith is but an exception which proves the point. From the vantage ground of an early enthusiasm and a disappointment with much in the *Aufklärung*, he could readily appreciate the German point of view.

31. The last words of this sentence are quoted by Carlyle, *Diderot* [III], p. 234, and in *Novalis* [II], p. 54.

32. Richter, *Levana* (anon. transl.), London, 1840, pp. 55-57. The last words of this passage are applied in *Novalis* [II], p. 54. *Cf.* Richter, *Levana*, Stuttgart, etc., 1845, pp. 38-41.

33. Schiller, *Works* (2 vols. in one), Philadelphia, 1870, p. 327; *cf.* Schiller, *Werke*, ed. H. Kunz, Hildburghausen, 1868-70, IX, p. 112, etc. Carlyle adopts some of Schiller's words in *Sartor*, p. 104: "Teufelsdröckh gives us long details of his 'fever-paroxysms of Doubt.'"

34. See Fichte, *Characteristics of the Present Age*, transl. W. Smith, London, 1847, Lectures I, II ("General Delineation of the Third Age"), V ("Farther Delineation of the Third Age"), VI ("Scientific Condition of the Third Age"), VIII ("Mysticism as a Phenomenon of the Third Age"). *Cf.* Fichte, *Werke*, VII.

35. Carlyle applied this last sentence in his discussion of Reason and Understanding in his *State of German Literature* [I], p. 83, and cited Schelling's pages.

36. Schelling, *Methode des akademischen Studiums* [V], p. 258. Carlyle apparently read the first edition of the *Methode*, since he omits, as Schelling does in the first edition, the final "s" on the word Studium. See footnote to page 83 of *State of German Literature* [I].

37. Friedrich Schlegel, *Lectures on the History of Literature, Ancient and Modern* (anon. transl.), London, 1871 (Bohn Library), p. 316 *ff.*, especially pp. 321, 323, etc. *Cf.* Schlegel, *Werke*, Wien, 1822-23, II ("Geschichte der alten und neuen Litteratur"), pp. 206-228. Carlyle attributes the last sentence of the paragraph to August Wilhelm Schlegel: "This is August Wilhelm Schlegel's verdict; given in words equivalent to these." *Cf. State of German Literature* [I], p. 80. Friedrich Schlegel's words, in the original, run as follows: "Denn seit Hume ist nichts weiter geschehen, als dass man durch allerlei Bollwerke den schädlichen praktischen Einfluss jener skeptischen Denkart abzuwehren und durch verschiedene Stützwerke, und Nothhülfen das Gebäude aller sittlichen nothwendigen Überzeugungen aufrecht zu erhalten suchte" (II, p. 215).

38. Quoted by Carlyle in *Novalis* [II], p. 35; *cf.* Novalis, *Werke*, II ("Die Lehrlinge zu Sais"), pp. 35-36.

39. Novalis, *Werke*, IV (Die Christenheit oder Europa), pp. 138-39.

40. Kant, *Critique of Pure Reason*, transl. and ed. Norman Kemp Smith, London, 1929, "Preface to the Second Edition," p. 32.

41. *Id.*, p. 29.

42. Quoted by Carlyle in *Jean Paul Friedrich Richter Again* [II], p. 154. *Cf.* Richter, *Werke*, Berlin, 1879, VII ("Hesperus, oder 45 Hundsposttage"), pp. 17-18.

43. *Cf. State of German Literature* [I], pp. 77-85; *Novalis* [II], pp. 22-29.

44. *State of German Literature* [I], pp. 77-78.

45. *Id.*, p. 67.

46. *Id.*, p. 66.

47. *State of German Literature* [I], pp. 74-75.

48. Novalis, *Werke*, III ("Fragmente"), p. 52.

49. *Lectures on Literature*, p. 205.

50. *Life of Schiller*, p. 110.

51. *Goethe's Works* [II], pp. 438-43.

52. *Cf.* Baumgarten, p. 6; H. H. Boyeson, *Essays on German Literature*, N. Y., 1892, p. 83, etc.; L. Kellner, "Goethe und Carlyle," *Die Nation*, XIII (1896), pp. 380-83, 399-403; Carré, *Goethe en Angleterre*, p. 103; etc. . . .

53. *Goethe's Works* [II], pp. 435-43.

54. *State of German Literature* [I], pp. 65-66; *Goethe's Works* [II], p. 437.

55. *Goethe's Works* [II], pp. 436-37, 439-40, 442. *Cf.* Carré, pp. 134-36, 153-54.

56. See, for example, Carré's treatment of Goethe's development (pp. 143-44, 157-60).

57. *Goethe's Works* [II], pp. 430 *ff.* Carlyle sees Goethe's development as beginning in the "pestilential fever of Scepticism" (*Werther*), progressing through "the wild apocalypse of *Faust*" into the second, "Pagan or Ethnic," period (the *Lehrjahre, Epigramme aus Venedig*, etc.), then into the final period of "melodious Reverence" (the *Wanderjahre*, the *West-Oestlicher Divan*, the *Zahme Xenien*, etc.). Any discussion of Goethe's religion is, of course, subject to numerous qualifications. It is hardly necessary to remember that he was at various moments a pantheist, polytheist, realist, as it suited his mood or occupation. Goethe changed and developed in his view of Nature and in his attitude toward Christianity. In his old age he approached a neo-Christian point of view. *Cf.* K. J. Obenauer, *Goethe in seinem Verhältnis zur Religion*, Jena, 1921, pp. 31 *ff.*; 121, etc.

For other views on Goethe's relation to religious doctrines, and on the principle of his life-development, see F. Gundolf, *Goethe*, Berlin, 1922; E. A. Boucke, *Goethes Weltanschauung auf historischer Grundlage*, Stuttgart, 1907; G. Simmel, *Goethe*, Leipzig, 1913; etc.

58. See, for example, Susanne Howe, *Wilhelm Meister and his English Kinsmen*, pp. 88-90, 106, etc.; Boyeson, p. 83; etc. . . .

59. J. M. Seely, *Goethe Reviewed after Sixty Years*, London, 1894, p. 160.

60. *State of German Literature* [I], p. 77.

61. *Id.*, p. 77.

62. Franz Horn, *Umrisse zur Geschichte und Kritik der Schönen Literatur*, etc., p. 54.

63. *Cf.* Josiah Royce, *The Spirit of Modern Philosophy*, Boston, 1892, pp. 173-74 *ff.*; F. Thilly, *History of Philosophy*, N. Y., 1914, pp. 448-49.

64. Garnett, *Thomas Carlyle*, p. 52. (Quotation condensed.)

65. *Novalis* [II], p. 21.
66. *Id.* [II], pp. 21, 42.—"Read *Novalis Schriften* for the second time some weeks ago, and wrote a Review of them. A strange, mystic, unfathomable Book; but full of matter for most earnest meditation. . . ." *Two Notebooks*, p. 135.
67. *Characteristics* [III], pp. 40-41.
68. *Id.*, p. 35.
69. *Id.*, p. 41.

NOTES TO CHAPTER IV

1. Novalis, *Werke*, III, pp. 115-16: "So ist die Welt in der That eine Mitteilung, Offenbarung des Geistes." *Cf. Faust*, Part I, Studierzimmer, l. 1217: "Wir sehnen uns nach Offenbarung."
2. Allingham, p. 247.
3. Dugald Stewart, *Works*, V, "The Idealism of Berkeley," p. 88. See Carlyle, *Novalis* [II], p. 23. Carlyle seems to have consulted this essay of Stewart's for the passage here cited from *Novalis*. His mention of Berkeley, Jones, and other writers suggests Stewart's discussion. "Our Bishop Berkeley," Carlyle writes, "seems to have adopted it [the denial of the existence of matter] from religious inducements: Father Boscovich was led to a very cognate result, in his *Theoria Philosophiae Naturalis*, from merely mathematical considerations. Of the ancient Pyrrho, or the modern Hume, we do not speak: but in the opposite end of the Earth, as Sir W. Jones informs us, a similar theory, of immemorial age, prevails among the theologians of Hindostan." It is interesting now to turn to Stewart's argument (pp. 87-108). Stewart denies the success of Boscovich's treatment of matter, as a futile attempt to discover the *nature* of matter when only its laws are within human comprehension. On the next page he surveys the old theory of the world as a dream, quotes the *Tempest* lines in a footnote, and mentions Plato, Voltaire, etc. He employs the term "Pyhrronists" in relation to Hume (p. 90), the skeptics, and the idealists. But just as he had opposed the doctrine of Boscovich, he also treats adversely the views of Jones, Malebranche, the Hindoos, and Leibnitz. The discussion sets out from an inquiry into Turgot's doctrine that our belief in an external world resolves itself into a belief in the continuance of the laws of nature. It is here that Stewart states his own view that external objects have reality on

the same footing with natural laws; the essence of neither can ever be known, but only their operation. Then follows the passage which Carlyle seems to have had in mind: "The same doctrine [that objects are merely 'phenomènes bien réglés'] is obviously involved in the physical theory of Boscovich, as well as in some of the metaphysical reveries of Malebranche and of Leibnitz . . . The creed, said to be so prevalent among the Hindoos, with respect to the nature of *Matter*, would seem to be grafted on a conception nearly similar. If we may rely on the account given by Sir William Jones, it has not the most distant affinity, in its origin or tendency, to the system of idealism, as it is now commonly understood in this part of the world; the former taking its rise from a high theological speculation, the latter being deduced as a skeptical consequence from a particular hypothesis concerning the origin of our knowledge, inculcated by the Schoolmen, and adopted by Locke and his followers." Sir William Jones is now quoted by the author, and brief mentions are made of *Maya*, the *Vedanta*, and various Indian doctrines. The discussion ends with Stewart attempting to show how these doctrines differ from Hume, and to point out that the fault with both sides in the argument is that they pronounce dogmatically on a mystery placed beyond the reach of our faculties.

Thus Stewart did not give Carlyle a plain case against materialism, but only a skeptical case, showing that matter cannot be known but must, however, be regarded as real "as far as the happiness of creatures can be affected by" it. On the other hand Stewart's willingness to grant the unknowability of matter, its essential mystery, and his insistence on our obligation to understand the *operations*, rather than the essence, of matter and of our knowledge, may have been what led Carlyle to regard "the assiduous study of [Stewart's] Works as the best preparation for studying those of Kant." (*State of German Literature* [I], p. 79.) Stewart's passage has relevance here chiefly in revealing one of the probable sources for Carlyle's habit of reading into several philosophies a greater common element than is sometimes warranted. (*Cf. Two Notebooks*, p. 112.)

4. *Cf.* Carlyle, *Jean Paul Friedrich Richter Again* [II], p. 154; Allingham, p. 247; *Wahrheit aus Jean Pauls Leben*, II, Breslau, 1827: "Eindruck bei Plattner der Stelle aus dem Sturm:

> . . . We are such stuff
> As dream [*sic*] are made on, and our little life
> Is rounded with a sleep.

> . . . Wir sind solcher Zeug
> Wie der zu Träumen [*sic*] und diese kleine Leben
> Umfasst ein Schlaf.

Die Stelle im Shakespeare: 'mit Schlaf umgeben,' von Plattner ausgesprochen, erschuf ganze Bücher von mir."

5. Allingham, p. 247; Cf. *Wotton*, p. 98, and *Heroes*, pp. 42, 79, 86, 127; the dream-grotto passage in *Sartor*, p. 46.

6. See *Psalms* cii, 26 (quoted in *Hebrews* i, 11, 12), civ, 2; *Job* xxxviii, 9; *Isaiah* i, 9, li, 6; etc.

7. See Swift, *Tale of a Tub* . . ., ed. A. C. Guthkelch and D. Nichol Smith, Oxford, 1920, pp. 77-78 *ff.* (in Section II) : "The Worshippers of this Deity had also a system of their Belief, which seemed to turn upon the following Fundament. They held the Universe to be a large *Suit of Cloaths* which *invests* every thing: that the Earth is *invested* by the air; the Air is *invested* by the Stars and the Stars are *invested by the Primum Mobile.* Look on this Globe of Earth, you will find it to be a very compleat and fashionable *Dress.* What is that which some call *Land*, but a fine coat faced with Green? or the Sea, but a Waistcoat of Water-Tabby? Proceed to the particular Works of the Creation, you will find how curious *Journeyman* Nature hath been, to trim up the *vegetable* Beaux: Observe how sparkish a Periwig adorns the head of a *Beech*, and what a fine Doublet of white Satin is worn by the *Birch*. To conclude from all, what is Man himself but a *Micro-Coat*, or rather a compleat Suit of Cloaths with all its Trimmings? As to his Body, there can be no dispute; but examine even the acquirements of his Mind, you will find them all contribute in their Order, towards furnishing out an exact Dress: To instance no more; Is not Religion a *Cloak*, Honesty a *Pair of Shoes*, worn out in the Dirt, Self-love a *Surtout*, Vanity a *Shirt*, and Conscience a *Pair of Breeches*, which, tho' a Cover for Lewdness as well as Nastiness, is easily slipt down for the Service of both . . .?"

See, also, Pascal for a conception of Nature as the *symbolical* dress of the Invisible: "Comme la nature est une image de la grâce, il [Dieu] a fait dans les biens de la nature ce qu'il devait faire dans ceux de la grâce, afin qu'on jugeât qu'il pouvait faire l'invisible, puisqu'il faisait bien le visible . . . . La Nature a des perfections pour montrer qu'elle est l'image de Dieu, et des défauts pour montrer qu'elle n'en est que l'image." (Pascal, *Oeuvres Complète*, ed. F. Strowski, Paris, 1931, III, pp. 187, 202-03.)

Also, Richter, *Levana*, Stuttgart u. Tübingen, 1845, p. 242: "Der Körper ist der Panzer und Kürass der Seele . . ."

It is noteworthy, too, that in the old fable of *Reinecke Fuchs* Carlyle found a "wild Parody of Human Life," "a World-Saturnalia," an "air-pageant from Fancy's dream-grotto," "under grotesque shadows . . . the saddest picture of Reality," and all "in strict accuracy of costume." (See *Early German Literature* [II], pp. 325-29.) Carlyle was familiar with the versions of Gottsched and Goethe, and reviewed D. W. Soltau's translation of 1830 in October, 1831, for the *Foreign Quarterly Review*. He seems also to have known the fable in the versions offered by eighteenth century chap books, and avers that "perhaps many a reader of these pages may, like the writer of them, recollect the hours, when, hidden from the unfeeling gaze of pedagogue, he swallowed *The most pleasant and delightful History of Reynard the Fox*, like stolen waters, with a timorous joy" (*Early Germ. Lit.* [II], pp. 324-25). He probably refers to the edition of 1723 (London), in the title of which is the word "pleasing" rather than "pleasant." Writing in his Journal in 1833, he noted: "If I consider it well, there is hardly any book in the world that has sunk so deep into me as 'Reinecke Fuchs.' It co-operates with other tendencies. Perhaps my whole speculation about 'clothes' arose out of that. It now absolutely haunts me, often very painfully, and in shapes that I will not write even here. Yet, again, how beautiful, how true, is this other: 'Man is an incarnate word.' Both these I habitually feel." (See Froude, *Carlyle, First Forty Years*, London, 1882, II, p. 372.) Thus, while the fable afforded him no specific image or language for a "Garment philosophy," it lay the foundation for Carlyle's habitual conception of the "beast-godhood" in man, the "divine-infernal" nature of life, and his general combination of descendentalism and transcendentalism as seen in the very name of the hero in *Sartor*, Diogenes (transcendental) Teufelsdröckh (descendental). As Barrett has pointed out, "*Reinecke Fuchs* was his 'Orbis Pictus,' in which, as in a wondrous life-vision or 'World-Saturnalia,' human passions in the guise of animals made strange masquerade" (J. A. S. Barrett, *Sartor*, London, 1916, p. 32). The fable reminded Carlyle that it was the "human passions," the soul, that remained the same, whether clothed in human or animal form; the very form of the latter accentuated the fragility and mask-like nature of bodily substance. The fable, however, was only a general or germinal source: Carlyle's clothes philosophy, as he admits, only "arose *out* of it."

8. *Heroes*, p. 42.

9. St. Chrysostom's definition. See Helen Flanders Dunbar, *Symbolism in Medieval Thought*, New Haven, 1929, p. 158. *Cf.* Schiller's little poem, *An die Mystiker* (*Werke*, I, p. 268):

> Das ist eben das wahre Geheimniss, das Allen vor Augen
> Liegt, euch ewig umgiebt, aber von Keinem gesehen.

10. "Wem die Natur ihr offenbares Geheimniss zu enthüllen anfängt, der empfindet eine unwiderstehliche Sehnsucht nach ihrer

würdigsten Auslegerin, der Kunst." (Goethe, *Maximen und Reflexionen*, ed. Hecker, no. 201.)

11. Dunbar, p. 16.

12. *Faust*, Part I, l. 509.

13. *Id.*, "Nacht" (first scene), ll. 501-09. The symbolic value of clothing is stressed in the "Pedagogical Province" in the *Wanderjahre* (pp. 156-57, ed. 1821) ; see Kraeger, *Carlyle's Stellung*, etc., p. 53. In the *Lehrjahre*, likewise, the "fair saint" and her sister "looked upon the body as a foreign substance, as we look upon a garment" (I, p. 454, Carlyle's transl.). *Cf.* Hensel, pp. 86-87; and Kraeger, "Zu Carlyles Sartor Resartus," *Anglia*, X (1899), pp. 12-13 (possible influence of Christian Franz Paullini, German writer of the 17th century).

14. *Sartor*, p. 48.

15. *Maximen u. Reflexionen*, ed. M. Hecker, Weimar, 1907, no. 810. (Freely translated.)

16. Goethe, *Gedichte*, IV, p. 4. (Freely translated.)

17. *Maximen u. Reflexionen*, no. 619. (Freely translated.)

18. *Max. u. Refl.*, nos. 375, 262, 263, 264. (Freely translated.)

19. Carlyle, *Voltaire* [I], p. 424.

20. Carlyle, *Cagliostro* [III], p. 273.

21. Novalis, III, p. 114.

22. Fichte, *Über das Wesen des Gelehrten* (*Werke*, VI), p. 386; *Fichte's Popular Works*, transl. W. Smith, London, 1873, p. 172: "this phase of the Divine Thought [manifestation through the individual's performance of duty] . . . is the only true living being within me; all else, though looked upon even by myself as belonging to my being, is dream, shadow, nothing . . ."

23. Carlyle, *Novalis* [II], p. 23, 27-28; *Faust*, Part I, Marthens Garten, ll. 3456-57.

24. Smith, *Fichte's Pop. Works*, p. 138; *Über das Wesen* [VI], p. 351. *Cf.* Carlyle, *State of German Literature* [I], p. 58; *Heroes* (MacMechan), 179; *On Richter Again* [II], p. 159; etc. Fichte's words are as follows:

"Die gesammte Sinnenwelt mit allen ihren Verhältnissen und Bestimmungen, und insbesondere das Leben der Menschen in dieser Sinnenwelt sind keinesweges an sich und in der That und Wahrheit dasjenige, als welches sie dem ungebildeten und natürlichen Sinne der Menschen erscheinen; sondern es ist etwas höheres und verborgenes, welches der natürlichen Erscheinung bloss zum Grunde liegt. Man kann diesen höheren Grund der Erscheinung in seiner höchsten Allgemeinheit sehr schicklich nennen: die göttliche Idee . . ."

25. Smith, pp. 145-46. (Italics added.) *Cf. Über das Wesen* [VI], p. 359:

"Sodann pflegt man Vorträge dieser Art zu tadeln, wegen ihrer vermeinten Unverständlichkeit. So denke ich mir,—keinesweges Sie, M. H., sondern irgend einen vollendeten Gelehrten in der Bedeutung des Scheines, dem etwa die soeben angestellte Betrachtung unter die Augen käme, als hintretend, hin und her zweifelnd, und endlich tiefsinnig ausbrechend: die Idee, *die göttliche Idee, dasjenige, was der Erscheinung zu Grunde liegt*: was soll nun das bedeuten? . . . ."

26. These two phrases have been freely translated. The long quotation is from Smith, pp. 148-50, 153, 155, condensed without change of wording or alteration of meaning. *Cf. Über das Wesen* [VI], pp. 361, 362-63, 367-68:

"Nun *äussert* sich dieses göttliche Leben, tritt heraus, erscheinet, und stellt sich dar, als solches, als göttliches Leben: und diese seine Darstellung, oder sein Daseyn und äusserliche Existenz ist die Welt . . . es tritt daher zwischen sein wahres inneres Seyn, und seine äussere Darstellung keinesweges etwa eine grundlose Willkühr in die Mitte, zufolge welcher es sich nur theilweise hergäbe, theilweise aber verbärge . . . .

"So wie das Seyn aufgeht und erschöpft ist in dem göttlichen Leben, so gehet das Daseyn, oder die Darstellung jenes göttlichen Lebens auf in dem gesammten menschlichen Leben, und ist durch dasselbe rein und ganz erschöpft. Sodann: das göttliche Leben wird in seiner Darstellung zu einem ins unendliche sich fortentwickelnden, und nach dem Grade der inneren Lebendigkeit und Kraft immer höher steigenden Leben . . . .

"Sie haben an dem so eben aufgestellten Begriffe der Schranken, wenn sie denselben recht scharf in das Auge fassen und erwägen, den Begriff der objectiven und materiellen Welt; oder der sogennanten Natur. Diese ist nicht lebendig, so wie die Vernunft, und einer unendlichen Fortentwicklung fähig, sondern todt, ein starres und in sich beschlossenes Daseyn. Sie ist das,—das Zeitleben anhaltende und hemmende; und allein durch diese Hemmung zu einer Zeit ausdehnende, was ausserdem mit Einem Schlage als ein ganzes und vollendetes Leben hervorbrechen würde. Sie soll ferner durch das vernünftige Leben in seiner Entwicklung selber belebt werden; sie ist darum der Gegenstand und die Sphäre der Thätigkeit und der Kraft-Äusserung des ins unendliche sich fort entwickelnden menschlichen Lebens . . . .

"Und so ist denn, m.H., für unseren Zweck hinreichend erklärt, wie der Welt die göttliche Idee zu Grunde liege, und inwiefern und wie diese dem gemeinen Auge verborgene Idee dem gebildeten Nachdenken begreiflich und zugänglich werde, und ihm notwendig erscheinen müsse, als dasjenige, was der Mensch durch freie That in der Welt hervorbringen solle.

"Ebenso, die das Leben der Menschen das einzige unmittelbare Werkzeug und Organ ist der göttlichen Idee in der Sinnenwelt, so ist dasselbe menschliche Leben auch der erste und unmittelbare Gegenstand dieser Wirksamkeit. Die Fortbildung der menschlichen Gattung hat die göttliche Idee . . . zum Ziele."

27. *Two Notebooks*, p. 151.—On Carlyle's departure from Fichte's doctrine of the Divine Idea, see Margaret Storrs, *The Relation of Carlyle to Kant and Fichte*, Bryn Mawr, Pennsylvania, 1929, pp. 62-73.—*Cf.* Smith, p. 448 (*The Doctrine of Religion*): "Thus may Matter in Space,—Time,—a fixed system of Worlds . . . be deduced with perfect clearness from the laws of reflexion." (Fichte, *Werke*, V, p. 460.)

It is worth noting, before leaving the subject of *Offenbarung*, that Carlyle of course found the doctrine on all hands in contemporary German thought. He notes (*Cf.* Wilson, II, p. 208) that it is common to Goethe, Schiller, Lessing, Herder, and Jacobi. In Schlegel, likewise, he found the following: "Gott erblicken wir nicht, aber überall erblicken wir göttliches; zunächst und am eigentlichsten jedoch in der Mitte eines sinnvollen Menschen, in der Tiefe eines lebendigen Menschenwerks. Die Natur, das Universum kannst du unmittelbar fühlen, unmittelbar denken; nicht also die Gottheit. Nur der Mensch unter Menschen kann göttlich dichten und denken und mit Religion leben. Sich selbst kann niemand auch nur seinem Geiste direckter Mittler sein, weil dieser schlechthin Objekt sein muss, dessen Centrum der Anschauende ausser sich setzt . . ." (*Cf.* F. v. Schlegel, *Ideen*, in A. W. u. F. v. Schlegel, *Athenaeum: Eine Zeitschrift*, Berlin, 1798-1800, III, pp. 11-12.)

28. *Sartor*, p. 236.—The old legend of Fortunatus must not be forgotten as one of the miscellaneous but fundamental sources for Carlyle's attitude toward space and time. It lent Kant's doctrines a peculiarly familiar quality. *Cf. Sartor*, pp. 141, 236, 239; Fehr, p. 93.

29. It is curious that the only lines from Kant which Carlyle actually quotes are not from the first *Critique*, but from the *Critique of Practical Reason*. In *Shooting Niagara* [V], p. 29, n., he wrote: " 'Two things,' says the memorable Kant, deepest and most logical of Metaphysical Thinkers, 'Two things strike me dumb: the infinite Starry Heaven; and the Sense of Right and Wrong in Man.' *Visible* Infinities, both; *say* nothing of them; don't try to 'account for them'; for you can say nothing wise." Carlyle is here obviously employing Kant in the service of his gospel of Silence. Kant, however,

really wrote as follows: "Zwei Dinge erfüllen das Gemüth mit immer neuer und zunehmender Bewunderung und Ehrfurcht, je öfter und anhaltender sich das Nachdenken damit beschäftigt: der bestirnte himmel über mir und das moralische Gesetz in mir." *Kritik der praktischen Vernunft*, "Beschluss," opening sentence.

Two passages from Allingham will illustrate the quite unmetaphysical approach of Carlyle to Kant: "Death and the Future. We know nothing—must leave all that alone. I often think of Kant's notion—no real Time or Space, these are only appearances—and think it is true . . ." "Kant's notions of time and space struck me very much: I had felt greatly oppressed in thinking of the long duration of Time Past, and Kant offered a relief in the suggestion that Time may be something altogether different from what we imagine. I have no kind of definite belief or expectation whatever as to the Future—only that all will be managed with wisdom, the very flower of wisdom." (Allingham, pp. 202, 273.)

30. Kant, *Critique of Pure Reason*, transl. N. K. Smith, p. 71; *Kritik der reinen Vernunft* [III], p. 55: "Der Raum ist nichts anders, als nur die Form aller Erscheinungen äusserer Sinne, d. i. die subjektive Bedingung der Sinnlichkeit . . . ."

31. N. K. Smith, pp. 73-74; *Kritik* [III], p. 57.

32. N. K. Smith, p. 77; *Kritik* [III], p. 59.

33. N. K. Smith, p. 82; *Kritik* [III], p. 65:

"Wir haben also sagen wollen: dass alle unsere Anschauung nichts als die Vorstellung von Erscheinung sei: dass die Dinge, die wir anschauen, nicht das an sich selbst sind, wofür wir sie anschauen, noch ihre Verhältnisse so an sich selbst beschaffen sind, als sie uns erscheinen, und dass, wenn wir unser Subjekt oder auch nur die subjektive Beschaffenheit der Sinne überhaupt aufheben, alle die Beschaffenheit, alle Verhältnisse der Objekte im Raum und Zeit, ja selbst Raum und Zeit verschwinden würden, und als Erscheinungen nicht an sich selbst, sondern nur in uns existieren können. Was es für eine Bewandtnis mit den Gegenständen an sich und abgesondert von aller dieser Rezeptivität unserer Sinnlichkeit haben möge, bleibt uns gänzlich unbekannt. Wir kennen nichts, als unsere Art sie wahrzunehmen, die uns eigentümlich ist, die auch nicht notwendig jedem Wesen, obzwar jedem Menschen zukommen muss. Mit dieser haben wir es lediglich zu tun. Raum und Zeit sind die reinen Formen derselben, Empfindung überhaupt die Materie."

34. N. K. Smith, pp. 84-85; *Kritik* [III], p. 67:

"So werden wir zwar den Regenbogen eine blosse Erscheinung bei einem Sonnregen nennen, diesen Regen aber die Sache an sich selbst, welches auch richtig ist, sofern wir den letztern Begriff nur physisch verstehen, als das, was in der allgemeinen Erfahrung unter allen verschiedenen Lagen zu den Sinnen, doch in der Anschauung so und nicht anders bestimmt ist. Nehmen wir aber dieses Empirische überhaupt, und fragen, ohne uns an die Einstimmung desselben mit jedem Menschensinne zu kehren, ob auch dieses einen Gegenstand an sich selbst (nicht die Regentropfen, denn die sind dann schon, als Erscheinungen empirische Objekte) vorstelle, so ist die Frage von der Beziehung der Vorstellung aus den Gegenstand transzendental, und nicht allein diese Tropfen sind blosse Erscheinungen, sondern selbst ihre runde Gestalt, ja sogar der Raum, in welchem sie fallen, sind nichts an sich selbst, sondern blosse Modifikationen, oder Grundlagen unserer sinnlichen Anschauung, das transzendentale Objekt aber bleibt uns unbekannt."

35. N. K. Smith, p. 89; *Kritik* [III], p. 71: "Es wäre meine eigene Schuld, wenn ich aus dem, was ich zur Erscheinung zählen sollte, blossen Schein machte."

36. Carlyle, *Novalis* [II], pp. 25-26.

37. *Id.* [II], p. 8; *State of German Literature* [I], p. 83.

38. Fehr (p. 82, n.), for instance, hints that Carlyle really comprehended Kant's doctrines; *cf.* C. F. Harrold, "Carlyle's Interpretation of Kant," *Studies in Philology*, VII (1928), p. 345, n.

39. Wellek notes rightly, however (*Kant in England*, p. 197), that Carlyle in *Sartor* (p. 48, etc.) understands that time and space are modes of our human sense, and not of our thought or understanding.

40. N. K. Smith, p. 79; *Kritik* [III], p. 62: "Nun sind Veränderungen nur in der Zeit möglich, folglich ist die Zeit etwas Wirkliches. Die Beantwortung hat keine Schwierigkeit. Ich gebe das ganze Argument zu. Die Zeit ist allerdings etwas Wirkliches, nämlich die wirkliche Form der inneren Anschauung. Sie hat also subjektive Realität in Ansehung der Inneren Erfahrung, d. i. ich habe wirklich die Vorstellung von der Zeit und meinen Bestimmungen in ihr. Sie ist also wirklich nicht als Objekt, sondern als die Vorstellungsart meiner selbst als Objekts anzusehen. Wenn aber ich selbst, oder ein ander Wesen mich, ohne diese Bedingung der Sinnlichkeit, anschauen könnte, so würden eben dieselben Bestimmungen, die wir uns jetzt als Veränderungen vorstellen, eine Erkenntnis geben, in welcher die Vorstellung die Zeit, mithin auch der Veränderung gar nicht vorkäme. Es bleibt also ihre empirische Realität als Bedingung aller unserer Erfahrungen."

41. *Cf. Sartor*, pp. 236, 239; *Wotton*, p. 98, etc.

42. *Sartor*, p. 239. (Quotation slightly condensed.)

43. "Think well, thou too wilt find that Space is but a mode of our human Sense, so likewise Time; there *is* no Space and no Time:

We are—we know not what;—light-sparkles floating in the aether of Deity!" (*Sartor*, p. 48.)

44. *Sartor*, p. 223. (Quotation slightly condensed.)—For Kant on man's glimpsing reality higher than mere Appearance, see N. K. Smith, p. 650; *Kritik* [III], pp. 536-37:

"Nein, die Überzeugung ist nicht logische, sondern moralische Gewissheit, und, da sie auf subjektiven Gründen (der moralischen Gesinnung) beruht, so muss ich nicht einmal sagen: es ist moralisch gewiss, das ein Gott sei usw., sondern ich bin moralisch gewiss usw. Das heisst: der Glaube an einen Gott und eine andere Welt ist mit meiner moralischen Gesinnung so verwebt, dass, sowenig ich Gefahr laufe, die erstere einzubüssen, ebensowenig besorge ich, dass mir der erste jemals entrissen werden könne."

45. *Sartor*, pp. 240, 59 (condensed). In my discussion of Kant's dualism and Carlyle's "monism," I have followed Miss Storrs' excellent treatment (pp. 29-33, etc.).

46. *Sartor*, pp. 238, 48; *State of German Literature* [I], pp. 58-59; *Heroes*, pp. 3-4; etc.

47. What Kant here says of time, he of course would say of space. *Cf.* N. K. Smith, p. 78; *Kritik* [III], p. 61:

"Unsere Behauptungen lehren demnach empirische Realität der Zeit, d. i. objektive Gültigkeit in Ansehung aller Gegenstände, die jemals unseren Sinnen gegeben werden mögen. Und da unsere Anschauung jederzeit sinnlich ist, so kann uns in der Erfahrung niemals ein Gegenstand gegeben werden, der nicht unter die Bedingung der Zeit gehörte. Dagegen streiten wir die Zeit allen Anspruch auf absolute Realität, da sie nämlich, auch ohne auf die Form unserer sinnlichen Anschauung Rücksicht zu nehmen, schlechthin den Dingen als Bedingung oder Eigenschaft anhinge. Solche Eigenschaften, die den Dingen an sich zukommen, können uns durch die Sinne auch niemals gegeben werden, Hierin besteht also die transzendentale Idealität der Zeit, nach welcher sie, wenn man von den subjektiven Bedingungen der sinnlichen Anschauung abstrahiert, gar nichts ist, und den Gegenständen an selbst (ohne ihr Verhältnis auf unsere Anschauung) weder subsistierend noch inhärierend beigezählt werden kann."

With this passage in mind, it is interesting to remember, with Fehr (p. 85), that Carlyle "wirft . . . Raum, Zeit und Materie in denselben Topf."

48. Carlyle, *Novalis* [II], p. 26.

49. *Sartor*, p. 48.

50. *Diderot* [III], p. 181; *Varnhagen von Ense* [IV], p. 109; *Biography* [III], p. 52; *Johnson* [III], p. 88.

51. *Sartor*, pp. 47-48; *Novalis* [II], p. 26, etc. For further discussion of Carlyle's conception of time, see Chapter VI, sect. 4.

52. Novalis, *Werke*, III, p. 53.

53. *Novalis* [II], pp. 24-25.

54. Smith, *Fichte's Popular Works* ("Vocation of Man"), p. 241; *Bestimmung des Menschen* [II], p. 172.

55. George Berkeley, *Works*, ed. A. C. Fraser, Oxford, 1871, I, p. 167.

56. Berkeley, *Works*, I, p. 292.

57. See Fichte, *Werke*, IV, pp. 123, 144, 147, 149, 153, 215, etc.; Storrs, p. 67; Fehr, pp. 86-87.

58. Margaret Storrs, *The Relation of Carlyle to Kant and Fichte*, p. 67.—It is only fair to remember, however, that Carlyle has left a brief, rather laconic, record of his reaction to such a passage as the one we have just noted. In his copy of Smith's *Fichte's Popular Works* (London, 1848), which now lies in the Carlyle House in Chelsea, we note his marginal comment to the following sentence of Fichte's: "But as these attitudes are in every case voluntarily assumed by the Ego, it is itself the only real existence, and the Non-Ego, as well as the varied aspects attributed to it, are but different forms of the activity of the Ego" (p. 77). To these last words, Carlyle's marginal reply is: "Dubious!" By the next paragraph, Carlyle apparently had become wearied of Fichte's discourse on the Ego, for to Fichte's remarks on its opposition to, and use of, the Non-Ego, Carlyle notes marginally, "A clever Ego!" How much of irony or admiration there may be in this ambiguous ejaculation, the reader may judge for himself.

59. Storrs, p. 67.

60. Carlyle, *Novalis* [II], p. 35; Novalis, *Werke*, II, 35.

61. Novalis, III, p. 55. (Freely translated.) Also, p. 53.

62. Carlyle, *Diderot* [III], p. 181.

63. Novalis, III, pp. 53-54.

64. *Id.*, p. 54.

65. *Id.*, p. 90. *Cf.* Fichte, *Vocation of Man* (ed. Smith), p. 295; *Werke*, II, pp. 229-30. (The ego projecting its world.)

It is important to remember, at this point, that we are more concerned with Carlyle's idea than with Fichte's. This is not the place to discuss in detail Fichte's distinction between the *Ich* and the *Nicht-Ich*, in which he was more interested in the former than in the latter, and in which he has nothing to say of the *symbolical* nature of the *Nicht-Ich* in terms which Carlyle would have understood. For Fichte, moreover, the *Nicht-Ich* was only a partial representation of the

Absolute Ego.—From Novalis's language, as from Carlyle's, the *Ich* obviously refers here to the pure ego of man (*das reine Ich*), the *Nicht-Ich* to "the sensualized material" of his destiny, the symbol or *evidence* of his activity as a free moral spirit. It is Novalis rather than Fichte who is properly the background for Carlyle on this point.

66. *Sartor*, p. 155. (Condensed.)

67. *Id.*, p. 149.

68. *Id.*, pp. 46, 58; Fehr, p. 94; Novalis, III, pp. 59-60.

69. *Cf.* N. K. Smith, p. 32; see, also, pp. 244 *ff.* "Refutation of Idealism."

70. *Sartor*, p. 46.

71. *Faust*, II, ll. 12104-05 (final lyric).

72. *Sartor*, p. 199. It may be well to have before us other passages from *Sartor* on this subject: "In a Symbol there is concealment and yet revelation . . . by Silence and Speech acting together . . .

"Of Symbols, however, I remark farther, that they have both an extrinsic and intrinsic value; oftenest the former only . . . as the accidental Standards of multitudes . . . the stupidest heraldic Coats-of-arms, military banners . . . Nevertheless through all these there glimmers something of a Divine Idea . . . the Divine Idea of Duty, of heroic Daring. . . .

"Another matter it is, however, when your Symbol has intrinsic meaning . . . Let but the Godlike manifest itself to Sense; let but Eternity look, more or less visibly, through the Time-figure . . . Of this latter sort are all true Works of Art . . . god-inspired Men . . . Death . . . religious Symbols . . . .

"But, on the whole, as Time adds much to the sacredness of Symbols, so likewise in his progress he at length defaces, or even desecrates them; and Symbols, like all terrestrial Garments, wax old . . . ." (Book III, Ch. III).

73. *Cf.* Josiah Royce, *Spirit of Modern Philosophy*, Boston, 1892, p. 175; Schelling, *Werke*, III, pp. 399-454, etc.

74. Schelling. *Methode des akademischen Studiums* [V], p. 325: ". . . in allen Dingen Ein Leben, die gleiche Macht zu sein, dieselbe Legirung durch die Ideen. Es ist keine reine Leiblichkeit in ihr, sondern überall Seele in Leib symbolisch umgewandelt, und für die Erscheinung nur ein Uebergewicht des einen oder andern . . ."

75. *Cf.* Schelling, *Methode* [V], p. 293: "Die Ideen einer auf Anschauung des Unendlichen im Englichen gerichteten Religion müssen vorzugsweise im Seyn ausgedrückt seyn, die Ideen der entgegengesetzen, in der alle Symbolik nur dem Subject angehört, können allein durch Handeln objectiv werden. Das ur-

sprüngliche Symbol aller Anschauung Gottes in ihr ist die Geschichte, aber diese ist endlos, unermesslich, sie muss also durch eine zugleich unendliche und doch begränzte Erscheinung repräsentirt werden, die selbst nicht wieder real ist, wie die Staat, sondern ideal, und die Einheit aller im Geist bei der Getrenntheit im Einzelnen als unmittelbare Gegenwart darstellt. Diese symbolische Anschauung ist die Kirche, als lebendiges Kunstwerk."

Cf., also, p. 319: "Es ist klar, dass die empirische Ansicht nicht über die Körperlichkeit erhebt und diese als etwas, das an sich selbst ist, betrachtet, da jene dagegen sie nur als das in ein Reales (durch den Akt der Subjekt-Objektivirung) verwandelte Ideale begreift. Die Ideen symbolisiren sich in den Dingen, und da sie an sich Formen des absoluten Erkennens sind, erscheinen sie in diesen als Formen des Seyns, wie auch die plastische Kunst ihre Ideen tödtet, um ihnen die Objektivität zu geben . . ."

76. *Cf. Sartor,* pp. 202-04, etc.

77. *Maximen u. Reflexionen,* ed. Hecker, no. 1113. Goethe was fond of indirect and imaginative ways of setting forth a truth. See for instance, *Meister* (Carlyle's transl.) II, p. 273: "When [a truth] embodies itself in a common, customary, comprehensible figure, so that it meets us as if alive, present, actual; so that we can seize it, appropriate, retain it, live with it as with our equal,—this is a second sort of miracle . . ."

78. Novalis, III, p. 90; also: "So versteht man das Ich nur, insofern es vom Nicht-Ich repräsentiert wird. Das Nicht-Ich ist das Symbol des Ich, und dient nur zum Selbstverständnis des Ich."

79. Schiller, *Werke,* ed. Kunz, etc., IX ("Philosophische Briefe"), p. 118 *ff.*:
"Das Universum ist ein Gedanke Gottes. Nachdem dieses idealische Geistesbild in die Wirklichkeit hinübertrat und die geborene Welt den Riss ihres Schöpfers erfüllte—erlaube mir diese menschliche Vorstellung—so ist der Beruf aller denkenden Wesen, in diesem vorhandenen Ganzen die erste Zeichnung widerzufinden, die Regel in der Maschine, die Einheit in der Zufammensetzung, das Gesetz in dem Phänomen aufzusuchen und das Gebäude rückwärts auf seinen Grundriss zu übertragen. Also giebt es für mich nur eine einzige Erscheinung in der Natur, das denkende Wesen. Die grosse Zusammensetzung, die wir Welt nennen, bleibt mir jetzo nur merkwürdig, weil sie vorhanden ist, mir die mannigfaltigen Äusserungen jenes Wesens symbolisch zu bezeichnen."

80. Carlyle's translation, in *Novalis* [II], p. 40; *cf.* Novalis, III, p. 195: "Der Mensch hat immer symbolische Philosophie seines

Wesens in seinen Werken und in seinem Tun und Lassen ausgedrückt. Er verküundigt sich und sein Evangelium der Natur. Er ist der Messias der Natur."

81. *Sartor*, p. 234; *Wotton*, pp. 75, 98.

82. Novalis, III, p. 116.

83. Schelling, *Methode* [V], p. 246: "Die Natur ist für uns ein uralter Autor, der in Hieroglyphen geschrieben hat, dessen Blätter kolossal sind, wie der Künstler bei Goethe sagt." *Cf.* Goethe's two poems, *Sendschreiben*, and *Künstler-lied*.

84. Schiller, *Werke*, IX, p. 118:

"Alles in mir und ausser mir ist nur Hieroglyphe einer Kraft, die mir ähnlich ist. Die Gesetze der Natur sind die Chiffern, welche das denkende Wesen zusammenfügt, sich dem denkenden Wesen verständlich zu machen—das Alphabet, vermittelst dessen alle Geister mit dem vollkommensten Geist und mit sich selbst unterhandeln."

As another reminder that German doctrines were only supplementary to ideas which Carlyle drew from many other sources, we should turn, in this connection, to Sir Thomas Browne on Nature as a "universal and publick manuscript":

"Thus there are two Books from whence I collect my Divinity: besides that written one of God, another of His servant Nature, that universal and publick Manuscript, that lies expans'd unto the Eyes of all . . . . Surely the Heathens knew better how to joyn and read these mystical Letters than we Christians, who cast a more careless Eye on these common Hieroglyphicks . . . . The Finger of God hath left an Inscription upon all His works . . . ." In another connection, the author speaks of flesh as a garment: "Now, for these walls of flesh . . . it is nothing but an elemental composition, and a Fabric . . . ." (*Religio Medici*, ed. C. H. Herford, Everyman edition, London, 1906, pp. 17-18, 42, 67-68.)

Cf., also, Goldsmith: "The volume of nature is the book of knowledge" (*Citizen of the World*, London, 1774 (3rd ed.), I, p. 13); Hazlitt: "You cannot read the book of nature without being perpetually put to the trouble of translating it for the benefit of others" (*On Going a Journey*; etc.).

85. Carlyle, *Novalis* [II], p. 39; *cf.* Novalis, IV, p. 20: "Was ist die Natur? Ein enzyklopädischer, systematischer Index, oder Plan unsers Geistes. Warum wollen wir uns mit dem blossen Verzeichnis unsrer Schätze begnügen? Lasst sie uns selbst besehn, und sie mannigfaltig bearbeiten und benutzen."

86. *Cf.* Cazamian, p. 100.

87. Noted by Lehman, pp. 111-12. See *Faust*, transl. A. G. Latham, Everyman's Library, London, 1908, p. 10; *Faust* I, ll. 336-49:

"Der Herr. Du darfst auch da nur frei erscheinen;
Ich habe deinesgleichen nie gehasst.
Von allen Geistern, die verneinen,
Ist mir der Schalk am wenigsten zur Last.
Des Menschen Tätigkeit kann allzuleicht erschlaffen,
Er liebt sich bald die unbedingte Ruh;
Drum geb' ich gern ihm den Gesellen zu,
Der reizt und wirkt und muss als Teufel schaffen.
Doch ihr, die echten Göttersöhne,
Erfreut euch der lebendig reichen Schöne!
Das Werdende, das ewig wirkt und Lebt,
Umfass' euch mit der Liebe holden Schranken,
Und was in schwankender Erscheinung schwebt,
Befestiget mit dauernden Gedanken!"

88. See *Fraser's Magazine*, VII (1833), pp. 539-40.
89. *Fichte's Pop. Works*, p. 178; *Über das Wesen* [VI], p. 393: "Gott hat die Welt überhaupt gedacht, nicht nur wie sie ist und sich findet, sondern auch also, wie sie sich durch sich selbst weiter gestalten soll; ausserdem, was sie ist, liegt in dem göttlichen Gedanken von ihr noch das Princip einer ewigen Fortentwickelung, und zwar einer Fortentwickelung aus dem Höchsten, was in derselben sich findet, aus den vernünftigen Wesen in ihr, vermittelst derselben Freiheit."
90. Carlyle, *Boswell's Life of Johnson* [III], p. 79.
91. Carlyle, *Characteristics* [III], p. 28. Schiller, likewise, gave encouragement to this view; *cf.* Schiller, *Werke*, IX ("Phil. Briefe"), pp. 125-126.
92. *Biography* [III], p. 56.
93. See Carré's excellent statement of this point (p. 173).
94. Carlyle, *Death of Goethe* [II], p. 375.
95. *Sartor*, p. 197, etc.; *Heroes*, p. 45; Fichte, *Pop. Wks.* (Smith's translation), pp. 378, 393; Fichte, *Characteristics of the Present Age*, transl. W. Smith, etc., p. 249; Novalis, IV, p. 39; Schiller, IX, pp. 119-20.
96. Carlyle's version, *Fraser's Mag.*, etc., pp. 539-40. *Cf.* J. A. S. Barrett's ed. of *Sartor*, p. 271, n.; Carlyle's essay on *Werner* [I], p. 143. Goethe's poem, *Vermächtnis*, written as a complement to *Eins und Alles*, suggests the Phoenix doctrine—"Kein Wesen kann zu Nichts zerfallen!" etc. Goethe, *Werke*, II, p. 245.

97. Smith, *Fichte's Pop. Works*, p. 378; *Bestimmung des Menschen* [II], p. 317: "Aller Tod in der Natur ist Geburt, und gerade im Sterben erscheint sichtbar die Erhöhung des Lebens." This passage is one of a number which suggest that Carlyle knew the *Vocation of Man*. *Cf. Characteristics of the Present Age*, p. 249.

98. *Cf.* Fichte (Smith's translation), pp. 378, 393.

99. *Sartor*, p. 223.

100. See, for example, Novalis, III, pp. 90, 114.

101. *Cf.* G. v. Schulze-Gaevernitz, *Carlyle's Welt-und Gesellschaftanschauung*, Dresden, 1893; H. Taine, *L'Idéalisme Anglais*, Paris, 1864, p. 72 *ff*.

102. As we have seen in Section 4, "Nature."

103. *Sartor*, p. 171.

104. *Id.*, p. 48.

105. Schelling, *Werke*, III (Entwurf eines Systems der Naturphilosophie), pp. 274-75: "Die Naturphilosophie is speculative Physik."

106. Schelling, *Methode* [V], p. 219: "Alles nun, was unmittelbar aus dem Absoluten als seiner Wurzel stammt, ist selbst absolut, demnach ohne Zweck ausser sich, selbst Zweck. Das Wissen, in seiner Allheit, ist aber die eine, gleich absolute, Erscheinung des Einen Universum, von dem das Sein oder die Natur die andere ist. Im Gebiet des Realen herrscht die Endlichkeit, im Gebiet des Idealen die Unendlichkeit; jenes ist durch Nothwindigkeit das, was es ist, dieses soll es durch Freiheit sein. Der Mensch, das Vernunftwesen überhaupt, ist hingestellt, eine Ergänzung der Welterscheinung zu seyn: aus ihm, aus seiner Thätigkeit soll sich entwickeln, was zur Totalität der Offenbarung Gottes fehlt, da die Natur zwar das ganze göttliche Wesen, aber nur im Realen, empfängt; das Vernunftwesen soll das Bild derselben göttlichen Natur, wie sie an sich selbst ist, demnach im Idealen ausdrücken." Later Schelling writes (p. 219): "Die Natur des Absoluten ist: als das absolut Ideale auch das Reale zu sein. In dieser Bestimmung liegen die zwei Möglichkeiten, dass es als Ideales seine Wesenheit in die Form, als das Reale, bildet, und dass es, weil diese in ihm nur eine absolute seyn kann, auf ewig gleiche Weise auch die Form wieder in das Wesen auflöst, so dass es Wesen und Form in vollkommener Durchdringung ist. . . ."

107. Schelling, *Methode* [V], p. 216:
"Aber eben diese erste Voraussetzung aller Wissenschaften, jene wesentliche Einheit des unbedingt Idealen und des unbedingt Realen is nur dadurch möglich, dass dasselbe, welches das eine ist, andere ist. Dieses aber ist die Idee des Absoluten, welche die ist: dass die Idee in Ansehung seiner auch das Seyn ist. So dass das Absolute auch jene oberste Voraussetzung des Wissens und das erste Wissen selbst ist."

108. *Id.*, p. 320:

"Die rein-endliche Auffassung hebt an und für sich schon alle organische Ansicht auf, und setzt an die Stelle derselben die einfache Reihe des Mechanismus, so wie an die Stelle der Construktion die Erklärung."

See, also, Novalis, IV, p. 38: "Aller Anfang des Lebens muss antimechanisch, gewaltsamer Durchbruch, Opposition gegen den Mechanism sein; absolute Materie—primitives Element des Geistes-Seele."

109. *Sartor*, pp. 130-31. Carlyle's context concerns love, but the principle applies, in his teachings, to everything else.

110. Fichte warns us that "we must not be blinded or led astray by a philosophy assuming the name of *natural*, which pretends . . . to elevate Nature into Absolute Being, and into the place of God." This is Fichte's rejection of Schelling. (*Nature of the Scholar*, Smith's transl., p. 150; *Über das Wesen* [VI], pp. 363-64.) Carlyle himself ruminates in his Journal: "Annihilation of the Subject.—Spinozism and Materialism." (*Two Notebooks*, p. 112.)

111. *Sartor*, pp. 63-64 (quotation condensed); *cf.* Richter, *Flower, Fruit and Thorn Pieces*, transl. A. Ewing, London, 1888, p. 471: "Life and Force are at work, with power, everywhere. The grave hillock and the mouldering body are each a *world* of powers at work. We *change* our stage, but do not *retire* from it." (Richter, *Blumen-Frucht-und Dornenstücke*, . . . Berlin, 1818, IV, p. 69.) *Sartor*, p. 63: "The withered leaf is not dead and lost, there are Forces in and around it, though working in inverse order; else how could it *rot*?"

112. *Sartor*, p. 223.

113. *Cf.* F. Thilly, "The World View of a Poet," *Hibbert Journal*, VI (1908), p. 539; G. Santayana, *Three Philosophical Poets*, pp. 139-40, 195, etc.

114. *Sartor*, p. 52. *Cf.* Schiller's *Don Carlos*, Act III, Scene X, as translated by Carlyle (*Life of Schiller*, p. 74):

> "Him the maker we behold not; calm
> He veils himself in everlasting laws,
> Which and not him the sceptic seeing exclaims,
> 'Wherefore a God? The World itself is God.'
> And never did a Christian's adoration
> So praise him as this sceptic's blasphemy."

115. *Cf.* Goethe, *Maximen u. Refl.*, no. 201.

116. Quoted by Carlyle, *Diderot* [III], p. 233; *cf.* Goethe, *Proömion* (in *Werke*, II, p. 239):

> "Was wär ein Gott, der nur von aussen stiesse,
> Im Kreis das All am Finger laufen liesse!

Ihm ziemt's, die Welt im Innern zu bewegen,
Natur in Sich, Sich in Natur zu hegen,
So dass, was in Ihm lebt und webt und ist,
Nie Seine Kraft, nie Seinen Geist vermisst."

117. *Heroes*, pp. 91-92; *Wotton*, p. 60, etc.
118. Dunbar, p. 158.
119. Hensel, p. 68: "Seine [Carlyle's] Lehre ist nicht Pantheismus, sondern Panentheismus."
120. Cazamian, p. 49.
121. Carré, pp. 168-171.

NOTES TO CHAPTER V

1. *State of German Literature* [I], p. 81.
2. H. L. Stewart, "Carlyle's Place in Philosophy," *The Monist*, XXIX (1919), p. 173.
3. *Early Letters*, I, p. 210. Just what Carlyle means by "Experience" here may be open to question. Does he mean "empirical" or "religious" experience? He probably refers to the experience of religious faith.
4. *Cf.* J. H. Muirhead, *The Platonic Tradition in Anglo-Saxon Philosophy*, p. 137 *ff.*, etc.
5. *State of Germ. Lit.* [I], p. 79, n.
6. Stewart, *Works*, III (Philosophy of the Human Mind), p. 9. *Cf.* Stewart's other quotation from Locke in this connection (p. 10): "the two most different things I know in the world, a logical chicaner from a man of reason" (Locke, *Conduct of the Understanding*, London, 1762, p. 20).
7. *Id.*, p. 10.
8. *Id.*, p. 11.
9. *Id.*, p. 13. Quoted also by Coleridge, *Biographia Literaria*, ed. Shawcross, I, p. 109. Carlyle thus found the distinction, as made by Milton, in two different places besides *Paradise Lost*.
10. Stewart, III, p. 14. It is noteworthy, however, that Stewart, like Milton, regards Understanding as a *part* of Reason. Carlyle, probably following the Germans, thought of them as more distinct.
11. Carlyle, *Voltaire* [I], pp. 457-458: "Our fathers were wiser than we, when they said in deepest earnestness, what we often hear

in shallow mockery, that Religion is 'not of Sense, but of Faith'; not of Understanding, but of Reason." *Cf.* Novalis [II], p. 22. Dugald Stewart's chief charge against Kant was that his doctrines, celebrated for their originality, were anticipated by Cudworth and the Cambridge Platonists.

12. Muirhead, *Coleridge as a Philosopher*, p. 66; Plato, *Dialogues*, ed. B. Jowett, Oxford, 1892, IV (Theaetetus), pp. 244-250.

13. Muirhead, *Coleridge*, pp. 65-67; C. Howard, *Coleridge's Idealism*, Boston, 1924, p. 25 *ff.*; Wellek, *Kant in England*, p. 103 *ff.*; A. O. Lovejoy, "Kant and the English Platonists," *Essays Philosophical and Psychological in Honor of William James*, N. Y., 1908, pp. 265-302.

14. Howard, p. 32; Cudworth, *Eternal and Immutable Morality*, London, 1831, IV, i, 1; Muirhead, *Platonic Tradition*, etc., pp. 13-14, 38 *ff.*—Though Howard's treatment of Coleridge, Kant, and the Cambridge Platonists has been criticised as not properly adequate on the critical position (*cf.* Wellek, *Kant in England*, p. 282), there is nevertheless a significant amount of truth in his demonstration that the English Platonists, though "lacking the rigidly logical, systematic and taxonomic propensity of Kant," did in fact attempt to determine the forms of thought under which the material of the senses must be subsumed. It is interesting to turn to Henry More's statement: "There are a multitude of Relative Notions or Ideas in the Mind of Man, as well Mathematical as Logical, which if we prove cannot be the Impressions of any Material Object from without, it will necessarily follow that they are from the Soul herself within, and are the natural Furniture of the Human Understanding. Such are these, Cause, Effect, Whole and Part, Like and Unlike . . ." (Henry More, *Philosophical Writings*, London, 1712, p. 18, quoted by Howard, pp. 33, 34, etc.). Lovejoy has likewise pointed out some anticipations of Kant. "For us men," says Burthogge, "things are nothing save in so far as they are known by us, and they are known by us only as they exist in the sense or imagination or thought; in a word, as they exist in our faculties . . . Each faculty takes a part, though not an exclusive part, in the production of its immediate object; as the eye produces colors and is said to see, as the ear produces sounds and the imagination images, so the understanding produces the ideas or conceptions under which it apprehends and beholds things. So that all the immediate objects of human thought are *entia cogitationis,* or appearances only; they being not properly and (if I may be allowed to use a school-term) *formally* in the things themselves . . . but only in the faculties of the intellect." (*Cf.* Lovejoy, p. 279.) How far Carlyle

was actually acquainted with this line of philosophic thought, it is impossible to determine; but it is safe to say that he was affected by it at least through Dugald Stewart and Coleridge.

15. Howard, p. 37.

16. Hooker, *Works*, ed. J. Keble, Oxford, 1888, I (*Laws of Ecclesiastical Polity*), pp. 227-28. *Cf. John*, i, 9.

17. Hooker, I, p. 234.

18. Howard, p. 39.

19. *Biographia Literaria*, ed. Shawcross, I, p. 109. Hooker, II, p. 145.

20. *Novalis* [II], p. 27; *State of Germ. Lit.* [I], pp. 81-82.

21. Coleridge, *The Friend*, in *Works*, II, p. 176. "Kantian thought and terminology permeates all the reflective parts of The Friend. Everything is there: the threefold division of the mind, space and time as forms, the categories, the Ideas of Reason (though their exact number is not respected), the a priori, the grounds of coincidence between reason and experience, the dictate of practical reason with all the paraphernalia of the maxim, the end-in-itself, the ethics of motives, the moral proof of immortality, etc." (Wellek, *Kant in England*, p. 108.)

22. *Aids to Reflection*, ed. Derwent Coleridge, London, 1859, pp. 168-69.

Of this work, it may be truthfully said that "no pretence is here made of an interpretation of Kant, but still Kantian thought is permeating the whole book. . . . Reason has lost almost all its Kantian meaning . . . yet the distinction inside of Reason is still Kantian . . . Understanding has dropped to the lowest place and the intuitions of sensibility have been put next to the intuitions of Reason, though on a lower plane." (Wellek, pp. 124, 125, 126, 127, 128.)

23. *The Friend* [II], p. 144.

24. Lütgert, *Die Religion des deutschen Idealismus und ihr Ende*, Part II, p. 27.

25. Carlyle, *Novalis* [II], p. 205.

26. *Cf.* F. H. Jacobi, *Werke*, Leipzig, 1812-25, IV, p. 237; A. W. Crawford, *The Philosophy of Jacobi*, p. 18.—Jacobi's philosophy is best found by turning to Vol. II of the *Werke*, especially to the *Vorrede*.

27. Jacobi, I, p. 365; *Cf.* Carlyle, *Reminiscences*, p. 281: "the foul and vile and soul-murdering Mud-gods of my Epoch," etc.

28. *Cf.* Crawford, p. 19.

29. Crawford, p. 20.

30. Jacobi, II, p. 317; Crawford, p. 22.

31. Jacobi, II, p. 314; Crawford, p. 25.

32. Crawford, p. 27.

33. L. Lévy-Bruhl, *La Philosophie de Jacobi*, Paris, 1894, pp. 74-75.
34. Crawford, pp. 30-31, etc.; Carlyle, *Characteristics* [III], p. 27.
35. Lütgert, II, pp. 20-27; Wellek, p. 134 (Coleridge's dilemma), p. 201 (Carlyle and Jacobi).
36. *Cf. Two Notebooks*, p. 142: "Understanding is to Reason as the talent of a Beaver . . ."
37. *Cf.* Storrs, p. 36 *ff.*
38. *Critique of Pure Reason*, ed. N. K. Smith, p. 93; *Kritik* [III], p. 75; also pp. 119 *ff.*, 86 *ff.*, 133 *ff.*, 108, for Kant's original statements on the principles mentioned; and Smith, pp. 164, 106, 180, 152.
39. *Critique*, ed. Smith, pp. 264-65; Kritik [III], pp. 207-08:
"Hieraus fliest nun unwidersprechlich: dass die reinen Verstandesbegriffe niemals von transzendentalem, sondern jederzeit nur von empirischem Gebrauche sein können, und dass die Grundsätze des reinen Verstandes nur in Beziehung auf die allgemeinen Bedingungen einer möglichen Erfahrung auf Gegenstände der Sinne, niemals aber auf Dinge überhaupt, (ohne Rücksicht auf die Art zu nehmen, wie wir sie anschauen mögen), bezogen werden können . . . . dass der Verstand *a priori* niemals mehr leisten könne, als die Form einer möglichen Erfahrung überhaupt zu antizipieren . . . . dass er die Schranken der Sinnlichkeit, innerhalb denen uns allein Gegenstände gegeben werden, niemals überschreiten könne. Seine Grundsätze sind bloss Prinzipien der Exposition der Erscheinungen . . . Der bloss transzendentale Gebrauch also der Kategorien ist in der That gar kein Gebrauch und hat keinen bestimmten, oder auch nur der Form nach bestimmbaren Gegenstand."
40. *Last Words of Thomas Carlyle*, pp. 60-63.
41. *State of Germ. Lit.* [I], pp. 82-83. Carlyle cites Schelling's *Methode* for the remark about the French exaltation of Understanding. Schelling's words ([V], p. 258) are as follows: "Man wird zugeben müssen, dass es keine Nation in dieser Erhebung eines räsonnirenden Verstandes über die Vernunft weiter gebracht hat, als die französische. . . ."
42. *Novalis* [II], pp. 26-28. See, also, *Sartor*, pp. 60, 66; *Two Notebooks*, p. 83; "The Tale," *Misc. Ess.*, II, pp. 450-51: Carlyle attempts here to interpret Goethe's *Märchen* with the aid of "Reason" and "Understanding"—"*Light* must signify human insight . . . Meditation, Intellectual Research, Understanding . . . As to the Man with the Lamp, . . . I see what you might name the celestial Reason of Man (Reason as contrasted with Understanding, and superordinated to it), the purest essence of his seeing Faculty; which manifests itself as the Spirit of Poetry, of Prophecy . . . the Poetic Vision that lies at the bottom of all other Knowledge or Action; and is the source and cre-

ative fountain of whatsoever mortals *ken* or *can*, and mystically and miraculously guides them forward whither they are to go." Carlyle's admiration for, and interpretation of, Goethe's "Tale" was not one of his happiest critical reactions. He undoubtedly read more into the story than Goethe intended to convey, and his employment of Reason and Understanding has little expository value. *Cf.* Kraeger, *Carlyle's Stellung*, p. 88 *ff.*

43. *The Friend* [II], p. 176.
44. *Aids to Reflection*, p. 181.
45. *Sartor*, p. 78. (Quotation rearranged.) This attitude toward names is curiously unidealistic in Carlyle and Coleridge. It recalls the Nominalist or Baconian position. Yet it is to be noted that it is the Understanding, the apprehender of the Apparent-Real, which deals with names, and not the Reason, which pierces behind them to Reality. —The passage in *Sartor* possibly goes back to *Tristram Shandy*, I, Ch. 19, etc.
46. Storrs, pp. 45-46.
47. Jacobi, II, p. 14.
48. *Aids to Reflection*, p. 190.
49. Storrs, p. 44; *Critique*, ed. Smith, pp. 115-116.
50. *Aids to Reflection*, p. 174. The other two items are as follows:

1. Understanding is discursive.	2. Reason is fixed.
3. Understanding is the faculty of reflection.	3. Reason of contemplation. Reason indeed is much nearer to Sense than to Understanding: for Reason (says our great Hooker) is a direct aspect of truth, and inward beholding, having a similar relation to the intelligible or spiritual, as Sense has to the material or phenomenal.

51. The other three, of course, are Quantity, Quality, and Modality. *Cf. Critique*, Analytic of Conceptions, Chapter I, Section II.
52. *Characteristics* [III], p. 27.
53. *Cf.* Fichte, *Bestimmung des Menschen* [II], p. 304; Jacobi, II, p. 53: "Aber auch diese Bewunderung, die alleinige des menschlichen Erkenntnissvermögens, würde verschwinden, wenn es einem Küunstigen Hartley, Darwin, Condillac oder Bonnet wirklich gelänge, uns eine Mechanik des Menschlichen Geistes vor Augen zu legen, die eben so allumfassend, begreiflich, einleuchtend wäre, als die Newtonische des Himmels. Wir würden dann weder Kunst noch hohe Wissenschaft, noch irgend eine Tugend mehr wahrhaft und besonnen ehren, sie

erhaben finden, mit anbetung sie betrachten können"; also IV, p. xxx; II, p. 101 *ff.* Coleridge, of course, has a memorable passage on Wonder: "In wonder all philosophy began; in wonder it ends: and admiration fills up the interspace" (*Aids*, p. 185). He acknowledges Aristotle and Plato as the sources of this view, in *The Friend* [II], p. 468. Carlyle was also probably acquainted with Jean Paul's remark: "Ohne Wunder gibt's keinen Glauben; und der Wunderglaube selber ist ein innres." (*Levana*, p. 56.) *Cf. Sartor*, pp. 60, 245.

54. *Cf. Sartor*, p. 59; Storrs, p. 38.

55. *Two Notebooks*, p. 142.

56. *Novalis* [II], p. 54; *Two Notebooks*, p. 114. *Cf.* Jean Paul, *Levana*, p. 39: ". . . aus der Welt wurde uns ein Weltgebäude, aus dem Aether ein Gas, aus Gott eine Kraft, aus der zweiten Welt ein Sarg." In this same work, Richter laments the self-consciousness of the age, the triumph of Understanding . . . "und die geistigen Fallsüchtigen der französischen Philosophie haben, wie körperliche, kein Bewusstsein ihres Uebels, sondern nur Stolz und Kraft" (p. 40). On other German writers and their attitude toward the supremacy of Understanding, see Chapter III, Section 3.

57. *Novalis* [II], p. 27.

58. *State of Germ. Lit.* [I], pp. 79, 81-83; *Novalis* [II], pp. 27, 29. In the period in which Carlyle was writing on German literature, on Novalis, Werner, etc., he was assiduously studying Tasso, and becoming fascinated in mysticism. "Tasso was a *Mystic*, as we should call him: Must not every true poet be so? . . ." (*Two Notebooks*, p. 125). In 1827 he planned an essay on Tasso, but wrote the article on Werner instead. He read Tasso's *Del Poema Eroico*, and noted in his Journal: "Curious division of Theology. The *mistico* much the same as *Vernunft?*" (*Two Notebooks*, pp. 124-26.) We have here the general background of reading out of which came Carlyle's mention of Tasso and the *Teologia Mistica* in his discussion of Reason. (*Cf.* Tasso, *Discorsi del Poema Heroico*, Naples [1597], Libro Secondo, p. 29 ff.) The identification of Tasso's conception of mystical knowledge, as derived from the Pseudo-Dionysius, with the Kantian "Reason," is of course highly arbitrary. For a discussion of the mystical aspect of Carlyle's thought, see C. F. Harrold, "The Mystical Element in Carlyle: 1827-1834," *Modern Philology*, XXIX (1932), pp. 459-75.

59. *Critique*, ed. Smith, p. 533; *Kritik* [III], pp. 427-28: "Ich behaupte demnach: die transzendentalen Ideen sind niemals von konstitutiven Gebrauche, so, dass dadurch Begriffe gewisser Gegenstände gegeben würden, und in dem Falle, dass man sie so versteht, so sind es bloss vernünftelnde (dialektische) Begriffe. Dagegen aber haben sie einen vortrefflichen und unentbehrlich notwendigen regula-

tiven Gebrauch, nämlich den Verstand zu einem gewissen Ziele zu richten, in Aussicht auf welches die Richtungslinien aller seiner Regeln in einen Punkt zusammenlaufen, der, ob er zwar nur eine Idee (focus imaginarius), d. i. ein Punkt ist, aus welchem die Verstandesbegriffe wirklich nicht ausgehen, indem er ganz ausserhalb den Grenzen möglicher Erfahrung liegt, dennoch dazu dient, ihnen die grösste Einheit neben der grössten Ausbreitung zu verschaffen." See, also, Smith, p. 536 *ff.*; *Kritik* [III], p. 430 *ff.*

60. *Critique*, pp. 533, 309-14; *Kritik* [III], pp. 244-50, and 428: "Nun entspringt uns zwar hieraus die Täuschung, als wenn diese Richtungslinien von einem Gegenstande selbst, der ausser dem Felde empirisch möglicher Erkenntnis läge, ausgeschlossen wären (so wie die Objekte hinter der Spiegelfläche gesehen werden), allein diese Illusion (welche man doch hindern kann, dass sie nicht betrügt) ist gleichwohl unentbehrlich notwendig, wenn wir ausser den Gegenständen, die uns vor Augen sind, auch diejenigen zugleich sehen wollen, die weit davon uns im Rücken liegen, d. i. wenn wir, in unserem Falle, den Verstand über jede gegebene Erfahrung (dem Teil der gesamten möglichen Erfahrung) hinaus, mithin auch zur grösstmöglichen und äussersten Erweiterung abrichten wollen."

61. We have seen, of course, that Carlyle admired the famous passage about the "starry heavens" and the moral law in man. *Cf. Shooting Niagara* [V], p. 29.

62. *The Metaphysic of Ethics*, in H. Calderwood's translated edition (transl. J. W. Semple), Edinburgh, 1871, p. 25; *Grundlegung zur Metaphysik der Sitten* [IV], p. 412.

63. Calderwood, p. 69; *Grundlegung* [IV], p. 456.

64. *Id.*, pp. 97-98; *Kritik der praktischen Vernunft* [V], p. 31.

65. *Id.*, p. 100; *Krit. der p. Vernunft* [V], p. 33.

66. Storrs, p. 39.

67. Calderwood, p. 109; *Krit. der p. Vernunft* [V], p. 71.

68. *Id.*, pp. 95-96; Storrs, p. 43; *Krit. der p. Vernunft* [V], p. 29.

69. E. Caird, *Critical Philosophy of Kant*, 1889, II, pp. 163, 191, etc.

70. *Boswell's Life of Johnson* [III], p. 110.

71. Calderwood, p. 97; *Krit. der p. Vernunft* [V], p. 30.

72. For a fuller demonstration that Carlyle's moral imperative owed little to Kant's categorical imperative, see Margaret Storrs, pp. 47-52.

73. See, for instance, Leopold (p. 59), who conjectures Schelling's *Urwissen.*—Professor Hill Shine of Maryville College, Tennessee, has discovered what would seem to be a German source for Carlyle's use of *Urwahr,* equally significant to Madame de Staël's: Reinhold's *Beyträge zur leichtern Uebersicht des Zustandes der Philosophie beym*

Anfange des 19 Jahrhunderts, Hamburg, 1801-03, 6 vols. In Reinhold's first volume, the word is used in various phrases with the very meaning which Carlyle attached to it. In discussing the opposition of empiricism and rationalism, as represented by Bacon and Descartes, Gassendi and Malebranche, the author refers to *das Urwahre nichts anderes als die Gottheit*, and to *das Wahre* as the *denkenden und materiellen Wesen unter Gott*. In other words, the "truth" of the philosophers, whether empiricism or rationalism, is only truth of a sort; final truth is the Truth beyond truth—the "primitively True." Such a point of view explains Carlyle's contempt for metaphysics, and his hope that the new German thought would yield him a foundation for a renewal of religion. Popularizers of philosophy, such as Reinhold, would naturally commend themselves to Carlyle, and a term like *Urwahr*, as employed by such writers, would seem appropriate when applied to some of the doctrines of Fichte, Schelling, Novalis. (*Cf.* Reinhold, *Beyträge*, I, pp. 12, 13, 72-73, 75-76, etc.)

74. De Staël, *Germany*, III, p. 64.
75. *Id.*, p. 73. (Italics added to "primitive truths.")
76. Jacobi, II, p. 16.
77. *Aids to Reflection*, p. 174.
78. *Fichte's Pop. Works*, p. 363 (Vocation of Man, Book III); *Bestimmung des Menschen* [II], p. 302: "Aber das eigentliche Gesetz der Venunft an sich ist nur das praktische Gesetz, das Gesetz der übersinnlichen Welt, oder jener erhabene Wille."
79. Calderwood, p. 3; *Grundlegung zur Metaphysik der Sitten* [IV], p. 393.
80. Calderwood, pp. 23-24; *Grundlegung* [IV], p. 411.
81. *Id.*, pp. 98-99; *Krit. der p. Vernunft* [V], p. 32.
82. *Critique*, pp. 318-19.
83. *Aids to Reflection*, p. 208.
84. *Id.*, p. 168.
85. Jacobi, II, p. 9.
86. *State of Germ. Lit.* [I], p. 83.
87. Carlyle, *Novalis* [II], p. 40; cf. Novalis, IV, p. 78: "Der erste Mensch ist der erste Geisterseher. Ihm erscheint alles als Geist. Was sind Kinder anders, als erste Menschen? Der frische Blick des Kindes ist überschwenglicher als die Ahndung des entschiedensten Sehers." Quoted by Carlyle in *Novalis* as cited above.
88. Jacobi, II, pp. 74, 55-56: "ein geistiges Auge für geistige Gegenstände . . . eine Kraft unmittelbar aus Gott." *Cf.* Crawford, pp. 21-22.
89. *The Friend* [II], p. 144.
90. Jacobi, II, p. 11; Crawford, pp. 27-28.

91. *Fichte's Pop. Works*, pp. 317-18, 359; *Cf. Bestimmung des Menschen* [II], pp. 253-55:

"Ich verstehe dich jetzt, erhabener Geist. Ich habe das Organ gefunden, mit welchem ich diese Realität, und mit dieser zugleich wahrscheinlich alle andere Realität ergreife. Nicht das Wissen ist dieses Organ; kein Wissen kann sich selbst begründen und beweisen; jedes Wissen setzt ein noch Höheres voraus, als seinen Grund, und dieses Aufsteigen hat kein Ende. Der Glaube ist es; dieses freiwillige Beruhen bei der sich uns natürlich darbietenden Ansicht, weil wir nur bei dieser Ansicht unsere Bestimmung erfüllen können; er ist es, der dem Wissen erst Beifall giebt, und das, was ohne ihn blosse Täuschung sein könnte, zur Gewissheit, und Ueberzeugung erhebt. Er ist kein Wissen, sondern ein Entschluss des Willens, das Wissen gelten zu lassen.

"So halte ich denn auf immer an diesem Ausdrucke fest, was keine blosse Unterscheidung in den Ausdrücken, sondern eine wahre tiefgegründete Unterscheidung ist, von der wichtigsten Folge für meine ganze Gesinnung. Alle meine Ueberzeugung ist nur Glaube, und sie kommt aus der Gesinnung, nicht aus dem Verstande. . . . Aus dem Gewissen allein stammt die Wahrheit . . . . Aber selbstthätige Vernunft ist Wille. Das Gesetz der übersinnlichen Welt wäre sonach ein Wille."

92. Novalis, III, pp. 88, 116; also p. 182: "Vernunft, Gemüt, Ernst und Wissenschaft sind von der Sache Gottes unabtrennlich."

93. *Bestimmung des Menschen* [II], p. 254.

94. *Characteristics* [III], p. 8.

95. Carlyle's translation (except first sentence), *Novalis* [II], p. 42. *Cf.* Novalis, III, p. 183: "Aller Glaube ist wunderbar und wundertätig . . . . Können Wunder Überzeugung wirken? Oder wäre nicht Wahrhafte Überzeugung, diese höchste Funktion unsers Gemüts und unsrer Personalität, das einzige, wahre, Gott verkündende Wunder?"

96. Carlyle, *Novalis* [II], p. 36; *cf.* Novalis, *Schriften*, ed. Tieck u. Schlegel, Berlin, 1837-46, II, pp. 108-09: "Die gewöhnliche Logik ist die Grammatik der höhern Sprache, oder des Denkens; sie enthält bloss die Verhältnisse der Begriffe unter einander, die Mechanik des Denkens, die reine Physiologie der Begriffe. Die logischen Begriffe verhalten sich aber zu einander, wie die Worte ohne Gadanken.—Die Logik beschäftigt sich bloss mit dem todten Körper der Denklehre.— Die Metaphysik ist die reine Dynamik des Denkens, sie handelt von den ursprünglichen Denkkräften, sie beschäftig sich mit der blossen Seele der Denklehre . . . ." See, also, Novalis, III, p. 52.

97. *Novalis* [II], pp. 28-29.

98. *Death of Goethe* [II], pp. 376, 377.
99. *Biography* [III], p. 57.
100. *Johnson* [III], p. 110.
101. See, for example, *Characteristics of the Present Age*, p. 33; *cf. Die Grundzüge* [VII], pp. 34-35: "Die Vernunft geht auf das Eine Leben, das als Leben der Gattung erscheint . . ."
102. *Cf.* Schelling, *Methode* [V], p. 280.
103. *Two Notebooks*, p. 151.
104. A. W. u. F. v. Schlegel, *Athenaeum*, III (F. von Schlegel's *Ideen*), p. 5.
105. *Sartor*, p. 131.
106. *Id.*, pp. 197-201 (rearranged).
107. Fehr, p. 96 *ff.*
108. Richter, *Wahrheit aus Jean Pauls Leben*, I, pp. 62-65, 97-100, 107, etc.; on Novalis, see Friedell, *Novalis als Philosoph*, München, 1904, pp. 42-44.
109. *Wahrheit*, I, p. 59.
110. Schelling, *Methode* [V], p. 267; Schiller, IX, p. 326 *ff.*
111. *Cf.* C. F. Harrold, *Carlyle and Novalis*, p. 57, n.; Fichte, *Werke*, I, pp. 204-05.
112. *Cf.* Stewart, *Works*, III, p. 264; Richter, *Aesthetische Vorschule* (in *Werke*, 1826-38, etc., XL (1827), pp. 9 *ff.*).
Carlyle no doubt observed that with Jean Paul, phantasy played a great part in the aesthetic act; it operated as a shaping and plastic element in creativeness, uniting the parts into a whole. (*Cf.* W. Harich, *Jean Paul*, pp. 617-18; E. Berend, *Jean Pauls Ästhetik*, pp. 113-14, 128.) Insofar, however, as Jean Paul followed Fr. von Schlegel in regarding phantasy as a higher (spiritual) faculty for knowledge, he undoubtedly received a kind of influence, less specific than confirmatory. (*Cf.* Berend, p. 131.)
Novalis wrote that "Vernunft und Phantasie ist Religion; Vernunft und Verstand is Wissenschaft . . . Praktische Vernunft ist reine Einbildungskraft . . . Der Phantasiebegriff ist die Anschauung . . ." (Novalis, III, pp. 75, 114.)
In Werner, likewise, is phantasy an organ of the "God-like." (See F. Poppenberg, *Zacharias Werner, Mystiker und Romantik*, p. 19.)
113. F. Schlegel, *Ideen*, p. 5: ". . . Ganz recht, die Fantasie ist das Organ des Menschen für die Gottheit."
114. *Wilhelm Meisters Lehrjahre*, II, p. 259.
115. *Cf.* Goethe, *Maximen u. Refl.*, ed. Hecker, no. 1207: "Das schönste Glück des denkenden Menschen ist, das Erforschliche erforscht zu haben und das Unerforschliche ruhig zu verehren." *Cf.*, also the *West-Oestlicher Divan*, pp. 22, 341.

116. *Faust I*, l. 3432 *ff.*

117. Novalis, III, p. 62: "Sollte nicht am Ende jede Frage: Was ist das? und Warum? eine dumme Frage sein?"

118. *Cf.* Fichte, *Bestimmung des Menschen* [II], pp. 258, 303-04; Richter, *Levana*, p. 52; Crawford, p. 40; etc.

119. *Characteristics* [III], p. 17.

120. *Faust I*, ll. 1830-33.

121. *Wilhelm Meisters Apprenticeship* (Carlyle's translation), Bk. VIII, Ch. V, p. 120; *Lehrjahre*, II, p. 312.

122. Carlyle, *Characteristics* [III], p. 37; *Cagliostro* [III], p. 251. *Cf.* Coleridge, *Aids to Reflection*, p. 157: "The life, we seek after, is a mystery; but so both in itself and in its origin is the life we have." "To *know*," says Carlyle in *Heroes* (pp. 65-66), "to get into the truth of anything, is ever a mystic act,—of which the best Logics can but babble on the surface."

123. Carlyle, *Life of Sterling*, p. 59. *Cf. Heroes*, p. 122: ". . . what we call imagination, fancy, understanding, and so forth, are but different figures of the same Power of Insight."

NOTES TO CHAPTER VI

1. J. B. Black, *The Art of History*, London, 1926, p. 14.

2. *Id.*, pp. 15-17.

3. Lord Bolingbroke, *Works*, Philadelphia, 1841, II, p. 433: ". . . because I look upon these things to be of the greatest use to the readers, as they will open a large field of noble, and profitable examples." Bolingbroke is following Dionysius of Halicarnassus; *cf. Omnia Opera*, transl. E. Spelman, London, 1758, IV, pp. 248-49, etc.

4. Carlyle, *On History* [II], p. 84.—It may be said here that there is curiously little in Carlyle's essays, *On History* and *On History Again*, which suggest any of the German doctrines concerning history.

5. *Cf.* Black, pp. 98, 101, 104, etc. E. Fueter, *Geschichte der neueren Historiographie*, pp. 364-71.—Of Carlyle's remarks on the British historians, we have the greatest number on Gibbon. Carlyle is "alternately delighted and offended by the gorgeous colouring with which [Gibbon's] fancy invests the rude and scanty materials of his narrative; sometimes fatigued by the learning of his notes, occasionally amused by their liveliness, frequently disgusted by their obscenity, and admiring or deploring the bitterness of his skilful irony." On the

other hand, Hume has greater "elegance and distinction," and Robertson possesses excellent "talents for general disquisition." All three, however, are "abundantly destitute of virtuous feeling—or indeed of any feeling at all. I wonder," adds Carlyle, "what benefit is derived from reading all this stuff." Yet "history . . . is the basis of all true knowledge, and Gibbon is the most strong-minded of all historians." It appears that Carlyle disliked Gibbon less for his irony and skepticism than for his "coarse and vulgar heart," in spite of his "keen logic and glowing imagination and lordly irony: he worships power and splendour; and suffering virtue . . . if unsuccessful, unarrayed in the pomp and circumstance of outward glory, has little of his sympathy." (See *Early Letters*, I, pp. 143-44; *Love Letters*, I, p. 186, etc.)

6. *Cf.* Lütgert, I, pp. 153 *ff*.

7. *Id.*, pp. 154-57.

8. *Cf.* Robert Flint, *The Philosophy of History in France and Germany*, London, 1874, Bk. II, Ch. III.

9. *Two Notebooks*, pp. 72-73. *Cf.* Flint, p. 379 *ff*. Fueter, pp. 407-11.

10. Schiller, *Werke*, VII, pp. 366-82; Carlyle, *On History* [II], pp. 86-87, 88-89, 90, etc.; Flint, p. 405 *ff*.; Lütgert, p. 167 *ff*. *Cf.* *Wahrheit aus Jean Pauls Leben*, II, pp. 51-52.

11. *Life of Schiller*, p. 98.

12. *Id.*, pp. 84-85. For further discussion of Carlyle's actual practice in the writing of *The French Revolution*, see C. F. Harrold, "The Method and Sources of Carlyle's French Revolution," *Publications of the Modern Language Association*, XLIII (1928), pp. 1150-69. It will be seen, from my examination, that Carlyle's procedure is remarkably like that suggested by Schiller, though at the time of writing, I had not yet made the comparison.

13. *Life of Schiller*, pp. 85-86.

14. *Id.*, pp. 100-01.

15. See Sections 3, 4, and 5 of the present chapter.

16. Schlegel, *Lectures on the History of Literature*, p. 302; *Werke*, II, Ch. XIII, pp. 151-54, and *passim*.

17. Schlegel, *Hist. of Lit.*, etc., pp. 302, 317-20; *Werke*, II, p. 206 *ff*., etc.—It is necessary, of course, to bear in mind that whatever philosophy of history Carlyle may have attained, it was not a conscious formulation. We are reminded of this fact from his derision of any philosophy of history in a conversation with Henry James, Sr., as reported by Lewis G. James, "Carlyle's Philosophy of History," *Westminster Review*, CXXXII (1889), p. 415.

18. Novalis, III, p. 192.

19. See, for example, Miss Storrs, p. 74, for an excellent and exhaustive comparison of Carlyle and Fichte on history; also, Hensel, pp. 114-46, Lehman, p. 108 *ff.*; etc. All authorities are also agreed on the prominent place occupied by *Über das Wesen des Gelehrten.* In Hensel, however, the parallel between Carlyle and Fichte is carried to unwarrantable limits: Carlyle is made to conceive history on Fichte's five-fold plan, etc. (*Cf. Storrs*, pp. 80-81, n.)

20. *Jean Paul Friedrich Richter Again* [II], p. 113, n.; *cf. Wahrheit aus Jean Pauls Leben*, III, pp. 45-46:

"Paul's ursprünglichen Widerwillen gegen das Historische und seine nachfolgende gerechtere Würdigung desselben kann man nicht besser erklären, oder darstellen, als er selbst es in einem Brief an einen seiner vertrautesten Freunde am 9ten Febr. 1795 gethan hat, in welchem er sagte: 'die ganze Geschichte ist, insofern sie ein Gewächs des Gedächtnisses ist, nichts als eine saft-und kraftlose Distel für pedantische Stieglitze, aber insofern ist sie, wie die Natur, alles werth, in wiefern wir, wie aus dieser, den unendlichen Geist errathen und ablesen, der mit der Natur und Geschichte wie mit Buchstaben an uns—schreibt. Wer einen Gott in der physischen Welt findet, findet auch einen in der moralischen, welches die Geschichte ist: die Natur dringet unserm Herzen einen Schöpfer, die Geschichte eine Vorsehung auf.' "

21. *Levana*, p. 343.

22. Schiller, *Resignation*, next to last stanza.

23. *Meister* (Carlyle's transl.) II, pp. 267-68, 269.

24. *Cf. Sartor*, pp. 194-95, etc.

25. *Cf. Über das Wesen* [VI], pp. 369-71; *Grundzüge* [VII], pp. 11-15.

26. *Grundzüge* [VII], p. 7: "Der Zweck des Erdenlebens der Menschheit ist der, dass sie in demselben alle ihre Verhältnisse mit Freiheit nach der Vernunft einrichte." *Cf. Characteristics of the Present Age*, p. 5.

27. *Char. of the Pres. Age*, p. 33; *Grundzüge* [VII], p. 34: "Die Vernunft geht auf das Eine Leben, das als Leben der Gattung erscheint . . . ."

28. *Signs of the Times* [II], p. 72.

29. *Cf. Storrs*, pp. 74-78; *Past and Present*, pp. 12, 25: "This Universe *has* its Laws. If we walk according to the Law, the Law-Maker will befriend us; if not, not." Etc., etc. Carlyle's theism became more and more explicit from about 1840 onward.

30. *Characteristics* [III], pp. 13-14.

31. *Char. of the Pres. Age*, pp. 2, 3; *Grundzüge* [VII], pp. 5, 6: "Der Philosoph, der sich die Aufgabe einer solchen Beschreibung setzte, würde unabhängig von aller Erfahrung einen Begriff des Zeit-

alters, der als Begriff in gar keiner Erfahrung vorkommen kann, aufsuchen, und die Weisen, wie dieser Begriff in der Erfahrung eintritt, als die notwendigen Phänomene dieses Zeitalters darlegen . . . . Jede einzelne Epoche der gesammten Zeit, deren wir soeben erwähnten, ist Grunbegriff eines besonderen Zeitalters."

32. *Past and Present*, p. 240.

33. Novalis, III, p. 192: "Der Historiker muss im Vortrag oft Redner werden. Er trägt ja Evangelium vor, denn die ganze Geschichte ist Evangelium." *Cf. Sartor*, p. 230.

34. Novalis, III, p. 57: "Das grösste Geheimnis ist der Mensch sich selbst. Die Auflösung dieser unendlichen Aufgabe in der Tat ist die Weltgeschichte." *Cf.* Carlyle, *Biography* [III], pp. 46-47, 48.

35. Novalis, III, pp. 187-88: "Lässt sich nicht die Verfertigung mehrerer Evangelium denken? Muss es durchaus historisch sein. Oder ist die Geschichte nur Vehikel? Nicht auch ein Evangelium der Zukunft?"

36. Novalis, III, p. 190: "Was bildet den Mensch, als seine Lebensgeschichte? Und so bildet den grossartigen Menschen nichts, als die Weltgeschichte."

37. Schelling, *Methode* [V], p. 291, 309-10: "Auch die wahre Historie beruht auf einer Synthesis des Gegebenen und Wirklichen mit dem Idealen, aber nicht durch Philosophie, da diese die Wirklichkeit vielmehr aufhebt und ganz ideal ist, Historie aber ganz in jener und doch zugleich ideal seyn soll. Dieses ist nirgends als in der Kunst möglich, welche das Wirkliche ganz bestehen lässt, wie die Bühne reale Begebenheiten oder Geschichten, aber in einer Vollendung und Einheit darstellt, wodurch sie Ausdruck der höchsten Ideen werden. Die Kunst also ist es, wodurch die Historie, indem sie Wissenschaft des Wirklichen als solchen ist, zugleich über dasselbe auf das höhere Gebiet des Idealen erhoben wird, auf dem die Wissenschaft steht; und der dritte und absolute Standpunkt der Historie ist demnach der der historischen Kunst."

38. On the other hand, it should be remembered that Carlyle's philosophy of history contained a great deal more symbolism than either Fichte's or Schelling's. Fundamentally there is very little *development* in history for Carlyle; history is less a progressive, organic revelation of God than a symbol of an eternal and perfect Being. The historian and the hero are to *read* the symbols, and humanity learns their meaning by *experience*. Though Carlyle occasionally toyed with the idea of evolution in history, and even though the doctrine of *Becoming* meant, at one time, a great deal to him, nevertheless history, as well as nature, struck him as the *handwriting of God*.

39. Fichte, *Grundzüge* [VII], p. 244.

40. *Char. of the Pres. Age*, pp. 4, 11; *Grundzüge* [VII], pp. 7-13: "Erdenleben der Menschheit gilt uns hier für das gesammte Eine Leben, und die irdische Zeit für die gesammte Zeit. . . . für den höheren Aufschwung der Speculation ist das menschliche Erdenleben und die irdische Zeit selbst nur eine nothwendige Epoche der Einen Zeit, und des Einen ewigen Lebens . . . . Die Wissenschaft endlich setzt über alle Zeit und alle Zeitalter hinweg, indem sie die Eine, sich selber gleiche Zeit als den höheren Grund aller Zeitalter erfasst, und ihrer freien Betrachtung unterwirft."

41. Hensel notes Carlyle's curious treatment of time and eternity, and conjectures that Carlyle derived his conception of an "Eternal Here and Now" from Meister Eckardt, through the writings of Schelling. Certainly Carlyle and the mystic are alike in their insistence that we should strive to lift ourselves above time and space, to eternity and infinity. Yet, as Hensel points out, Carlyle also conceives *Ewigkeit* in a second manner, especially when alluding to the present as "the conflux of two Eternities." In this latter sense he means *Unendlichkeit*, or, according to Carlyle's phrasing, the vesture of God's *Ewigkeit*. Of the two conceptions, Carlyle was the more fascinated by *Unendlichkeit*; it lent the past the pathos he always felt, and offered the limitless future as the "seedfield" for moral endeavor. (*Cf.* Hensel, p. 67; Carlyle, *Johnson* [III], p. 79: "Consider all that lies in that one word *Past!* What a pathetic, sacred, in every sense *poetic*, meaning is implied in it . . .")

Again, Carlyle seems to have adopted, for moments at least, Schlegel's conception of time as the original disturbance (*Zerrüttung*) of the peace of eternity. Time is the *Zeitgeist*, the spirit of evil, the devourer (*cf. Characteristics* [III], p. 34). But there is little reason for thinking that Carlyle understood the real meaning and implication of Schlegel's doctrine. (*Cf.* Wellek, "Carlyle and German Romanticism," p. 386.)

42. *Diderot* [III], p. 247.

43. *Characteristics* [III], p. 38.

44. *Char. of the Pres. Age*, pp. 61, 87-88; *Grundzüge* [VII], pp. 62, 88: "So, sagte ich, windet die ewig sich selbst ganz erfassende, in sich selber lebende, und aus sich selber lebende Eine Idee sich fort durch den Einen Strom der Zeit. Und, setze ich hinzu, in jedem Momente dieses Zeitstroms erfasst sie sich ganz, und durchdringt sich ganz, wie sie ist, in dem ganzen unendlichen Strome; ewig und immer sich selber allgegenwärtig. Was in ihr in jedem Momente vorkommt, *ist* nur, inwiefern *war*, was vergangen ist, und weil da *seyn soll*, was in alle Ewigkeit werden wird. Nichts geht in diesem System ver-

loren. . . . nichts wahrhaft Gutes geht in dem Strome der Zeiten verloren."

45. *Sartor*, p. 117.

46. There is no implication meant here, of course, that Fichte's notions of time and act were more influential than—or even equal to—those of Goethe on the theory and practice of Carlyle. When all possible German influences are considered, in connection with this problem, Carlyle clearly shows the predominent influence of Goethe's teachings regarding the *"seedfield"* of *time*, and action as the mighty seed of the future. Fichte's passage may be found in the *Char. of the Pres. Age*, p. 258; *Grundzüge* [VII], p. 242: "In der religiösen Ansicht werden schlechthin alle Erscheinungen in der Zeit, eingesehen als nothwendige Entwickelungen des Einen, in sich seligen, göttlichen Grundlebens, mithin jede einzelne als die nothwendige Bedingung eines höheren und vollkommneren Lebens in der Zeit, das aus ihr entspriessen soll."

47. The solution which Carlyle drew from *Wilhelm Meister*. Cf. *Meister* II, p. 225: "Nature then appears to us in the form of a Sibyl, who has beforehand laid down a testimony of what had been determined from Eternity, and was not to be realised till late in Time": *Wanderjahre*, ed. 1821, p. 73.

48. Novalis, III, p. 190: "Manche Menschen leben besser mit der vergangenen Zeit und der zukünftigen, als mit der gegenwärtigen."

49. *Characteristics* [III], p. 37.

50. *Char. of the Pres. Age*, p. 3; *Grundzüge* [VII], p. 5.

51. *Cf. Grundzüge* [VII], pp. 11-12, for a brief summary:
"Es gibt, zufolge dieser Auseinandersetzung, fünf Grundepochen des Erdenlebens; deren jede, da sie doch immer von Individuen ausgehen, aber, um Epoche im Leben der Gattung zu sein, allmählich alle ergreifen und durchdringen muss, eine geraume Zeit dauern, und so das Ganze zu sich scheinbar durchkreuzenden, und zum Teil nebeneinander fortlaufenden Zeitaltern, ausdehnen wird. 1. Die Epoche der unbedingten Herrschaft der Vernunft durch den Instinkt: *der Stand der Unschuld des Menschengeschlechts*. 2. Die Epoche, da der Vernunftinstinkt in eine äusserlich zwingende Autorität verwandelt ist: das Zeitalter positiver Lehr- und Lebenssysteme, die nirgends zurückgehen bis auf die letzten Gründe, und deswegen nicht zu überzeugen vermögen, dagegen aber zu zwingen begehren, und blinden Glauben, und unbedingten Gehorsam fordern: *der Stand der anhebenden Sünde*. 3. Die Epoche der Befreiung, unmittelbar von der gebietenden Autorität, mittelbar von der Botmässigkeit des Vernunftinstinkts und der Vernunft überhaupt in jeglicher Gestalt: das Zeitalter der absoluten Gleichgültigkeit gegen alle Wahrheit, und der völligen Ungebundenheit

ohne einigen Leitfaden: *der Stand der vollendeten Sündhaftigkeit.* 4. Die Epoche der Vernunftwissenschaft: das Zeitalter, wo die Wahrheit als das Höchste anerkannt, und am höchsten geliebt wird: *der Stand der anhebenden Rechtfertigung.* 5. Die Epoche der Vernunftkunst: das Zeitalter, da die Menschheit mit sicherer, und unfehlbarer Hand sich selber zum getroffenen Abdrucke der Vernunft aufbauet: *der Stand der vollendeten Rechtfertigung und Heiligung.*—Der gesamte Weg aber, den zufolge dieser Aufzählung die Menschheit hienieden macht, ist nichts anderes, als ein Zurückgehen zu dem Punkte, auf welchem sie gleich anfangs stand, und beabsichtigt nichts, als die Rückkehr zu seinem Ursprunge. Nur soll die Menschheit diesen Weg auf ihren eigenen Füssen gehen; mit eigener Kraft soll sie sich wieder zu dem machen, was sie ohne alles ihr Zutun gewesen; und *darum* musste sie aufhören es zu sein." (*Cf. Char. of Present Age*, pp. 9-10.)

52.   *Cf. Characteristics* [III], p. 10 *ff.*, for Carlyle's two-fold division.

53.   *Char. of the Pres. Age*, p. 6; *Grundzüge* [VII], p. 8:

"Durch diese Bemerkung zerfällt zuvörderst, nach dem aufgestellten Grundbegriffe, das Erdenleben des Menschengeschlechts in zwei Hauptepochen und Zeitalter: die Eine, da die Gattung lebt und ist, ohne noch mit Freiheit ihre Verhältnisse nach der Vernunft eingerichtet zu haben; und die andere, da sie diese vernunftmässige Einrichtung mit Freiheit zu Stande bringt."

We must remember, of course, in comparing Fichte's philosophy of history with Carlyle's, that the concept of rhythm in history cannot strictly be applied to Fichte's doctrine, which sets forth a single progressive pattern which is not repeated. Although Carlyle never *expressly* states his belief in periodicity, it is implicit in many of his remarks, as we shall note, and Fichte's theory was undoubtedly of suggestive value only.

It is not difficult to discern a possible influence from Fichte on Carlyle in respect to Carlyle's idea of the Enlightenment. Virtually every charge which Carlyle levelled at that period can be found in Fichte's *Grundzüge* (Chapters II, V, VI, VIII, etc.). Like Fichte, Carlyle deplores the exaltation of "Understanding as the highest tribunal," the obedience to "Public Opinion," the excessive fondness for periodical literature and reviews rather than for creative productions. The whole epoch struck both thinkers as the apotheosis of frivolity and *persiflage*: "Die Finsternis," said Fichte, "ist die Gedankenlosigkeit, die Frivolität, der Leichtsinn der Menschen." The period was the antithesis of both the "blind instinct" of Fichte's Reason of the First Age, and Carlyle's "unconscious Faith" of earlier and more creative ages. It is probable, however, that Carlyle owed some debt also to

Rousseau for his notion of an earlier and superior age which dwelt wholly in unselfconsciousness and productivity. (*Cf. Grundzüge* [VII], p. 248; Carlyle, *Characteristics* [III], pp. 13-14.)

54. *Novalis* [II], pp. 37-38.

55. Novalis, III, pp. 36-38; *Novalis* [II], p. 38.

56. *Diderot* [III], pp. 247, 248.

57. *Cf.* Goethe, *West-Oestlicher Divan* (italics added), pp. 247-48: "Israel in der Wüste." This Note is devoted to a discussion of the reasons for the misfortunes of the Israelites after the death of Joseph. Goethe suggests that "the last four books of Moses" show the triumph of "unfaith," apathy, weakness, after a period of supremely positive action. World-history, in general, Goethe concludes, shows this unceasing oscillation between faith and negation.

58. *Sartor,* p. 102; also *Heroes,* p. 235: ". . . that great universal war which alone makes-up the true History of the World,—the war of Belief against Unbelief!"

59. Schiller, *Resignation.*

60. *Meister* II, p. 270; *Wanderjahre,* ed. 1821, p. 181: "Vor dem ethischen Richtstuhle, vor dem Richterstuhl des Gottes des Völker, wird nicht gefragt, ob es die beste, die vortrefflichste Nation sey, sondern nur ob sie daure, ob sie sich erhalten habe."

61. Carré has noted (p. 175) Goethe's application of this idea to the Christian religion, in a manner which must have been highly congenial to Carlyle's mind. In the Notes to the *West-Oestlicher Divan,* we find one on "Mahmud von Gasna," which includes the following reflection: "Dagegen gebührt der christlichen [religion] das höchste Lob, deren reiner, edler Ursprung sich immerfort dadurch betätigt, dass nach den grössten Verirrungen, in welche sie der dunkle Mensch hineinzog, eh' man sich's versieht, sie sich in ihrer ersten lieblichen Eigentümlichkeit, als Mission, als Hausgenossen-und Brüderschaft zu Erquickung des sittlichen Menschenbedürfnisses immer wieder hervortut" (pp. 175-76).

62. *Cf. Heroes,* p. 165: "Give a thing time; if it can succeed, it is a right thing"; *Past and Present,* p. 12: "In all battles, if you await the issue, each fighter has prospered according to his right. His right and his might, at the close of the account, were one and the same. He has fought with all his might, and in exact proportion to all his right he has prevailed. His very death is no victory over him. He dies indeed; but his work lives, very truly lives." Occasionally, however, Carlyle verges on the other and more unpleasant interpretation of his principle (p. 190): " . . . . Mights which do in the long-run, and forever will in this just Universe in the long-run, mean Rights."

63. Novalis, III, p. 191.

64. Novalis, *ibidem.*

65. *Id.*, III, p. 190.

66. Another and very interesting passage in Novalis deserves brief notice. Novalis speculates on history in terms of *anecdotes* (III, p. 233):
"Geschichte ist eine grosse Anekdote. Eine Anekdote ist ein historisches Element, ein historisches Molekül oder Epigramm. Eine Geschichte in Anekdoten—etwas Ähnliches hat Voltaire geliefert—ist ein höchst interessantes Kunstwerk. Die Geschichte in gewöhnlicher Form ist eine zusammengeschweiste, oder ineinander zu einem Kontinuo geflossene Reihe von Anekdoten."
Though Carlyle does not include these sentences among those *Fragmente* which he translated in his essay on Novalis, it is interesting to remember that Carlyle's *French Revolution*, his *Frederick the Great*, and *The Diamond Necklace* are all. written on the principle that historical anecdotes, well assembled and verified for truth and accuracy, can re-create for us the reality of the past. Indeed, Carlyle's histories are a glorious tissue of anecdotes, a cento of episodes from histories and memoirs, rather than the usual conventional narrative in which the sources have been completely assimilated by the author and removed from the reader's view. (*Cf.* C. F. Harrold, "Carlyle's Method and Sources," etc., p. 1150 *ff.*, and "Carlyle and Novalis," pp. 59-60.)

67. *Cf.* Lütgert, I, 132.

68. *Methode* [V], p. 309, etc.

69. *Id.* [V], p. 310:
"In solcher Darstellung kann die Geschichte die Wirkung des grössten und erstaunenswürdigsten Drama nicht verfehlen, das nur in einem unendlichen Geiste gedichtet sein kann."

70. *Id.* [V], pp. 310-11: "Es versteht sich, dass der Historiker nicht, einer vermeinten Kunst zu lieb, den Stoff der Geschichte verändern kann, deren oberstes Gesetz Wahrheit seyn soll. Ebensowenig kann die Meinung seyn, dass die höhere Darstellung den wirklichen Zusammenhang der Begebenheiten vernachlässige, es hat vielmehr hiermit ganz dieseble Bewandtniss, wie mit der Begründung der Handlungen im Drama, wo zwar die einzelne aus der vorhergehenden und zuletzt alles aus der ersten Synthesis mit Nothwendigkeit entspringen muss, die Auseinanderfolge selbst aber nicht empirisch, sondern nur aus einer höheren Ordnung der Dinge begreiflich seyn muss. Erst dann erhält die Geschichte ihre Vollendung für die Vernunft, wenn die empirischen Ursachen, indem sie den Verstand befriedigen, als Werkzeuge und Mittel der Erscheinung einer höheren Nothwendigkeit gebraucht werden. In solcher Darstellung kann die Geschichte

die Wirkung des grössten und erstaunenswürdigsten Drama nicht
verfehlen, das nur in einem unendlichen Geiste gedichtet sein kann.
"Wir haben die Historie auf die gleiche Stufe mit der Kunst gesetzt.
Aber, was diese darstellt, ist immer eine Identität der Nothwendigkeit
und Freiheit, und diese Erscheinung, vornehmlich in der Tragödie,
ist der eigentliche Gegenstand unserer Bewunderung. Diesselbe Identität aber ist zugleich der Standpunkt der Philosophie und selbst der
Religion für die Geschichte, da diese in der Vorsehung nichts anderes,
als die Weisheit erkennt, welche in dem Plane der Welt die Freiheit
der Menschen mit der allgemeinen Nothwendigkeit und umgekehrt
diese mit jener vereinigt. Nun soll aber die Historie wahrhaft weder
auf dem philosophischen noch auf dem religiösen Standpunkt stehen.
Sie wird demnach auch jene Identität der Freiheit und Nothwendigkeit
in dem Sinne darstellen müssen, wie sie vom Gesichtspunkt der Wirklichkeit aus erscheint, den sie auf keine Weise verlassen soll. Von
diesem aus ist sie aber nur als unbegriffene und ganz objektive
Identität erkennbar, als Schicksal."

71. *Id.* [V], pp. 311-12.

72. *Id.* [V], p. 312: "Die ersten Urbilder des historischen Styls
sind das Epos in seiner ursprünglichen Gestalt und die Tragödie;
denn wenn die universalle Geschichte, deren Anfänge, wie die Quellen
des Nils, unerkennbar, die epische Form und Fülle liebt, will die
besondere dagegn mehr concentrisch um einen genmeinschaftlichen
Mittelpunkt gebildet seyn; davon zu schweigen, dass für den Historiker die Tragödie die wahre Quelle grosser Ideen und der erhabenen
Denkungsart ist, zu welcher er gebildet sein muss."

73. Lehman, *Carlyle's Theory of the Hero*, p. 168 *ff.*

Notes to Chapter VII

1. *Early Letters*, II, 56-57. For other foreshadowings of Carlyle's
doctrine of the hero, see *Sartor*, pp. 161, 228; *State of German Literature* I, pp. 59-60, 66, and his exaltation of Fichte, p. 77.

2. B. H. Lehman, *Carlyle's Theory of the Hero*, Chapters I, IV,
and V.

3. Fichte, *Über das Wesen des Gelehrten* [VI], p. 427.

4. *Heroes*, p. 1.

5. *Char. of the Pres. Age*, pp. 40, 45. (Slightly rearranged.) *Cf.*
Grundzüge [VII], p. 41:

"Alles grosse und gute, worauf unsere gegenwärtige Existenz sich stützet, wovon sie ausgeht, und unter dessen alleiniger Voraussetzung unser Zeitalter sein Wesen treiben kann, wie es dasselbe treibt, ist lediglich dadurch wirklich geworden, dass edle und kräftige Menschen allen Lebensgenuss für Ideen aufgeopfert haben; und wir selber mit allem, was wir sind, sind das Resultat der Aufopferung aller früheren Generationen, und besonders ihrer würdigsten Mitglieder."

6. *Char. of the Pres. Age.*, p. 84; *Grundzüge*, p. 91 [VII], p. 85:

"Offenbar, wird man sagen, die Helden des Zeitalters, die Vorfechter, in denen der Zeitgeist am herrlichsten sich offenbart hat."

7. *State of German Literature* [I], pp. 59-61; *cf. Über das Wesen des Gelehrten* [VI], pp. 353, 354-55, 358-60:

"Wir unseres Orts gedenken hier die Sache keinesweges nach dem äusseren Scheine zu betrachten, sondern nach der Wahrheit. Uns gelte daher von nun an für den ganzen Lauf dieser Vorlesungen nur derjenige für einen Gelehrten, der durch die gelehrte Bildung des Zeitalters hindurch zur Erkenntniss der Idee wirklich gekommen ist, oder wenigstens zu derselben zu kommen lebendig und kräftig strebt. Wer, ohne dadurch zu der Idee zu kommen, diese Bildung erhalten hat, ist nach der Wahrheit, so wie wir hier die Sache zu betrachten haben, gar Nichts; er ist ein zweideutiges Mittelding zwischen dem Besitzer der Idee, und dem von der gemeinen Realität kräftigst gestützten und getragenen:—über dem vergeblichen Ringen nach der Idee hat er versäumt, die Geschicklichkeit, die Realität zu ergreifen, in sich auszubilden, und schwebt nun zwischen zwei Welten, ohne einer von beiden anzugehören . . . .

"Noch giebt es aus einem anderen Gesichtspuncte eine andere Eintheilung im Begriffe des Gelehrten, welche für uns zu allernächst fruchtbar ist. Nemlich, entweder hat der Gelehrte die ganze göttliche Idee, inwiefern sie vom Menschen zu fassen ist, oder auch einen besonderen Theil dieses an ihr zu erfassenden,—was freilich nicht ohne eine wenigstens klare Uebersicht des Ganzen möglich ist,—schon wirklich ergriffen, durchdrungen, und sich vollkommen klar gemacht, so dass sie sein, zu jeder Zeit in derselben Gestalt zu erneuerndes Besitzthum und ein Bestandtheil seiner Persölichkeit geworden sey; so ist er ein vollendeter und fertiger Gelehrter, ein Mann, der ausstudirt hat; oder derselbe ringt noch und strebt die Idee überhaupt, oder den besonderen Theil und Punct, von welchem aus Er für seine Person das Ganze durchdringen will, sich vollkommen klar zu machen; einzelne Lichtfunken springen schon von allen Seiten ihm entgegen, und schliessen eine höhere Welt vor ihm auf, aber sie vereinigen sich ihm noch nicht zu einem untheilbaren Ganzen; sie verschwinden ihm eben so unwillkürlich wieder, als sie ihm kamen, und er kann sie noch nicht unter die Botmässigkeit seiner Freiheit bringen,—so ist er ein angehender und sich bildender Gelehrter, ein Studirender.—Dass es wirklich die Idee sey, die besessen oder angestrebt werde, ist beiden gemeinschaftlich: geht das Streben bloss auf die äussere Form und den Buchstaben der gelehrten Bildung, so erzeugt sich, wenn die Runde durchgemacht ist, der vollendete, wenn sie noch nicht durchgemacht ist, der angehende Stümper. Der letztere is noch immer erträglicher, als der erstere; denn noch lässt sich hoffen, dass er, bei der Fortsetzung seines Weges etwa in einem künftigen Puncte von der Idee ergriffen werden könne; an dem ersten aber ist alle Hoffnung verloren . . . .

"An Betrachtungen der Art, wie diese heutige war, und wie die folgenden insgesammt ausfallen werden, pflegt man gewöhnlich zu tadeln: zuvörderst die Strenge; sehr oft in der gutmüthigen Voraussetzung, dass der Vortragende es nur nicht gewusst habe, dass seine Bestimmtheit uns misfallen werde, dass wir dies ihm nur freimüthig sagen müssten, und er sodann wohl in sich gehen, und seine Sätze mildern werde. So haben wir gesagt: wer durch die gelehrte Bildung nicht zur Kenntniss der Idee gekommen sey, oder diese Kenntniss erstrebe, sey eigentlich gar Nichts, und später haben wir gesagt: er sey ein Stümper. Dies ist in der Weise jener unbarmherzigen Aeusserungen, die man den Philosophen so übel nimmt.—Um von dem vorliegenden Falle absehend, sogleich der Maxime im Ganzen zu begegnen, so erinnere ich, dass diese Denkart, ohne entschiedene Kraft, der Wahrheit alle Achtung zu versagen, von derselben nur etwas herunterzuhandeln und abzumarkten sucht, um wohlfeileren Kaufes zu einiger Achtung für sich selber zu kommen. Aber die Wahrheit, die nun einmal ist, so wie sie ist, und nichts in ihrem Wesen wandeln kann, geht ihren Weg gerade fort; und es bleibt ihr in Rücksicht derer, die sie nicht rein darum, weil sie wahr ist, haben wollen, nichts anderes übrig, als dieselben stehen zu lassen, gerade also, als ob sie nie geredet hätten.

"Sodann pflegt man Vorträge dieser Art zu tadeln, wegen ihrer vermeinten Unverständlichkeit. So denke ich mir,—keinesweges Sie, meine Herren, sondern irgend einen vollendeten Gelehrten in der Bedeutung des Scheines, dem etwa die soeben angestellte Betrachtung unter die Augen käme, als hintretend, hin und her zweifelnd, und endlich tiefsinnig ausbrechend: die Idee, die göttliche Idee, dasjenige, was der Erscheinung zu Grunde liegt: was soll nun das bedeuten? Ich würde einen solchen Frager zurückfragen: was soll denn diese Frage bedeuten?—Untersucht man das letztere genau, so bedeutet sie in den meisten Fällen nicht mehr, als folgendes: unter welchem anderen Namen, und in welchen anderen Formeln kenne ich denn

schon dieselbe Sache, die Du mit einem so sonderbaren und mir so
unbekannten Zeichen ausdrückst; und darauf wäre denn, abermals
in den meisten Fällen, die einzig passende Antwort folgende: Du
kennst diese Sache überhaupt nicht, und hast während Deines ganzen
Lebens nie etwas von ihr vernommen, weder unter diesem, noch unter
einem anderen Namen, und falls Du zur Kenntniss derselben kommen
sollst, so musst Du eben jetzt von vorne anfangen, dieselbe kennen zu
lernen; und dann am schicklichsten unter derjenigen Benennung,
unter der sie Dir zuerst angetragen wird. So wird das heute
gebrauchte Wort Idee in den folgenden Vorlesungen allerdings weiter
bestimmt und erklärt, und, wie ich hoffe, zur vollkommenen Klarheit
herauf erklärt werden; aber das ist keinesweges das Geschäft einer
einzigen Stunde."

8. *Das Wesen* [VI], pp. 367-71, 374.

9. *Nature of the Scholar*, p. 154; *Das Wesen* [VI], p. 368:
"Die ursprüngliche göttliche Idee von einem bestimmten Standpuncte
in der Zeit lässt grössentheils sich nicht eher angehn, als bis der von
Gott begeisterte Mensch kommt, und sie ausführt." (*Cf. Past and
Present,* Book I, Chapter VI, "Hero-Worship.")

10. *Über das Wesen* [VI], p. 375; *Nat. of the Scholar*, p. 161.

11. *Nat. of the Scholar*, pp. 210-11; *Über das Wesen* [VI], p. 427:
"Unmittelbar sichtbar aber, und wahrnembar durch alle auch äussere
Sinne, erscheinet die Gottheit, und tritt ein in die Welt in dem Wandel
göttlicher Menschen. In diesem Wandel stellt sich dar die Unver-
änderlichkeit des göttlichen Wesens in der Festigkeit und Uner-
schütterlichkeit des menschlichen Wollens . . . . Ein göttlicher Wandel
ist der entscheidendste Beweis, den Menschen für das Daseyn Gottes
führen können."

12. *Nat. of the Scholar*, p. 143 (slightly rearranged); *Über das
Wesen* [VI], p. 356:
"Dieser Mensch liebt die Idee, und lebt in der Idee, da es doch, nach
der Wahrheit, die Idee selbst ist, welche an seiner Stelle, und in
seiner Person lebt und sich liebt, und seine Person lediglich die sinnliche Erscheinung dieses Daseyns der Idee ist . . . . In dem wahrhaften
Gelehrten hat die Idee ein sinnliches Leben gewonnen, welches sein
persönliches Leben völlig vernichtet, und in sich aufgenommen hat."

13. *Heroes*, pp. 1-2, 15, 49, 52, 91.

14. *Über das Wesen* [VI], p. 368.

15. *Heroes*, pp. 49, 90.

16. Lehman, pp. 126-28.

17. *Char. of the Pres. Age*, p. 121; *Grundzüge* [VII], p. 119:
". . . und sodann treibt [die Idee] unmittelbar zum Handeln, strömt
aus in das persönliche Leben des Menschen, vernichtend alle seine sinn-

lichen Triebe und Begierden; und der Mensch ist Künstler, Held, Wissenschaftlicher, oder Religioser . . . ."

18. *Nature of the Scholar*, p. 160; *Über das Wesen* [VI], p. 374: ". . . so wird doch in der Erscheinung der wirklich sich äussernde, und etwas erfassende Trieb immer sich darstellen, als Trieb für eine besondere Seite der Einen an sich untheilbaren Idee, oder—wie man zu folge der Erörterung in unserer lezten Vorlesung, ohne Missverständniss zu befürchten, auch sagen kann:—als Trieb für eine besondere Idee in der Sphäre aller möglichen Ideen; oder, wenn dieser Trieb Genie genannt wird,—das Genie wird immer erscheinen als ein besonderes Genie, für Philosophie, Poesie, Naturbeobachtung, Gesezbegebung und dergleichen, keinesweges aber bloss im Allgemeinen als Genie."

At the end of Lecture II, Fichte specifies five different ways in which the Divine Idea manifests itself through men in the world of sense; in Legislation, or the art of maintaining the essential unity of society; Science, or the art of subjecting nature to human purposes; Religion, or the "gladdening consciousness" of the true source of man's existence; the Knowledge of the Divine Idea; and the "Art or Skill actually to make manifest in the world the Idea which is thus clearly seen and understood."

19. *Heroes*, p. 51; *Über das Wesen* [VI], pp. 382-90: "diese gründliche Rechtschaffenheit . . .," etc.

20. *Über das Wesen* [VI], p. 373; *Heroes*, pp. 133, 56: "There is the seeing eye, the mildly understanding heart."

21. *Nat. of the Scholar*, p. 206 (slightly rearranged); *Über das Wesen* [VI], p. 423:
"Der Regent nach unserem Bilde blickt in seiner Würdigung des Geschlechts über dasjenige, was sie *wirklich* sind, hinaus, auf das, was sie im *göttlichen Begriffe* sind, und diesem zufolge werden können, werden sollen . . . ."

22. Similar to Fichte's notion of insight as insight into "what ought to be," is Carlyle's favorite idea that "All Power is Moral" (*Heroes*, p. 35). *Cf.* Goethe's Maxim: "Wo ich aufhören muss, sittlich zu sein, habe ich keine Gewalt mehr" (no. 678 [Hecker]); Schlegel's *Idee*: "Wo Politik ist oder Oekonomie, da ist keine Moral" (*Ideen*, p. 22).

23. In spite of Carlyle's earlier admiration for Napoleon, he finally declared: "I find no such *sincerity* as in Cromwell . . . No silent walking . . . with the Awful Unnamable of this Universe . . ." (*Heroes*, p. 274.)

24. *Nat. of the Scholar*, p. 210 (Smith's translation here is rather free): *Über das Wesen*: "*Nur* die Idee treibt ihn . . . So lange ihm

diese schweigt, schweigt auch Er, denn nur für sie hat er die Sprache."
(VI, p. 426.)
    25. *Nat. of the Scholar*, p. 165; *Über das Wesen* [VI], p. 379:
"Das Talent selbst weiss am allerwenigsten von sich selber; es ist schon
und wirkt und waltet mit stiller Macht fort, ehe es zum Bewusstseyn
selbst kommt."
    26. Carlyle, *Life of Schiller*, pp. 198-99; *cf*. Schiller, *Werke*, IX
("Über naïve und sentimentalische Dichtung"), pp. 450-51 (the first
paragraph contains Schiller's ideas on genius in respect to spontaneity,
instinct, intuition, unselfconsciousness, etc. The third paragraph is
that which Carlyle translated):
    "Naïv muss jedes wahre Genie sein, oder es ist keins. Seine
Naïvetät allein macht es zum Genie, und was es im Intellektuellen
und Ästhetischen ist, kann es im Moralischen nicht verleugnen.
Unbekannt mit den Regeln, den Krücken der Schwachheit und den
Zuchtmeistern der Verkehrtheit, bloss von der Natur oder dem
Instinkt, seinem schützenden Engel, geleitet, geht es ruhig und sicher
durch alle Schlingen des falschen Geschmackes, in welchen, wenn es
nicht so klug ist, sie schon von weitem zu vermeiden, das Richtgenie
unausbleiblich verstrickt wird. Nur dem Genie ist es gegeben, ausserhalb des Bekannten noch immer zu Hause zu sein und die Natur zu
erweitern, ohne über sie hinauszugehen. Zwar begegnet letzteres
zuweilen, auch den grössten Genies, aber nur, weil auch diese ihre
phantastischen Augenblicke haben, wo die schützende Natur sie
verlässt, weil die Macht des Beispiels sie hinreisst oder der verderbte
Geschmack ihrer Zeit sie verleitet.
    "Die verwickeltsten Aufgaben muss das Genie mit anspruchloser
Simplicität und Leichtigkeit lösen; das Ei des Kolumbus gilt von
jeder genialischen Entscheidung. Dadurch allein legitimiert es sich
als Genie, dass es durch Einfalt über die verwickelte Kunst triumphiert.
Es verfährt nicht nach erkannten Prinzipien, sondern nach Einfällen
und Gefühlen; aber seine Einfälle sind Eingebungen eines Gottes
(alles, was die gesunde Natur thut, ist göttlich) seine Gefühle sind
Gesetze für alle Zeiten und für alle Geschlechter der Menschen.
    "Den kindlichen Charakter, den das Genie in seinen Werken abdrückt,
zeigt es auch in seinem Privatleben und in seinen Sitten. Es ist
schamhaft, weil die Natur dieses immer ist; aber es ist nicht decent,
weil nur die Verderbnis decent ist. Es ist verständig, denn die Natur
kann nie das Gegenteil sein; aber es ist nicht listig, denn das kann nur
die Kunst sein. Es ist seinem Charakter und seinen Neigungen treu,
aber nicht sowohl, weil es Grundsätze hat, als weil die Natur bei
allem Schwanken immer wieder in die vorige Stelle rückt, immer das
alte Bedürfnis zurückbringt. Es ist bescheiden, ja blöde, weil das

Genie immer sich selbst ein Geheimnis bleibt; aber es ist nicht ängst-
lich, weil es die Gefahren des Weges nicht kennt, den es wandelt. Wir
wissen wenig von dem Privatleben der grössten Genies, aber auch das
Wenige, was uns z. B. von Sophokles, von Archimed, von Hippokrates
und aus neueren Zeiten von Ariost, Dante und Tasso, von Raphael,
von Albrecht Dürer, Cervantes, Shakespeare, von Fielding, Sterne und
andern ausbewahrt."
The idea of the unselfconscious genius, of the superiority of intuition and instinct over reason and social conventions, goes back, of
course, beyond Schiller. We need only remember Rousseau in this
connection. How far Carlyle felt the influence of Rousseau, however,
has been open to question. From his remarks on Rousseau in
Heroes (Lecture V), one may gather a strong impression of how
uncongenial to Carlyle was Rousseau's general point of view. (*Cf.*
Cazamian, pp. 35-36.)
27. *Nat. of the Scholar*, p. 163; *Über das Wesen* [VI], p. 377:
"Wo das Genie nur wirklich eingetreten, da findet sich der Fleiss von
selber."
28. *Nat. of the Scholar*, p. 169; *Über das Wesen* [VI], p. 383:
"Der Mensch soll etwas seyn und thun, sein zeitliches Leben soll ein
unvergängliches und ewiges Resultat hinterlassen in der Geisterwelt.."
29. *Über das Wesen* [VI], 394; *Nat. of the Scholar*, p. 179.
30. *Heroes*, p. 233.
31. *Nat. of the Scholar*, p. 205; *Über das Wesen* [VI], p. 421:
"Der Regent besitzt zuföderst einen lebendigen Begriff von dem-
jenigen Verhältnisse überhaupt, worüber er die Aufsicht übernimmt,
weiss, was es eigentlich an sich ist, bedeutet und soll . . . Er kennt
die bestimmte Gestalt, welche es in der Gegenwart angenommen, und
weiss, durch welche neue Gestalten hindurch es dem an sich unerreich-
baren Ideale immer mehr angenähert werden müsse. . . . Er kennt
das Ganze, von welchem jenes Verhältniss ein Theil ist . . . Sein
Blick vereinigt immerfort die Theile und das Ganze, und das letztere
im Ideale und in der Wirklichkeit."
32. *Nat. of the Scholar*, p. 192; *Über das Wesen* [VI], p. 408:
"Und doch kann dieser Trieb zur Versuchung werden, das Heilige
gemein darzustellen, damit es an die Gemeinheit komme, und so es zu
entheiligen. Was ist edler, als die tiefste Achtung für das Heilige,
und die Nichtachtung und Vernichtung alles Gemeinen jenem
gegenüber?"
33. *Nat. of the Scholar*, p. 207; *Über das Wesen* [VI], p. 423:
". . . dies erfüllt ihn mit Achtung für ein Geschlecht von dieser
erhabenen Bestimmung. Liebe ist nicht einem Jeden anzumuthen; es
ist sogar, wenn man tiefer denkt, eine Anmaassung, dass ein Regent

sich herausnehme, die gesammte Menschheit, oder auch nur seine gesammte Nation, zu lieben, und sie seiner Liebe zu versichern und sie von derselben abhängig zu machen. Diese Liebe wird dem von uns geschilderten Regenten erlassen; sein Respect für die Menschheit, als das Bild und den Schützling der Gottheit, ersetzt dieselbe im Uebermaasse."

34. *Heroes*, p. 225.

35. *Über das Wesen* [VI], pp. 169, 427.

36. *Nat. of the Scholar*, p. 211; *Über das Wesen*: ". . . und ganze besonders muss den Regenten, als den höchsten Anordnern der menschlichen Verhältnisse daran gelegen seyn." ([VI], p. 427.)

37. *Ibid.* [VI], p. 428: ". . . wir werden in ihren Werken Gott sehen von Angesicht zu Angesicht, und keines anderen Beweises bedürfen; Gott ist, werden wir sagen, denn sie sind, und er ist in ihnen."

38. *Nat. of the Scholar*, p. 209; *Über das Wesen* [VI], p. 425: "Jedermann bedarf der Religion, jedermann kann sie an sich bringen, jedermann erhält mit ihr unmittelbar die Seeligkeit: ganz vorzüglich bedarf sie, wie sich schon oben ergeben hat, der Regent. Ohne in ihrem Lichte sein Geschäft zu verklären, kann er es gar nicht mit gutem Gewissen treiben."

39. *Char. of the Pres. Age*, p. 46; *Grundzüge* [VII], p. 48: "Auch musste . . . das gebildete herrschen, und das ungebildete dienen, wenn geschehen sollte, was Rechtens ist. Diese Idee lebte schon seit langem in den edleren griechischen Gemüthern, bis sie in Alexander zur lebendigen Flamme wurde, welche sein individuelles Leben bestimmte, und aufzehrte. Rechne man mir nun nicht vor die Tausende, die auf seinem Zuge fielen, erwähne man nicht seines eigenen frühzeitig erfolgten Todes; was konnte er denn nun, nach Realisierung der Idee, noch grösseres tun, als sterben?"

40. Goethe, *Werke*, I, pp. 208, 217. Carlyle, *Goethe's Works* [II], p. 441:

"Diesem Amboss vergleich' ich das Land, den Hammer dem Herrscher,
Und dem Volke das Blech, das in der Mitte sich krümmt.
Wehe dem armen Blech! wenn nur willkürliche Schläge
Ungewiss treffen, und nie fertig der Kessel erscheint.

Alle Freiheitsapostel, sie waren mir immer zuwider:
Willkür suchte doch nur jeder am Ende für sich.
Willst du Viele befrein, so wag' es, Vielen zu dienen.
Wie gefährlich das sei, willst du es wissen? Versuch's!"

41. *Heroes*, p. 187.
42. *Über das Wesen* [VI], pp. 444, 446.
43. *Heroes*, p. 193.—Like many of the other ideas of Carlyle regarding heroes and men of letters, the notion of the poet as a priest goes far back into antiquity. *Cf.* the Hebraic conception of the poet as prophet, and *vice versa*.
44. *Über das Wesen* [VI], p. 435; *Nat. of the Scholar*, p. 219.
45. *Nat. of the Scholar*, p. 220; *Über das Wesen* [VI], p. 437.
46. *Nat. of the Scholar*, p. 229; *Über das Wesen* [VI], pp. 445-46: "Begeistert wird er durch diese Idee, zu einer würdigen und heiligen Ansicht des schriftstellerischen Berufes. . . . Das Werk des Schriftstelers . . . ist in sich selber ein Werk für die Ewigkeit."
Novalis, also, has interesting things to say on the man of letters (III, pp. 236-242, etc.), but aside from echoing several points of Fichte, he does not seem to have any significant bearing on the present problem.
47. *Char. of the Pres. Age*, pp. 85, 88 *ff.*; *Grundzüge* [VII], pp. 86, 89 *ff.*, etc.— Not too much emphasis should be placed on these minor parallels between Carlyle and Fichte. The ideal of a Republic of Letters was not peculiar to Fichte. *Cf.* the title of one of Klopstock's works: *Die Deutsche Gelehrtenrepublik*, . . . Hamburg, 1777.
48. Novalis, III, p. 137.
49. *Nat. of the Scholar*, p. 141; *Über das Wesen* [VI], p. 354: "Ihre Tugend besteht in pünktlichem Gehorsam und der Vermeidung alles Selbstdenkens, und über ihr Geschäft Selbsturtheilens."
50. Carlyle, *Novalis* [III], p. 39; Novalis, III, p. 136: "Es gibt nur einen Tempel in der Welt, und das ist der menschliche Körper. Nichts ist heiliger, als diese hohe Gestalt. Das Bücken vor Menschen ist eine Huldigung dieser Offenbarung im Fleisch. Man berührt den Himmel, wenn man einen Menschenleib betastet."
It is a question how much spiritual content Novalis meant these words to suggest. They have a possibly sensual meaning which Carlyle, of course, would have ignored if he recognized it, in order to interpret the words in accordance with his Clothes Philosophy.
51. *Char. of the Pres. Age*, pp. 12-13; *Grundzüge* [VII], p. 15: "Übrigens geht die Zeit ihren festen, ihr von Ewigkeit her bestimmten Tritt, und es lässt in ihr durch einzelne Kraft sich nichts übereilen, oder erzwingen. Nur die Vereinigung aller, und besonders der inwohnende ewige Geist der Zeiten und der Welten vermag zu fördern."
52. Lehman, p. 122.
53. *State of Germ. Lit.* [I], p. 58. See Miss Storrs' more detailed treatment of this point (pp. 83-90).

54. Storrs, p. 88.—Carlyle's peculiar treatment of Fichte's Scholar, and the possibility that he never read all of Fichte's lectures on the subject, gain a certain significance when we note that all of Carlyle's quotations and summaries of Fichte's theory are drawn from the first lecture. (See footnote to Storrs, p. 88.)

55. Storrs, p. 90. For Carlyle's reference to Fichte's lectures, see *Heroes*, pp. 179-81. Fichte is here said to have lectured on "the Nature of the Literary Man." The man of letters, says Carlyle further, "is sent hither especially that he may discern for himself, and make manifest to us, this same Divine Idea . . . Such is Fichte's phraseology." Throughout the paraphrase of Fichte, Carlyle uses the expression "Literary Man" (meaning poet, man of letters, etc.) for Fichte's *Gelehrter*, which meant not only Literary Man but also Teacher, Ruler, etc. After discussing Fichte's notions regarding the Hodman and the Bungler, Carlyle again refers to the "Literary Man," —"It means, in its own form, precisely what we here mean." Thus it is clear, that although Carlyle seems to have followed Fichte in showing the Hero as appearing in the forms of Poet, Priest, King, etc., he emphasized, at least momentarily, the supremacy of the literary man over the other heroic types. Here, again, appears Carlyle's characteristic ambiguity and lack of systematic formulation of ideas. (We have seen that Carlyle translates Fichte's passage in *The State of German Literature* [I], pp. 59-61. See note 7 to the present chapter.)

Notes to Chapter VIII

1. *Sartor*, p. 4; *Lehrjahre*, II, p. 326: "Nur alle Menschen machen die Menschheit aus . . ." Cf. *Meister* (Carlyle's translation), II, p. 131.

2. *Characteristics* [III], p. 37.

3. *Sartor*, p. 58; Richter, *Blumen-Frucht-und Dornenstücke,* . . . Berlin, 1818, III, pp. 286-87: "Es gibt schauerliche Dämmeraugenblicke in uns, wo uns ist, als schieden sich Tag und Nacht—als würden wir gerade geschaffen, oder gerade vernichtet . . . und wir sehen uns darin an und fragen uns: 'was bist Du jetzo, Ich?'—Wenn wir so fragen: so gibt es ausser uns nichts Grosses oder Festes für uns mehr—alles wird eine unendliche nächtliche Wolke . . . und nur hoch über der Wolke gibt es einen Glanz, und der ist Gott, und tief unter ihr ist ein lichter Punkt, und der ist ein Menschen-Ich." (The

English transl. is by A. Ewing, London, 1888 [Bohn's Library], p. 429.)

4. See *Sartor*, pp. 46, 58, etc.

5. *Richter* [II], p. 111; *Wahrheit*, I, p. 53:

"Nie vergess ich die noch keinem Menschen ehzählte Erscheinung in mir, wo ich bei der Geburt meines Selbbewusstseins stand, von der ich Ort und Zeit anzugeben weiss. An einem Vormittag stand ich als ein sehr junges Kind unter der Hausthüre und sah links nach der Holzlege, als auf einmal das innere Gesicht, ich bin ein Ich, wie ein Blitzstrahl vom Himmel vor mich fuhr, und seitdem leuchtend stehen blieb: da hatte mein Ich zum erstenmale sich selber gesehen und auf ewig. Täuschungen des Erinnerns sind hier schwerlich gedenkbar, da kein fremdes Erzählen sich in eine bloss im verhangnen Allerheiligsten des Menschen vorgefallne Begebenheit, deren Neuheit allein so alltäglichen Nebenumständen das Bleiben gegeben, mit-zusätzen mengen konnte." *Cf.* Leopold, p. 55, on this passage in relation to Carlyle's "conversion."

6. Novalis, III, p. 195: "Der Mensch . . . ist der Messias der Natur." *Cf.* Carlyle, *Novalis* [II], p. 40; *Sartor*, p. 200.

7. Novalis, III, pp. 182, 241, etc.: "Jedes Menschen Geschichte soll eine Bibel sein; wird eine Bibel sein . . . In jedem Menschen kann mir Gott erscheinen . . . Unter Menschen muss man Gott suchen. In den menschlichen Begebenheiten, in menschlichen Gedanken und Empfindung offenbart sich der Geist des Himmels am helsten."

8. *Corn-Law Rhymes* [III], p. 155; *Varnhagen von Esne* [IV], p. 109.

9. *Cf.* Goethe, *Faust* I, ll. 1347-58.

10. See Chapter IV, Section 4.—The *locus classicus* for the expression of the idea of the two-fold self is in *Faust* I, ll. 1112-17:

> "Zwei Seelen wohnen, ach! in meiner Brust,
> Die eine will sich von der andern trennen:
> Die eine hält, in derber Liebeslust,
> Sich an die Welt mit klammernden Organnen;
> Die andre hebt gewaltsam sich vom Dust
> Zu den Gefilden hoher Ahnen."

11. *Sartor*, p. 67; *Lehrjahre*, I, p. 113; *Meister* (Carlyle's translation), I, p. 131.

12. *Vocation of Man* (transl. W. Smith), pp. 361, 362, 363; *Die Bestimmung des Menschen* [II], pp. 299-301:

"Dieser Wille verbindet mich mit sich selbst; derselbe verbindet mich mit allen endlichen Wesen meines Gleichen, und ist der allgemeine Vermittler zwischen uns Allen. Das ist das grosse Geheimniss der unsichtbaren Welt, und ihr Grundgesetz, in wiefern sie Welt oder System von mehreren einzelnen Willen ist: jene Vereinigung, und unmittelbare Wechselwirkung mehrerer selbstständiger und unabhängiger Willen mit einander; ein Geheimniss, das schon im gegenwärtigen Leben klar vor Aller Augen liegt. . . . Kurz, diese gegenseitige Erkenntniss und Wechselwirkung freier Wesen schon in dieser Welt, ist nach Natur- und Denkgesetzen völlig unbegreiflich, und lasst sich erklären lediglich durch das Eine, in dem sie zufammenhängen, nach dem sie für sich getrennt sind, durch den unendlichen Willen, der alle in seiner Sphäre hält und trägt."

13. *Characteristics* [III], p. 12; *Burns* [I], p. 280. *Cf.* Richter, *Levana*, p. xxiii ("Vorrede zur ersten Auflage") : "Weisheit, Sittlichkeit sind kein Ameisenhaufen abgetrennter zusammentragender Thätigkeiten, sondern organische Eltern der geistigen Nachwelt . . . Wir kehren die Unwisisenheit der Wilden, welche Schiesspulver säeten, anstatt es zu machen, bloss um, wenn wir etwas zusammen setzen wollen, was sich nur entfalten lässt."

14. *Wanderjahre*, p. 548; *Meister* (Carlyle's translation), II, p. 415; *cf.* Sartor, Book III, Chapter V, "The Phoenix," as elaborating Carlyle's conviction that "society is the want of the age."— Allied to the thought that "all men make up mankind," is Carlyle's doctrine that society rests largely on habit, imitation, and the uniting of the individual with the mass. *Cf. Sartor*, p. 119, where Teufelsdröckh is to establish habit-contacts with his fellows, to "unite himself with somewhat." Carlyle is here quoting the *Wanderjahre*, 196: "Doch macht eine besondere Eigenheit der menschlichen Natur eine genauere Beurteilung gewissermassen schwierig: es ist der Nachahmungsgeist, die Neigung sich anzuschliessen. . . ."

15. Novalis, III, p. 180: "Noch ist keine Religion . . . Religion muss gemacht und hervorgebracht werden durch die Vereinigung mehrerer Menschen." *Cf.* Carlyle, *Two Notebooks*, p. 149. Carlyle's idea of society as mystically a fusion of spirit reflects Coleridge's idea of *Schwärmerei* (*cf.* the Conclusion of the *Aids to Reflection*, p. 326). It must be remembered, of course, that this notion of religion as the basis of society is of considerable age. See, for instance, Bacon's essay, "Of Unity in Religion"; religion, says Bacon, is "the chief band of human society." *Essays*, ed. Selby, p. 5. *Cf. Sartor*, pp. 194-97.

16. *Characteristics* [III], pp. 11-12.

17. Though Carlyle records his estimate of the structure of the *Lehrjahre*, he nowhere gives us his impression of the increasingly recondite and symbolical nature of the *Wanderjahre*. Of the former he writes (*Goethe* [I], p. 225) :

"It is wonderful to see with what softness the scepticism of Jarno, the commercial spirit of Werner, the reposing polished manhood of Lothario and the Uncle, the unearthly enthusiasm of the Harper, the gay animal vivacity of Philina, the mystic, ethereal, almost spiritual nature of Mignon, are blended together in this work; how justice is done to each, how each lives freely in his proper element, in his proper form; and how, as Wilhelm himself, the mild-hearted, all-hoping, all-believing Wilhelm, struggles forwards towards his world of Art through these curiously complected influences, all this unites itself into a multifarious, yet so harmonious Whole; as into a clear poetic mirror, where man's life and business in this age, his passions and purposes, the highest equally with the lowest, are imaged back to us in beautiful significance."

"This *Wanderjahre*," he writes further (I, p. 233), "seems to us a most estimable work." In his remarks on Goethe (*Meister*, I, p. 32), he admits that "these *Travels* will surprise and disappoint the reader . . . and perhaps the reader of the *Apprenticeship* will be more surprised than any other." Carlyle is silent on the bewildering and incoherent chapters with which the novel closes. We can only imagine what he thought of "Who Can the Traitor Be?", or the narratives of the Nut-brown Maid, the Man of Fifty Years, etc. In the Preface of the second edition (1839), he mentions some of the subjects touched upon in the novel (*Meister*, I, pp. 1-2):

"In the second Translation, *Meister's Travels*, two years later in date, I have changed little or nothing: I might have added much; for the Original, since that time, was as it were taken to pieces by the Author himself in his last years, and constructed anew; and in the Final Edition of his Works appears with multifarious intercalations, giving a great expansion both of size and of scope. Not Pedagogy only, and Husbandry and Art and Religion and Human Conduct in the Nineteenth Century, but Geology, Astronomy, Cotton-Spinning, Metallurgy, Anatomical Lecturing, and much else, are typically shadowed forth in this second form of the *Travels*; which, however, continues a Fragment like the first, significantly pointing on all hands towards infinitude; not more complete than the first was, or indeed perhaps less so."

18. *Cf.* M. Wundt, *Goethes Wilhelm Meister und die Entwicklung des Modernen Lebensideals*, Berlin, 1913, pp. 211, 226, 233, 239-52. Wundt characterises *die schöne Seele* as representing "die religiöse Humanität"; the Uncle, "die aesthetische Humanität"; Natalia, "die sittliche Humanität"; and Lothario, Jarno, Therese, and the Abbé as exemplifying "das Leben der Tat."

19. *Sartor*, p. 109. (Slightly rearranged.)

20. *Cf.* Aristotle, *Ethics*, Book X, c. 9, sect. 1; *Sartor*, p. 143; *Wotton Reinfred*, p. 10; *Lehrjahre*, II, p. 163; *Meister*, I, pp. 454-55. See, also, *Ecclesiastes*, ix, 10, and *John*, ix, 4.

21. *Wallenstein's Lager*, Prolog, last line; *cf.* Baumgarten, pp. 66-69.

22. *Lehrjahre*, II, p. 357; *Meister*, II, p. 157; Carlyle possibly had in mind also such a passage as the following (*Lehrjahre*, II, p. 152) : ". . . ohne Ernst ist in der Welt nichts möglich, und unter denen, die wir gebildete Menschen nennen, ist eigentlich wenig Ernst zu finden . . ." *Cf.* Carlyle, *Meister*, I, p. 446.

23. *Lehrjahre*, II, p. 163; Carlyle, *Meister*, I, pp. 454-55.

24. Schiller, *Werke*, I, p. 268.

25. *Jean Pauls Briefe und bevorstehender Lebenslauf*, Gera und Leipzig, 1799, p. 282.

26. *Nature of the Scholar*, p. 169; *Über das Wesen* [VI], p. 383.

27. *Nat. of the Scholar*, p. 171; *Über das Wesen* [VI], p. 386: "Auf alle Fälle ist es der göttliche Wille, dass jeder in der Lage, in die die Nothwendigkeit ihn gesetzt hat, alles thue, was in derselben geschehen soll."

28. *Vocation of Man*, p. 313; *Bestimmung* [II], p. 249: "Nicht blosses Wissen, sondern nach deinem Wissen *Thun* ist deine Bestimmung."

29. *Bestimmung* [II], p. 261.

30. *Id.* [II], p. 263: "Von jenem Bedürfnisse des Handelns geht das Bewusstsein der wirklichen Welt aus, nicht umgekehrt vom Bewusstsein der Welt das Bedürfniss des Handelns; dieses ist das erste, nicht jenes, jenes ist das abgeleitete. Wir handeln nicht, weil wir erkennen, sondern wir erkennen, weil wir zu handeln bestimmt sind; die praktische Vernunft ist die Wurzel aller Vernunft. Die Handelsgesetze für vernünftige Wesen sind *unmittelbar* gewiss; ihre Welt ist gewiss nur *dadurch, dass jene gewiss sind*. Wir können den erstern nicht absagen, ohne dass uns die Welt, und mit ihr wir selbst, in das absolute Nichts versinken; wir erheben uns aus diesem Nichts, und erhalten uns über diesem Nichts lediglich durch unsre Moralität."

That Carlyle's doctrine of work owed little, however, to Fichte can be seen by noting Fichte's emphasis on a "moral striving" rather than upon the more specific "duty" which Carlyle had in mind. Fichte's doctrine is the result of a rational deduction. For a detailed contrasting of Carlyle and Fichte on this point, see Miss Storrs' admirable discussion (pp. 92-96).

31. *Lehrjahre*, I, p. 93; *Meister*, I, p. 114. *Sartor*, p. 172. Carlyle had undoubtedly found elsewhere, also, the notion that "man's unhap-

piness . . . comes from [the] Infinite in him." It is stated, for example, in Hooker's *Ecclesiastical Polity* (*Works*, ed. J. Keble, Oxford, 1888, I) Bk. I, Ch. XI, sect. 4, pp. 257-58. See, also, *Faust I*, ll. 300-01.

32. *Wanderjahre*, p. 416: ". . . weil man sich, wohin man auch gelange, immer wieder in einer bedingten Welt befindet . . ."

33. Novalis, III, p. 62: "Wir suchen über all das Unbedingte, und finden immer nur Dinge."

34. *Lehrjahre*, II, p. 81; *Meister*, I, p. 386; *Sartor*, p. 177: "Most true is it, as a wise man teaches us, that 'Doubt of any sort cannot be removed except by Action.' "

35. *Lehrjahre*, II, p. 233 (Carlyle, *Meister*, II, p. 54):
"Und die Leiden unserer Freunde bringen wir nicht in Anschlag?

"Auch unsere Freunde tun wohl, wenn sie sich bald finden, wenn sie sich sagen: Da, wo du bist, da, wo du bleibst, wirke, was du kannst, sei tätig und gefällig, und lass dir die Gegenwart heiter sein."

36. *Wanderjahre*, p. 301 (*Meister*, II, p. 321): "Wir sehen unsere Schüler, sagte der Aufseher, sämmtlich als Schwimmer an, welche, mit Verwunderung, im Elemente das sie zu verschlingen droht, sich leichter fühlen, von ihm gehoben und getragen sind; und so ist es mit allem dessen sich der Mensch unterfängt." Carlyle was fond of this figure. *Cf.* "New Letters of Carlyle," ed. W. A. Speck, *Yale Review*, July, 1926, p. 6.

37. *Lehrjahre*, II, p. 119 (Meister, I, p. 418):
"Aber da ich endlich nach tausendfältigem Streit, nach immer wiederholter Betrachtung auch scharfe Blicke auf das Band warf, das mich an ihn festhielt, entdeckte ich, dass es nur schwach war, dass es sich zerreissen lass. Ich erkannte auf einmal, dass es nur eine Glasglocke sei, die mich in den lustleeren Raum sperrte: nur noch so viel Kraft, sie entzweizuschlagen, und du bist grettet!"
Cf. Sartor, p. 222, for Carlyle's application of the figure of the glass bell.

38. *Maximen u. Refl.*, nos. 442-43:
"Wie kann man sich selbst kennen lernen? Durch Betrachten niemals, wohl aber durch Handeln. Versuche, deine Plicht zu thun, und du weisst gleich, was an dir ist.

"Was aber ist deine Pflicht? Die Forderung des Tages."
Cf. Sartor, p. 177: "*Do the Duty which lies nearest thee* . . ."
The contrast between Goethe and Carlyle here, however, should not be forgotten: "For Goethe it was a practical maxim, promoting self-development and culture. For Carlyle, on the other hand, it was a categorical imperative—the Infinite Nature of Duty—and his labour was that of a lonely, great soul, striving to obey an unseen Ruler, in

the midst of an unknown and unknowable Immensity."—J. A. S. Barret, "Carlyle's Debt to Goethe," *Hibbert Journal*, XXX (1931), p. 69.

39. *Sartor*, p. 149.

40. *Id.*, p. 149: "Between vague wavering Capability and fixed indubitable Performance, what a difference!" *Cf. Lehrjahre*, II, p. 289 (Carlyle, *Meister*, II, p. 100):

"Er behaupte: das Erste und Letzte am Menschen sei Tätigkeit, und man könne nichts tun, ohne die Anlage dazu zu haben, ohne den Instinkt, der uns dazu treibe, . . ., aber wenn man es genau betrachtet, so wird jede, auch nur die geringste Fähigkeit uns angeboren, und es gibt keine unbestimmte Fähigkeit."

41. *Lehrjahre*, II, p. 325 (Carlyle, *Meister*, II, p. 130):

"Man soll sich, fuhr Jarno fort, indem er auf die Rolle sah, vor einem Talente hüten, das man in Vollkommenheit auszuüben nicht Hoffnung hat. Man mag es darin soweit bringen, als man will, so wird man doch immer zuletzt, wenn uns einmal das Verdienst des Meisters klar wird, den Verlust von Zeit und Kräften, die man auf eine solche Pfuscherei gewendet hat, schmerzlich bedauern."

42. *Lehrjahre*, II, p. 82 (Carlyle, *Meister*, I, pp. 386-87):

"Für den Menschen, sagte er, sei nur das eine ein Unglück, wenn sich irgendeine Idee bei ihm festsetze, die keinen Einfluss ins tätige Leben habe oder ihn wohl gar vom tätigen Leben abziehe."

43. *Sartor*, p. 184.

44. *Lehrjahre*, II, pp. 259-60; Carlyle, *Meister*, II, p. 76.

45. *Id.*, II, p. 323: ". . . und dass man sich selbst eigentlich nur in der Tätigkeit zu beobachten und zu erlauschen im stande sei." (Carlyle, *Meister*, II, p. 129.)

46. *Ibidem*, pp. 323-24:

"Nicht allen Menschen ist es eigentlich um ihre Bildung zu tun, viele wünschen nur so ein Hausmittel zum Wohlbefinden, Rezepte zum Reichtum und zu jeder Art von Glückseligkeit. Alle diese, die nicht auf ihre Füsse gestellt sein wollten, wurden mit Mystifikationen und anderm Hokus-Pokus teils aufgehalten, teils beiseite gebracht." This passage in the *Lehrjahre* was one of the most revelatory to Carlyle. In his *Lectures on Literature* (ed. J. R. Greene, London, 1892, p. 202), he told how, in the novel, "a number of applications for advice were daily made to the association, which were answered thus and thus, but that many people wrote in particular for recipes of happiness; all that, he adds, 'was laid on the shelf, and not answered at all!' Now this thing gave me great surprise when I read it. 'What!' I said, 'is it not the recipe of happiness that I have been seeking all my life; and isn't it precisely because I have failed in finding it that I am now miserable and discontented?' "—This is undoubtedly the Goethean source for Carlyle's position on "the happiness question."

47. *Lehrjahre*, II, pp. 150-51 (Carlyle, *Meister*, I, pp. 444-45) : "Ich werde, sagte er darauf, auch auf meine eigenste Weise, ohne Veränderung des Tons fortfahren können. Des Menschen grösstes Verdienst bleibt wohl, wenn er die Umstände soviel als möglich bestimmt und sich sowenig als möglich von ihnen bestimmen lässt. Das ganze Weltwesen liegt vor uns, wie ein grosser Steinbruch vor dem Baumeister, der nur dann den Namen verdient, wenn er aus diesen zufälligen Naturmassen ein in seinem Geiste entsprungenes Urbild mit der grössten Ökonomie, Zweckmässigkeit und Festigkeit zusammenstellt. Alles ausser uns ist nur Element, ja, ich darf wohl sagen auch alles an uns; aber tief in uns liegt diese schöpferische Kraft, die das zu erschaffen vermag, was sein soll, und uns nicht ruhen und rasten lässt, bis wir es ausser uns oder an uns, auf eine oder die andere Weise, dargestellt haben . . . . Ich verehre den Menschen, der deutlich weiss, was er will, unablässig vorschreitet, die Mittel zu seinem Zwecke kennt und sie zu ergreifen und zu brauchen weiss. . . ."

48. Kraeger, "Carlyle's Stellung," etc., p. 49.

49. *Lehrjahre*, II, pp. 181-82 (Carlyle, *Meister*, II, p. 11) : "O, mein Freund! fuhr Lothario fort, das ist ein Hauptfehler gebildeter Menschen, dass sie alles an eine Idee, wenig oder nichts an einen Gegenstand wenden mögen. Wozu habe ich Schulden gemacht? warum habe ich mich mit meinen Oheim entzweit, meine Geschwister so lange sich selbst überlassen, als um einer Idee willen? In Amerika glaubte ich zu wirken, über dem Meere glaubte ich nützlich und notwendig zu sein; war eine Handlung nicht mit tausend Gefahren umgeben, so schien sie mir nicht bedeutend, nicht würdig. Wie anders seh' ich jetzt die Dinge, und wie ist mir das Nächste so wert, so teuer geworden.

"Ich erinnere mich wohl des Briefes, versetzte Jarno, den ich noch über das Meer erhielt. Sie schrieben mir: Ich werde zurückkehren und in meinem Hause, in meinem Baumgarten, mitten unter den Meinigen sagen: hier, oder nirgends ist Amerika!

"Ja, mein Freund, und ich wiederhole noch immer dasselbe; und doch schelte ich mich zugleich, dass ich hier nicht so tätig wie dort bin. Zu einer gewissen gleichen, fortdauernden Gegenwart brauchen wir nur Verstand, und wir werden auch nur zu Verstand, so dass wir das Ausserordentliche, was jeder gleichgültige Tag von uns fordert. . . ."

Cf. Novalis, III, p. 90.

Lehrjahre, II, p. 170 (Carlyle, *Meister*, II, p. 2):

"Darin irren Sie sich; alles, was uns begegnet, lässt Spuren zurück, alles trägt unmerklich zu unserer Bildung bei; doch es ist gefährlich, sich davon Rechenschaft geben zu wollen. Wir werden dabei entweder stolz und lässig, oder niedergeschlagen und kleinmütig, und eins ist für die Folge so hinderlich als das andere. Das Sicherste bleibt immer, nur das Nächste zu tun, was vor uns liegt, und das ist jetzt, fuhr er mit einem Lächeln fort, dass wir eilen, ins Quartier zu kommen." *Cf. Two Notebooks*, p. 155. Carlyle wishes to go to Weimar; and to collect data for a *Life of Luther*. But, remembering Goethe's maxim, he adds, "Take the task which is *nearest* thee!"

50. *West-Oestlicher Divan*, p. 55:

"Mein Erbteil wie herrlich, weit und breit! Die Zeit ist mein Besitz, mein Acker ist die Zeit."

Carlyle alters these verses, both in copying and in translating, as is evident from their appearances in *Sartor* (as motto), in the *Miscellaneous Essays*, and in the social writings. See *Characteristics* [III], p. 43.

51. Novalis, III, pp. 65, 150.—Considering Carlyle's emphasis on action, it would be interesting to know what he thought of Faust's alteration of the Johannine line, "In the beginning was the Word," to "In the beginning was the Deed." *Faust I*, ll. 1224-37:

"Geschrieben steht: 'Im Anfang war das Wort!'
Hier stock' ich schon! Wer hilft mir weiter fort?
Ich kann das Wort so hoch unmöglich schätzen,
Ich muss es anders übersetzen,
Wenn ich vom Geiste recht erleuchtet bin.
Geschrieben steht: Im Anfang war der Sinn.
Bedenke wohl die erste Zeile,
Dass deine Feder sich nicht übereile!
Ist es der Sinn, der alles wirkt und schafft?
Es sollte stehn: Im Anfang war die Kraft!
Doch, auch indem ich dieses niederschreibe,
Schon warnt mich was, dass ich dabei nicht bleibe.
Mir hilft der Geist! auf einmal seh' ich Rat
Und schreibe getrost: Im Anfang war die Tat!"

Cf. John, i, 1.

52. *Wanderjahre*, p. 332; *Meister*, II, p. 334; *Sartor*, pp. 173-74.—The question of Carlyle's transformation of Goethe's "Renunciation," "Reverence for Sorrow," "Divine Depth of Sorrow," and "Sanctuary

of Sorrow," requires a somewhat detailed discussion. Certain Carlyleans have held that Carlyle remained faithful to the essential meaning in Goethe's passage (J. A. S. Barrett, "Carlyle's Debt to Goethe," *Hibbert Journal*, XXX (1931), pp. 61-75) ; others, however, have charged Carlyle with ignoring the greater part of Goethe's meaning, of over-emphasizing the religious elements of the *Wanderjahre*, of reading an ascetic meaning into *Entsagen*, and of giving disproportionate emphasis to the passages on "Reverence" and "Sorrow." (*Cf.* Seely, *Goethe Reviewed After Sixty Years*, p. 149; S. Howe, *Wilhelm Meister and his English Kinsmen*, p. 89, etc.; Carré, p. 143, etc.) It will be seen that there is much truth in both views, and also a certain amount of error, chiefly in emphasis.

53. *Vocation of Man*, p. 354; *Bestimmung* [II], p. 292:
"Den Sinn, mit welchem man das ewige Leben ergreift, erhält man nur dadurch, dass man das Sinnliche und die Zwecke desselben wirklich aufgiebt, und aufopfert für das Gesetz, das lediglich unsern Willen in Anspruch nimmt, und nicht unsre Thaten."

54. *Way towards the Blessed Life*, pp. 515, 516; *Anweisung* [V], p. 518 (and 519-20) : "Diese Selbstvernichtung ist der Eintritt in das höhere, dem niedern, durch das Daseyn eines Selbst bestimmten Leben, durchaus entgegengesetzte Leben; . . .," etc.

55. *Sartor*, pp. 169, 173-74.

56. *Wanderjahre*, pp. 13-14. References to Renunciation—and Renunciants—occur also on pp. 81, 251, 292, 294, 296, etc.

57. *Wanderjahre*, p. 332 (*Meister*, II, p. 334) : "Einige Stellen . . . deuten auf den hohen Sinn des Entsagens, durch welche der eigentliche Eintritt ins Leben erst denkbar ist."

58. Bielschowsky, *Life of Goethe*, transl. W. A. Cooper, London, 1907, III, p. 195; *cf.*, also, Baumgarten, p. 90.—Carlyle recognized "Goethe the Heathen" as much as any of his contemporaries, it seems. He wrote to Emerson (*Carlyle-Emerson Correspondence*, ed. C. E. Norton, London, 1883, I, p. 40) : "On the whole, I suspect you yet know only Goethe the Heathen (Ethnic) ; but you will know Goethe the Christian by and by, and like that one far better."

59. *Sartor*, p. 169.

60. Ströle, p. 64.

61. *Novalis* [II], p. 39; Novalis, III, p. 32:
"Der echte philosophische Akt ist Selbsttödtung; dies ist der reale Anfang aller Philosophie, dahin geht alles Bedürfnis des philosophischen Jüngers, und nur dieser Akt entspricht allen Bedingungen und Merkmalen der transzendentaen Handlung."

62. *Novalis* [II], p. 15.

63. *Werner* [I], pp. 106, 116-17.
64. *Werner* [I], p. 112; Z. Werner, *Werke*, Grimma, 1840-44, V, pp. 184-189, especially, p. 189:

> "Da fiel es ihm wie Schuppen von den Augen:
> Es schwand der Wahn, zu werden Ein und Etwas;
> Sein Wesen war in's grosse All zerronnen . . ."

65. *Werner* [I], pp. 117-18; Z. Werner, *Werke*, V, pp. 205-06:

> "Der Tod,—so dämmert's mir—er soll vielleicht,
> Er, der von uns so gar nichts übrig lässt—
> Vielleicht Symbol sein dieser Selbstverläugnung—
> Vielleicht noch mehr . . . vielleicht—Ich hab' es, Alter!
> Die krüpplichte Unsterblichkeit—nicht wahr?—
> Die unser eignes jämmerliches Ich
> So dünn und kläglich—so mit allem Unrath
> Nur fortspinnt in's Unendliche—nicht wahr?—
> Auch sie muss sterben?—unser schales Selbst—
> Wir sind in Ewigkeit nicht d'ran genagelt?
> Wir können es, wir müssen es verlieren,
> Um einst in aller Kraft zu schwelgen!—
>
> ADAM
> (*freudig in das Innere Höhle rufend*)
> Brüder,
>
> Er hat entsagt—er hat es selbst gefunden!"

66. *Werner* [I], p. 118.
67. *Two Notebooks*, p. 265.
68. *Sartor*, Book II, Chapter IX, p. 179.
69. *Id.*, p. 177.
70. See *Sartor*, pp. 171-79.
71. *Id.*, p. 179; *Ecclesiastes*, ix, 10, and *John*, ix, 4.
72. *Lectures on Lit.*, ed. J. R. Greene, p. 207.
73. *Wanderjahre*, pp. 168-76; Carlyle, *Meister*, II, p. 268.
74. *Id.*, pp. 191-92 (*Meister*, II, p. 275):
"Jene letzte Religion, die aus der Ehrfurcht vor dem, was unter uns ist, entspringt, jene Verehrung des Widerwärtigen, Verhassten, Fliehenswerten geben wir einem jeden man nur ausstattungsweise in die Welt mit, damit er wisse, wo er dergleichen zu finden hat, wenn ein solches Bedürfnis sich in ihm regen sollte. Ich lade Euch ein, nach Verlauf eines Jahres wiederzukehren, unser allgemeines Fest zu besuchen und zu sehen, wie weit Euer Sohn vorwärts gekommen;

alsdann sollt auch Ihr in das Heiligtum des Schmerzes eingeweiht werden." "Erlaubt mir eine Frage," versetzte Wilhelm. "Habt ihr denn auch, so wie ihr das Leben dieses göttlichen Mannes als Lehr- und Musterbild ausstellt, sein Leiden, seinen Tod gleichfalls als ein Vorbild erhabener Duldung herausgehoben?"—"Auf alle Fälle," sagte der Älteste. "Hieraus machen wir kein Geheimnis; aber wir ziehen einen Schleier über diese Leiden, eben weil wir sie so hoch verehren. Wir halten es für eine verdammungswürdige Frechheit, jenes Martergerüst und den daran leidenden Heiligen dem anblick der Sonne auszusetzen, die ihr Angesicht verbarg, als eine ruchlose Welt ihr dies Schauspiel aufdrang mit diesen tiefen Geheimnissen, in welchen die göttliche Tiefe des Leidens verborgen liegt, zu spielen, zu tändeln, zu verzieren und nicht eher zu ruhen, bis das Würdigste gemein und abgeschmackt erscheint. . . ."

It should be noted that Chapter X of the *Wanderjahre* has no mention of the "Reverence for Sorrow"; and that Chapter XI touches on it only in connection with "the Reverence of what is beneath us," ending on a discussion of the symbolism of clothes as employed in the Pedagogical Province. The idea of "sorrow" is in no way the general subject or theme of these two chapters. (*Cf. Werke*, XIX, pp. 191-92.)

75. *Wanderjahre*, pp. 176-77 (Carlyle, *Meister*, II, p. 268):

"Ein solches Bekenntnis, auf diese Weise entwickelt, befremdet mich nicht," versetzte Wilhelm; "es kommt mit allem überein, was man im Leben hie und da vernimmt, nur dass euch dasjenige vereinigt, was andere trennt." Hiernach versetzten jene: "Schon wird dieses Bekenntnis von einem grossen Teil der Welt ausgesprochen, doch unbewusst."

"Wie denn und wo?" fragte Wilhelm. "Im Kredo!" riefen jene laut. "Denn der erste Artikel ist ethnisch und gehört allen Völken; der zweite christlich, für die mit Leiden Kämpfenden und in Leiden Verherrlichten; der dritte zuletzt lehrt eine begeisterte Gemeinschaft der Heiligen, welches heisst: der im höchsten Grad Guten und Weisen." (*Cf. Werke*, XIX, pp. 183-84.)

Carlyle was very fond of the notion of the "communion of saints" as represented in the united action of all virtuous men of all times. In his Journal, on January 21, 1832, he wrote that to him it was a "grand perennial" thought. (*Two Notebooks*, p. 246.) *Cf. Sartor*, p. 224: ". . . the Wise Man stands ever encompassed, and spiritually embraced, by a cloud of witnesses and brothers; and there is a living, literal *Communion of Saints*, wide as the World itself, and as the

History of the World." (See, also, p. 230.) *Cf.* Article IX of the *Creed*, and *Hebrews*, xii, 22, 23. Goethe's *Symbolum* should also be remembered; the "Sages, the Worlds, and the Ages" bid the reader to remember that

"Hier flechten sich Kronen
In ewiger Stille;
Die sollen mit Fülle
Die Tätigen lohnen!
Wir heissen euch hoffen."
—*Werke*, II, pp. 231-32.

76. Froude, *Carlyle*: *A Hist. of his Life in London*, etc., London, 1884, II, p. 17.

77. *Wanderjahre*, pp. 174-75 (Carlyle, *Meister*, II, p. 267):

"Nun ist aber von der dritten Religion zu sprechen, gegründet auf die Ehrfurcht vor dem, was unter uns ist; wir nennen sie die christliche, weil sich in ihr eine solche Sinnesart am meisten offenbart; es ist ein Letztes, wozu die Menschheit gelangen konnte und musste. Aber was gehörte dazu, die Erde nicht allein unter sich liegen zu lassen und sich auf einen höhern Geburtsort zu berufen, sondern auch Niedrigkeit und Armut, Spott und Verachtung, Schmach und Elend, Leiden und Tod als göttlich anzuerkennen, ja Sünde selbst und Verbrechen nicht als Hindernisse, sondern als Fördernisse des Heiligen zu verehren und liebzugewinnen!" (*Cf. Werke*, XIX, pp. 182-83.)

78. Carré, p. 178.

79. *Novalis* [II], p. 42; Novalis, III, pp. 180, 183.

80. *Goethe* [I], p. 242.

81. *Wanderjahre*, p. 176 (Carlyle, *Meister*, II, p. 267):

"und man darf sagen, dass die christliche Religion, da sie einmal erschienen ist, nicht wieder verschwinden kann, da sie sich einmal göttlich verkörpert hat, nicht wieder aufgelöst werden mag." (*Cf. Werke*, XIX, p. 183.)

82. *Lehrjahre*, II, p. 259; Carlyle, *Meister*, II, p. 76.

83. *Wahrheit*, II, p. 89.

84. *Char. of the Pres. Age*, p. 62 (transl. W. Smith); Grundzüge [VII], 63:

"Möge die Schlummerer in der Wiege für das ewige Leben zuweilen ein freudigerer Traum aus jenem Leben erquicken; mögen von Zeit zu Zeit Verkündigungen an ihr Ohr treffen, dass es ein Licht gebe, und einen Tag."

85. On this tendency in Carlyle, see C. F. Harrold, "The Mystical Element in Carlyle: 1827-1834," *Modern Philology*, XXIX (1932), p. 466, etc.

86. Italics added. *Wanderjahre*, p. 54; *Meister*, II, p. 216. *Cf.*
Wotton, p. 65.

87. *Lehrjahre*, II, pp. 259-60; (*Meister*, II, pp. 75-76). The
Lehrbrief as whole is worth noting at this point:

Lehrbrief.

"Die Kunst ist lang, das Leben kurz, das Urteil schwierig, die
Gelegenheit flüchtig. Handeln ist leicht, denken schwer; nach dem
Gedachten handeln unbequem. Aller Anfang ist heiter, die Schwelle
ist der Platz der Erwartung. Der Knabe staunt, der Eindruck
bestimmt ihn, er lernt spielend, der Ernst überrascht ihn. Die
Nachahmung ist uns angeboren, das Nachzuahmende wird nicht leicht
erkannt. Selten wird das Treffliche gefunden, seltner geschätzt. Die
Höhe reizt uns, nicht die Stufen; den Gipfel im Auge, wandeln wir
gerne auf der Ebene. Nur ein Teil der Kunst kann gelehrt werden,
der Künstler braucht sie ganz. Wer sie halb kennt, ist immer irre
und redet viel; wer sie ganz besitzt, mag nur tun und redet selten
oder spät. Jene haben keine Geheimnisse und keine Kraft, ihre Lehre
ist wie gebackenes Brot, schmackhaft und sättigend für einen Tag;
aber Mehl kann man nicht säen, und die Saatfrüchte sollen nicht
vermahlen werden. Die Worte sind gut, sie sind aber nicht das Beste.
Das Beste wird nicht deutlich durch Worte. Der Geist, aus dem wir
handeln, ist das Höchste. Die Handlung wird nur vom Geiste
begriffen und wieder dargestellt. Niemand weiss, was er tut, wenn er
recht handelt, aber des Unrechten sind wir uns immer bewusst. Wer
bloss mit Zeichen wirkt, ist ein Pedant, ein Heuchler oder ein Pfuscher.
Es sind ihrer viel, und es wird ihnen wohl zusammen. Ihr Geschwätz
hält den Schüler zurück, und ihre beharrliche Mittelmässigkeit
ängstigt die Besten. Des echten Künstlers Lehre schliesst den Sinn
auf, denn wo die Worte fehlen, spricht die Tat. Der echte Schüler
lernt aus dem Bekannten das Unbekannte entwickeln, und nähert sich
dem Meister."

It need hardly be said that Carlyle's doctrine of silence does not
rest on Goethe alone. Like most of the other principles for which
he seems heavily indebted to German writers, this doctrine can be
traced to many races and times.

88. Carlyle, *Life of Schiller*, pp. 50-51. *Cf. Sartor*, p. 76. Schiller,
Werke, VII ("Geisterseher"), p. 134:

"Was hat denn die wohlthätigen Empfindungen verdrangt, die einst
der Genuss und die Richtschnur Ihres Lebens waren? Saaten für
die Zunkunft zu pflanzen, einer hohen ewigen Ordnung zu dienen—

"Zukunft! Ewige Ordnung!—Nehmen wir hinweg, was der Mensch aus seiner eigenen Brust genommen und seiner eingebildeten Gottheit als Zweck, der Natur als Gesetz untergeschoben hat—was bleibt uns dann übrig?—Was mir vorherging und was mir folgen wird, sehe ich als zwei schwarze undurchdringliche Decken an, die an beiden Grenzen des menschlichen Lebens herunterhängen und welche noch kein Lebender aufgezogen hat. Schon viele hundert Generationen stehen mit der Fackel davor und raten und raten, was etwa dahinter sein möchte. Viele sehen ihren eigenen Schatten, die Gestalten ihrer Leidenschaft, vergrössert auf der Decke der Zukunft sich bewegen und fahren schaudernd vor ihrem eigenen Bilde zusammen. Dichter, Philosophen und Staatenstifter haben sie mit ihren Träumen bemalt, lachender oder finsterer, wie der Himmel über ihnen trüber oder heiterer war; und von weitem täuschte die Perspektive. Auch manche Gaukler nützten diese allgemeine Neugier und setzten durch seltsame Vermummungen die gespannten Phantasien in Erstaunen. Eine tiefe Stille herrscht hinter dieser Decke, keiner, der einmal dahinter ist, antwortet hinter ihr hervor; alles, was man hörte, war ein hohler Widerschall der Frage, als ob man in eine Gruft gerufen hätte. Hinter diese Decke müssen alle, und mit Schaudern fassen sie an, ungewiss, wer wohl dahinter stehe und sie in Empfang nehmen werde; *quid sit id, quod tantum morituri vident.* Freilich gab es auch Ungläubige darunter, die behaupteten, dass diese Decke die Menschen nur narre und dass man nichts beobachtet hätte, weil auch nichts dahinter sei; aber um sie zu überweisen, schickte man sie eilig dahinter."

89. *Faust I*, ll. 3430-58:

"Margarete.   So glaubst du nicht?
Faust. Misshör' mich nicht, du holdes Angesicht!
Wer darf ihn **nennen?**
Und wer bekennen:
Ich glaub' ihn?
Wer empfinden,
Und sich unterwinden
Zu sagen: ich glaub' ihn nicht?
Der Allumfasser,
Der Allerhalter,
Fasst und erhält er nicht
Dich, mich, sich selbst?
Wölbt sich der Himmel nicht dadroben?
Liegt die Erde nicht hierunten fest?
Und steigen freundlich blickend
Ewige Sterne nicht herauf?

Schau' ich nicht Aug' in Auge dir,
Und drängt nicht alles
Nach Haupt und Herzen dir,
Und webt in ewigem Geheimnis
Unsichtbar sichtbar neben dir?
Erfüll' davon dein Herz, so gross es ist,
Und wenn du ganz in dem Gefühle selig bist,
Nenn' es dann, wie du willst,
Nenn's Glück! Herz! Liebe! Gott!
Ich habe keinen Namen
Dafür! Gefuhl ist alles;
Name ist Schall und Rauch,
Umnebelnd Himmelsglut."

Carlyle's constant use of Faust's question is too well known to require complete citation. It is frequent in his correspondence. *Cf. Letters to Mill, Sterling,* etc., p. 193.

90. *Sartor*, p. 146.

91. Carlyle's translation, as taken from *Past and Present*, end of Book III. *Cf.* Goethe, *Loge: Symbolum*:

"Des Maurers Wandeln
Es gleicht dem Leben,
Und sein Bestreben,
Es gleicht dem Handeln
Der Menschen auf Erden.

"Die Zukunft decket
Schmerzen und Glücke.
Schrittweis dem Blicke,
Doch ungeschrecket
Dringen wir vorwärts.

"Und schwer und ferner
Hängt eine Hülle,
Mit Ehrfurcht. Stille
Ruhn oben die Sterne
Und unten die Gräber.

"Betracht' sie genauer!
Und siehe, so melden
Im Busen der Helden
Sich wandelnde Schauer
Und ernste Gefühle.

"Doch rufen von drüben
Die Stimmen der Geister,
Die Stimmen der Meister:
Versäumt nicht, zu üben
Die Kräfte des Guten!

"Hier flechten sich Kronen
In ewiger Stille,
Die sollen mit Fülle
Die Tätigen lohnen!
Wir heissen euch hoffen."

Cf. Kuno Francke, "Carlyle, and Goethe's Symbolum," *Philological Quarterly*, VI (1927), pp. 97-101, for a short but illuminative treatment of Carlyle's transformation of Goethe's poem, as "a masterpiece of divinatory interpretation." The author conjectures that inasmuch as Goethe's greater ideas are read into this rather mediocre poem, Carlyle must have read it after he had studied *Faust* and *Wilhelm Meister* (p. 97).

BIBLIOGRAPHY

Allingham, W.: A *Diary*. London, 1907.

Aristotle: *Ethica Nicomachea*. Transl. by W. D. Ross. Oxford, 1925.

Bacon: *Essays*. Edited by F. G. Selby. London, 1890.

Barrett, J. A. S.: Carlyle's Debt to Goethe. *Hibbert Journal*, XXX (1931), pp. 61-75.

Batt, Max.: Carlyle's Life of Schiller. *Modern Philology*, I (1903-04), pp. 391-92.

Baumgarten, O.: *Carlyle und Goethe*. Tübingen, 1906.

Bentham, Jeremy: *An Introduction to the Principles of Morals and Legislation*. London, 1789.

Berend, E.: *Jean Pauls Ästhetik*. (Forschungen zur neueren Literaturgeschichte, XXXV), Berlin, 1909.

Berkeley, G.: *Collected Works*. Edited by A. C. Fraser. Oxford, 1871. 4 Vols.

Bielschowsky, A.: *Life of Goethe*. Translated by W. A. Cooper. London, 1907. 3 Vols.

Black, J. B.: *The Art of History: A Study of Four Great Historians of the Eighteenth Century* [Voltaire, Hume, Robertson, and Gibbon]. London, 1926.

Boeuf, Marie [*Pseud.* Bos, Camille]: Le Kantisme de Carlyle. *Archiv für Geschichte der Philosophie*, XV (Neue Folge Bnd. VIII) (1902), pp. 32-41.

Boucke, E. A.: *Goethes Weltanschauung auf historischer Grundlage*. Stuttgart, 1907.

Boyeson, H.: *Essays on German Literature*. New York, 1892.

Browne, Sir Thomas: *Religio Medici*. Everyman's Library. London, 1906.

Caird, E.: *The Critical Philosophy of Kant*. Glasgow, 1889. 2 Vols.

Carlyle, Thomas: *Works of*. Centenary Edition, edited by H. D. Traill. London, 1896-99. 30 Vols. (Note: All references to Carlyle have been to this edition, except in the cases of *Sartor Resartus* and *On Heroes*, which have been cited as given below.)

————: *Sartor Resartus*. Edited by Archibald MacMechan. Boston, 1896.

Sartor Resartus. Edited by J. A. S. Barrett. London, 1916.

————: *On Heroes, Hero-Worship, and the Heroic in History*. Edited by Archibald MacMechan. Boston, 1901.

———: *Lectures on the History of Literature, delivered by, April to July 1838*. Edited by J. Reay Greene. London, 1892.

———: *Correspondence of, and Ralph Waldo Emerson*. London, 1883. 2 Vols.

———: *Early Letters of*. Edited by Charles Eliot Norton. London, 1886. 2 Vols.

———: *Letters of, 1826-1836*. Edited by Charles Eliot Norton. London, 1889.

———: *The Love Letters of, and Jane Welsh Carlyle*. Edited by Alexander Carlyle. London, 1909. 2 Vols.

———: *Reminiscences by*. Edited by Charles Eliot Norton. Everyman's Library. London, 1932.

———: *Last Words of*. London, 1892. (Contains *Wotton Reinfred, Excursion (Futile Enough) To Paris*, and a number of letters.)

———: *Two Note Books of, from 23d March to 16th May 1832*. Edited by Charles Eliot Norton. Grolier Club. New York, 1898.

———: *Faustus. New Edinburgh Review*, II (1822), pp. 316-34.

———: *New Letters of, to Eckermann*. Edited by W. A. Speck. *Yale Review*, July, 1926, pp. 1-22.

Carré, J.-M.: Quelques lettres inédites de William Taylor, Coleridge, Carlyle à H. C. Robinson sur la littérature allemande. *Revue Germanique*, VIII (1912), pp. 40 *et seq.*

———: *Goethe en Angleterre*. Paris, 1920, pp. 101-87.

Cazamian, L.: *Carlyle*. Paris, 1913.

Coleridge, S. T.: *Aids to Reflection*. Edited by Derwent Coleridge. Eighth Edition. London, 1859.

———: *Biographia Literaria*. Edited by J. Shawcross. Oxford, 1907. 2 Vols.

———: *The Friend*. In Vol. II of the *Complete Works*. Edited by Shedd. New York, 1853. 7 Vols.

Craig, R. S.: *The Making of Carlyle*. London, 1908.

Crawford, A. W.: *The Philosophy of Jacobi*. New York, 1905.

Dilthey, W.: Thomas Carlyle. *Archiv für Geschichte der Philosophie*, IV (1891), pp. 260-85.

Dunbar, Helen Flanders: *Symbolism in Medieval Thought, and its Consummation in Dante's Divine Comedy*. New Haven, 1929.

Fehr, B.: Der deutsche Idealismus in Carlyles Sartor Resartus. *Germanisch-romanische Monatsschrift*, V (1913), pp. 81-101.

Fichte, J. G.: *Sämmtliche Werke*. Edited by J. H. Fichte. Berlin, 1845-46. 8 Vols.

———: *Popular Works*. Translated by William Smith. London, 1873. (Contains *On the Nature of the Scholar* [pp. 133-231],

The Vocation of Man [pp. 235-379], and *The Way towards the Blessed Life; or The Doctrine of Religion* [pp. 383-564].)

————: *Characteristics of the Present Age.* Translated by William Smith. London, 1847.

Flint, Robert: *The Philosophy of History in France and Germany.* London, 1874.

Fraser's Magazine, VII (1833), pp. 532-54. ("Hayward's Translation of Goethe's Faust.")

Fridell, Egon: *Novalis als Philosoph.* München, 1904.

Froude, J. A.: *Thomas Carlyle: A History of the First Forty Years of His Life: 1795-1835.* London, 1882. 2 Vols.

————: *Thomas Carlyle: A History of His Life in London: 1834-1881.* London, 1884. 2 Vols.

Fueter, E.: *Die Geschichte der neueren Historiographie.* Berlin, 1911.

Garnett, R.: *Life of Thomas Carlyle.* London, 1887.

Geissendoerfer, T.: Carlyle and Jean Paul Friedrich Richter. *Journal of English and Germanic Philology,* XXV (1926), pp. 540-53.

Gibbon, E.: *Memoirs of His Life and Writings.* Edited by George Birkbeck Hill. London, 1909.

Goethe: *Sämtliche Werke.* Jubiläums-Ausgabe. Stuttgart und Berlin, 1902-07. 40 Vols.

————: *Wilhelm Meisters Wanderjahre, oder die Entsagenden.* Stuttgart, 1821.

————: *Maximen und Reflexionen.* Edited by H. Hecker. Goethe-Gesellschaft, Vol. 21. Weimar, 1907.

Gundolf, F.: *Goethe.* Berlin, 1922.

Hagberg, K.: *Thomas Carlyle: Romantik och Puritanism i Sartor Resartus.* Stockholm, 1925.

Harich, W.: *Jean Paul.* Leipzig, 1925.

Harrold, Charles Frederick: Carlyle's Interpretation of Kant. *Philological Quarterly,* VII (1928), pp. 345-57.

————: Carlyle and Novalis. *Studies in Philology,* XXVII (1930), pp. 47-63.

————: The Mystical Element in Carlyle: 1827-34. *Modern Philology,* XXIX (1932), pp. 459-75.

————: Carlyle's General Method in The French Revolution. *Publications of the Modern Language Association of America,* XLIII (1928), pp. 1150-69.

Hartley, David: *Observations on Man.* London, 1791.

Hauhart, W. F.: *The Reception of Goethe's Faust in England in the First Half of the Nineteenth Century.* New York, 1909.

328   *Carlyle and German Thought: 1819–1834*

Hensel, P.: *Carlyle.* Stuttgart, 1922. (Third revised edition.)
Hibben, J. G.: *The Philosophy of the Enlightenment.* London, 1910.
Hildebrand, A.: *Carlyle und Schiller.* Berlin, 1913.
Höffding, H.: *A History of Modern Philosophy.* Translated by
    B. E. Meyer. London, 1900. 2 Vols.
Hooker, R.: *Works.* Edited by John Keble. Seventh Edition.
    Oxford, 1888. 3 Vols.
Horn, Franz.: *Umrisse zur Geschichte und Kritik der Schönen
    Literatur Deutschlands, während der Jahre 1790 bis 1818.* Berlin,
    1821.
Howard, C.: *Coleridge's Idealm.* Boston, 1924.
Howe, Susanne: *Wilhelm Meister and his English Kinsmen.* New
    York, 1930.
Hume, David: *A Treatise of Human Nature.* Edited by L. A.
    Selby-Bigge. Oxford, 1896.
———: *An Enquiry Concerning the Human Understanding.* Edited
    by L. A. Selby-Bigge. Oxford, 1894.
Jacobi, F. H.: *Werke.* Leipzig, 1812-25. 6 Vols.
James, L. G.: Carlyle's Philosophy of History. *Westminster Review,*
    CXXXII (1889), pp. 414-28.
Kant: *Gesammelte Schriften.* Herausgegeben von der Königlich
    Akademie der Wissenschaften. Berlin, 1902-13. 15 Vols.
———: *Critique of Pure Reason.* Translated by Norman Kemp
    Smith. London, 1929.
———: *The Metaphysic of Ethics.* Translated by J. W. Semple.
    Edited by H. Calderwood. Edinburgh, 1871. (Contains a trans-
    lation of the *Grundlegung zur Metaphysik der Sitten,* and parts
    of the *Kritik der praktischen Vernunft,* etc.)
Kellner, L.: Goethe und Carlyle. *Die Nation,* XIII (1896), pp.
    380-83, 399-403.
———: *Die Englische Literatur der neuesten Zeit, von Dickens bis
    Shaw.* Leipzig, 1921.
Kraeger, H.: Carlyles deutsche Studien und der "Wotton Reinfred."
    Anglia. Beiblatt, IX (1898), pp. 193-219.
———: Carlyle's Stellung zur deutschen Sprache und Literatur.
    Anglia, XXII (1899), pp. 145-343.
———: Zu Carlyles Sartor Resartus. *Anglia.* Beiblatt, X (1899),
    pp. 12-13.
Küchler, F.: Carlyle und Schiller. *Anglia,* XXVI (1903), pp. 1-93,
    393-446.
Lehman, B. H.: *Carlyle's Theory of the Hero: Its Sources, Develop-
    ment, History, and Influence on Carlyle's Work.* Durham, N. C.,
    1928.

Leopold, W.: *Die Religiöse Wurzel von Carlyles Literarischer Wirksamkeit, dargestellt an seinem Aufsatz "State of German Literature"* (*1827*). Halle, 1922.

———: Carlyle and Franz Horn. *Journal of English and Germanic Philology,* XXVIII (1929), pp. 215-19.

Lévy-Bruhl, L.: *La Philosophie de Jacobi.* Paris, 1894.

Locke, John: *The Conduct of the Understanding.* London, 1762.

Lovejoy, A. O.: Kant and the English Platonists. *Essays Philosophical and Psychological in Honor of William James.* New York, 1908, pp. 265-302.

Lütgert, W.: *Die Religion des deutschen Idealismus und ihr Ende.* Erste Teil, Zweite Teil. Gütersloh, 1923, 1929.

Masson, David: *Edinburgh Sketches and Memories.* London, 1892.

Morgan, W.: Carlyle and German Thought. *Queen's Quarterly,* XXIII (1915-16), pp. 438-52.

Morley, Edith J.: Carlyle in the Diary, Reminiscences, and Correspondence of Henry Crabb Robinson. *London Mercury,* VI (1922), p. 617, etc.

———: *Crabb Robinson in Germany: 1800-1805. Extracts from his Correspondence.* Oxford, 1929.

Muirhead, J. H.: *Coleridge as a Philosopher.* London, 1930.

———: *The Platonic Tradition in Anglo-Saxon Philosophy.* London, 1931.

Murray, R. H.: *Studies in the English Social and Political Thinkers of the Nineteenth Century.* Cambridge, 1929. 2 Vols.

Neff, E.: *Carlyle.* New York, 1932.

Novalis: *Werke.* Edited by H. Friedemann. Berlin, 1908. 4 Vols.

Obenauer, K. J.: *Goethe in seinem Verhältnis zur Religion.* Jena, 1921.

Pascal: *Oeuvres Complète.* Edited by F. Strowski. Paris, 1931.

Plato: *Dialogues.* Edited by Jowett. Oxford, 1892. 4 Vols.

Poppenberg, F.: *Zacharias Werner: Mystik und Romantik in den "Sohnen des Thals."* Berlin, 1893.

Reinhold, K. L.: *Briefe über die Kantische Philosophie.* Leipzig, 1790-92.

Richter, Jean Paul Friederich: *Werke.* Berlin, 1879. 60 Vols.

———: *Blumen- Frucht- und Dornenstücke: oder Ehestand, Tod, Hochzeit des Armenadvokaten F. St. Siebenkäs.* Berlin, 1818. 4 Vols. in two.

———: *Flower, Fruit, and Thorn Pieces* . . . Translated by Alexander Ewing. Bohn's Library. London, 1888.

———: *Hesperus.* Anonymous translation. Boston, 1865.

———: *Levana: oder Erziehlehre.* Stuttgart und Tübingen, 1845.

———: *Levana, or the Doctrine of Education.* Anonymous translation. London, 1840.

———: *Jean Pauls Briefe und bevorstehender Lebenslauf.* Gera, Leipzig, 1799.

———: *Wahrheit aus Jean Pauls Leben.* Breslau, 1826-33. 8 Vols.

Roe, F. W.: *Carlyle as a Critic of Literature.* New York, 1910.

Royce, Josiah: *The Spirit of Modern Philosophy.* Boston, 1892.

Sagar, S.: *Round by Repentance Tower: A Study of Carlyle.* London, 1930.

St. John, H., Lord Bolingbroke: *Works.* Philadelphia, 1841. 4 Vols.

Santayana, G.: *Three Philosophical Poets.* Cambridge, Mass., 1910.

Schanck, N.: *Die Sozial-Politischen Anschauungen Coleridges und sein Einfluss auf Carlyle.* Bonn, 1924.

Schelling, F. W. J. von: *Sämmtliche Werke.* Stuttgart und Augsburg, 1859-61. 10 Vols.

Schiller, F. von: *Sämmtliche Werke.* Edited by H. Kurz. Hildburghausen, 1868-70. 9 Vols.

Schlegel, A. W. and F. von: *Athenaeum.* Berlin, 1798-1800.

Schlegel, F. von: *Sämmtliche Werke.* Wien, 1822-23. 10 Vols.

———: *Lectures on the History of Literature, Ancient and Modern.* Anonymous translation. Bohn's Library. London, 1871.

Schulze-Gaevernitz, G. von: *Thomas Carlyle's Welt- und Gesellschaftsanschauung.* Dresden, 1893.

Seely, J. M.: *Goethe Reviewed After Sixty Years.* London, 1894.

Simmel, G.: *Goethe.* Leipzig, 1913.

Smith, Adam: *The Theory of the Moral Sentiments.* London, 1774. (Fourth Edition.)

Smith, Norman Kemp: *A Commentary to Kant's Critique of Pure Reason.* London, 1923.

Staël, Madame de: *Germany.* London, 1813. 3 Vols.

Stephen, Leslie: *A History of English Thought in the Eighteenth Century.* London, 1876. 2 Vols.

Stewart, Dugald: *Works.* Edited by Sir William Hamilton. Edinburgh, 1854-58. 10 Vols.

Stewart, H. L.: Carlyle's Conception of Religion. *American Journal of Theology,* XXI (1917), pp. 43-57.

———: Carlyle's Place in Philosophy. *The Monist,* XXIX (1919), pp. 161-189.

Storrs, Margaret: *The Relation of Carlyle to Kant and Fichte.* Bryn Mawr, Pa., 1929.

Ströle, A.: *Thomas Carlyle's Anschauung vom Fortschritt in der Geschichte.* Gütersloh, 1909.

Swift, Jonathan: *Tale of a Tub* . . . Edited by A. C. Guthkelch and D. Nichol Smith. Oxford, 1920.

Taine, H.: *L'Idéalisme Anglais*: *Étude sur Carlyle*. Paris, 1864.

Tasso: *Discorsi del Poema Heroico*. Naples [1597].

Thilly, F.: *The World View of a Poet* [Goethe]. *Hibbert Journal*, VI (1907-08), pp. 530-48.

Vaughan, C. E.: Carlyle and his German Masters. *Essays and Studies by Members of the English Association*. Oxford, 1910, pp. 168-96.

Wellek, R.: Carlyle and German Romanticism. *Xenia Pragensia*: Sumptibus societatis neophilologorum. Prague, 1929. Pp. 375-403.

——: *Immanuel Kant in England*: *1793-1838*. Princeton, N. J., 1931. Pp. 183-202.

Werner, Zacharias: *Sämmtliche Werke*. Grimma [1840-44]. 13 Vols.

Wilm, E. C.: *The Philosophy of Schiller in its Historical Relations*. Boston, 1912.

Wilson, D. A.: *Carlyle Till Marriage*. London, 1923.

——: *Carlyle to The French Revolution*. London, 1924.

Wundt, M.: *Goethes Wilhelm Meister und die Entwicklung des Modernen Lebensideal*. Berlin, 1913.

INDEX